Robert M. Francescotti (Ed.)
Companion to Intrinsic Properties

Companion to Intrinsic Properties

Edited by
Robert M. Francescotti

DE GRUYTER

ISBN 978-3-11-055452-6
e-ISBN 978-3-11-029259-6

Library of Congress Cataloging-in-Publication Data
A CIP catalog record for this book has been applied for at the Library of Congress.

Bibliografische Information der Deutschen Nationalbibliothek
Die Deutsche Nationalbibliothek verzeichnet diese Publikation in der Deutschen Nationalbibliografie; detaillierte bibliografische Daten sind im Internet über http://dnb.dnb.de abrufbar.

© 2017 Walter de Gruyter GmbH, Berlin/Boston
This volume is text- and page-identical with the hardback published in 2014.
Printing: CPI books GmbH, Leck

♾ Gedruckt auf säurefreiem Papier
Printed in Germany

www.degruyter.com

Contents

Editor's Introduction —— 1

Rae Langton, David Lewis
Defining 'Intrinsic' —— 17

Peter Vallentyne
Intrinsic Properties Defined —— 31

Stephen Yablo
Intrinsicness —— 41

Brian Weatherson
Intrinsic Properties and Combinatorial Principles —— 69

David Denby
Essence and Intrinsicality —— 87

D. Gene Witmer
A Simple Theory of Intrinsicality —— 111

Carrie Figdor
What's the Use of an Intrinsic Property? —— 139

Vera Hoffmann-Kolss
Is the Intrinsic/Extrinsic Distinction Hyperintensional? —— 157

Robert Francescotti
Intrinsic/Extrinsic: A Relational Account Defended —— 175

Dan Marshall
Yablo's Account of Intrinsicality —— 199

Alexander Skiles
Primitivism about Intrinsicality —— 221

Michael Esfeld
Physics and Intrinsic Properties —— 253

M. Eddon
Intrinsic Explanations and Numerical Representations —— 271

Contributors —— 291

Name Index —— 293

Editor's Introduction

Talk of intrinsic properties is meant to draw attention to those features that something has "in itself," that is, independently of the condition of other things. These intrinsic features are intuitively described as those a thing has in virtue of the way it alone and nothing else is, properties whose exemplification by some item does not consist in how it relates to any distinct things. The word 'extrinsic' is generally considered an antonym of 'intrinsic'; any property of an item that does not fit the descriptions above is usually considered one of its extrinsic features.

The distinction between intrinsic and extrinsic properties plays a major role in a variety of philosophical debates and in many different areas of philosophy. In the field of ethics, talk of *intrinsic value* has long been a topic of debate. Do actions as well as individuals have intrinsic value? Assuming individuals have intrinsic value, which ones have it and why? Are only rational beings included? Or do the bearers of intrinsic value include sentient beings generally, ... anything with a life, nature itself?

In the philosophy of physics, there is the question of whether the causal powers of objects supervene on their intrinsic features, whether the relational properties of physics require an intrinsic ground, and whether all or even any fundamental physical properties are intrinsic. And assuming that fundamental physical items have an intrinsic nature, how can we ever have knowledge of that intrinsic nature given that we can only be aware of the effects? In metaphysics, there is the question of what constitutes genuine change (which seems to require a change in intrinsic properties), and whether change in the intrinsic properties of an individual is compatible with its *enduring* through time (being numerically identical at different times). Philosophers of mind wonder whether the content of our mental states supervenes on our intrinsic features or whether mental content is partly a function of the external items toward which our thoughts are directed. There is also the issue of whether consciousness extends beyond the intrinsic features of one's brain or even the rest of one's body. For the philosopher of art, there is the issue of whether aesthetic value is an intrinsic feature of an object, and if not, what relations to which external items ground aesthetic properties; and in epistemology, there is the long-standing question of whether the justification of one's beliefs is solely a function of one's intrinsic features.

Despite the significant role that talk of intrinsic properties has played in the philosophical literature, there has been great difficulty capturing the intuitive idea of an intrinsic property in a sufficiently plausible definition. In section 1 of this introduction, I review some of the most popular and influential attempts to define intrinsicality (with a few of these essays reprinted in this anthology). In section 2, I introduce the exciting new essays that have been written for this collection.

1 Earlier Work on Intrinsicality

In his discussion of intrinsic value, G. E. Moore offers a two-part analysis of intrinsic nature.

> When I say, with regard to any particular kind of value, that the question whether and in what degree anything possesses it *depends solely on the intrinsic nature of the thing in question*, I mean to say two different things at the same time. I mean to say (1) that it is *impossible* for what is strictly *one and the same* thing to possess that kind of value at one time, or in one set of circumstances, and *not* to possess it at another; and equally *impossible* for it to possess it in one degree at one time, or in one set of circumstances, and to possess it in a different degree at another, or in a different set.... (2) The second part of what is meant is that if a given thing possesses any kind of intrinsic value in a certain degree, then not only must the same thing possess it, under all circumstances, in the same degree, but also anything *exactly like* it, must, under all circumstances, possess it in exactly the same degree. Or to put it in the corresponding negative form: It is *impossible* that of two exactly similar things one should possess it and the other not, or that one should possess it in one degree, and the other in a different one. (1922, pp. 260–1)

According to part (1) of Moore's analysis, to say that a property of an item, e.g., a certain sort of value, depends on its intrinsic nature is to say that it's impossible for the item to have that property at one time and lack it at another. This implies that one's intrinsic properties are those that one has *necessarily*, those without which one cannot exist. It is arguable, however, that being intrinsic is not the same as being necessary. Michael Dunn (1990, p. 181) notes that there is a tendency for some philosophers to conflate the notion of being intrinsic with the notion of being necessary or essential. This conflation is a mistake since some properties we regard as intrinsic are contingent features of the items that have them, features the items can exist without. The mass of the rock, or any other physical object, would seem to be one of its intrinsic properties, although the rock could arguably continue to exist despite some changes in its mass. Also, some essential features seem to be extrinsic. Being a product of that particular sperm and egg is arguably an essential feature of you, although this feature is had by you in virtue of your relations to distinct individuals (and times).

Moore's condition (2) is a more plausible requirement for being intrinsic. Since intrinsic properties are those something has "in itself," they would seem to be those whose instantiation does not depend on one's relation to other things. It would seem to follow that no matter what environmental differences there are between x and y, so long as x and y are duplicates, they will have all the same intrinsic properties. It is tempting, then, to think that a property F is an intrinsic property of x just in case F is had by all possible duplicates of x.

Of course, by 'duplicate' here one cannot mean what has *all* the same properties, for whatever has all the same properties as x will have all of x's *extrinsic* properties. Features shared by all duplicates are guaranteed to be intrinsic only when the features duplicated are restricted to those that are intrinsic. So it seems that the notion of duplication that's relevant to defining 'intrinsic' is itself a notion to be understood in terms of intrinsic properties. As David Lewis notes, "things are perfect duplicates iff they have the very same intrinsic properties" (1983a, p. 197).

One way to avoid the circularity is suggested in the passage from Moore quoted above: "if a given thing possesses any kind of intrinsic value in a certain degree," then anything exactly like it "must, *under all circumstances*, possess it in exactly the same degree." The emphasis is mine, and I emphasize 'under all circumstances' to highlight the idea that an object's intrinsic properties are ones it would have no matter what changes were made to its environment. If this is an accurate way to think of intrinsic properties, then we should expect an object to retain its intrinsic properties even when all items external to it are removed. Borrowing from Chisholm's idea of a property being *rooted outside the times* at which it is had, Kim (1982) introduces the idea of a property being rooted *outside the objects* that have it. A property F is rooted outside the objects that have it just in case, necessarily, any object x has F only if some contingent object wholly distinct from x exists—where a wholly distinct object is one that is not identical with x and not identical with any of x's proper parts. Kim then defines an "internal" property as one that is "neither rooted outside times at which it is had nor outside the objects that have it" (p. 60). Replacing 'internal' with 'intrinsic', the proposal is that intrinsic properties are those an object can exemplify while being alone in the world (i.e., without any wholly distinct contingent objects).[1] As Lewis expresses the idea, "extrinsic properties are those that imply accompaniment, whereas intrinsic properties are compatible with loneliness" (1983a, p. 198). Yet, as Lewis notes, there is an obvious flaw with this proposal—*loneliness,*

---

[1] Without the word 'contingent' no properties would qualify as intrinsic (assuming there are necessary beings). Since necessary beings cannot fail to exist, no properties can be had in the absence of necessary beings (assuming there are necessary beings).

being alone in the world, is extrinsic, "yet certainly it does not imply accompaniment and certainly it is compatible with itself" (p. 199).

Being compatible with loneliness is not sufficient for being intrinsic, but there is the more sophisticated notion of being *independent of accompaniment* which comes closer to defining what it is to be intrinsic. Rae Langton and Lewis introduce the notion in their famous 1998 essay, "Defining 'Intrinsic'," reprinted in this collection.[2] A property is independent of accompaniment just in case its *presence or absence* is compatible with *either loneliness or accompaniment*. That is, F is independent of accompaniment if and only if (i) a lonely object can have F, (ii) a lonely object can lack F, (iii) an accompanied object can have F, and (iv) an accompanied object can lack F. If intrinsic properties are characterized as those that satisfy (i)-(iv), then the property of being lonely is correctly classified as extrinsic, since being lonely does not meet conditions (ii) or (iii). Langton and Lewis recognize that we need a bit more than (i)-(iv) to ensure that a property is intrinsic. They note the disjunctive property, being *either cubical and lonely or else non-cubical and accompanied*. This property is independent of accompaniment. It can be had or lacked by either a lonely object or an accompanied one; it's had by a lonely cube and an accompanied circular object, and it's lacked by a lonely circular object and an accompanied cube. Yet, it seems that this disjunctive property does not qualify as intrinsic since each disjunct contains a conjunct that is extrinsic. (Likewise, the negation of this disjunctive property also seems to be extrinsic, although it, too, meets conditions (i)–(iv).)

To correctly classify problematic disjunctive properties, Langton and Lewis (hereafter, "L & L") amend the account by appealing to *natural* properties. Lewis (1983b) offered a duplication account that relied heavily on the notion of a natural property, defining duplicates as those that have exactly the same perfectly natural properties,[3] and then proposing that a property is intrinsic just in case it can never differ between duplicates.[4] In the L & L account, the reliance on the notion of a natural property is not as heavy. They define a disjunctive property as one that is not natural while its disjuncts are; or if naturalness admits of degrees, the property is less natural than the disjuncts. Then they define *basic intrinsic* properties as those that are independent of accompaniment,

---

[2] Reprinted with permission of Rae Langton and Stephanie Lewis, and with permission of Wiley & Sons, Inc.
[3] A *perfectly natural* property is a fundamental physical property.
[4] Lewis (1986) later requires that duplicates not only share perfectly natural properties, but also that "their parts can be put into correspondence in such a way that corresponding parts have exactly the same perfectly natural properties, and stand in the same perfectly natural relations" (p. 61).

not disjunctive properties, and not negations of disjunctive properties. By defining duplicates as those that have exactly the same basic intrinsic properties, they are then able to define an intrinsic property as one that can never differ between duplicates. Now the property of being *either cubical and lonely or else non-cubical and accompanied* is correctly classified as extrinsic since it is a property that can differ between duplicates (i.e., between those with the exact same basic intrinsic properties).

The reliance on the notion of naturalness has been a main source of complaint with the L & L account (and with Lewis' 1983b and 1986).[5] Peter Vallentyne (1997) offers a definition that relies on the idea of intrinsic properties being those one can have all alone in the world, while managing to avoid any appeal to the controversial notion of a natural property. His essay, "Intrinsic Properties Defined," is reprinted in this collection.[6] Here's a brief preview. We have the notion of what a world might be like where everything remains the same except that a few objects or times are removed. Now imagine a *maximal* contraction of a world, where we remove from a world as much as we can while leaving a certain object x at a certain time t. Then we have what Vallentyne calls an "x-t contraction." With the notion of an x-t contradiction, Vallentyne shows how to capture the idea that intrinsic properties are those whose presence or absence does not depend on what the rest of the world is like. He proposes that a property F is intrinsic just in case for any world w, object x, and time t, if x has F in w at t, then x has F at t in each x-t contraction of w, and likewise for the negation of F (i.e., if x has not-F in w at t, it does so at each x-t contraction of w).

This analysis correctly classifies the disjunctive properties that caused trouble for the L & L account without having to rely on natural properties. Being *either cubical and lonely or else non-cubical and accompanied* is correctly classified

---

[5] Stephen Yablo warns: "there is something uncomfortable about taking an intrinsicness-fact that is very clearcut ... and putting it at the mercy of something as controversial, and (apparently) irrelevant, as the relative naturalness" of a disjunction and its disjuncts (1999, p. 2). Gene Witmer, William Butchard, and Kelly Trogdon (2005) question whether we even have a concept of naturalness. While Lewis (2001) insists that the cost of doing without the notion of naturalness is too great, Witmer et al. reply: "The problem here is not a matter of having a concept and assessing the costs and benefits of using it. Rather, the problem is a matter of having no clear concept the costs and benefits of which can even begin to be assessed" (p. 329). At least this much seem correct, "If we want to clarify a notion which is a relatively ordinary one, presumably the notions we use to provide that clarification ought to be in better shape than the one to be clarified" (p. 331), but intrinsicality seems to be a notion better understood than naturalness. Although, see Ted Sider's (1996) defense of relying on a primitive notion of naturalness.

[6] Reprinted with permission of Peter Vallentyne and Springer.

as extrinsic on Vallentyne's account, for an accompanied non-cube lacks the disjunctive property in x-t contractions where it is lonely. Another merit of Vallentyne's account is that by not relying on the notion of duplicates, his definition is able to correctly classify *non-qualitative* properties (those whose specification requires reference to particular items, e.g., *liking Norman* vs. *liking some human*). L & L admit that their definition applies only to *qualitative* properties, since intrinsic properties are not had by all of one's duplicates if they are non-qualitative. And it seems that there are intrinsic non-qualitative properties, e.g., the property of being *identical with Alice*. Vallentyne's account gives the apparently correct result that being identical with Alice is intrinsic since any x that has this property (i.e., Alice herself) has it in all x-t contractions, and any x that has the negation of this property (anyone or anything other than Alice) has the negation of the property in all x-t contractions.

Vallentyne relies on the idea that taking stuff away from the world should not affect whether an item has some intrinsic property F. Stephen Yablo (1999) appeals to the idea that *adding more* to the world should not affect whether one has F. If F is an intrinsic property of object x in one world, then it should be a property that x retains in a world with all the same stuff plus some more items. Yablo also notes that there are intimate connections between the part-whole relation and intrinsicality; e.g., there is the fact that if x is part of y, then x cannot change intrinsically without y changing intrinsically as well, and the fact that if x is part of y, then x and y have a region of intrinsic match. Inspired by these considerations, Yablo proposes as an initial attempt that a property F is intrinsic iff for any individual x, and possible worlds w_1 and w_2, such that x is a proper part of w_1 and w_1 is a proper part of w_2, x has F in w_1 iff x has F is w_2. Like Vallentyne's account, this proposal gives the intuitively correct results in many cases. An added benefit is that unlike Vallentyne's account, Yablo goes on to develop the core idea just expressed in a way that allows that some of our essential properties are extrinsic. Vallentyne recognizes that some apparently extrinsic essential features (e.g., having a particular origin—some specific date or zygote) are classified as intrinsic on his account, and while he does defend the idea that such properties are intrinsic,[7] it would seem desirable to have a definition that allows essential properties to be extrin-

---

[7] Vallentyne contends that it is not so implausible to regard such properties as intrinsic since they are "metaphysically glued" to each of their bearers, and therefore, "in an important sense, there is no dependence since there is no room for variation on what the rest of the world is like" (1997, p. 217).

sic. And in this respect at least, Yablo's account is preferable.⁸ His essay, "Intrinsicness," is reprinted here.⁹

The last reprint in this collection is Brian Weatherson's "Intrinsic Properties and Combinatorial Principles."¹⁰ In this essay Weatherson develops the basic idea of L & L that intrinsicality is a matter of independence of accompaniment, but he develops it in a way that avoids three main objections to the L & L account. One objection is Yablo's complaint (mentioned in fn. 5) that the theory rests on "controversial, and (apparently) irrelevant" judgments about relative naturalness. Another objection to the L & L account that Weatherson's analysis answers is presented by Dan Marshall and Josh Parsons (2001). Marshall and Parsons mention the property of being *such that there is a cube*. This property (like various other quantificational properties) is independent of accompaniment and seems to be non-disjunctive; so it is implausibly classified as intrinsic on the L & L account.¹¹ Another threat to the L & L account is what Ted Sider (2001) calls "maximal" properties, i.e., properties of an object that are not had by the object's proper parts. Being a rock is maximal since no undetached portion of a rock is itself a rock. However, if that portion were set free by having the surrounding sandstone chipped away, then it would be a rock. So x's being rock depends on the way things are outside of x: it depends on the absence of any rock that contains x as a proper part. This suggests that being a rock is extrinsic. But it would seem to count as intrinsic on the L & L account, since it is independent of accompaniment, and being quite natural it also seems non-disjunctive in the L & L sense.¹²

---

8 However, there are some apparently extrinsic properties that are necessary features not just of some objects, but of everything that exists. These *universally necessary* features (or "*indiscriminately necessary*," as Weatherson and Marshall 2013 call them) include being *such that either Socrates is wise or Socrates is not wise* (as Dunn 1990, p. 184 mentions) and *coexisting with a number* (assuming numbers exist necessarily). These two seem to be extrinsic, yet each of the accounts mentioned above (including Yablo's – and Weatherson's, which is introduced next) classifies all indiscriminately necessary properties as intrinsic.
9 Reprinted with permission of Yablo and Edward Minar (editor of *Philosophical Topics*).
10 Reprinted with permission of Weatherson and Wiley & Sons.
11 Being such that there is a cube can be rephrased as the disjunctive property, being either a cube or accompanied by a cube, but being such that there is a cube does not appear to be disjunctive in L & L's sense of being less natural than each of the disjuncts (since being such that there is a cube seems no less natural than being accompanied by a cube).
12 Incidentally, Vallentyne's account gives the arguably correct result that being a rock is extrinsic. If something is a rock, it is a rock in all x-t contractions, but this is not true of the negation of being a rock. Yablo's account also allows that being a rock qualifies as extrinsic. Both accounts also give the apparently correct result that being such that there is a cube is extrinsic.

Like the L & L definition of intrinsicality, Weatherson's account is "combinatorial" in that it analyzes being intrinsic by specifying principles regarding which combinations of intrinsic properties are possible. There is the L & L principle that intrinsic properties are independent of accompaniment. Weatherson adds a few more combinatorial principles. One is a Boolean closure principle, according to which: (B) if F and G are intrinsic properties, then so are *F-and-G*, *F-or-G*, and *not-F*. Another principle is: (T) If F and G are intrinsic and there is a possible world with n + 1 pairwise distinct things, and something in some world is F and something in some world is G, then there is a world with exactly n + 1 pairwise distinct things such that one is F and the other n are G" (p. 373). The basic idea of (T) is that any two intrinsic properties that can be instantiated can be instantiated together any number of times. With these two combinational principles, we get the right result that being *such that there is a cube* is not intrinsic. Suppose that the property is intrinsic. Then by (B), not being such that there is a cube is also intrinsic. Now, it's possible for being such that there is a cube to be instantiated and also possible for its negation to be instantiated. So given (T) it follows that there is a world in which something is such that there is a cube and something is not such that there is a cube. This is impossible. So with Weatherson's combinational principles we get the right result that being such that there is a cube is not intrinsic. Weatherson offers further combinatorial principles to classify being a rock as extrinsic and to classify certain problematic disjunctive properties (e. g., those of the form *being F and lonely or non-F and accompanied*) as extrinsic without appealing to naturalness. (However, Weatherson does admit the need to appeal to naturalness to get the intuitively correct results in certain special cases.)

2 New Essays

In addition to the classic essays mentioned above, this anthology contains several new papers on intrinsic properties. The first is David Denby's "Essence and Intrinsicality."

In earlier works, Denby (2006, 2010) offers a combinational account, utilizing the notion of being independent of accompaniment. Yet, whereas L & L spoke of properties had independently of other *objects*, Denby focuses on properties had independently of other *properties*. He proposes that an object's intrinsic properties are independent of the properties of other items, but they are not independent of the intrinsic properties the object itself has. An object's extrinsic properties, on the other hand, always depend on intrinsic properties of other individuals. To make these ideas precise, he relies on the notions of *internal* and *external independence*, where (very roughly and omitting Denby's detail) F is internally independent of G when x's having or lacking F is independent of x's having or lacking G, and F is externally independent of G when x's having or lacking F is independent of the presence or absence of G for items other than x. An intrinsic property is then characterized as a property that fails to be internally independent of some other intrinsic property, but is externally independent of every property.

In his "Essence and Intrinsicality," written for this collection, rather than defining intrinsicality, Denby uses the concept of an intrinsic property to define what it is for a property to be *essential*. A property's being necessary does not entail that it is intrinsic: being accompanied by the number 9 is a necessary feature of you and me (assuming numbers exist necessarily) but it is not intrinsic. There is also the fact, as Kit Fine (1994) highlights, that a property's being necessary does not entail that it is essential; being a member of the singleton set, {Socrates}, is a necessary feature of Socrates but it seems it is not part of his essence. So essential properties should not be defined as those had necessarily. Denby proposes, instead, to define essential properties as those necessary features that are also intrinsic. He defends this provocative proposal against anticipated objections, and in the second half of his essay, he further supports the analysis of essential in terms of intrinsic by revealing how the family of intrinsic properties has a certain structure that helps us understand some important facts about the nature of essences.

The second new essay in this collection is Gene Witmer's, "A Simple Theory of Intrinsicality." It's helpful to understand Witmer's simple theory against the background of the less simple theory he developed with William Butchard and Kelly Trogdon. Witmer, Butchard, and Trogdon (2005) offer a definition that relies on the idea that intrinsic properties are independent of accompaniment, but unlike the L & L account, theirs does not depend in any way on the notion of a natural property. They add to the "Simple Independence" requirement (that intrinsic properties are those that are independent of accompaniment) the "Strong Independence" constraint that intrinsic properties are not had *in virtue of* any properties that are not independent of accompaniment. They propose: "Property P is intrinsic iff, for any possible individual x, if x has P, x has P in an intrinsic fashion," where "x has P in an intrinsic fashion iff (i) P is independent of accompaniment and (ii) for any property Q, if x has P in virtue of having Q, Q is also independent of accompaniment" (2005, p. 333).[13]

---

[13] While the disjunctive property, being *either cubical and lonely or non-cubical and accompanied*, is independent of accompaniment, neither disjunct is independent of accompaniment.

The Strong Independence Constraint relies on the notion of properties had *in virtue of* other properties. With this talk of being had *in virtue of*, Witmer et al. are appealing to a dependence relation of major interest in recent metaphysics—the *grounding* relation. In Witmer's essay for this anthology, the idea of independence from accompaniment is eliminated, with the notion of grounding now doing all the work. The result is a more elegant theory, and with plausible results in a wider range of cases.

One intriguing component of Witmer's essay is his defense of the view that the *global* notion of an intrinsic property should be viewed as more basic than the *local* notion. The global notion is employed when we speak of a property itself being intrinsic, and the local notion is used when we talk about a property had intrinsically (or extrinsically) by some individual at some time. As Dunn instructs, there is a difference between "*being an intrinsic property* (as a kind), and *intrinsically being a property of a given individual* (as a specific happening)" (1990, p. 183, original emphasis). Dunn illustrates by noting that a square object has the property of being *square-or-accompanied* intrinsically, even though the property itself is often considered extrinsic (since it is possible for it to be had extrinsically, e.g., by accompanied circular objects). Lloyd Humberstone (1996) introduces the labels 'local' and 'global' in the context of intrinsic properties and illustrates the distinction with the example of *being either made of tin or adjacent to something made of tin*. This property would seem to count as an intrinsic feature of tin objects but it is an extrinsic feature of adjacent tinless items. Now, it is tempting to define the global notion in terms of the local: a property is plausibly defined as intrinsic just in case it is always exemplified intrinsically. As Humberstone puts it, "the intrinsic properties are precisely those which are locally intrinsic to all their possessors" (1996, p. 228). Witmer, however, argues that despite this tempting and standard view, the global notion is more basic, with the local notion to be defined in terms of it.

The idea that the global notion is the more fundamental is quite contrary to the thoughts on intrinsicality expressed by Carrie Figdor. In her 2008 essay, "Intrinsically/Extrinsically," Figdor reveals that those mixed cases, in which a prop-

---

Since an object has the disjunctive property either in virtue of having the first disjunct or in virtue of having the second, the Witmer et al. analysis gives the intuitively correct result that the disjunctive property is never had intrinsically. Their analysis also gives the presumably correct result that being a rock is extrinsic, for while being a rock is independent of accompaniment, an object has that property at least partly in virtue of the absence of surrounding material of the same kind, which is not independent of accompaniment. Being such that there is a cube is also correctly classified as extrinsic on their account since while it is independent of accompaniment, the property is had by non-cubes in virtue of being accompanied by distinct cubical objects.

erty is had intrinsically and also extrinsically, are not confined to the designer properties of metaphysicians (e.g., being made of tin or next to something made of tin). When we focus on less contrived properties, we also find many mixed cases. Figdor considers (among others) the properties of being witty and being a good basketball player. Some individuals have these properties solely in virtue of what they are like in themselves, independently of their environments. Others have them only because they are in the right external circumstances (e.g., being in the company of another witty person, or being on the court with a superstar). With the help of these mixed cases, Figdor (2008) argues that we should understand the I-ly/E-ly distinction (having a property intrinsically vs. having a property extrinsically) independently of the I/E distinction. Talk of having properties I-ly, she claims, indicates independence from contextually relevant counterfactual circumstances. When we ask whether something has value intrinsically, "we are asking whether it would still be valuable in relevant counterfactual circumstances, not where its value is spatiotemporally located" (2008, p. 698). Which counterfactual circumstances are relevant and when depends on our explanatory purposes, as she describes in detail. If these ideas are correct, then there is reason to suspect that in addition to mixed-cases in which one individual or object has a property intrinsically and another has it extrinsically, there are ultra-mixed cases in which the very same item has the same property intrinsically and extrinsically at the very same time. In her essay, "What's the Use of an Intrinsic Property?," written for this anthology, Figdor makes it clear that these ultra-mixed cases can and do obtain. Consider, for instance, an item that is valuable due to its internal properties and at the same time valuable also because it is valued by others. As Figdor explains, such cases threaten the global notion of intrinsicality, especially the exclusivity of the global notion (the implication that a property cannot be both intrinsic and extrinsic). She further argues that we can legitimately question whether the global notion is of any philosophical value, and in the latter half of her essay she illustrates by showing how the global notion fails to illuminate various metaethical debates.

Even if one denies that the same property can be had both intrinsically and extrinsically, one might still allow that in some cases *necessarily coextensive* properties differ in their intrinsicality. The intrinsic/extrinsic distinction certainly is *intensional* since there are coextensive predicates, 'F' and 'G', where 'F' denotes an intrinsic property and 'G' denotes an extrinsic property (suppose 'F' = 'being an aardvark' and 'G' = 'belonging to my friend Tony's favorite animal type'). The intrinsic/extrinsic distinction would also be *hyperintensional* if it were the case that there are necessarily coextensive (cointensive) predicates, 'F' and 'G', such that 'F' denotes an intrinsic property and 'G' denotes an extrinsic property. As M. Eddon (2011) demonstrates, a strong case can be made that the intrinsic/extrinsic distinction is hyperintensional. And yet, each of the highly influential accounts mentioned in section 1, along with the analysis Vera Hoffmann-Kolss offers in her 2010 book, *The Metaphysics of Extrinsic Properties*, entail that the intrinsic/extrinsic distinction is *not* hyperintensional.[14] Hoffmann-Kolss defends this consequence in her essay, "Is the Intrinsic/Extrinsic Distinction Hyperintensional?," written for this collection. She argues that as typically construed, the intrinsic/extrinsic distinction involves two dependence claims: that intrinsic properties are those whose instantiation by any x depends only on what x is like, whereas extrinsic properties are those whose instantiation by some x depends on what individuals distinct from x are like. With these dependence claims, Hoffmann-Kolss shows how Eddon's conclusion can plausibly be resisted.

Despite Hoffmann-Kolss' compelling defense, in my "Intrinsic/Extrinsic: A Relational Account Defended," written for this collection, I grant (for the sake of discussion) that intrinsicality is hyperintensional and I try to decide whether a *grounding* approach is best suited to capture this hyperintensionality, or whether the appeal to *identity* (of instances of intrinsic properties with instances of internal properties) described in my 1999 definition of 'intrinsic' is preferable. Perhaps not surprisingly, I defend the latter (with the help of Marshall's 2013 critique of grounding analyses), and I also respond to some objections that have been raised to my 1999 account.

In section 1, I mentioned the 2001 essay that Marshall wrote with Parsons, where they show that the L & L analysis has trouble with quantificational properties, e. g., being such that there is a cube, that seem to be extrinsic even though they are independent of accompaniment. In his 2009 essay, Marshall argues that (in the absence of any special assumptions about properties) an adequate definition of 'intrinsic' in terms of only broadly logical notions is bound to fail. By "broadly logical" notions, Marshall includes those that can be expressed with the vocabulary of first-order predicate logic, the modal notions of possibility and necessity, the mereological notions of part and whole, and the notions of identity and set membership. In his paper, "Yablo's Account of Intrinsicality," which he wrote for this anthology, Marshall argues specifically against Yablo's (1999) broadly logical analysis. He considers Yablo's analysis in its concretist

---

14 In *The Metaphysics of Extrinsic Properties*, she presents a *relational* analysis of the intrinsic/extrinsic distinction. The basic idea underlying a relational account is that F is extrinsic just in case one has F due to one's relations to distinct items; otherwise F is intrinsic. In her book, Hoffmann-Kolss develops a sophisticated relational account that, she argues, improves on other relational accounts (including my 1999 definition) and also improves on various non-relational (e. g., duplication and combinatorial) analyses.

form (with the assumption that possible worlds are concrete items) and in its neutral form (compatible with all accounts of possible worlds), and shows that in either form Yablo's account and various modifications of it are unsuccessful.

Given the failure of previous attempts to characterize intrinsicality, one might wonder whether there is a coherent notion here to be defined at all.[15] Alternatively, one might wonder whether the failure to successfully define 'intrinsic' is due to the notion's being *primitive*. In "Primitivism about Intrinsicality," presented here, Alexander Skiles addresses some important issues that have received little attention in the literature on intrinsic properties. There is the basic issue of what it could be, exactly, for intrinsicality to qualify as primitive, and what a viable primitivist account of intrinsicality could and should look like. There is also the question of what reasons there are to believe that primitivism about intrinsicality is true, and whether compelling arguments can be given to oppose the view. Skiles' clear and detailed exploration of these issues is of great service to those wondering about the prospects of primitivism, and his discussion is one that should also be minded by those who continue to search for an adequate reductionist analysis.

The final two essays in this anthology are not concerned with defending or refuting any particular approach to defining intrinsicality. What they reveal, instead, is what the physical sciences can tell us about intrinsic properties. In an earlier paper, Michael Esfeld (2003) describes how quantum theory provides evidence that the fundamental physical properties are not intrinsic. Since physics can only reveal the way in which things are related to one another, we can believe either that (i) there are fundamental physical properties of the intrinsic variety, but we cannot know them, or that (ii) at the level of basic physics, there are only the relations that items bear to each other. Esfeld (2003) points out that while purely philosophical considerations cannot decide between these two positions, quantum theory provides reason to accept (ii) rather than (i). In his new paper, "Physics and Intrinsic Properties," Esfeld further develops the argument that quantum theory supports (ii). He describes a view of the physical world in which matter is primitive stuff distributed in space, and the properties of physics are dispositions that fix the temporal development of the distribution of matter in space. As Esfeld explains, in classical mechanics, these physical properties can be thought of as the intrinsic properties of particles. However, quantum physics suggests that there is only one structure or holistic property that relates

---

15 Note Dennett's (1988, p. 67) suspicions about the notion.

all matter and fixes the temporal development of its distribution in space, and therefore that none of the basic properties of physics are intrinsic.

Earlier in this section I mentioned Eddon's (2011) compelling defense of the view that intrinsicality is hyperintensional. In "Intrinsic Explanations and Numerical Representations," which she wrote for this anthology, Eddon defends Hartry Field's support of "intrinsic explanations" of physical phenomena. Field argued that with his treatment of quantity, (i) we are able to provide intrinsic explanations of a variety of physical phenomena and (ii) we are also able to provide intrinsic explanations of why certain numerical representations of quantities are acceptable and others are not. Eddon refutes arguments that have been offered against both claims, arguments that rely on the fact that our numerical representations of quantitative features are largely a matter of convention. It is true that the numerical representations of quantitative features that we employ are conventional. Yet, Eddon shows, the conventionality of these numerical representations does not entail the conventionality of the features themselves. The conventionality of our numerical representations is perfectly compatible with (i)'s being true. Eddon does agree that Field's framework fails to establish (ii). She shows, however, that we can modify his framework so that we can provide intrinsic explanations for why some numerical representations are better than others.

Much thanks to the authors who have contributed to this collection—David Denby, Maya Eddon, Michael Esfeld, Carrie Figdor, Vera Hoffmann-Kolss, Dan Marshall, Alex Skiles, and Gene Witmer. Their addition to the literature on the intrinsic/extrinsic distinction is of great value to all of us who are trying to understand the nature of intrinsicality. Thanks, also, to Rae Langton, Peter Vallentyne, Brian Weatherson, and Stephen Yablo for agreeing to have their important work on intrinsic properties reprinted here.[16]

---

[16] I am grateful, also, to Gertrud Grünkorn, Christoph Schirmer, and the rest of the Philosophy Editorial Staff at De Gruyter. I also thank Peter Atterton, Steven Barbone, and Tom Weston at San Diego State for their advice on formatting, and much thanks to Kimberly Unger for all her help with proof-reading. And special thanks to Blanca Francescotti for her undying emotional support.

References

Denby, David A. (2006). "The Distinction between Intrinsic and Extrinsic Properties." *Mind* 115(457): pp. 1–17.
Denby, David A. (2010). "Intrinsic and Extrinsic Properties: A Reply to Hoffmann-Kolss." *Mind* 119(475): pp. 773–782.
Dennett Daniel (1988). "Quining Qualia." In A. J. Marcel and E. Bisiach (eds.), *Consciousness in Contemporary Science* (pp. 42–77). New York: Oxford University Press.
Dunn, J. Michael (1990). "Relevant Predication 2: Intrinsic Properties and Internal Relations." *Philosophical Studies* 60(3): pp. 177–206.
Eddon, Maya (2011). "Intrinsicality and Hyperintensionality." *Philosophy and Phenomenological Research* 82(2): pp. 314–336.
Esfeld, Michael (2003). "Do Relations Require Underlying Intrinsic Properties?: A Physical Argument for a Metaphysics of Relations." *Metaphysica:* 4(1): pp. 5–25.
Fine, Kit (1994). "Essence and Modality." *Philosophical Perspectives* 8: pp. 1–16.
Figdor, Carrie (2008). "Intrinsically/Extrinsically." *The Journal of Philosophy*, 105(11): pp. 691–718.
Francescotti, Robert (1999). "How to Define Intrinsic Properties." *Noûs* 33(4): pp. 590–609.
Hoffmann-Kolss, Vera (2010). *The Metaphysics of Extrinsic Properties.* Frankfurt: Ontos-Verlag
Humberstone, I. Lloyd (1996). "Intrinsic/Extrinsic." *Synthese* 108(2): pp. 205–267.
Kim, Jaegwon (1982). "Psychophysical Supervenience." *Philosophical Studies* 41(1): pp. 51–70.
Langton, Rae and David Lewis. (1998). "Defining 'Intrinsic'." *Philosophy and Phenomenological Research* 58(2): pp. 333–345.
Lewis, David (1983a). "Extrinsic Properties." *Philosophical Studies* 44(2): pp. 197–200.
Lewis, David (1983b). "New Work for a Theory of Universals." *Australasian Journal of Philosophy* 61(4): pp. 343–377.
Lewis, David (1986). *On the Plurality of Worlds.* Oxford: Blackwell.
Lewis, David (2001). "Redefining 'Intrinsic'." *Philosophy and Phenomenological Research* 63(2): pp. 381–398.
Marshall, Dan (2009). "Can 'Intrinsic' Be Defined Using Only Broadly Logical Notions?" *Philosophy and Phenomenological Research* 78(3): pp. 646–672.
Marshall, Dan (2013). "Intrinsicality and Grounding." *Philosophy and Phenomenological Research*. Early view: published online, 3 July 2013.
Marshall, Dan and Josh Parsons (2001). "Langton and Lewis on 'Intrinsic'." *Philosophy and Phenomenological Research* 63(2): pp. 347–351.
Moore, G. E. (1922). *Philosophical Studies.* London: Routledge and Kegan Paul.
Sider, Theodore (1996). "Intrinsic Properties." *Philosophical Studies* 83(1): pp. 1–27.
Sider, Theodore (2001). "Maximality and Intrinsic Properties." *Philosophy and Phenomenological Research* 63(2): pp. 357–364.
Vallentyne, Peter. (1997). "Intrinsic Properties Defined." *Philosophical Studies* 88(2): pp. 209–219.
Weatherson, Brian. (2001). "Intrinsic Properties and Combinatorial Principles." *Philosophy and Phenomenological Research* 63(2): pp. 365–380.

Weatherson, Brian and Dan Marshall (2013). "Intrinsic vs. Extrinsic Properties." In E. N. Zalta (ed.), *The Stanford Encyclopedia of Philosophy* (Spring 2013 edition). http://plato.stanford.edu/archives/spr2013/entries/intrinsic-extrinsic/

Witmer, D. Gene, William Butchard and Kelly Trogdon (2005). "Intrinsicality without Naturalness." *Philosophy and Phenomenological Research* 70(2): pp. 326–350.

Yablo, Stephen. (1999). "Intrinsicness." *Philosophical Topics* 26(1/2): pp. 479–505.

Rae Langton, David Lewis
Defining 'Intrinsic'*

Something could be round even if it were the only thing in the universe, unaccompanied by anything distinct from itself. Jaegwon Kim once suggested that we define an intrinsic property as one that can belong to something unaccompanied. Wrong: unaccompaniment itself is not intrinsic, yet it can belong to something unaccompanied. But there is a better Kim-style definition. Say that *P is independent of accompaniment* iff four different cases are possible: something accompanied may have *P* or lack *P*, something unaccompanied may have *P* or lack *P*. *P is basic intrinsic* iff (1) *P* and *not-P* are non-disjunctive and contingent, and (2) *P* is independent of accompaniment. Two things (actual or possible) are *duplicates* iff they have exactly the same basic intrinsic properties. *P is intrinsic* iff no two duplicates differ with respect to *P*.

I Kim and Lewis

Jaegwon Kim defined an *intrinsic* property, in effect, as a property that could belong to something that did not coexist with any contingent object wholly distinct from itself.[1] Call such an object *lonely* or *unaccompanied;* and call an object *accompanied* iff it does coexist with some contingent object wholly distinct from itself. So an intrinsic property in the sense of Kim's definition is a property compatible with loneliness; in other words, a property that does not imply accompaniment.[2]

Published in *Philosophy and Phenomenological Research* 58: 333–345 (1998).
* We thank C. A. J. Cody, Allen Hazen, Richard Holton, Peter Menzies, George Molnar, Denis Robinson, Barry Taylor, and those who discussed this paper when it was presented at the 1996 Australasian Association of Philosophy conference. We also thank the Boyce Gibson Memorial Library. One author owes a particular debt to Lloyd Humberstone, who prompted her interest in contemporary (as opposed to eighteenth century) work on the metaphysics of intrinsic properties. Preliminary versions of some of the ideas in the present paper were raised in Langton's 'Defining "Intrinsic"', Appendix 2 of *Kantian Humility*, Princeton University Doctoral Dissertation, 1995. They are applied to Kant in the dissertation, and in a book, tentatively titled *Kantian Humility*, Oxford University Press (1998).
1 Jaegwon Kim, 'Psychophysical Supervenience', *Philosophical Studies* 41 (1982, pp. 51–70).
2 This way of putting it simplifies Kim's formulation by foisting on him a view he is not in fact committed to: the view that things that persist through time consist of wholly distinct temporal parts at different times. Given that view, one way for you-now to be accompanied is for you to persist through time, so that you-now coexist with your past or future temporal parts. But Kim himself remains neutral about the metaphysics of temporal parts; so what he actually says is as follows. Property *G* is *rooted outside the time at which it is had* iff, necessarily, for any object *x* and time *t*, *x* has *G* at *t* only if *x* exists at some time before or after *t*; *G* is *rooted outside the things*

David Lewis objected that loneliness itself is a property that could belong to something lonely, yet it is not an intrinsic property. He concluded that Kim's proposal failed. He also conjectured that nothing resembling Kim's definition would work, and if we want to define 'intrinsic' we had best try something altogether different.[3]

II A Kim-style Definition

That sweepingly negative judgement was premature. Though Kim's definition does indeed fail, a definition in much the same style may succeed.

First step. One intuitive idea is that an intrinsic property can be had by a thing whether it is lonely or whether it is accompanied. It is compatible with either; it implies neither.

Second step. Another intuitive idea is that, although an intrinsic property is compatible with loneliness, a thing's being lonely is not what makes the thing have that property. Lacking the property also is compatible with loneliness. And likewise with accompaniment: if a property is intrinsic, being accompanied is not what makes something have that property. Lacking the property also is compatible with accompaniment.

Putting the first and second steps together, we have that all four cases are possible. A lonely thing can have the property, a lonely thing can lack the property, an accompanied thing can have the property, an accompanied thing can lack the property. For short: having or lacking the property is *independent* of accompaniment or loneliness.

So can we define an intrinsic property as one that is independent in this way?—Subject to some qualifications, yes; but not in full generality.

A first qualification is that the proposed definition, and likewise all that follows, is to be understood as restricted to pure, or qualitative, properties—as opposed to impure, or haecceitistic, properties. There may be impure extrinsic properties, such as the property of voting for Howard (as opposed to the pure extrinsic property of voting for someone). There may be impure intrinsic properties, such as the property of being Howard, or having Howard's nose as a proper part (as opposed to the pure intrinsic property of having a nose as a proper

---

that have it iff, necessarily, any object x has G only if some contingent object wholly distinct from x exists; G is *intrinsic* – Kim's term is 'internal' – iff G is neither rooted outside times at which it is had nor outside the things that have it. We shall ignore this complication henceforth.
3 David Lewis, 'Extrinsic Properties', *Philosophical Studies* 44 (1983, pp. 197–200).

part).[4] These impure properties are had only by Howard, and not by Howard's duplicates, or even (perhaps) his counterparts. Our proposal is offered as a way of distinguishing amongst the pure, or qualitative properties, those which are intrinsic, and those which are extrinsic. Impure properties are set aside as falling outside the scope of the present discussion. To be sure, we might eventually wish to classify impure properties also as intrinsic or extrinsic. But that is a task for another occasion.

III The Problem of Disjunctive Properties

Our proposed definition, as it stands, plainly does not work for disjunctive properties. Consider the disjunctive property of being either cubical and lonely or else non-cubical and accompanied. This property surely is not intrinsic. Yet having or lacking it is independent of accompaniment or loneliness: all four cases are possible.

So we require a second qualification: our definition should be deemed to fall silent about disjunctive properties. All it does is to divide non-disjunctive intrinsic properties from non-disjunctive extrinsic properties.

(The same goes for any definition that selects some one or two or three of the four cases, and says that a property is intrinsic iff all the selected cases are possible. Again, the property of being cubical and lonely or else non-cubical and accompanied will be misclassified as intrinsic.)

If a property is independent of accompaniment or loneliness, its negation also is independent. Yet if a property is intrinsic, so is its negation; and if a property is not intrinsic, neither is its negation. So we would expect trouble with negations of disjunctive properties. The property of being neither cubical and lonely nor non-cubical and accompanied is independent of accompaniment or

---

4 Pure and impure relational properties are described in E. J. Khamara, 'Indiscernibles and the Absolute Theory of Space and Time', *Studia Leibnitiana* 20 (1988, pp. 140–59). The notion of pure and impure intrinsic properties, by analogy with Khamara's distinction, was raised by Rae Langton (in conversation) and discussed by Humberstone in 'Intrinsic/Extrinsic', *Synthese* 108 (1996, pp. 205–67) (accepted for publication in 1992), and in Langton's *Kantian Humility* (Princeton University Doctoral Dissertation, 1995). The notion of an 'interior property' attributed by Humberstone to J. M. Dunn includes both impure and pure intrinsic properties (J. M. Dunn, 'Relevant Predication 2: Intrinsic Properties and Internal Relations', *Philosophical Studies* 60 (1990, pp. 177–206)). Humberstone distinguishes the family of duplication-related concepts of intrinsicness from the interiority conception, and from a notion he calls non-relationality of properties.

loneliness: all four cases are possible. Yet it is not intrinsic. So the definition proposed so far fails in this case too.[5]

What is a disjunctive property? Not just any property that can be expressed as a disjunction! Any property at all can be expressed as a disjunction: something is *G* iff either it is *G*-and-*H* or else it is *G*-and-not-*H*. But we think most philosophers will be willing to help themselves to some version or other of the distinction between 'natural' and 'unnatural' properties. Given that distinction, we can go on to capture our intuition that some properties are 'disjunctive' in a way that other properties are not.

Some of us will help ourselves to some sort of primitive notion of naturalness of properties. Others will accept an ontology of sparse universals, or of sparse tropes, that has a built-in distinction between natural properties and other properties. Still others will wish to characterize the natural properties as those that play some interesting special role in our thinking—but for our present purposes, even this vegetarian metaphysics will suffice. One way or another, most of us will be prepared to grant such a distinction.[6] Here we must say farewell to those who will not make so free, and carry on without them.

What matters for now is not how we begin, but how we continue. Given some or other notion of natural properties, let us define the *disjunctive* properties as those properties that can be expressed by a disjunction of (conjunctions of)[7] natural properties; but that are not themselves natural properties. (Or, if naturalness admits of degrees, they are much less natural than the disjuncts in terms of which they can be expressed.) That done, we can cash in our previous partial success, as follows.

Third step: the *basic intrinsic* properties are those properties that are (1) independent of accompaniment or loneliness; (2) not disjunctive properties; and (3) not negations of disjunctive properties.

The basic intrinsic properties are some, but not all, of the intrinsic properties. Other intrinsic properties include disjunctions or conjunctions of basic in-

---

[5] A neater example is due to Peter Vallentyne ('Intrinsic Properties Defined', *Philosophical Studies* 88 (1997, pp. 209–19)): the property of being the only red thing. This is the negation of the disjunctive property of being either non-red or else both red and accompanied by another red thing.

[6] See *inter alia* David Lewis, 'New Work for a Theory of Universals', *Australasian Journal of Philosophy* 61 (1983, pp. 343–77); David Lewis, 'Against Structural Universals', *Australasian Journal of Philosophy* 64 (1986, pp. 25–46, especially p. 26); Barry Taylor, 'On Natural Properties in Metaphysics', *Mind* 102 (1993, pp. 81–100); Mary Kathryn McGowan, *Realism or Non-Realism: Undecidable in Theory, Decidable in Practice* (Princeton University Doctoral dissertation, 1996).

[7] The point of the parenthetical insertion is to remain neutral on the question whether all conjunctions of natural properties are themselves natural.

trinsic properties; and, indeed, arbitrarily complicated, even infinitely complicated, truth-functional compounds of basic intrinsic properties.

IV Duplication

Now we pause to recall a familiar pair of definitions. Two things (actual or possible) are (intrinsic) *duplicates* iff they have exactly the same intrinsic properties. (That is: iff all and only the intrinsic properties of one are intrinsic properties of the other.) *Intrinsic properties*, on the other hand, are those properties that never can differ between duplicates. A tight little circle—and, like all circles of interdefinition, useless by itself. But if we can reach one of the interdefined pair, then we have them both.

And we can. For how could two things differ in their disjunctive properties if they differed not at all in their non-disjunctive properties? And that goes for their disjunctive and non-disjunctive intrinsic properties as it does for their disjunctive and non-disjunctive properties in general. Likewise for all other forms of truth-functional combination, even infinitely complicated forms of truth-functional combination. So we have this:

Fourth step: two things are (intrinsic) *duplicates* iff they have exactly the same basic intrinsic properties.

Fifth step: a property is *intrinsic* iff it never can differ between duplicates; iff whenever two things (actual or possible) are duplicates, either both of them have the property or both of them lack it.

So our definitional circle has opened out into a little spiral. Those intrinsic properties that were left out at the third step, for instance because they were disjunctive, are admitted at the fifth step. The basic intrinsic properties afford a basis upon which all the intrinsic properties supervene. We have our definition.

V The Problem of Strong Laws

The modal status of laws of nature has become a matter of controversy. Some deny that laws are mere regularities; rather, laws are said to be regularities that hold by necessity.[8] In other words, it is impossible for them to have counter-

---

[8] See, for instance, Sydney Shoemaker, 'Causality and Properties' in *Time and Cause,* ed. Peter van Inwagen (Reidel, 1980); Chris Swoyer, 'The Nature of Natural Laws', *Australasian Journal of Philosophy* 60 (1982, pp. 203–23).

instances. But independence of accompaniment or loneliness is a modal notion. If laws are strong, maybe fewer properties than we think will turn out to be independent of accompaniment or loneliness. Then must we conclude that fewer properties than we think are intrinsic?

Suppose, for instance, that the only way that the laws permit for a star to be stretched out into an ellipsoid is for it to orbit around another massive star, and undergo distortion by the tidal effects of its companion. The property of being an ellipsoidal star would seem offhand to be an intrinsic property. In fact, it would seem to be a basic intrinsic property. However, this property is incompatible—nomologically incompatible—with loneliness.

But isn't that the wrong sort of incompatibility?—Not if laws are strong! In that case, if an ellipsoidal lonely star is nomologically impossible, it is impossible *simpliciter*. That would mean that the property of being an ellipsoidal star is not a basic intrinsic property—indeed, not any kind of intrinsic property—after all!

Some friends of strong laws may agree: they may say that our intuitions of what is intrinsic are made for a loose and separate world, and it is only to be expected that a world of necessary connections will defy these intuitions.

Well, that is one option. But there is another, perhaps better, alternative. If a theory of strong laws is to be credible, it had better provide not only a sense of 'possible' in which violations of laws are impossible, but also another sense in which violations of laws are possible. Perhaps that second sense cannot be provided. In that case the doctrine of strong laws is not credible enough to deserve consideration. Or perhaps that second sense can somehow be provided. (Friends of strong laws might think it a hoked-up, artificial sense.[9] But no harm done, provided they acknowledge the possibility of lonely ellipsoidal stars, or whatnot, in some sense or other.) If so it is this sense of possibility, whatever it may be, that a friend of strong laws should use in defining 'intrinsic'.

The doctrine that God exists necessarily is problematic in a similar way to the doctrine of strong laws. Suppose it to be true. The property of being divinely

---

9 They might say that it is a matter of truth in all not-quite-literally-possible world-stories; or that it should be explained in terms of what possible worlds there are according to a certain Humean fiction. On fictionalist treatments of possibility, see Gideon Rosen, 'Modal Fictionalism', *Mind* 99 (1990, pp. 327–54), and 'Modal Fictionalism Fixed', *Analysis* 55 (1995, pp. 67–73); and for yet another slightly artificial sense in which violations of strong laws may count as possible, see Denis Robinson, 'Epiphenomenalism, Laws and Properties', *Philosophical Studies* 69 (1993, p. 31). And in working out these hoked up possibilities, they had better heed Allen Hazen's warning not to do so in a way that makes the definition circular, by using a principle of recombination stated in terms of intrinsic properties.

created turns out, surprisingly, to be a basic intrinsic property. How so?—Surely this property requires accompaniment by a divine creator, wherefore it is a property incompatible with loneliness.—No. An accompanied thing, we said, coexists with a contingent object distinct from itself. So accompaniment by necessarily existing God does not count.

What to do? If we change the definition of accompaniment by striking out the word 'contingent', it will turn out that if anything at all exists necessarily, whether it be God or the number 17, then loneliness is impossible, so no property at all is compatible with loneliness. That cure only makes matters worse.

Or we might accept the conclusion that if God exists necessarily, then the property of being divinely created is intrinsic; and we might deem this conclusion to be a swift *reductio ad absurdum* against the idea of God's necessary existence. Altogether too swift! Or we might accept the bankruptcy of intuition in the face of divine mysteries.

Perhaps a better alternative is again to distinguish senses of necessity. Perhaps God's existence may be supposed to be necessary in some sense. Yet in a second sense, it still might be contingent. (We could expect disagreement about which sense is straightforward and which sense is artificial.) A conviction that the property of being divinely created is not intrinsic would then be evidence, for those of us who are prepared to take the supposition of God's necessary existence seriously, that it is the second sense and not the first that should be used in defining 'intrinsic'.

VI The Status of Dispositions

Some authors take for granted that dispositional properties, such as fragility, should turn out to be intrinsic. Others are equally sure they are extrinsic. Where do we stand?

The answer implicit in our definition is: it depends. We remain neutral (here) between rival theories about what it means to be a law of nature. Different theories of lawhood will yield different answers about whether dispositions are intrinsic in the sense of the definition. A satisfactory situation, we think.

Let us assume that a disposition (or at least, any disposition that will concern us here) obtains in virtue of an intrinsic basis together with the laws of nature. Then whether the disposition is intrinsic boils down to whether the property of being subject to so-and-so laws is intrinsic. We have three cases.[10]

---

10 Ignoring the possibility that not all laws have the same status.

Case 1. The laws are necessary, in whatever sense should be used in defining 'intrinsic'. Then the property of being subject to so-and-so laws is automatically intrinsic. (See Section VII.) Dispositions are likewise intrinsic.

Case 2. The laws are contingent, in whatever is the appropriate sense; and further, the laws to which something is subject can vary independently of whether that thing is accompanied or lonely. Then being subject to so-and-so laws will presumably turn out to be a basic intrinsic property.

Case 3. The laws are contingent; but the property of being subject to so-and-so laws (or perhaps the conjunction of that property with some aspect of intrinsic character) is not independent of accompaniment or loneliness. Suppose, for instance, that laws are regularities that hold throughout a large and diverse cosmos. Then a lonely thing (unless it were itself of cosmic size) would be subject to no laws, for lack of a cosmos to serve as lawmaker. Or suppose that laws of nature are divine decrees, but that the law-making gods are lowly gods and exist contingently. Then a lonely thing, unaccompanied by a law-making god (and not itself a god) would again be subject to no laws. Under either of these suppositions, something unaccompanied by a lawmaker would be subject to no laws. So dispositions would in this case be extrinsic.

Those who take for granted that dispositions are intrinsic may just be dismissing Case 3 out of hand. Or they may instead have a concept of intrinsic properties that is best captured not by our definition but by a version amended so as to ensure that dispositions (with intrinsic bases) will count as intrinsic, no matter what the correct metaphysical theory of lawhood may be.[11]

Likewise, those who take for granted that dispositions are extrinsic may just be dismissing Cases 1 and 2. Or they may instead have a concept of intrinsic properties that is best captured not by our definition but by a version amended so as to ensure that dispositions will count as extrinsic, no matter what the correct theory of lawhood may be.[12]

---

[11] Amended as follows: at the fifth step, after saying what it is for two things to be duplicates, end by saying that a property is intrinsic iff it never can differ between duplicates *provided that these duplicates are subject to the same laws*. Here we have adapted a suggestion put forward by Lloyd Humberstone in 'Intrinsic/Extrinsic', which in turn is an adaptation of a notion he finds in Kim's informal discussion, 'Psychophysical Supervenience', pp. 66–8. (Humberstone offers a nomologically sensitive notion of intrinsicness, according to which something is nomologically intrinsic – 'Kim+-intrinsic', in his terms – iff duplicates in worlds with the same laws never differ with respect to it.)

[12] Amended as follows: wherever 'lonely' appears in the first and second steps of our definition, put instead 'lonely *and lawless*', where 'lawless' means 'subject to no laws'. (We might need to resort to some hoked-up sense of possibility to ensure that lonely and lawless things are

VII Consequences of our Definition

A property which necessarily belongs to everything never differs between any two things; *a fortiori* it never differs between duplicates. Therefore the necessary property (or, if you prefer to individuate properties more finely than by necessary coextensiveness, *any* necessary property) turns out to be intrinsic under our definition. Likewise, the (or any) impossible property turns out to be intrinsic.

Here is another way to make the point: necessary and impossible properties supervene on the basic intrinsic properties in the trivial way that non-contingent matters supervene on any basis whatever. There can be no difference in the supervenient without a difference in the basis, because there can be no difference in the supervenient at all.

Is this consequence acceptable?—We think so. True, the distinction between intrinsic and extrinsic is of interest mostly when applied to *contingent* properties: that is, properties that are neither necessary nor impossible. But it is harmless to apply it more widely. True, necessary or impossible properties can be specified in ways that make gratuitous reference to extraneous things—but the same is true of all properties. (As witness the property of being cubical and either adjacent to a sphere or not adjacent to a sphere.)

As already noted, the basic intrinsic properties are some, but not all, of the intrinsic properties. Intrinsic properties that are disjunctive, or that are negations of disjunctive properties, are not basic intrinsic. We have just seen that non-contingent properties also are intrinsic, but of course they are not basic intrinsic. (A property that cannot be lacked at all cannot be lacked by lonely or by accompanied things; one that cannot be had at all cannot be had by lonely or by accompanied things.) But are these the only cases in which the intrinsic properties outrun the basic intrinsic properties?—Our answer is a qualified 'yes'.

Suppose we assume that every accompanied thing has a lonely duplicate, and every lonely thing has an accompanied duplicate. (Here we are speaking of possible things that may or may not be actual.) That assumption may be controversial: on the one hand, it is part of an attractive combinatorial conception of possibility;[13] but for that very reason it will be open to doubt from friends of strong laws, unless they devise a special sense in which violations of strong laws are 'possible'.

---

possible.) Here we have adapted a suggestion put forward in Vallentyne, 'Intrinsic Properties Defined'.

13 Such as that advanced on pp. 87–92 of David Lewis, *On the Plurality of Worlds* (Blackwell, 1986); or in D. M. Armstrong, *A Combinatorial Theory of Possibility* (Cambridge University Press, 1989).

Without that assumption, we cannot answer the question before us. Making the assumption, we answer the question as follows. If a property is contingent, not disjunctive, not the negation of a disjunctive property, and intrinsic, then it is basic intrinsic.

> Since the property is contingent, some possible thing x has it and some possible thing y lacks it. By our assumption about duplication, x has a duplicate x' which is lonely iff x is accompanied. Since the property is intrinsic and never differs between duplicates, x' also has it. Likewise y has a duplicate y' which is lonely iff y is accompanied, and y' also lacks the property. So the property is independent of accompaniment or loneliness. Therefore it is basic intrinsic. QED.

Recall our starting point: loneliness itself is a property compatible with loneliness, hence intrinsic according to Kim's definition; yet Lewis judged loneliness not to be intrinsic. We would want our definition to classify loneliness, and likewise accompaniment, as extrinsic properties. And so it does. (At least, given our assumption that every accompanied thing has a lonely duplicate, and every lonely thing has an accompanied duplicate.) For loneliness and accompaniment are not basic intrinsic properties; they are not disjunctive properties or negations thereof; and they are contingent properties.

The same goes (subject to the obvious provisos) for properties that imply accompaniment or loneliness: the property of being an accompanied cube, the property of being a lonely sphere, the property of being a daughter, the property of being an entire cosmos are all of them extrinsic. So far, no surprises and no problems.

Other examples are more questionable: ontological categories, posited by contentious metaphysical systems, which may (or may not) be reserved for accompanied entities. Could there be a change without something to undergo that change? If not, and if the change and the changing thing are counted as distinct coexisting entities, then the property of being a change is a property that implies accompaniment. Likewise *mutatis mutandis* for the category of events more generally; for the category of immanent universals;[14] and for the category of states of affairs.[15]

A straightforward option is to follow wherever our definition may lead. That would mean deciding to say, for instance, that the property of being a change was extrinsic—and so likewise was any more specific property of being so-and-so sort of change. But mightn't we want to classify properties of changes

---

14 See D. M. Armstrong, *Universals and Scientific Realism* (Cambridge University Press, 1978).
15 See D. M. Armstrong, *A World of States of Affairs* (Cambridge University Press, 1997).

in a way that conflicts with that decision? Some changes are sudden, others are gradual; some changes are foreseen, others are unexpected. Wouldn't we want to say that the property of being a sudden change, unlike the property of being a foreseen change, is an *intrinsic* property of changes? But then we had better not also say that the property of being so-and-so sort of change always counts as *extrinsic*.

A timid option is to limit the scope of our definition, declaring that it is meant to apply only to properties of things, not to properties of entities in other categories. That would keep us safe from misclassification, at the cost of cutting us off from some applications of the intrinsic/extrinsic distinction. (Think, for instance, of those familiar discussions in philosophy of mind that attempt to delineate the intrinsic from the extrinsic aspects of brain events. Well lost?—We doubt it.)

A laborious option might be to tinker with the notion of distinctness. When something changes, the thing and the change coexist, and in some sense these are two wholly distinct entities. But perhaps there is room for another, more relaxed sense in which the thing and its change do *not* count as distinct. In that relaxed sense, a sudden change to something in an otherwise empty universe could count as lonely, even though it remains true that the change and the changing thing coexist. We get the desired result that being sudden qualifies as an intrinsic property of changes. A foreseen change, however, could not possibly count as lonely even in the relaxed sense.

What makes this option laborious is that the work of tinkering with the notion of distinctness may have to be done over, category by category and metaphysical system by metaphysical system. A tall order! Nevertheless, probably the best alternative.

All the more so, because there is another side to the problem—a difficulty that the other options fail to address. Unless somehow we can block the conclusion that a changing thing and its changes are distinct coexisting entities, not only does it turn out that the changes are accompanied by the thing, but also that the thing is accompanied by its changes. Then a changing thing cannot be lonely; so the property of changing is not basic intrinsic, and presumably not intrinsic at all! Never mind what we do or do not want to say about the properties of changes; the trouble now is that we are misclassifying a property of ordinary things. The laborious option offers a remedy. The straightforward option and the timid option do not.

VIII Relations

Relations, like properties, can be classified as intrinsic or extrinsic. Consider, for example, the case of a two-place relation. (The case of a more-than-two place relation is similar. The case of a one-place relation is just the case of a property.)

The ordered pair of x and y is *accompanied* iff it coexists with some contingent object wholly distinct both from x and from y. (Equivalently, wholly distinct from the mereological sum of x and y, assuming that they have a sum.) Otherwise the pair is *lonely*. A relation is *independent* of accompaniment or loneliness iff all four cases are possible: a lonely pair can stand in the relation, a lonely pair can fail to stand in the relation, an accompanied pair can stand in the relation, an accompanied pair can fail to stand in the relation.

For relations, as for properties, we distinguish pure from impure (qualitative from haecceitistic) relations, and we set aside the latter. We also distinguish natural from unnatural relations; that enables us to distinguish disjunctive relations from others. Now, the *basic intrinsic relations* are those (pure) relations that are (1) independent of accompaniment or loneliness; (2) not disjunctive relations; (3) not negations of disjunctive relations. Two ordered pairs are *duplicates* iff they stand in exactly the same basic intrinsic relations. A relation is *intrinsic* iff it never can differ between duplicate pairs.

So far, just a transposition of what we already said about properties. But we end with a distinction that has no parallel in the case of properties. Some relations are *internal*: they supervene on the intrinsic properties of their relata. A relation of match in intrinsic respects, for example congruence of shape, is an internal relation. A spatio-temporal distance relation is an intrinsic relation (unless nature holds surprises), but not an internal relation. The relation of aunt to niece is not an intrinsic relation at all.[16]

We can show that the internal relations are some, but perhaps not all, of the intrinsic relations.

> If x and x' are duplicates, and so are y and y', it follows that x stands to y in exactly the same internal relations as x' stands to y'. Yet it does not follow that the pair of x and y and the pair of x' and y' are duplicate pairs; so it does not follow that x and y stand in all the same intrinsic relations. Suppose, on the other hand, that the pair of x and y and the pair of x' and y' are duplicate pairs: they stand in all the same intrinsic relations. Then x and x' have the same basic intrinsic properties, and so likewise do y and y'. Suppose, for instance, that x has basic intrinsic property F. Let R be the relation that anything

---

[16] Beware: our use of the term 'internal relation' is not to be conflated with that of the British Idealists. For a different terminology, see Lewis, 'New Work for a Theory of Universals', p. 356 (fn. 16): a relation 'intrinsic to its relata' versus a relation 'intrinsic to its pairs'.

having F stands in to everything, and anything else stands in to nothing. R is not a disjunctive relation or the negation of a disjunctive relation; since F is independent of accompaniment and loneliness, so is R; so R is a basic intrinsic relation; so R is an intrinsic relation. Since x has F, x stands in R to y; so x′ stands in R to y′; so x′ also has F. Likewise for all other basic intrinsic properties of x, x′, y, and y′. So the two duplicate pairs stand in the same internal relations. Since internal relations never can differ between duplicate pairs, they are intrinsic relations. QED.

IX Lewis

When Lewis objected to Kim's definitions of 'intrinsic' and advised that we should try something completely different, the line he took was as follows.[17] Having become persuaded by D. M. Armstrong that we should be willing to help ourselves to a distinction between natural properties and other properties, he put forward the hypothesis that all perfectly natural properties are intrinsic; and further, that two things are duplicates iff they have exactly the same perfectly natural properties. Then he said (just as we have) that a property is intrinsic iff it never can differ between duplicates—and he was done.

That definition is simpler than our present one. So far as we can see, it does not conflict with our present one. What's wrong with it? True, Lewis had to help himself to a distinction between natural properties and others—but so did we.

Reply: Lewis's burden of commitments was, nevertheless, much heavier than ours. All we need is enough of a distinction to sort out the disjunctive properties from the rest. We need not insist that it makes sense to single out a class of *perfectly* natural properties, as opposed to a larger class of *natural-enough* properties; or that the members of our élite class will all, without exception, strike us as intrinsic; or that the élite class will serve as a basis on which the complete qualitative character of everything there is, and everything there could have been, supervenes. You can believe all that if you like. Indeed, Lewis still does believe all that. But for present purposes, at least, we can get by with much less; and if we get by with much less, we have a definition we can offer to philosophers more risk-averse than Lewis.

---

[17] David Lewis, 'New Work for a Theory of Universals', pp. 355–57.

X Vallentyne

Peter Vallentyne considered the definition of an intrinsic property as a property independent of accompaniment or loneliness, and rejected it for the reasons we have considered.[18] He then turned in a different direction.

Vallentyne helps himself to the notion of a duplicate, and considers in particular the lonely duplicates of things. He says, in effect,[19] that G is an intrinsic property iff G never can differ between a thing and a lonely duplicate of that thing.

This is not far away from something familiar: the half of the tight little circle that we've already seen which says that an intrinsic property is one that never can differ between duplicates.

The restriction to the case where one of the duplicates is lonely makes no difference, provided we may assume that everything has a lonely duplicate.

> Suppose G never can differ between duplicates at all. *A fortiori*, G never can differ between a thing and its lonely duplicate. Conversely, suppose G never can differ between a thing and its lonely duplicate. Let x and y be duplicates. We have assumed that there exists a lonely duplicate of x, call it z. By transitivity of duplication, z is a duplicate also of y. *Ex hypothesi* G does not differ between x and z, or between y and z. So G does not differ between x and y. QED.

You might think the definitional circle between 'intrinsic' and 'duplicate' is too tight to be enlightening; or you might think it's worth something. We think it's worth something, but we think a definition that starts at a greater distance from its target is worth more. But, either way, Vallentyne's new twist on the tight circle—his attention to the special case of the lonely duplicate—seems not to make much difference. So, while we don't suggest that Vallentyne's definition fails to work, it seems to us that our rival definition has something more to offer.

---

[18] Vallentyne, 'Intrinsic Properties Defined'. Vallentyne's work was independent of ours and approximately simultaneous.

[19] This is a simplification of Vallentyne's actual formulation. Further complications arise because (1) Vallentyne, like Kim, remains neutral about the metaphysics of temporal parts; (2) his definition covers impure as well as pure properties; and (3) he uses a version of the 'lonely and lawless' amendment considered in Section VI (note 12) in order to classify 'law-constituted' properties – e.g. dispositions – as extrinsic.

Peter Vallentyne
Intrinsic Properties Defined

Intuitively, a property is intrinsic just in case a thing's having it (at a time) depends only on what that thing is like (at that time), and not on what any wholly distinct contingent object (or wholly distinct time) is like. A property is extrinsic just in case it is non-intrinsic. Redness and squareness are intrinsic properties. Being next to a red object is extrinsic.

Distinguishing intrinsic from extrinsic properties is important for at least two reasons. First, we want to distinguish real change from mere Cambridge change. A change in intrinsic properties is a real change in an object, whereas change in extrinsic properties isn't. Second, we want to distinguish qualitatively, but not numerically, identical objects (i.e. duplicates) from numerically identical objects. Distinct duplicate objects, we want to say, share all their intrinsic properties, but not all their extrinsic properties. (For reasons given below, this second desideratum is reasonable only if somewhat modified.)

Giving a precise and adequate definition of intrinsicness has turned out to be extremely difficult. David Lewis, for example, has criticized a definition of intrinsic properties developed by Jaegwon Kim (who was building on one by R.M. Chisholm), and rightly finds it lacking.[1] He conjectures that no adequate definition is possible within the usual logical framework. We need, he suggests, to expand our framework by recognizing an irreducibly new primitive notion of intrinsicness or something related to it (such as naturalness).

I agree. I shall argue, however, that an enlightening definition of intrinsicness can be given in terms of the notion of a contraction of a world (roughly a world obtained by removing some of the objects in the original world). Although this concept is not part of the usual logical framework, it is an intuitively familiar concept, and appealing to it, I claim, permits an adequate definition of intrinsicness.[2]

Published in *Philosophical Studies* 88: 209–219 (1997).
1 See, David Lewis, "Extrinsic Properties," *Philosophical Studies* 44 (1983, pp. 197–200), and Jaegwon Kim, "Psychological Supervenience," *Philosophical Studies* 41 (1982, pp. 51–70).
2 Throughout, I restrict my attention to monadic properties, but it is possible to extend the definition to relations. Following David Lewis *On the Plurality of Worlds* (Oxford: Basil Blackwell, 1986, p. 62), we can say that a relation is intrinsic to its relata *taken individually* just in case it is entailed by the having of intrinsic properties of its relata (e.g., being taller is intrinsic in this sense, since it is entailed by intrinsic height properties). A relation is intrinsic to its relata *taken together* just in case it meets the proposed definition with the relata being treated as an object (e.g., being aware of is intrinsic in this, but not the former, sense, since for any two objects it is

To motivate the definition I give, I shall first review Lewis's criticism of Kim's definition, and then suggest and criticize an imperfect improvement. Then I shall give the final definition.

Let A be the property of being accompanied in the world by at least one distinct object. Here and below, for brevity, understand references to a *distinct* object as references to an object that is *wholly* distinct (i.e., having no parts in common) and *contingent* (i.e., that exists in some but not all possible worlds).

Kim's definition, Lewis shows, comes to the following:

1. P is intrinsic =df Px is compatible with ~Ax.

The intuitive idea is that P can be had by an object even in a world with no other distinct objects.

Lewis criticizes this characterization on the grounds that it classifies ~A (i.e., being unaccompanied in the world by any wholly distinct contingent object) as intrinsic, but intuitively ~A is extrinsic. After all, an object has that property only if there are no other distinct objects.

It might seem that Lewis's counterexample could be sidestepped with a little fiddling with Kim's definition. And indeed it can. But, as I shall show, this still won't free Kim's account of its troubles. In fact, by seeing that Kim's definition cannot be salvaged with a few changes to avoid these counterexamples, we will see that it contains a fundamental flaw in its understanding of "independence".

Kim's definition can be improved so as to avoid Lewis's counter-example as follows:

2. P is intrinsic =df Px is compatible with Ax and with ~Ax, and so is ~Px.

That is, P is intrinsic just in case neither the presence nor absence of P entails the presence, or the absence, of some wholly distinct contingent object.

~A is rightly classified as extrinsic on this account, since it is not compatible with A. And similarly, A is rightly classified as extrinsic. Redness and squareness are rightly classified as intrinsic. But there is still a problem. Let S be squareness and R be redness. Then (S&A)v(R&~A) is wrongly classified as intrinsic, since any accompanied square (non-square) object has (lacks) it, and any unaccompanied red (non-red) object has (lacks) it. But intuitively this property is extrinsic, since a square, non-red object has it *only if* accompanied. The having of this property

---

unaltered in the contraction). The relation of having more siblings, on the other hand, is not intrinsic in either sense, since it depends on how many siblings (which are distinct objects) each of the relata has.

depends on whether there are other objects present, and is thus extrinsic. The above definition gets it wrong.

The property of being the only red object is also wrongly classified as intrinsic. For it is compatible with being accompanied (by non-red objects) and with being unaccompanied, and its negation is compatible both with being accompanied and with being unaccompanied (when not red).

The problem with this second definition is that it is formulated in terms of logical independence (compatibility), and this fails to capture the relevant notion of independence. It fails, for example, to capture the idea that being the only red object in the world depends on what other objects are present and what they are like. It fails to capture the idea that an object can cease to be the only red object in the world by the "mere addition" of a red object to the world.[3]

In order to capture the relevant notion of dependency, we shall appeal to the notion of a *contraction* of a given world, which is to be understood as a world "obtainable" from the original one solely by "removing" objects from it. For example, starting with a world that contains just two red squares, the world "obtainable" by "removing" one of the squares is a contraction of the original world. Although the idea of contractions is not part of the standard logical framework, it is a notion with which we are intuitively familiar.

We shall appeal to certain sorts of *maximal* contractions, which contract as much as possible while still leaving a specified object existing at a specified time. More specifically, we shall appeal to the notion of an *x-t-contraction* of a given world, where x is an object and t is a time. The intuitive idea is that such a contraction is a world "obtainable" from the original one by, to the greatest extent possible, "removing" all objects wholly distinct from x, all spatial lo-

---

[3] One possible way of capturing the relevant notion of dependence is to appeal to relevance logic (according to which, roughly, A relevantly implies B only if A can be used non-vacuously to derive B). Michael Dunn defends this view in "Relevant Predication 2: Intrinsic Properties and Internal Relations," *Philosophical Studies* 60 (1990, pp. 177–206), and "Relevant Predication 1: The Formal Theory," *Journal of Philosophical Logic* 16 (1987, pp. 347–381). Ted Sider criticizes (successfully, I believe) Dunn's approach in "Intrinsic Properties," *Philosophical Studies* 83 (1996, pp. 1–27). (Sider argues more generally in favor of Lewis's claim that no reductive definition of the intrinsicness is possible solely in terms quasi-logical vocabulary.) Here I shall not attempt to assess the adequacy of this approach. Instead, I shall provide a definition that makes no use of relevance logic, and argue that it is adequate. I should mention also that Rae Langton and David Lewis are in the process of developing another approach which takes the second definition of intrinsicness as its starting and then appeals to an independent distinction between disjunctive and non-disjunctive properties. Their paper "Defining 'Intrinsic'" will be presented at the 1996 annual conference of the Australasian Association of Philosophy.

cations not occupied by x, and all times (temporal states of the world) except t, from the world. An x-t-contraction of a world is typically a small world if x and t are small. It typically has just one time, t, and just one object (and its parts). As will be noted below, the qualifications "to the greatest extent possible" and "typically" are needed to cover some cases where it may not be metaphysically possible to remove all wholly distinct objects.

Intrinsic properties are those the having, or lacking, of which does not depend on what the rest of the world is like. The notion of an x-t contraction will help us capture this notion, but if it is to do so, it must be understood as also involving the "removal" of any laws of nature governing the behavior of objects. For the intrinsic properties of an object in a given world do not depend on what the laws of nature happen to be in that world. For laws are part of the "rest of the world". Because an object can have an exact duplicate in a world with different laws of nature, x-t contractions must be understood as involving the removal of laws, as well as wholly distinct objects, and times. An x-t contraction will thus typically be a lawless world.

It should be noted that we are not presupposing that there is a unique x-t contraction. It may be that the existence of x at t requires the existence of other objects or times without requiring the existence of any *particular* other objects or times. In such a case, there will be several distinct ways of maximally removing objects (or times or laws) from a world. We shall return to this point below.

We are now ready for the final definition of intrinsicness:

3. P is intrinsic =df for any world w, any time t, and any object x: (a) if Px at t in w, then Px at t in each x-t contraction of w, and (b) likewise for ~P.[4]

Redness (R) and squareness (S) are rightly classified as intrinsic, since contractions don't change an object's color. Being accompanied by a wholly distinct contingent object (A), and its negation (~A), are rightly classified as extrinsic, since at least sometimes (and typically) objects lack A in contracted worlds.

---

4 This definition captures the notion of being intrinsic *relative to an instant of time*, which is the most common notion. Being 10 years old is not intrinsic on this conception, since having it depends on existence at prior times. The definition could be modified to capture the notion of being intrinsic *relative to an object* by dropping the temporal specification in the contraction condition, and replacing it with a temporal contraction to just those points at which the specified object exists. Being 10 years old would be intrinsic in that sense. One could also capture other notions of intrinsicness by modifying the definition to make it relative to a duration of time, or a set of times.

The property (R&A)v(S&~A) is rightly classified as extrinsic, since at least sometimes (and typically) an R&A object will lack it in contracted worlds. And being the only red object in the world is rightly classified as extrinsic, since its negation (i.e., not being red or being accompanied by a distinct red object) is lost in some contractions for a red object accompanied by other red objects.[5]

That completes the development of the basic idea. The idea is that by appealing to x-t contractions we can identify those properties the having or lacking of which does not depend on the presence or absence of other objects or times. This, of course, presupposes that we have a grasp of the notion of x-t contractions, and I claim that we do. We know what a given world would be like if nothing changed except that certain objects were removed. The notion of an x-t contraction is simply the limiting case where as many objects are removed as possible compatibly with x existing at t.

It should be emphasized, however, that the definition of intrinsicness given in terms of x-t contractions is completely inadequate as a *reductive* definition of intrinsicness in terms of standard logical notions. For the idea of a contraction is not a standard logical notion, nor is it definable in such terms. For one world is a contraction of a second world just in case it is *exactly like it* except that first has some objects in it that the second doesn't. This notion is obviously very close to the notion duplication (it's duplication minus some objects). So the definition fails as a reductive definition. Nonetheless, the idea of a contraction is intuitively clear and familiar, and the definition of intrinsicness in terms of contractions is enlightening because it captures some connections that have not been adequately appreciated.

I turn now to some complexities and problems with the account. One objection is that it seems to classify secondary qualities, such as redness, as extrinsic, which seems wrong. For secondary qualities are response-dependent, and if the responders are removed from the world, objects will cease, it seems, to have the secondary qualities. We need, however, to distinguish between two sorts of response-dependence. On a *rigid* response-dependent account, the responses of some fixed set of beings not necessarily in the world of the object (e.g., us as we are here and now) determines what secondary qualities are had. On this ac-

---

[5] Note that the definitions of intrinsicness given here are definitions of when a property is intrinsic – not of when a property is intrinsic *to a particular object*. Consequently, some extrinsic properties will in an intuitive sense be intrinsic to *whole worlds*. For example, containing some and all of the red objects in the world is classified as an extrinsic property, even though the property is in a sense intrinsic (internal) to any whole world that has it. Likewise, being in a world with certain sorts of laws is classified as extrinsic, even though when a world has that property, it depends on nothing outside that world.

count objects have secondary qualities even in worlds in which there are no responders. For the relevant responders are not beings in the world in question, but rather some independently specified and fixed set of responders. So there is no problem here. If, however, the response-dependence of secondary qualities is understood non-rigidly and as requiring responders in the same world, then the proposed account does indeed classify such secondary qualities as extrinsic. But so understood, they are intuitively extrinsic. For the having of such a property depends on what the rest of the world is like. So, there is no problem in this case either.[6]

A second objection to the contraction account of intrinsicness concerns law-constituted properties such as water-solubility. An object with a particular chemical composition (e.g., a sodium particle) that is water-soluble in a given world need not be water-soluble in a world that has different laws. Water and sodium may not be nomically related in the second world in the requisite manner. More specifically, an object, x, that is water-soluble in a given world at a time t, need not be (and typically is not) water-soluble in an x-t contraction of the given world (since there are no, or very few, laws). Consequently, water-solubility is not classified as an intrinsic property on the proposed account. And more generally, law-constituted properties are not classified as intrinsic.[7]

Is this a problem? Initially, water-solubility and the like might seem like intrinsic properties, but once one recognizes the dependence on what the laws of nature are, it seems more correct to classify such properties as extrinsic. A more serious worry, however, comes from the idea that *all* properties are law-constituted. This idea requires a more careful discussion than I can give it here, but a few remarks will at least help place the issue in perspective. First, although it is plausible that all, or at least most, properties are law-*governed* in the sense that the laws of nature control how they interact with other properties, it is far from clear that all are law-*constituted* in the sense that there are no properties if there are no laws. Of course, one might hold this view for a special sense of properties (e. g., as logically sparse natural properties or as universals, as opposed to logically abundant attributes), but that is not at issue here. Here we are concerned with properties in the logically abundant sense of anything that can be instantiated or which has a negation that can be instantiated. Even in lawless worlds there are properties in this sense (e.g., the property of being in a lawless world). So, it's doubtful that all properties are law-constituted.

---

[6] For further discussion of the difference between the two types of response-dependence see Peter Vallentyne, "Response-Dependence, Rigidification, and Objectivity," *Erkenntnis* 44 (1995), pp. 101–112).
[7] I owe this point to Walter Edelberg and Al Casullo.

Furthermore, even if all properties are law-constituted, the proposed account seems to be right in claiming that in such a case no properties are intrinsic. For in that case, all properties depend on what the rest of the world is like (namely what the laws of nature are). So, law-constituted properties are not counter-examples, at least not clear and compelling ones, to the proposed account.

A third objection to the account concerns non-qualitative properties such as being at a particular spatial or temporal location, or being identical to a particular individual. These are classified as intrinsic on the proposed account, since having them does *not* depend on whether any other objects exist, or what they are like. If any object, x, has in a given world, w, and at given time, t, the property of being located at a particular time, or of being identical with George Washington, then it will have those properties in any x-t contraction of w.[8] Thus the contraction account classifies them as intrinsic. This seems, however, mistaken. For it is generally held that intrinsic properties are shared by duplicates, but duplicates cannot share the sorts of properties just listed. An exact duplicate of George Washington does not have the property of being (numerically) identical to George Washington.

What this shows, I claim, is that we need to distinguish between two senses of intrinsicness. In the *broad sense*, a property is intrinsic just in case having it is appropriately independent of the existence of other objects. The above definition, I claim, captures this notion. This notion captures what is relevant for distinguishing real change from Cambridge change. In the *narrow sense*, a property is intrinsic just in case it is intrinsic in the broad sense *and is a qualitative property*. The property of being (numerically) identical to George Washington, and the like, are not qualitative properties in that they "involve", or "make an essential reference to" particular objects, times, or spatial locations. With this distinction, we can say that duplicate objects share all their broadly intrinsic *qualitative* properties, but not all their broadly intrinsic non-qualitative properties.[9]

---

8 Somewhat more precisely: On an absolutist conception of space and time, spatial and temporal location properties will turn out to be intrinsic on the proposed definition. On a relational conception of space and time, however, objects would (presumably) lack the property of being at a specific location in the contracted world, since the relevant relations to other times and locations will not hold. Consequently, on a relational theory such properties will not be classified as intrinsic on the proposed account. The problem remains even here, however, for identity properties (such as being identical to George Washington).

9 A related objection is that grueness (green at t and t is before 2000 A.D., or blue at t and t is on or after 2000 A.D.) is classified as intrinsic on the contraction account. Given the specific reference to 2000 A.D., this is a non-qualitative property as well. In "Intrinsic Properties" Ted Sider raises this problem for defining intrinsicness in general, but then sets it aside as non-

It turns out that giving a rigorous and enlightening definition of qualitativeness is extremely difficult. I do not know how to do any better than the hand-waving characterization just given. Consequently, I do not know how to give an enlightening and rigorous definition of intrinsicness in the narrow sense. Still, intrinsicness in the broad sense is an important notion. Changes in spatial or temporal location are more genuine changes in a thing than changes in the status of being the only red object.

More generally, there are two independent distinctions at work in the discussion of intrinsicness and duplicates: (1) the distinction between those properties the having or lacking of which is independent of the presence or absence of other objects (for the genuine/Cambridge change distinction), and (2) the distinction between qualitative and non-qualitative properties. Redness is qualitative and independent, being larger than some red object is qualitative and dependent, being identical with George Washington is non- qualitative and independent, and coexisting with George Washington is non-qualitative and dependent. The contraction account captures the "independence" notion, but does not capture the notion of intrinsicness as that which perfect duplicates share. But it can capture this notion if we presuppose the distinction between qualitative and non-qualitative properties. For duplicates share all their qualitative, "independent" (as characterized by the contraction account) properties.

A fourth objection comes from considering essential properties of objects. Suppose, for example, that having a particular date of origin is essential to Smith. Then there is no world and time with Smith in it at that time that doesn't also have Smith in it on that earlier date of origin. Consequently, any Smith-t contraction will include Smith on that date. (This is an example of how contraction may not reduce to a single time. Other examples might show how they may not reduce to the single object specified.) This might make it seem that having a particular date of origin will turn out be an intrinsic property on the contraction account, since Smith loses neither it, nor its negation, on contraction.[10] But this need not be so. For, although having a given date of origin may be essential for people (let's say), it may not be essential for other sorts of objects (such as rocks). As long as there is some object for which the having of a particular date of origin is not essential, then it can be lost on contraction. Because the contraction account of intrinsicness classifies a property as extrinsic (non-intrinsic)

---

qualitative. He agrees that the independence notion of intrinsicness is independent of the shared by duplicates notion.

10 I owe this point to David Braun and Ted Sider.

if it can be lost on contraction by some object, the property won't be classified as intrinsic.

We're not out of the forest yet, however. It all depends on whether there are any properties that are *universally* essential in the sense that every object either has it essentially or lacks it essentially. (Note that for lack of a better word, in the stipulated sense, universally essential properties can be lacked by some objects, but if they are, they are lacked essentially.) If there are universally essential properties, then such properties will indeed be classified as intrinsic on the contraction account. Thus, for example, if having a given date of origin is universally essential, then the contraction account classifies it as intrinsic (since neither it, nor its negation can be lost on contraction)—even though such a property relates to the past. This is admittedly most unsatisfying.

One line of defense would be to argue that there aren't any universally essential properties. Being of a particular species is, however, a fairly plausible candidate for being universally essential. Of course this particular universally essential property is not problematic for the proposed account, since intuitively it is intrinsic, and the account classifies it as intrinsic. The problematic universally essential properties are past-regarding, or future-regarding, universally essential properties, such as having a particular origin. Are there any such properties? Even here it seems that there are. For although having a particular origin may not be universally essential, something like being human and having a particular origin (e. g., date, or sperm and egg) may well be. The issues here are, of course, deep and murky, but it does not seem promising to answer the objection by denying the existence of such properties.

The best strategy, I think, is simply to acknowledge that if there are universally essential properties, it is not a mistake to classify them as intrinsic (even if past-regarding). For a universally essential property is such that either it, or its negation is "metaphysically glued" to every single object. If there are past-directed, or future-directed, universally essential properties, then times are not as independent as we intuitively think. For in that case, an object's existence at one time metaphysically requires that the object have certain features at another time. Consequently, in an important sense, there is no dependence (since there is no room for variation) on what the rest of the world is like. If this is right, then the problem of universally essential properties is a problem for *any* account of intrinsicness, and thus one that requires rethinking of our intuitive responses. Past-regarding, and future-regarding, universally essential properties are strange things, and once understood, it's not so crazy to classify them as intrinsic.

In closing, let us recall that the proposed definition of intrinsicness has two limitations. One is that it does not distinguish between qualitative and non-qualitative properties. So it fails to identify exactly those properties that exact duplicates share. Nonetheless, the definition captures the notion of being independent of what other objects there are and what they are like, and thus grounds an account of real (vs. Cambridge) change. The second limitation is that it does not yield of a reductive definition of intrinsicness solely in terms of standard logical notions. For it appeals to the notion of a contraction of a world, and that is not a standard notion. Still, the definition captures an important and underappreciated connection between intrinsicness and our intuitive idea of contractions. It is thus, I claim, an enlightening definition.[11]

---

[11] Thanks to David Braun, Albert Casullo, Walter Edelberg, David Lewis, Trenton Merricks, Gene Mills, Ted Sider, Raymond Woller, and an anonymous referee for this journal for helpful comments.

Stephen Yablo
Intrinsicness[1]

I Introduction

You know what an intrinsic property is: it's a property that a thing has (or lacks) regardless of what may be going on outside of itself. To be intrinsic is to possess the second-order feature of stability-under-variation-in-the-outside-world.

You probably know too why this is hopeless as a philosophical account of intrinsicness. "Variation in the outside world" has got to mean "variation in what the outside world is like *intrinsically*." Otherwise every property G is extrinsic; for a thing cannot be G unless the objects outside of it are *accompanied* by a G.[2]

But, although the naive account is circular, it is not beyond salvage. Leave aside for a minute the problem of saying what *in general* constitutes intrinsic variation in the outside world. A special case of the notion can be defined independently. This special case, suitably iterated, turns out to be enough; suitably iterated the special case *is* the general case.

II Analysis

Before introducing the special case, a word about motivation. A philosophical account of X ought if possible to bring out de jure relations between X and other notions. It is not enough if X covaries as a matter of fact with ABC, even if the de facto covariation is counterfactually robust. (I include here metaphysically necessary covariation as the limiting case.) How well has this condition—

Published in *Philosophical Topics* 26: 479–505 (1999).
[1] This paper repays an old debt to Sydney Shoemaker. Years ago, as editor of *Philosophical Review*, he allowed me to cite a manuscript on intrinsicness that I was unable to provide at the time. He asked for it again in 1994, when he taught a seminar on intrinsicness; all I could offer was a one-page sketch of the main idea. Now you've got it, Sydney! I had help from Sally Haslanger, Ned Hall, Rae Langton, Jennifer McKitrick, Gideon Rosen, Alan Sidelle, Ted Sider, Judy Thomson, and Ralph Wedgwood. I wish I could acknowledge a greater debt to Peter Vallentyne's "Intrinsic Properties Defined"; it would have saved me a lot of trouble to have seen it earlier. An implicit subtheme here is that there is more to Vallentyne's approach than Langton and Lewis give him credit for.
[2] Jaegwon Kim, "Psychophysical Supervenience," *Philosophical Studies* 41 (1982, pp. 51–70).

the "de jure condition," let's call it—on a successful analysis been respected in the literature on intrinsicness?

The first proposal worth mentioning is due to Jaegwon Kim. G is intrinsic according to Kim iff it is compatible with *loneliness:* the property of being unaccompanied by any (wholly distinct, contingently existing) thing.[3] It seems of the essence of intrinsicness that an intrinsic property should be possessable in the absence of other things; and so Kim's account does fairly well with the de jure condition. The problem with the account is that, as Lewis noticed back in 1983, it gives the wrong results.[4] Loneliness is as extrinsic as anything; but since it is a property compatible with loneliness (!), Kim would have to call it intrinsic.

What about Lewis's own account, according to which G is intrinsic iff given any x and y with the same natural properties, x is G iff y is G?[5] This gives more accurate results, but an element of de facto-ness has now intruded. If some natural property H should fail to be intrinsic, the account will overgenerate; it will call H "intrinsic" regardless. You may say that such a situation will never arise, and you may be right. The problem is that its never arising seems no more than a lucky accident.[6] There is no *in principle* reason why theorists of the quantum domain should not find themselves forced by nonlocality phenomena to count certain extrinsic properties as "ground floor" and natural. Because there is nothing in the nature of intrinsicness to prevent this, it is a matter of luck that Lewis's story succeeds as well it does.

A modified account developed with Rae Langton draws only on a particular aspect of naturalness, viz., nondisjunctiveness.[7] According to Langton and Lewis, G is "basic intrinsic" iff (i) G and its negation are independent of loneliness and accompaniment and (ii) G and its negation are nondisjunctive. The intrinsic properties are the ones that never distinguish between things with the same basic intrinsic properties.

If you think that nondisjunctiveness comes closer than naturalness to being in the same conceptual ballpark as intrinsicness, then the modified account is

---

3 Kim (1982).
4 David Lewis, "Extrinsic Properties," *Philosophical Studies* 44 (1983, pp. 197–200).
5 "New Work for a Theory of Universals," *Australasian Journal of Philosophy* 61 (1983, pp. 343–77). The formulation in the text leaves out some irrelevant complications.
6 "Accident" is meant to be compatible with a fact's holding necessarily. If God and the null set are both necessary beings, then it is impossible for either to exist without the other. Still the correlation is accidental in the sense I have in mind.
7 David Lewis and Rae Langton, "Defining 'Intrinsic'," *Philosophy and Phenomenological Research* 58 (1998).

more de jure than its predecessor. But an element of de facto-ness remains. Consider the property R of being the one and only round thing. R satisfies (i) and the first half of (ii); if it avoids being (basic) intrinsic, then, that is because it is the negation of the disjunctive property S of being nonround or else round and accompanied by a round thing.

Is S disjunctive, though? That it can be expressed in disjunctive terms doesn't count for much; roundness too can be expressed that way, e.g., as the disjunction of round-and-charged with round-and-not-charged. Better evidence of disjunctiveness would be a finding that S's "disjuncts"—the property of not being round, and that of being round and accompanied by something round—were perfectly natural. But they clearly are not, and so Langton and Lewis are led to maintain that S is at least much *less* natural than its "disjuncts." This means in particular that

S = accompanied by something round *if* round oneself

is much less natural than

T = accompanied by something round *and* round oneself.

It may well be. But there is something uncomfortable about taking an intrinsicness-fact that is very clearcut—the fact that R is not intrinsic—and putting it at the mercy of something as controversial, and (apparently) irrelevant, as the relative naturalness of S and T. One feels that it ought not to *matter* to the issue of R's intrinsicness where S and T come out on the naturalness scale.

Of course, we don't want to be in the position of asking too much. Who is to say that intrinsicness bears *any* worthwhile de jure relations to other notions? Or maybe it bears them only to notions less fundamental than itself—notions that ought to be explained in terms of intrinsicness rather than the other way around.

The answer to this is that intrinsicness *does* appear to line up in nonaccidental ways with something quite fundamental: the relation of part to whole. It seems, for instance, as de jure as anything that

if u is part of v, then u cannot change intrinsically without v changing intrinsically as well.

And that

if u is part of v, then u and v have a region of intrinsic match.

And that

if u is properly part of v, then u and v have intrinsic differences.

So the materials for a more principled account are not obviously lacking. What remains to be seen is whether we can parlay one-way conditionals like the above into a de jure biconditional with intrinsicness all by itself on the left hand side.

III Expansion

The last of our three conditionals says that if one thing is properly part of another, then the two are intrinsically unalike. If you believe that, then you'll agree with me that *one* good way to arrange for intrinsic variation in the world outside of x is to *expand it:* add on something new. This immediately gives a necessary condition on intrinsicness:

> (*) G is intrinsic only if necessarily, whether a thing is or is not G cannot be changed by adding a part to its containing world.

I say that the necessary condition is also sufficient. A counterexample would be a G that could be made to vary through intrinsic variation in the outside world, but not through the particular *sort* of intrinsic variation contemplated here: expansion. But for reasons about to be explained, such a G is not possible.

IV Why expansion is enough

Remember the intuition that we started with: If G is an extrinsic property, then it can be lost (gained) through intrinsic variation in the outside world. It follows from this that there are w and w' such that x has G in w but not w', and the changes rung on w to get w' are *outside* of x.

Because the part of w that lies within x is left absolutely untouched, w and w' have a part in common: a part extending at least to x's boundaries and possibly beyond. Focus now on this shared part. It could have existed all by itself; why not? Another way to put it is that there is a self-standing world (call it w'') consisting of the shared part and nothing else.

The question is, does G obtain in w'' or does it not? However you answer, there are worlds u and v such that (i) x is part of u is part of v, and (ii) G is either lost or gained as you move from u to v. Suppose first that G does obtain in w''; then G is lost as we move from $u = w''$ to $v = w'$. If, on the other hand, G doesn't obtain in w'', then G is gained as we move from $u = w''$ to $v = w$. Either way, G is sensitive to positive mereological variation in the outside world. Condition (*) is not just necessary for intrinsicness but a sufficient condition as well.

V Assumptions

A few implicit assumptions must now be brought to light. Or let me stress: *most of them are for simplicity only* and will eventually be given up. This applies in particular to assumptions (1)-(3), which together go under the name of "modal realism." Later on (see the appendix), we'll be abandoning possible worlds altogether. But for the time being our outlook is very close to that of David Lewis. We accept:

(1) *Pluralism:* This actual world is only one of a large number of possible worlds. It is possible that BLAH iff in at least one of these worlds, BLAH is the case.

(2) *Possibilism:* These other worlds exist—they are part of what there is—but they are no part of actuality.

(3) *Concretism:* Other possible worlds are entities of the same basic sort as this world. They are maximal concrete objects that just happen not to be the same maximal concrete object that we around here inhabit.

(4) *Mereologism:* There is only one part/whole relation worth taking seriously, a relation answering to the axioms of mereology.

(5) *Recombinationism:* The space of worlds is closed under arbitrarily reshuffling of world-parts. As Lewis puts it, "patching together parts of different possible worlds yields another possible world."[8]

Finally, a seeming corollary of (5),

(6) *Inclusionism:* Some worlds contain others as proper parts.

I said that our outlook was "close to" that of Lewis; I might have said that we are going to be more Lewisian than Lewis himself. For it turns out that Recombinationism is *not*, the quoted passage notwithstanding, a view that Lewis accepts. ("An attached head does not reappear as a separated head in some other world, because it does not reappear at all in any other world."[9]) Nor does Lewis accept Inclusionism. The reason is the same in both cases. Both assumptions represent worlds as having parts in common; and the sharing of parts is, according to Lewis, strictly forbidden. (A section of *Plurality of Worlds* is called "Against Overlap." What part of "Against" don't you understand?)

---

[8] David Lewis, *On the Plurality of Worlds* (London: Blackwell, 1986, pp. 87–88).
[9] Lewis (1986, p. 88).

VI Accidental Intrinsics

If one looks, however, at what Lewis actually says in "Against Overlap," his position turns out to be not quite as adamant as suggested:

> my main problem is not with the overlap itself. Things do have shared parts, as in the case of the Siamese twins' hand ... what I do find problematic—inconsistent, not to mince words—is the way the common part of the two worlds is supposed to have different properties in the one world and in the other.[10]

Reading on, we learn what the inconsistency is. According to friends of overlap,

> Humphrey, who is part of this world and here has five fingers on the left hand, is also part of some other world and there has six fingers on his left hand... . He himself—one and the same and altogether self-identical—has five fingers on the left hand, and he has not five but six. How can this be? You might as well say that the shared hand of the Siamese twins has five fingers as Ted's left hand, but it has six fingers as Ned's right hand! That is double-talk and contradiction. Here is the hand. Never mind what else it is part of. How many fingers does it have?[11]

Lewis calls this the *problem of accidental intrinsics*. What matters to us is that it is a problem raised by some cases of overlap, but not all.

The problem does not arise, Lewis says, for Humphrey's *essential* properties,[12] however intrinsic they may be. No explanation is needed of how Humphrey can have different essential properties in different worlds, because he doesn't.

"Neither [does] it arise for Humphrey's extrinsic properties, however accidental." A thing's extrinsic properties are, implicitly, relations it bears to its surroundings. And there is no contradiction whatever in bearing a relation to one set of surroundings (being shorter than anyone in those surroundings, say) that you do not bear to another.

---

[10] Lewis (1986, p. 199).
[11] Lewis (1986, pp. 199–200). This is not the first occurrence of "How many fingers?" in world literature; O'Brien puts the question to Winston in *1984*.
[12] Meaning the ones he has in every world that contains him.

VII Not all Overlap is Bad

As far as the main argument of "Against Overlap" goes, a part of one world *can* recur in another world *provided that its intrinsic properties do not vary between the two worlds*.

One place we might seek assurances on this score is in the nature of the shared item. If the item was of a sort that possessed its intrinsic properties *essentially*, there would be no danger of its changing in intrinsic respects between the one world and the other.

A second place assurances might be sought is in the nature of the *relation* between the two worlds. Even if the item did not retain its intrinsic properties across *all* worlds, it might stay intrinsically the same across certain particular *pairs* of worlds—such as, for example, those standing in the part/whole relation. If so, there would be no objection to saying that the item was shared by those particular pairs of worlds.

And now our cup overfloweth; for our interest here is in a *case* of overlap—the case where one of two worlds is included in the other—that eludes Lewis's strictures in *both* of the ways just mentioned.

It eludes them in the first way because worlds are generally understood to have all of their intrinsic properties essentially.[13] World-inclusion avoids the problem of accidental intrinsics because it is *world*-inclusion.

Also, though, it avoids the problem because it is world-*inclusion*. One world is not part of another unless it recurs in it with the same intrinsic properties it had qua self-standing world.[14] Example: a world just like this one up to five minutes ago, when irresponsible atom-smashing experiments occurred causing everything to pop out of existence *now*,[15] is *not* an initial segment of actuality—

---

[13] Some might say that worlds cannot vary extrinsically either. But our resistance to extrinsic variation is much weaker, or the branching conception of worlds would not be so popular. See John Bigelow, "The World Essence," *Dialogue* 29 (1990), pp. 205–17), for the view that a world's *intrinsic* nature is largely accidental to it.

[14] Advocates of the branching conception appear to take this for granted. A counterfactual world w' branches from the actual world @ at time t iff world w, which has the history of @ up to time *t* as its entire history, is an initial segment of w'. That the relevant intrinsic features of @ "carry over" into w and thence into w' goes without saying.

[15] To go by a recent report in *Scientific American*, this is not altogether out of the question. Atom-smashers have felt moved on occasion to calculate the chances of their experiment flipping the universe into "null-state."

whereas a world just like this one up to now, when everything *miraculously* pops out of existence, *is* an initial segment of actuality.[16]

VIII Definition

I said that G is intrinsic iff, supposing that x has (lacks) G in w, G cannot be canceled (introduced) by moving to w', where w' is w with the addition of a new part.

This may seem unnecessarily cagey. Why "canceled"? Why not just say that there can be no w' of the indicated type in which G fails to be exemplified by the original object x: the object that *did* exemplify G back in w?

One worry would be that x might not *persist* into w'. But if we stick to our policy of departing from Lewis's metaphysics or only when absolutely necessary, this eventuality can be ruled out.

Remember, Lewis is a *mereologist:* he maintains that there is only one containment relation worth taking seriously, a relation (partially) characterized by the axioms of mereology.[17]

How does mereologism eliminate the danger of x not surviving the trip to w'? The story so far is that w and w' have a part in common that contains x. If containment is mereological part/whole, this means that x is a mereological part of the mereological overlap between w and w'. But the overlap between w and w' is (trivially) part of w'. So we can conclude by the transitivity of part/whole that x is part of w', i.e., that w' contains x.

Now, if x persists into w', then it seems clear that x is the thing in w' that G had better still attach to, if G wants to be regarded as intrinsic.[18] This gives us our first official definition of intrinsicness ('<' stands for mereological inclusion):

(1) G is *intrinsic* iff:
     for all $x < w < w'$, x has G in w iff x has G in w'.

---

16 Lewis has other objections to overlap that are meant to apply even when there is no variation in intrinsic properties. He says, for instance, that overlap in the form of branching "conflicts with our ordinary presupposition that we have a single future" *(Plurality of Worlds*, p. 207). But these other objections are not advanced as decisive, and if overlap opens the door to a new account of intrinsicness, that would be an argument on the other side.
17 At least, none of relevance to us; set-membership is a potential counterexample that I would rather put aside.
18 Actually, perhaps it is not so clear. If x sits at a boundary of w, it could happen that x has a different shape in the larger w' than it had in x. Concessions about to be made in response to a different worry should alleviate this one as well.

Roundness is intrinsic, by this definition, because for any w including x and any elaboration w' of w, if it is round in either, it is round in the other. Accompaniment is extrinsic because w and its elaboration w' can overlap on x while differing in the amount of company they provide it.[19]

IX Essential Extrinsics

A consequence of (1) may give us pause. Call a property *absolutely essential* iff anything that has (lacks) it at all has (lacks) it in every world where it exists. Then *every absolutely essential property G is (1)-intrinsic*.[20] (If x has/lacks G essentially, there are not going to be *any* worlds in which x lacks/has G; so there are not going to be any that contain w as a part.) This result gives us pause because it falls afoul of well-known examples of essential properties due to Kripke and others.

Example 1: According to Kripke, I am essentially descended from a certain zygote Z; and it seems plausible as well that nothing can descend (in the relevant sense) from Z without being me. So *descending from Z* is an absolutely essential property. But on almost anybody's account, the zygote stopped existing before I started—whence *descending from Z* is an *extrinsic* property of mine. So how can (1) be believed when it tells us that extrinsicness and absolute essentiality are not compatible?

Example 2: Anything with the property of *being human* has that property essentially; and whatever lacks the property lacks it essentially as well. So *being human* is absolutely essential. But it is not intrinsic; how could it be when it involves an evolutionary lineage reaching back before the time not only of partic-

---

19 Does (1) make a material object's location intrinsic to it? I don't think so. The problem arises only if one is a substantivalist about space-time; it's only if location is the property of occupying such and such space-time points that x's location can be expected to "follow it" from w into the more inclusive w'. But for G to be intrinsic, it's not enough that it can't be lost through world-expansion; a further requirement is that it can't be gained that way either. And this gives us a way out. No one supposes that the space-time points a table occupies are to be counted among the table's *parts*. So the table should be able to survive intact into a world v from which those points had been removed. Consider now v and the more inclusive world v' with which we began. That the table *gains* the property of occupying such and such space-time points in the transition from v to v' tells us that location is not intrinsic according to the definition in the text. (See also n. 30 below.)

20 In this paper, "x has G essentially" means that x has G in every world where it exists. The door is left open to a counterpart-theoretic rejoinder to the argument of the main text.

ular humans but of humanity itself? So *being human* is extrinsic and absolutely essential, again contrary to (1).

Example 3: Consider the property of *being me*, that is, *being SY*. Part of what it takes to be SY is to have the other two properties mentioned; so if they are extrinsic, *being SY* is too. But we know from the necessity of identity (and distinctness) that *being SY* is absolutely essential. So *being SY* is an extrinsic and absolutely essential property, in defiance of (1).

Where are we? Lewis, recall, had his problem of *accidental intrinsics*—the problem being that accidental intrinsic properties are, initial appearances to the contrary, not possible. He "solved" this problem by caving in to it—x's intrinsic properties do indeed have to be essential in one sense: x has them in every world where it exists—and then reestablishing his intended subject matter elsewhere—intrinsic properties do *not* have to be essential in the alternative sense that x shares them with all its counterparts.

Our problem is something like the opposite of Lewis's. It has to do not with accidental intrinsics but *(absolutely) essential extrinsics.* The problem is that (absolutely) essential extrinsic properties, despite making clear intuitive sense, are threatening to come out impossible. Our solution, in the next section but one, will have a similar shape to Lewis's. First, there'll be the caving in: if we limit ourselves to entities of such and such a type, then, yes, absolutely essential properties do have to be intrinsic. (But that is no paradox because entities of the type in question *should* have intrinsic essences.) Second, there'll be the reconstitution elsewhere of our intended subject matter: if we let in entities of such and such *other* types, then absolutely essential extrinsics become once again possible.

X All-Not-Overlap is Bad

I just gave *being SY* as an example of an essential property that was extrinsic to its bearer. I didn't say that *all* identity properties—all properties of the form *being x*—had to be extrinsic. Such a claim would not be plausible, and it has rarely been defended in philosophy.[21] If anything, the tendency has been to fall into the opposite error: the error of seeing *being x* as the intrinsic property par excellence. The right thing to say, with that error now exposed, is that some identity properties are intrinsic and others are not.

---

[21] But see Graeme Forbes, *Metaphysics of Modality* (Oxford: Clarendon Press, 1985), and my review in *Journal of Philosophy* 85 (1988, pp. 329–37).

Take for instance a pair of protons, or two space-time points, or two identically shaped hunks of gunk. Do these have their (separate) identities intrinsically, or not? One can, of course, conceive of the first hunk being the hunk it is due, say, to its causal origins, which were different from the origins of the second hunk. But it takes imagination. The natural (and so presumably not absurd) thought is that the hunks are what they are as a purely intrinsic matter; each gets its identity from its gunk, and the gunk in hunk 1 is not numerically the same as the gunk in hunk 2. A venerable tradition even maintains that when you dig down to the ultimate building blocks of reality—the level of protons and the like, or perhaps a deeper level still—identity is *always* intrinsic. One may agree with the tradition or one may not. But intrinsic identity is certainly not an *incoherent* idea, and so we should take care to allow for it in our theory of intrinsicness.

Allowing for it will be difficult, if overlap is forbidden. The quickest way to see this is via a widely accepted principle of Lewis's connecting intrinsicness to duplication:

(#) the intrinsic properties are the ones that never distinguish duplicates—including, crucially, duplicates in different worlds.

Suppose that overlap is prohibited. Then the property of *being x* distinguishes *x* from its otherworldly duplicates; if the duplicates were also *x* then we'd have overlap. It follows that whatever *x* may be, it has its identity extrinsically.

This is what I am calling problematic. A theory of intrinsicness should not predict right out of the starting gate that there is no such thing as intrinsic identity. But it will predict this if it accepts (#) and rejects overlap.

One response to the difficulty, proposed by Langton and Lewis, is to treat the theory as rendering no judgment in cases like this; the theory defines intrinsicness for "pure" or "qualitative" properties, not "impure" properties like *being x*.

But we might have had hopes of a unitary treatment of intrinsicness that applied to pure and impure properties alike.[22] If so, then our choices are either to reject (#) or to reconcile ourselves to the possibility of overlap. There is nothing wrong with (#), so we need to make our peace with overlap.[23]

The goal is a unitary treatment of intrinsicness—a theory as comfortable with impure intrinsics like *being x* as it is with pure intrinsics. How are we to tell if our attempt at a unified theory has succeeded? It would help if we had examples of

---

[22] Lloyd Humberstone calls this intrinsicness-as-interiority. See his "Intrinsic/Extrinsic," *Synthese* 108 (1996, pp. 205–67).
[23] This is made easier by the fact that the principal objection to it doesn't apply to the kind of overlap we are contemplating.

intrinsic-natured items to test it against. Let's adopt for purposes of this paper the view that worlds are made up of intrinsic-natured atoms a, b, c, ...[24] And let's make it a condition of adequacy on our (eventual) theory that it recognize *being a* as intrinsic for each atom a.

XI Essentialism and Mereology

Back now to the issue we were dealing with before the digression. Analysis (1) may or may not succeed with accidental extrinsics; but to (absolutely) *essential* extrinsics, like *being human*, it is quite blind. All such properties are found by the analysis to be intrinsic.

Could it be that we have been pitching (1) to the wrong audience? A case can be made that the Kripke examples do not refute (1) so much as calling attention to one of its presuppositions. (1) is an analysis for *monolithic mereologists*—people who see no real competitors in the part/whole department to the relation of *mereological parthood*.[25] And a case can be made that the problem of essential extrinsics *does not arise* for the monotholic mereologist, because for her *there are no such properties*.

Why not, you ask? Among the laws of mereology is one called the *unique-sum principle*: take any objects x_1, x_2, x_3, ... you like, there is a unique object $S(x_i)$—their *sum*—with all the x_is as parts and all of whose parts overlap the x_is. If we accept this principle, then it becomes plausible to hold that an absolutely essential property has got to be intrinsic. What is the essence of the x_is' unique sum going to be, after all, if not

(a) to exist in exactly the worlds containing each x_i

(b) to exist at exactly the space-time positions occupied by any x_i

(c) to have the x_is as parts, and

(d) whatever is necessitated by (a)–(c)?[26]

---

[24] Not, I hasten to add, the same ones in every world; some worlds share atoms, others do not. Being composed of atoms a_1 ... a_n will come out intrinsic on our account. See Humberstone, "Intrinsic/Extrinsic," on the distinction between intrinsicness and nonrelationality.
[25] So-called because it is defined in large part by the fact that it satisfies the laws of mereology.
[26] Kit Fine, "Compounds and Aggregates," *Nous* 28 (1994, pp. 137–58). Compare also Judy Thomson's "some-fusions," in Thomson, "The Statue and the Clay," *Nous* 32 (1998, pp. 149–73).

Kit Fine calls the sum defined by (a)–(d) the *aggregate* of the x_is, and remarks that "it has ... often been supposed that aggregation is the only legitimate method of [summation]."[27] Whoever supposes that sums are aggregates and adopts our assumption above that every x is the sum, ultimately, of intrinsic-natured atoms, is well on the way to supposing that x's essential properties are one and all intrinsic to it. For they will find it hard to resist the following line of argument:

> Suppose that P is essential to x, where x is the sum of intrinsic-natured atoms x_i. Then P is necessitated by Q = the property of existing when and where the x_is do, with them as parts. Given the intrinsicness of *being x_i*, x possesses Q regardless of what goes on outside its boundaries. Hence it possesses P the same way; hence x has P intrinsically. Now, if a property essential to x is intrinsic to it, then a property that can *only* be had essentially (an absolutely essential property) can only be had intrinsically. A property that can only be had intrinsically, however, is an intrinsic property.[28] So every absolutely essential property is intrinsic.

The unique-sum principle thus sits very well with (1); for it gives us a basis on which to *reject* the absolutely essential, extrinsic, properties that were causing (1) so much trouble.

If you are with me this far, though, you will see that the unique-sum principle sits very *ill* with the Kripkean perspective. From that perspective it is going to seem unduly limiting to suppose that the essence of an x made up of $x_1, x_2, ...$ has got to be (a)–(d) above.

If we're going to have a sum $S(x_i)$ that exists in a world w iff *all* the x_is exist there, why not a sum $S^1(x_i)$ that exists iff *any* of the x_is exist? Why not a sum $S^2(x_i)$ whose existence in w requires only that *most* of the x_is exist? Why not a sum $S^3(x_i)$ which exists iff all and *only* the x_is exist?[29] Why for that matter should there not be *lots of* sums $S^a(x_i)$, alike in "ordinary" respects but differing in which of their properties they have essentially? And why should not some of these sums have extrinsic properties in their essences—as indeed one of the sums just mentioned already does?

These questions have no good answers, I think, or at least none that the Kripkean can be expected to find convincing. This is why I say that the moral

---

27 Fine, "Compounds and Aggregates," p. 138.
28 The relation between intrinsic *properties* (our topic here) and intrinsic *predication* (having a property intrinsically) is nicely elaborated by Humberstone.
29 That is, a sum $S^3(x_i)$ that exists iff all the x_is exist, and nothing disjoint from them exists.

of the Kripke examples is not that (1) is wrong, but that Kripkeans are not monolithic mereologists and so not among its intended audience.

XII Intrinsicness for the Rest of Us

Even if (1) can be defended as capturing *a* notion of intrinsicness—acceptable perhaps to monolithic mereologists—it remains to be seen how intrinsicness is to be defined for "the rest of us," in particular, those who are convinced by the Kripke examples that the properties essential to a thing need not be intrinsic to it, or intrinsic at all.

Suppose that x has an extrinsic property G essentially. Then purely mereological changes in the part of w outside of x may well have the effect of removing x from the scene. So x will not be there to "witness" G's extrinsicness in w'. How then is G's extrinsicness to be brought out?

The answer has got to be that it is not x but a *related* object x' whose G-ness in w' concerns us. An example will show what I mean. Suppose for argument's sake that creationists have got it partly right. The world did indeed spring into existence in 4004 B.C., complete with fossils, archeological remains, and other traps for the unwary. But, and this is where creationists overreach themselves, there was no act of God involved; the transition from nothing to something was a complete and utter ex nihilo miracle.

All of that given, it seems to me (and for the sake of the example, please let it seem to you, too) that it is essential to the kind *rabbit* that it originated more or less spontaneously, and, in particular, that it did not evolve from earlier kinds. It follows that Floppy here, who is essentially a rabbit, is essentially of a non-evolved kind. *Being of a non-evolved kind* is extrinsic, though; so the fact that Floppy has it essentially means that the property of *being identical to Floppy* is extrinsic as well.

Now consider a world w' that prefixes to w a long and complicated evolutionary history; w' is the sort of world that Darwinian types (wrongly) *believe* themselves to inhabit. When we look at the candidates for Floppyhood in w', we find that every one of them sits at the terminus of a continuous and biologically plausible developmental path tracking back to earlier species. Since it is essential to Floppy *not* to sit at such a terminus, Floppy does not exist in w'. What is it, then, that bears witness in w' to the extrinsicness of *being Floppy*? It has to be the "Darwinized" creature Floppy' that takes her place there.

Our challenge is to say how in general this x'—the object whose failure to exemplify G in w' reveals G as extrinsic—is to be identified. The outlines of the answer seem fairly clear: x' should be an object occupying exactly the piece or portion of w' that x occupied in w. But that still doesn't clue us in to the identity of the object x' that we want.

An advantage of the monolithically mereological approach was that it always made sense to speak of *the* occupant of the-x-portion-of-w-transplanted-into-w'. The disadvantage, of course, was that the occupant was x itself, leading to the unhappy (from a Kripkean vantage point) results just noted: results that led us to reconsider our attachment to monolithic mereologism.

But although mereology can be pushed too far, it stands to reason that we should try to hold on to as much of it as we can, compatibly with the Kripkean data we are trying to accommodate. Why not let the view be that worlds are mereological *at bottom* – at the level of their "stuff" or "matter" – with the non-mereological aspects superimposed? Then we can say that at the bottom level, where mereology reigns, essences are always intrinsic; while at the higher Kripkean levels, where any sort of property can be essential, mereology graciously steps aside. There may be various ways of implementing this divide-and-conquer strategy, but the following seven step plan looks attractive:

First, α-sums:
The x_is have a number of sums $S^α(x_i)$, exactly alike except in their essences, or (what comes to the same) their transworld careers.

Two, aggregates:
One of these α-sums is the *aggregate* $S^0(x_i)$; its essence is to exist iff each of the x_is do, when and where any of the x_is do.

Three, pieces:
x is a *piece* of y ($x <^0 y$) iff there are things z_i such that y is the aggregate of all of them, and x is the aggregate of some of them.

Four, portions:
The *stuff* of a world w is the aggregate of all its atoms. Pieces of w-stuff, that is, aggregates of some or all of w's atoms, are called *portions* of w.

Five, parts:
x is a *part* of y ($x < y$) iff there are α and z_i such that y is the α-sum of all of the z_is, and x is the α-sum of some of them.[30]

---

[30] Special cases aside, x is a part of y iff it occupies a subset of the space-time positions occupied by y. The special cases include, for instance, a bundle of compresent tropes vis à vis some particular trope t in the bundle; the bundle may occupy the same space-time position(s) as t, but it isn't part of t. Another example might be Casper the ghost passing through a mountain or a larger ghost. The special cases matter. An account of intrinsicness ought to distinguish the

Six, coincidence:
x and *y coincide* iff they have exactly the same parts—equivalently, iff *x* is part of *y* and vice versa.

Seven, existence:
To *exist* in a world *w* is to be (a) a portion of *w*, or (b) constituted by (strictly: coincident with) a portion of *w*.

As the seventh step suggests, coincidence is the notion we need, but the definitions read better when framed in terms of constitution. A word should thus be said about what it is for *x* to constitute *y*, and why it does little harm to substitute constitution for coincidence. The account I have in mind is a slight variant of one recently proposed by Judith Thomson.[31] The idea is that *x*, although possessed of the same parts as *y*, "hugs" those parts more closely than *y* does:

x constitutes *y* iff

(a) *x* coincides with *y*,

(b) any part of *x* essential to it has parts that are not essential to *y*, and

(c) no part of *y* essential to it fails to have parts that are essential to *x*.[32]

Because pieces of world-stuff hug their parts so very closely—*all* their parts are (modulo the coincidence relation) essential to them—almost anything coinciding with one is also constituted by it.[33] This is why not much harm can come of writing "*x* constitutes *y*" instead of "*x* is coincident with *y*" in the definitions to follow. When push comes to shove, however, it is always coincidence we really have in mind.

---

trope's intrinsic properties from those of the co-located bundle; likewise Casper and the co-located mountain-part. Intrinsicness is not a spatiotemporal notion except per accidens – the accident being that part/whole tends to be spatiotemporal.

31 Thomson, "The Statue and the Clay."

32 At the risk of oversimplifying, the difference between this definition and Thomson's is that she has "some" at the beginning of (b) where I have "any." This has the result, which I find unwelcome and she does not, that if Lumpl constitutes Goliath, then take any *z* you like (e.g., the planet Saturn), the fusion of Lumpl with *z* constitutes the fusion of Goliath with *z*.

33 For an example of something coincident with a piece *x* of world-stuff in *w* that *x* does *not* constitute in *w*, consider a *y* that is "just like" *x* in *w* but exists in no other worlds. Everything about *y* is essential to it, so condition (b) cannot be met.

XIII Intrinsicness and Constitution

All this time we have been grappling with a problem raised long ago for (1). The problem was that x may or may not carry over into w'. And if x does not exist in w', then it makes no sense to ask whether x is G in w iff x is G in w'. Our proposed solution was to say that the portion of w that constitutes x there—the x-portion of w—*does* carry over into w', where it constitutes an x' that *can* be assessed for G-ness in w'. If we modify (*) to take account of this solution, we get

(**)   G is intrinsic iff:
for all $x < w < w'$, x has G in w iff x' has G in w'—where x' is whatever is constituted in w' by the x-portion of w.

An intrinsic property, in other words, is one that never distinguishes between x in w, on the one hand, and what x's constituting matter goes on to constitute in expansions of w, on the other. Since constitution is itself explained in terms of part/whole, this brings us *close* to the sought-after reduction of intrinsicness to part/whole and modality.

XIV A Fork in the Road

But we are not there yet. The "whatever" in (**) hides a choice. There are going to be *lots* of things x' constituted in w' by the x-portion of w. Which of them have to be G for a verdict of intrinsicness?

The answers that come to mind are: *at least one* of them has to be G, and *each* of them has to be G. So there are two disambiguations of (**) to consider. These will be easier to read if we abbreviate "x' is constituted in w' by the x-portion of w" to "x' is a copy of x":

(2)   G is intrinsic iff
for all $x < w < w'$, x has G in w iff *some* copy x' of x has G in w'.

(3)   G is intrinsic iff
for all $x < w < w'$, x has G in w iff *every* copy x' of x has G in w'.

Before investigating how (2) and (3) differ, we should notice a way in which both of them improve on (1). They agree in allowing extrinsic properties to be essential.

Example: Suppose that w is the 4004 B.C. world described in section XII, imagined again as actual. And let w' be the more inclusive world that we wrongly *believe* to be actual. Our friend Floppy in w essentially possesses the property G of *not* sitting at the terminus of a long evolutionary history. But none of its copies in w' shares this property. It makes no difference, then, whether we go along with (2) in demanding that all of Floppy's copies be G, or with (3) in demanding that some of them be G. Either way, the demand is not going to be met. And so both definitions classify G as extrinsic.

XV Categoricals and Hypotheticals

Before trying to tease (2) and (3) apart, we need to fill in the background metaphysical picture some more, especially the all-important notion of coincidence. Coincidence theorists come in many shapes and sizes, but the relation I have in mind works as follows.

Imagine that we have before us the objects coincident in a world w with a portion p of w. These objects are, *categorically* speaking, just alike. To the extent that categorical properties fix perceptual appearance, they look just the same.[34] The differences between them are *modal*—one has essentially a property that another has only accidentally—or (to be a little more accurate) *hypothetical*—a matter of what they are like counterfactually, dispositionally, causally, or along any dimension that respects their behavior in other possible worlds.[35] By "casting our gaze" over these other worlds in imagination, we can "see" that the objects have different modal careers.

If this is how we understand coincidence, then (2) and (3) agree on the intrinsicness-status of categoricals. For let G be categorical. Then either *all* of the objects coincident in w' with x's w-stuff are G, or *none* of them is G. And so the hypothesis on the right-hand side of (2) is equivalent to the one on the right-hand side of (3). The question is, how do (2) and (3) compare in their classification of non-categoricals?

---

[34] Note that the compound of the x_is may well be categorically different from their aggregate. It is likely to have a shorter life since it goes out of existence when any of the x_is ceases to exist. This shows that Fine's compounding is not a sum operation in my sense (likewise Thomson's operation of all-fusion).

[35] I am not using "categorical" and "hypothetical" to help define "intrinsic." I am using them to work out the consequences of definitions (2) and (3) for people who, like me, think that coincidents (things with the same parts) are categorically alike and distinguished by their hypothetical properties.

XVI Generic vs. Specific Intrinsicness

Intrinsicness and categoricality are, of course, not the same. But there does seem to be a rather striking analogy between them. One can bring the analogy out like this: G is intrinsic iff whenever x has G in a world w, it has it in a manner insensitive to goings-on outside of x; and it is categorical iff whenever x has G in a world w, it has it in a manner insensitive to goings-on outside of w.

Someone who takes this analogy very seriously—someone who hears "outside of w" as standing to "outside of x" roughly as "outside of the galaxy" stands to "outside of this office"—will be tempted to conclude that sensitivity to circumstances outside of w is ipso facto sensitivity to circumstances outside of x. They will be tempted to conclude, in other words, that *hypothetical properties can never be intrinsic.* Call the notion of intrinsicness on which this is so—on which intrinsics have to be categorical—the *generic* notion. ("Generic" because it lumps other worlds in with other places as sources of extrinsicness.)

Whether they arrive at it by the indicated route or not, it is the generic notion that writers on intrinsicness often have in mind. Peter Vallentyne, for instance, says that "water-solubility and the like might seem like intrinsic properties, but once one recognizes [their] dependence on what the laws of nature are, it seems more correct to classify such properties as extrinsic."[36] After all, Vallentyne argues, the laws of nature "are part of 'the rest of the world'"—they are sensitive to changes in the world outside the object. If a lump of sugar can lose its solubility just by being placed in different surroundings, then solubility is not intrinsic.

Even if we agree, as not everyone does, that the laws in force at a given location depend on goings-on in "the rest of the world," Vallentyne's argument can be resisted. Dispositions are dispositions to behave in particular ways *in particular circumstances*. But if laws are circumstantial in the way that Vallentyne thinks, then there is no obvious reason why the circumstances should not be understood to include them.

An extrinsic disposition D_1 can almost always be made into a (more) intrinsic one D_2 by taking the external factors which make D_1 come and go, and loading them into D_2's triggering circumstances. This is one way—a very old-fashioned way, to be sure—of understanding the difference between weight and gravitational mass. An object's weight, on the old-fashioned account, is its disposition to depress a properly constructed scale so as to elicit a reading of so many pounds *in the local gravitational field, weak or strong as that field might*

---

[36] Peter Vallentyne, "Intrinsic Properties Defined," *Philosophical Studies* 88 (1997, pp. 209–19).

be. This nicely explains why weight is extrinsic: the reason your weight changes when you go to the moon, even though intrinsically you remain just the same, is that a different field becomes local. An object's mass, on the other hand—its disposition to elicit a reading of so many pounds *in a gravitational field of such and such strength, wherever a field of that strength might be*—is not extrinsic, or anyway not *as* extrinsic as its weight.

All of this is to suggest that the generic notion of intrinsicness is not the only one we understand, or the only one we have need of.[37] Sydney Shoemaker in a celebrated paper distinguishes two types of causal power:

> A particular key on my key chain has the power of opening locks of a certain design. It also has the power of opening my front door. It could lose the former power only by undergoing what we would regard as a real change, for example, a change in its shape. But it could lose the latter without undergoing such a change; it could do so in virtue of the lock on my door being replaced by one of a different design. Let us say that the former is an intrinsic power and the latter is a mere-Cambridge power.[38]

"Mere-Cambridge" powers are in later writings called "extrinsic" powers.[39] The point either way is the same: if the key's power to open a lock of such and such a type is intrinsic to it, then clearly we need a version of intrinsicness on which it does not entail categoricality. Since the reverse entailment does not hold in anyone's book, we want intrinsic/extrinsic to crosscut categorical/hypothetical in every possible way.

Another example to consider here is identity. Atoms have their identities as an intrinsic matter. But *being x* is always hypothetical, since one can imagine a distinct thing x^* that is indiscernible from x when we bracket their counterfactual careers (x^* might differ from x just in the fact that it exists in fewer worlds).[40] The property of *being a*, where *a* is an atom, is thus intrinsic and hypothetical.

Other examples could be mentioned, but they aren't really needed: it is obvious that we have, in addition to a generic notion of intrinsicness that entails categoricality, a *specific* notion that leaves an intrinsic property's status as cate-

---

[37] Some will see a different problem with the generic notion. They will object that the generic notion, far from being the *only* legitimate one, is in fact *illegitimate*, because dispositional properties are always intrinsic. See, e.g., David Lewis in "Finkish Dispositions," *Philosophical Quarterly* 47 (1991, pp. 142–58) and George Molnar, "Are Dispositions Reducible?," *Philosophical Quarterly* 49 (1999, pp. 1–17). Both the always-extrinsic and the always-intrinsic positions are rejected here as too extreme.

[38] Shoemaker, *Identity, Cause, and Mind* (London: Cambridge University Press, 1984, p. 221).

[39] E.g., at pp. 105–6 of *The First-Person Perspective and Other Essays* (London: Cambridge University Press, 1996).

[40] See my "Identity, Essence, and Indiscernibility," *Journal of Philosophy* 84 (1987, pp. 293–314).

gorical undecided. The specific notion is the more discriminating and hence (it seems to me) the more useful one. A generically intrinsic property is just a specifically intrinsic one that happens also to be categorical; defining specific intrinsicness in terms of generic would not be so easy.

XVII Intrinsicness$_3$ = Generic Intrinsicness

Suppose that the space of particulars is *full:* for any assignment F of (coinstantiated) categorical properties to worlds, there is something x_F existing in just the worlds in F's domain and exemplifying in each of those worlds the properties that F assigns to it. Then, since a property is hypothetical iff it can be made to vary by manipulating otherworldly categorical profiles, (3) makes all hypothetical properties extrinsic.

Why does (3) have this result? Setting w' in (3) equal to w, we see that G is intrinsic in the sense of (3) only if it never distinguishes coincidents in the same world. No hypothetical property can meet this condition. If H is hypothetical, then there is a world w containing an x such that (i) x is H in w, but (ii) an x' differing from x only in its categorical properties in other worlds would not be H in w. By fullness, such an x' is bound to exist. So for any hypothetical property H, H's hypotheticality is "witnessed" by a pair of H-discernible coincidents in some world w. It follows that H is not intrinsic.

Example: Imagine a statue Goliath composed of a hunk of wax Lumpl. Goliath is essentially of a certain intrinsic shape—it is essentially, let us say, so-shaped. But to be so-shaped is only accidental to Lumpl, which might never have been formed into a statue at all. Since Goliath is coincident with Lumpl, it follows that Goliath in w is a copy of something (Lumpl) in w that differs from Goliath in point of essential so-shapedness. So the property of being essentially so-shaped is not intrinsic.

XVIII Intrinsicness$_2$ = Specific Intrinsicness

Are hypothetical properties extrinsic in the sense given by (2)? Sometimes yes, sometimes no. Consider again the property of being essentially so-shaped. The reason this came out extrinsic$_3$ was that not everything coincident with Goliath in w' was essentially so-shaped; Lumpl, for one, was so-shaped only accidentally.

But all that (2) asks is that *something* coincident with Goliath be essentially so-shaped. And given fullness, this condition is met for any world w' containing

p = the Goliath-portion of w. For consider a super-Goliath stipulated to possess exactly the categorical properties of p in w' and to exist in no other worlds. Super-Goliath is an essentially so-shaped coincident of p. And that's precisely what is needed for essential so-shapedness to come out intrinsic$_2$.

XIX Doing it with Duplicates

A property is intrinsic, according to Lewis, iff it never distinguishes duplicates. This reduces the problem of defining intrinsicness to the problem of explaining duplication. Suppose that we like this reduction, but don't like Lewis's explanation of what it is for x and y to be duplicates.[41] If we could obtain duplication from part/whole, that would be a move in the right direction.

Above we defined x' in w' to be a *copy* of x in w iff (a) w is part of w' (this to ensure that the x-portion of w persists into w'), and (b) x' is constituted in w' by the transplanted x-portion. The copying relation joined with its converse will be called *immediate duplication*. Duplication is the ancestral of immediate duplication: the relation that x_1 in w_1 bears to x_n in w_n iff there is a string of x_is and w_is (1 ≤ i < n) such that x_{i+1} in w_{i+1} is an immediate duplicate of x_i in w_i.

Now we are almost there; all that remains is to distinguish two different kinds of transworld similarity to serve the needs of our two definitions. Say that x in u and y in v *agree* on a property G iff: x has ±G in u iff y has ±G in v. And say that they *concur* on G iff: x has coincidents with ±G in u iff y has coincidents with ±G in v. Then the following are equivalent to (2) and (3):

(2′)   G is intrinsic iff duplicates always concur on G.

(3′)   G is intrinsic iff duplicates always agree on G.

Exactly as before, (2′) gives us a modally neutral notion of intrinsicness—what above we called the specific notion—while (3′) defines the generic notion whereby an intrinsic property has got to be "modally intrinsic" or categorical.

---

[41] Lewis relies on a distinction between natural and unnatural properties that he treats as primitive. One can agree that a primitive notion of naturalness is needed in philosophy, without agreeing that it is needed for the definition of intrinsicness, or that its availability is enough of a reason to use it.

XX Conclusion

Lewis in "Extrinsic Properties" locates intrinsicness in "a tight little family of interdefinables," and muses about the possibility of breaking out. Later, in "New Work for a Theory of Universals," he sees his opening: reduce intrinsicness to duplication, and (the break-out point) duplication to naturalness. Still later, in "Defining 'Intrinsic'," he and Langton decide that they can make do with just an aspect or component of naturalness, viz., (relative) nondisjunctiveness.

But while that is certainly progress, neither of the proposed reducers—naturalness, nondisjunctiveness—*feels* like it has much to do with "what intrinsicness is." Another way to put it is that both of the Lewis definitions trade on de facto connections with intrinsicness rather than de jure ones. It might be doubted, of course, whether intrinsicness *has* any interesting de jure connections with other notions. But conditionals like

(%) x is a part of y only if x cannot change intrinsically without y changing intrinsically as well

show that this pessimism is unjustified. The de jure appearance of (%) led us to attempt a broadly mereological account of intrinsicness. Whether the account gives the right results in all cases, it does seem to lay the issue at a doorstep more in the right neighborhood.

The conditional (%), although putting us on the track of an account less accidental-feeling than Lewis's, also suggests a way in which our approach might be thought to fall short of his. Naturalness has no chance whatever of being explained in terms of intrinsicness; so a successful analysis of intrinsicness in terms of naturalness would probably amount to a reduction. One would truly have broken out of Lewis's "family of interdefinables."

An analysis in terms of part/whole, however, might or might not constitute a reduction, depending on whether part/whole was definable reversewise from intrinsicness. One is certainly accustomed to thinking of part/whole as the more basic of the two, but a look at (%) makes me wonder. Is a reversewise definition possible? If so, then we have at best enlarged Lewis's circle a little. If, on the other hand, part/whole deserves its reputation as primitive and undefinable, then perhaps we (too) can claim to have broken out.

Appendix

This appendix explores how far we can disentangle ourselves from the modal realism presupposed in the main body of the paper. I'll suppose that we are confronted with a series of three objectors. ARG says that the *argument* we gave for our account of intrinsicness presupposed modal realism. PAL says that argument or no argument, the account is not *plausible* without modal realism. EXP maintains that our account is not even *expressible* without modal realism.

ARG

A lot is riding on the idea that if one world is part of another, then this makes for an area of intrinsic match-up between them. The argument for this turned on Lewis's problem of accidental intrinsics. But as Lewis would be the first to admit, accidental intrinsics are a problem only for modal realists—only for those conceiving counterfactual worlds as big concrete objects on a par with the actual world. Modal realism is not a hugely popular doctrine.[42] How do you propose to defend your idea to the rest of us?

Reply: This misrepresents the argumentative strategy. Accidental intrinsics came in not to *support* any claim about parts and intrinsicness, but to quiet a certain worry that the modal realist might feel. I said: look, to the extent that your opposition to overlap is based on the problem of accidental intrinsicness, you needn't be worried about overlap of the specific sort envisaged here. That one world can be part of another wasn't argued for at all; it was taken for granted. Also taken for granted was the claim that if one thing overlaps another, there is going to be complete intrinsic similarity with respect to the shared part. Nobody would question this in the intraworld case; why would the transworld case be different?

PAL

I'll tell you why (it would be different in the transworld case). Not all transworld relations are created equal. On the one hand, you've got "genuine" transworld relations like *being the same color as*. These really do inherit the features of their intraworld originals. Transworld *same color as*, is transitive and entails *being colored*, just like the intraworld version.

---

[42] Not to mention that it has surprising consequences for intrinsicness. Assuming modal realism, accompaniment (as opposed to accompaniment by something you bear spatiotemporal relations to) comes out intrinsic; duplicates never differ with respect to it because *everything* is accompanied. Accompaniment has traditionally been the paradigm of an extrinsic property.

On the other hand, you've got "degenerate" transworld relations like *touching*. All it can mean to say that x in w touches y in w' is that when you get them together in the same world, say v, you find that x touches y there. Degenerate transworld relations do *not* inherit the features of their intraworld originals; transworld touching, for example, is compatible with toucher and touchee each being quite alone in their original worlds.

Now if modal realism is correct, then just *maybe* there is a non-degenerate relation of transworld parthood. Otherwise though, parthood is like touching; when you try to apply it between worlds, it goes degenerate.[43] If that is right, then the fact that intraworld parts have a region of intrinsic match with their containing wholes says nothing whatever about the transworld case.

Reply: Transworld parthood is *not* degenerate. If it were, then (i) to be transworld part of y, x would have to be intraworld part of y (in some salient world), and (ii) if x were intraworld part of y (in some salient world), x couldn't *avoid* being transworld part of y. I will argue that neither (i) nor (ii) is at all plausible.

Against (ii): The Kiwanis Picnic would have been considerably shorter had the world popped (miraculously!) out of existence just as the soda was being opened. Indeed, more is true: the picnic that would have been is a *proper part* of the picnic that actually was. According to (ii), though, this is impossible, for the picnic that was is a part of the picnic that would have been.

Why is that? Well, the picnic that would have been is none other than the picnic that actually took place; it is that picnic as it might have been rather than as it is. But if they are the same, then there is no question but that each intraworld includes the other; a thing always intraworld includes itself. By (ii), finally, this intraworld inclusion suffices for transworld inclusion. *The denier of genuine transworld parthood can thus make no sense of the idea that the picnic that would have been—the actual picnic with its tail end chopped off—is a proper part of the actual picnic.*

Against (i): The Rainbow Rally includes what *would* have been the entire Spartacus League demonstration – would have been, if a few Spartacist rowdies wrongly supposed to be out of town had not turned up to demonstrate *against* the Rally. According to (i), the *would-be* demonstration is part of the Rally only if the *actual* demonstration is. So, although the would-be demonstration precisely *omits* the rowdies, it still has to pay the mereological price for their behavior. That seems absurd; *the Spartacist demonstration as it would have been is wholly included in the Rally.*

---

[43] For discussion, see Nathan Salmon's *Reference and Essence* (Princeton: Princeton University Press, 1981, p. 121 ff.).

Degenerate transworld relations are a dime a dozen. Any "ordinary" relation R gives rise to a bunch of them by the formula: x in w bears transworld R^v to y in w' iff x bears R to y in v. But these degenerate R^v's are almost never what is meant by "transworld R." It would be one thing if there were no alternative to the degenerate interpretation. But in this case there clearly is: it's the interpretation we come to naturally when, e.g., we dispute with Lewis about whether there are counterfactual worlds with the actual world as a part. If "part" here stood for the degenerate relation, the answer would be obvious; it isn't, so it doesn't.

EXP

Your account is committed to counterfactual worlds by virtue of explicitly quantifying over them. And the worlds you quantify over had better be Lewisian concrete worlds. Because it seems very doubtful that ersatz worlds, e.g., sets of propositions, are going to stand in the requisite inclusion-relations.

Reply: You're right that the worlds of (2) and (3) are concrete. But just maybe the analysis can be (re)construed as speaking of worlds that, although they *could* have existed, as it happens do *not* exist—not even in a place bearing no spatio-temporal relations to the speaker.

The reason that the analysis appears to require existent concrete worlds is that it makes essential play with transworld relations such as transworld part/whole. How can the counterfactual picnic be (transworld) part of the actual one unless both are somehow *there,* in their containing worlds?

This is a fair question, but it has an answer; it had *better* have one, for colloquial English is thick with talk of transworld relations, and other worlds do not seem to come into the picture. You might say, for example, that

(i) the car I would have had, if I'd installed afterburners in my old 'Vette, is faster than the Camaro I do have.

Does this commit you to the existence of a (counterfactual world containing a) counterfactual car, fitted out with afterburners as your actual car is not? Not at all. Your claim in essence is that

(i′) it could have happened that I had a 'Vette that was faster than my Camaro is in actual fact.

And (i′) makes no mention of counterfactual objects except in the scope of a modal operator. What remains to be seen is whether the same can be done with (2) and (3), that is, whether they too can be restated in a way that avoids wide-scope quantification over things that (modal realism aside) do not exist.

Before attempting this, let me concede right off that a formulation as colloquial as (i′) is going to be hard to come up with. Our everyday modal devices are quickly pushed to their limits when the transworld comparisons become too involved, as in

(ii) the car I would have had if I'd installed afterburners in the 'Vette is intermediate in speed between the one I would have had if I'd supercharged my Camaro and the Camaro as it is actually.

About the best we can do with this is

(ii′) it could have happened that after supercharging my Camaro was such that [it could have happened that I had a 'Vette with afterburners such that {the Camaro was faster than the 'Vette was and the 'Vette was faster than the Camaro *is*}]

This may not be wonderful English, but it seems close enough in *spirit* to (i′) that it would be strange to discern here a qualitative change in subject matter—so that while (i′) gave a partly modal description of actuality, (ii′) described non-actual, merely possible, items, viz., other possible worlds and their inhabitants.

If that is right, then our next step should be to seek a Loglish-type regimentation of the language used in (i′) and (ii′), in the hope that it permits a noncommittal reformulation of transworld-part talk, and ultimately a noncommital reformulation of (2) and (3). A number of people have applied themselves to this sort of problem,[44] and they have had considerable success with a device called "multiple indexing." Rather than trying to explain the idea from scratch, let me illustrate it with translations of our two target sentences. Think of "c" as a proper name of my actual Camaro, and "B" and "S" as standing for the relevant sort of afterburner-enhanced 'Vette and supercharged Camaro:

(i″) possibly $(\exists y)(By$ & actually^c [y is faster than c]).

(ii″) possibly$_1$ $(\exists z)(z = c$ & Sz & possibly$_2$ $(\exists y)(By$ & actually$_1^z$ actually$_2^y$ actually^c [z is faster than y is faster than c]))

Now let's try the method out on

(iii) yesterday's Kiwanis picnic was only a part of the picnic we would have had if not for the interruption.

Here it is, nearly enough, in noncommittal English:

---

44 See Forbes, *Metaphysics of Modality*, p. 89 ff. and references there.

(iii′) it could have happened that we had a picnic of which the picnic we did have was a proper part.

And here it is in Loglish, with "k" standing for the picnic and "P" describing the relevant sort of prolonged picnic:

(iii″) possibly $(\exists y)$(Py & actually^k [k is a proper part of y]).

Now let's see what can be done with (2) and (3). I'll assume that, necessarily, there is one and only one world (which is not, of course, to say that "the world" is rigid). The letters "u" and "v" are world-variables, "p" and "q" range over world-portions, i.e., aggregates of atoms, "$\approx$" expresses the coincidence relation, and "$<$" stands for parthood:

(3″) G is *intrinsic* iff:
necessarily$_1$ $(\forall u)(\forall p < u)(\forall x \approx p)$ necessarily$_2$ $(\forall v)(\forall q < v)(\forall y \approx q)$ (actually$_1^{pu}$ actually$_2^{qv}$ $(p = q < u < v)$ → [actually$_1^x$ Gx ↔ actually$_2^y$ Gy])

G is intrinsic$_3$, in other words, when the following holds necessarily: if a mass of atoms that composes x would, had a more inclusive world obtained, have composed y, then x is G iff y would have been G. The definition of intrinsicness$_2$ is nearly the same, except that the two coincidence-quantifiers get moved to either side of the final biconditional:

(2″) G is *intrinsic* iff:
necessarily$_1$ $(\forall u)(\forall p < u)$ necessarily$_2$ $(\forall v)(\forall q < v)$(actually$_1^{pu}$ actually$_2^{qv}$ $(p = q < u < v)$ → [actually$_1$ $(\forall x \approx p)$ ±Gx ↔ actually$_2$ $(\forall y \approx q)$ ±Gy])

The ±Gs towards the end are to indicate a conjunction of two biconditionals, one with G unnegated on both sides, one with it negated. Translated into English, what (2″) says is that G is intrinsic$_2$ iff necessarily, any mass of atoms that composes only Gs (non-Gs) would still have composed only Gs (non-Gs), had a world obtained of which the actual world is only a part.

Brian Weatherson
Intrinsic Properties and Combinatorial Principles*

Abstract: Three objections have recently been levelled at the analysis of intrinsicness offered by Rae Langton and David Lewis. While these objections do seem telling against the particular theory Langton and Lewis offer, they do not threaten the broader strategy Langton and Lewis adopt: defining intrinsicness in terms of combinatorial features of properties. I show how to amend their theory to overcome the objections without abandoning the strategy.

Three objections have recently been levelled at the analysis of intrinsicness in Rae Langton and David Lewis's "Defining 'Intrinsic'". Stephen Yablo (1999) has objected that the theory rests on "controversial and (apparently) irrelevant" judgements about the relative naturalness of various properties. Dan Marshall and Josh Parsons (2001) have argued that quantificational properties, such as *being accompanied by a cube*, are counterexamples to Langton and Lewis's theory. And Theodore Sider (2001) has argued that maximal properties, like *being a rock*, provide counterexamples to the theory. In this paper I suggest a number of amendments to Langton and Lewis's theory to overcome these counterexamples. The suggestions are meant to be friendly in that the basic theory with which we are left shares a structure with the theory proposed by Langton and Lewis. However, the suggestions are not meant to be *ad hoc* stipulations designed solely to avoid theoretical punctures, but developments of principles that follow naturally from the considerations adduced by Langton and Lewis.

1 Langton and Lewis's Theory

Langton and Lewis base their theory on a combinatorial principle about intrinsicness. If a property F is intrinsic, then whether a particular object is F is independent of whether there are other things in the world. This is just a specific instance of the general principle that if F is intrinsic then whether some particular

---

Published in *Philosophy and Phenomenological Research* 63: 365–380 (2001)
* Thanks to John Hawthorne, David Lewis, Europa Malynicz, Dan Marshall, Daniel Nolan, Josh Parsons and Ted Sider for helpful discussions.

thing is *F* is independent of the way the rest of the world is. So if *F* is intrinsic, then the following four conditions are met:

(a) Some lonely object is *F*;

(b) Some lonely object is not-*F*;

(c) Some accompanied object is *F*; and

(d) Some accompanied object is not-*F*.

The quantifiers in the conditions range across objects in all possible worlds, and indeed this will be the quantifier domain in everything that follows (except where indicated). An object is 'lonely' if there are no wholly distinct contingent things in its world. The effect of including 'distinct' in this definition is that an object can be lonely even if it has proper parts; an object is not identical with its parts, but nor is it distinct from them. Following Langton and Lewis, I will say that any property that meets the four conditions is 'independent of accompaniment'.

All intrinsic properties are independent of accompaniment, but so are some extrinsic properties. For example, the property *being the only round thing* is extrinsic, but independent of accompaniment. So Langton and Lewis do not say that independence of accompaniment is sufficient for intrinsicness. However, within a certain class of properties, what we might call the *basic* properties, they do say that any property independent of accompaniment is intrinsic. A property is *basic* if it is neither *disjunctive* nor the negation of a disjunctive property. Langton and Lewis define the disjunctive properties as follows:

> [L]et us define the *disjunctive* properties as those properties that can be expressed by a disjunction of (conjunctions of) natural properties; but that are not themselves natural properties. (Or, if naturalness admits of degrees, they are much less natural than the disjuncts in terms of which they can be expressed.) (Langton and Lewis 1998: 336)

Langton and Lewis assume here that there is some theory of naturalness that can be plugged in here, but they are explicitly ecumenical about what the theory may be. They mention three possibilities: naturalness might be primitive; it might be defined in terms of which universals and tropes exist, if you admit such into your ontology; or it might be defined in terms of which properties play a special role in our theory. Call the first the primitivist conception, the second the ontological conception, and the third the pragmatic conception. (One can generate different versions of the pragmatic theory by altering what one takes to be 'our theory'. In Taylor (1993), which Langton and Lewis credit as the canonical statement of the pragmatic conception, naturalness is relativised to a theory, and the theories he focuses on are 'regimented common sense' and 'unified science'.) Langton and Lewis's intention is to be neutral as to the correct interpretation of naturalness whenever they appeal to it, and I will follow their policy.

With these concepts, we can now define intrinsicness. A property is *basic intrinsic* iff it is basic and independent of accompaniment. Two objects are *duplicates* iff they have the same basic intrinsic properties. And a property is *intrinsic* iff there are no two duplicates that differ with respect to it.

Langton and Lewis make one qualification to this definition: it is only meant to apply to *pure*, or qualitative, properties, as opposed to *impure*, or haeccceitistic, properties. One reason for this restriction is that if there are any impure intrinsic properties, such as *being John Malkovich*, they will not have the combinatorial features distinctive of pure intrinsic properties. If F is a pure intrinsic property then there can be two wholly distinct things in a world that are F. This fact will be crucial to the revised definition of intrinsicness offered below. However, it is impossible to have wholly distinct things in the same world such that each is John Malkovich. So for now I will follow Langton and Lewis and just say what it takes for a pure property to be intrinsic. As Langton and Lewis note, it would be nice to complete the definition by giving conditions under which impure properties are intrinsic, but the little task of working out the conditions under which pure properties are intrinsic will be hard enough for now.

2 Three Objections

Stephen Yablo (1999) criticises the judgements of naturalness on which this theory rests. Consider again the property *being the only round thing*, which is extrinsic despite being independent of accompaniment. If Langton and Lewis are right, this must not be a basic property. Indeed, Langton and Lewis explicitly say that it is the negation of a disjunctive property, since its negation can be expressed as: *being round and accompanied by a round thing or being not-round*. Yablo's criticism is that it is far from obvious that the existence of this expansion shows that *being the only round thing* is disjunctive. For simplicity, let us name all the salient properties:

$R =_{df}$ *being the only round thing*

$S =_{df}$ *being not the only round thing*

$T =_{df}$ *being round and accompanied by a round thing*

$U =_{df}$ *being not-round*

(Something is accompanied by an *F* iff one of its distinct worldmates is *F*.) Langton and Lewis claim that since *S* = *T* v *U*, and *S* is much less natural than *T* and than *U*, *S* is disjunctive, so *R* is not basic. Yablo notes that we can also express *S* as *being round if accompanied by a round thing*, so it differs from *T* only in that it has an *if* where *T* has an *and*. Given this expansion, we should be dubious of the claim that *S* is much less natural than *T*. But without that claim, *R* already provides a counterexample to Langton and Lewis's theory, unless there is some other expression of *R* or *S* that shows they are disjunctive.[1]

Dan Marshall and Josh Parsons (2001) argue that the same kind of difficulties arise when we consider certain kinds of quantificational properties. For example, let *E* be the property *being such that a cube exists*. This is independent of accompaniment, since a lonely cube is *E*, a lonely sphere is not *E*, each of us is accompanied and *E*, and each of Max Black's two spheres is accompanied and not *E*. So it is a counterexample to Langton and Lewis if it is basic. Marshall and Parsons note that, like all properties, it does have disjunctive expressions. For example *x* is *E* iff *x* is a cube or *x* is accompanied by a cube. And *E* is a less natural property than *being a cube*. But it is not at all intuitive that *E* is much less natural than the property *being accompanied by a cube*. This does not just show that Langton and Lewis have to cease being ecumenical about naturalness, because on some conceptions of naturalness it is not clear that *E* is much less natural than *being accompanied by a cube*. Rather, this example shows that there is no conception of naturalness that could play the role that Langton and Lewis want. The properties *E* and *being accompanied by a cube* seem just as natural as each other on the ontological conception of naturalness, on the pragmatic conception of naturalness, and, as far as anyone can tell, on the primitivist conception. This is not because *E* is particularly natural on any of these conceptions. It certainly does not, for example, correspond to a universal, and it does not play a special role in our thinking or in ideal science. But since there is no universal for *being accompanied by a cube*, and that property does not play a special role

---

1 It would be no good to say that Langton and Lewis should be more liberal with their definition of disjunctiveness, and say instead that a property is disjunctive iff it can be expressed as a disjunction. Any property F can be expressed as the disjunction F and G or F and not G, or for that matter, F or F, so this would make every property disjunctive.

I do not want to dismiss out of hand the possibility that there is another expression of S that shows it is disjunctive. Josh Parsons suggested that if we define T' to be *being accompanied by a round thing*, then S is T' v U, and there is some chance that T' is more natural than S on some conceptions of naturalness. So we cannot derive a decisive counterexample from Yablo's discussion. Still, Langton and Lewis need it to be the case that on any account of naturalness, there is an expression that shows S or R to be disjunctive, and unless T' is much more natural than S on all conceptions of naturalness, this task is still far from complete.

in our thinking or in ideal science, it seems likely that each property is as natural as the other.

Theodore Sider (forthcoming) notes that similar problems arise for *maximal* properties, like *being a rock*. A property F is maximal iff large parts of Fs are typically not Fs. For example, *being a house* is maximal; a very large part of a house, say a house minus one window ledge, is not a house, it is just a large part of a house. Purported proof: call the house minus one window ledge house-. If Katie buys the house she undoubtedly buys house-, but she does not thereby buy two houses, so house- is not a house. As Sider notes, this is not an entirely conclusive proof, but it surely has some persuasive force. Maximal properties could easily raise a problem for Langton and Lewis's definition. All maximal properties are extrinsic; whether *a* is a house depends not just on how *a* is, but on what surrounds *a*. Compare: House- would be a house if the extra window ledge did not exist; in that case it would be *the* house that Katie buys. But some maximal properties are independent of accompaniment. *Being a rock* is presumably maximal: large parts of rocks are not rocks. If they were then presumably tossing one rock up into the air and catching it would constitute juggling seventeen rocks, making an apparently tricky feat somewhat trivial. But there can be lonely rocks. A rock from our planet would still be a rock if it were lonely. Indeed, some large rock parts that are not rocks would be rocks if they were lonely. And it is clear there can be lonely non-rocks (like our universe), accompanied rocks (like Uluru) and accompanied non-rocks (like me).

Since *being a rock* is independent of accompaniment and extrinsic, it is a counterexample if it is basic. Still, one might think it is not basic. Perhaps *being a rock* is not natural on the primitivist conception. (Who is to say it is?) And perhaps it does not correspond to a genuine universal, or to a collection of tropes, so it is a disjunctive property on the ontological conception of naturalness. Sider notes, however, that on at least one pragmatic conception, where natural properties are those that play a special role in regimented common sense, it does seem particularly natural. Certainly it is hard to find properties such that *being a rock* can be expressed as a disjunction of properties that are more central to our thinking than *being a rock*. So this really does seem to be a counterexample to Langton and Lewis's theory.

3 The Set of Intrinsic Properties

It is a platitude that a property F is intrinsic iff whether an object is F does not depend on the way the rest of the world is. Ideally this platitude could be morphed into a definition. One obstacle is that it is hard to define *the way the rest of the world is* without appeal to intrinsic properties. For example, even if F is intrinsic, whether a is F is not independent of whether other objects have the property *not being accompanied by an F*, which I will call G. To the extent that having G is a feature of the way the rest of the world is, properties like G constitute counterexamples to the platitude. Since platitudes are meant to be interpreted to be immune from counterexamples, it is wrong to interpret the platitude so that G is a feature of the way the rest of the world is. The correct interpretation is that F is intrinsic iff whether an object is F does not depend on which *intrinsic* properties are instantiated elsewhere in the world.

If what I call the independence platitude is to be platitudinous, we must not treat independence in exactly the same way as Langton and Lewis do. On one definition, whether a is F is independent of whether the rest of the world is H iff it is possible that a is F and the rest of the world H, possible that a is not-F and the rest of the world H, possible that a is F and the rest of the world not-H, and possible that a is not-F and the rest of the world not-H. On another, whether a if F is independent of whether the rest of the world is H iff whether a is F is entirely determined by the way a itself, and nothing else, is, and whether the rest of the world is H is determined by how it, and not a, is. This latter definition is very informal; hence the need for the formal theory that follows. But it does clearly differ from the earlier definition in a couple of cases. The two definitions may come apart if F and H are excessively disjunctive. More importantly, for present purposes, they come apart if F is the necessary property (that everything has), or the impossible property (that nothing has). In these cases, whether a is F is entirely settled by the way a, and nothing else is, so in the latter sense it is independent of whether the rest of the world is H. But it is not the case that all four possibilities in the former definition are possible, so it is not independent of whether the rest of the world is H in that sense. Since there is some possibility of confusion here, it is worthwhile being clear about terminology. When I talk about independence here, I will always mean the latter, informal, definition, and I will refer to principles about which combinations of intrinsic properties are possible, principles such as Langton and Lewis's principle that basic intrinsic properties are independent of accompaniment, as combinatorial principles. So, in the terminology I am using, the combinatorial principles are attempts to formally capture the true, but elusive, independence platitude with which I opened this section.

Since the platitude is a biconditional with *intrinsic* on either side, it will be a little tricky to morph it into a definition. But we can make progress by noting that the platitude tells us about relations that hold between some intrinsic properties, and hence about what the set of intrinsic properties, which I will call *SI*, must look like.

For example, from the platitude it follows that *SI* is closed under Boolean operations. Say that *F* and *G* are intrinsic. This means that whether some individual *a* is *F* is independent of how the world outside *a* happens to be. And it means that whether *a* is *G* is independent of the way the world outside *a* happens to be. This implies that whether *a* is *F and G* is independent of the way the world outside *a* happens to be, because whether *a* is *F and G* is a function of whether *a* is *F* and whether *a* is *G*. And that means that *F and G* is intrinsic. Similar reasoning shows that *F or G*, and *not F* are also intrinsic. Call this condition *Boolean closure*.

Another implication of the independence platitude is that *SI* must be closed under various mereological operations. If *F* is intrinsic then whether *a* is *F* is independent of the outside world. If some part of *a* is *F*, that means, however the world outside that part happens to be, that part will be *F*. So that means that however the world outside *a* is, *a* will have a part that is *F*. Conversely, if *a* does not have a part that is *F*, that means all of *a*'s parts are *not F*. As we saw above, if *F* is intrinsic, so is *not F*. Hence it is independent of the world outside *a* that all of its parts are *not F*. That is, it is independent of the world outside *a* that *a* does not have a part that is *F*. In sum, whether *a* has a part that is *F* is independent of how the world outside *a* turns out to be. And that means *having a part that is F* is intrinsic. By similar reasoning, the property *Having n parts that are F* will be intrinsic if *F* is for any value of *n*. Finally, the same reasoning shows that the property, *being entirely composed of n things that are each F* is intrinsic if *F* is intrinsic. The only assumption used here is that it is independent of everything outside *b* that *b* is entirely composed of the particular things that it is composed of, but again this seems to be a reasonable assumption. So, formally, if *F* ∈ *SI*, then *Having n parts that are F* ∈ *SI*, and *Being entirely composed of n things that are F* ∈ *SI*. Call this condition *mereological closure*.

Finally, and most importantly, various combinatorial principles follow from the independence platitude. One of these, that all intrinsic properties are independent of accompaniment, forms the centrepiece of Langton and Lewis's theory. The counterexamples provided by Marshall and Parsons, and by Sider, suggest that we need to draw two more combinatorial principles from the platitude. The first is that if *F* and *G* are intrinsic properties, then whether some particular object *a* is *F* should be independent of how many other things in the world are *G*. More carefully, if *F* and *G* are intrinsic properties that are somewhere instantiated then, for any *n* such that there is a world with *n*+1 things, there is a world constituted by exactly *n*+1 pairwise distinct things, one of which is *F*, and the other *n* of which are all *G*. When I say the world is constituted by exactly *n*+1 things, I do not mean that there are only *n*+1 things in the world; some of the *n*+1 things that constitute the world might have proper parts.

What I mean more precisely is that every contingent thing in the world is a fusion of parts of some of these $n+1$ things. Informally, every intrinsic property is not only independent of accompaniment, it is independent of accompaniment by every intrinsic property. As we will see, this combinatorial principle, combined with the Boolean closure principle, suffices to show that Marshall and Parsons's example, *being such that a cube exists*, is extrinsic.

Sometimes the fact that a property F is extrinsic is revealed by the fact that nothing that is F can be worldmates with things of a certain type. So the property *being lonely* is extrinsic because nothing that is lonely can be worldmates with anything at all. But some extrinsic properties are perfectly liberal about which other properties can be instantiated in their world; they are extrinsic because their satisfaction excludes (or entails) the satisfaction of other properties in their immediate neighbourhood. Sider's maximal properties are like this. That a is a rock tells us nothing at all about what other properties are instantiated in a's world. However, that a is a rock does tell us something about what happens around a. In particular, it tells us that there is no rock enveloping a. If there were a rock enveloping a, then a would not be a rock, but rather a part of a rock. If *being a rock* were intrinsic, then we would expect there could be two rocks such that the first envelops the second.[2] The reason that *being a rock* is extrinsic is that it violates this combinatorial principle. (As a corollary to this, a theory which ruled out *being a rock* from the class of the intrinsic just because it is somehow unnatural would be getting the right result for the wrong reason. *Being a rock* is not a property like *being a lonely electron or an accompanied non-electron* that satisfies the independence platitude in the wrong way; rather, it fails to satisfy the independence platitude, and our theory should reflect this.)

So we need a second combinatorial principle that rules out properties like *being a rock*. The following principle does the job, although at some cost in complexity. Assume there is some world w_1, which has some kind of spacetimelike structure.[3] Let d_1 and d_2 be shapes of two disjoint spacetimelike regions in w_1 that stand in relation A. Further, suppose F and G are intrinsic properties such that in some world there is an F that wholly occupies a region with shape d_1, and in some world, perhaps not the same one, there is a G that wholly occupies a region with shape d_2. By 'wholly occupies' I mean that the F takes up all the

---

[2] I assume here that there are rocks with rock-shaped holes in their interior. This seems like a reasonable assumption, though without much knowledge of geology I do not want to be too bold here.

[3] Perhaps all worlds have some kind of spacetimelike structure, in which case this qualification is unnecessary, but at this stage it is best not to take a stand on such a contentious issue.

'space' in d_1 and does not take up any other 'space'. (There is an assumption here that we can identify shapes of spacetimelike regions across possible worlds, and while this assumption seems a little contentious, I hope it is acceptable in this context.) If F, G, d_1, d_2 and A are set up in this way, then there is a world where d_1 and d_2 stand in A, and an F wholly occupies a region of shape d_1 in that world, and a G wholly occupies a region of shape d_2 in that world. In short, if you could have an F in d_1, and you could have a G in d_2, and d_1 and d_2 could stand in A, then all three of those things could happen in one world. This kind of combinatorial principle has been endorsed by many writers on modality (for example Lewis 1986 and Armstrong 1989), and it seems something we should endorse in a theory on intrinsic properties.

In sum, the set of intrinsic properties, *SI*, has the following four properties:

(B) If $F \in SI$ and $G \in SI$ then *F and G* $\in SI$ and *F or G* $\in SI$ and *not F* $\in SI$

(M) If $F \in SI$ then *Having n parts that are F* $\in SI$ and *Being entirely composed of exactly n things that are F* $\in SI$

(T) If $F \in SI$ and $G \in SI$ and there is a possible world with $n+1$ pairwise distinct things, and something in some world is F and something in some world is G, then there is a world with exactly $n+1$ pairwise distinct things such that one is F and the other n are G.

(S) If $F \in SI$ and $G \in SI$ and it is possible that regions with shapes d_1 and d_2 stand in relation A, and it is possible that an F wholly occupy a region with shape d_1 and a G wholly occupy a region with shape d_2, then there is a world where regions with shapes d_1 and d_2 stand in A, and an F wholly occupies the region with shape d_1 and a G wholly occupies the region with shape d_2.

Many other sets than *SI* satisfy (B), (M), (T) and (S). That is, there are many sets I_k such that each condition would still be true if we were to substitute I_k for *SI* wherever it appears. Say that any such set is an *I*-set. Then *F* is intrinsic only if *F* is an element of some *I*-set. Is every element of every *I*-set intrinsic? As we will see, sadly the answer is *no*. However, most of the counterexamples proposed to Langton and Lewis's theory are not elements of any *I*-set, so we already have the resources to show they are extrinsic.

4 Responding to Counterexamples

Marshall and Parsons noted that *E*, the property *being such that a cube exists*, is independent of accompaniment. However, it is not part of any *I*-set. To see this, assume it is in I_k, which is an *I*-set. By (B), *not E* is also in I_k. So by (T), there is a world where something is *E*, and there are two things, one of which is *E* and the other of which is *not E*. But clearly this cannot be the case: if something in a world is *E*, so is everything else in the world. Hence I_k cannot be an *I*-set, contrary to our assumption. Intuitively, *E* is extrinsic because whether it is satisfied by an individual is not independent of whether other individuals satisfy it.

Some other quantificational properties, such as *being one of at most seventeen cubes*, require a different argument to show that they are not in any *I*-set. Call that property *E17*. (Note, by the way, that *E17* is independent of accompaniment, and not obviously disjunctive.) If *E17* is in an *I*-set, then by (T) there is a world containing exactly 18 things, each of which is *E17*. But this is clearly impossible, since everything that is *E17* is a cube, and everything that is *E17* is in a world containing at most seventeen cubes. So *E17* is not in any *I*-set, and hence is extrinsic. Similarly, *being the only round thing* cannot be in an *I*-set, because if it were by (T) there would be a world in which two things are the only round thing, which is impossible. So a definition of intrinsicness in terms of *I*-sets need not make the odd postulations about naturalness that Yablo found objectionable.

Assume, for *reductio*, that *being a rock* is in an *I*-set. There is a rock that is roughly spherical, and there is a rock that has a roughly spherical hollow in its interior. (Actually, there are many rocks of each type, but we only need one of each.) Let d_1 be the region the first rock takes up, and assume that the shape of the hollow in the second is also d_1. If it is not, we could always find another rock with a hollow this shape, so the assumption is harmless. Let d_2 be the region the second rock, the one with this nicely shaped hollow, takes up. If *being a rock* is an *I*-set, then by (S) there is a world where d_2 exactly surrounds d_1, there is a rock wholly occupying d_1 and a rock wholly occupying d_2. But this is impossible; if there were rock-like things in both d_1 and d_2, they would both be parts of a single large rock, that extends outside both d_1 and d_2 and if there were not a rock-like thing in one or the other region, then there would not be a rock in that region. So no set satisfying (S) contains *being a rock*, so that property is not in any *I*-set, and hence is extrinsic.

The first extrinsic property independent of accompaniment that Langton and Lewis consider is *CS: being spherical and lonely or cubical and accompanied*. This too is not in any *I*-set. Again, assume for reductio that it is. In the actual world, there are (accompanied) cubes that are entirely composed of eight smaller cubes.

Both the large cube and the eight smaller cubes are accompanied, so they are both *CS*. Hence there is a *CS* that is entirely composed of eight things that are *CS*. By (M), *being entirely composed of exactly eight things that are CS* is in the *I*-set. By (B), *being CS and entirely composed of exactly eight things that are CS* is in the *I*-set. So by (T), there is a world in which something has that property, and there is nothing else. (To see that (T) entails this, let *G* be any element of the *I*-set, and let *n* be zero.) That is, there is a lonely *CS* that is composed of eight things that are *CS*. But this is impossible. A lonely *CS* is a sphere, but its eight parts are not lonely, and are *CS*, so they must be cubes. And no sphere is entirely composed of exactly eight cubes. So *CS* cannot be in an *I*-set, and hence is extrinsic.

5 Problem Cases and Disjunctive Properties

Those five successes might make us think that only intrinsic properties are ever in *I*-sets. However there are still some extrinsic properties that can slip into *I*-sets. For an example, consider the property *LCS*, defined as follows:

x is *LCS* ↔ (*x* is cubical and not both lonely and simple) or (*x* is lonely, simple and spherical)

The smallest set containing *LCS* and satisfying (B) and (M) is an *I*-set. There is an important reason for this. Define a *simple world* as a world containing just one mereological simple, and a compound world as a world that is not a simple world. Whether a property satisfies (T) and (S) (or, more precisely, whether a set containing that property can satisfy (T) and (S)) depends on just how the property interacts with other properties in compound worlds and whether it is ever instantiated in simple worlds. Since the same things are *LCS* as are cubical in compound worlds, these two properties, *LCS* and *being cubical*, interact with other properties in compound worlds in the same way. And each property is instantiated in simple worlds, although they are instantiated in different simple worlds. In sum, the properties are similar enough to be indistinguishable by (T) and (S), and that means we will not be able to show that *LCS* is extrinsic using just those considerations.

Any property that agrees with an intrinsic property, like *being cubical*, in the compound worlds, and is somehow extended so it is instantiated in simple worlds, will be in an *I*-set. This is not just because we have not put enough restrictions on what makes an *I*-set. There are just no combinatorial principles we could deduce from the independence platitude that *LCS* violates. This is because any such principle would, like (T) and (S), be satisfied or not depending just on how the property interacts with other properties in worlds where there are things to interact with, i.e. the compound worlds, and whether it is instantiated in the simple worlds. It is to the good that our deductions from the independence platitude did not show that *LCS* is extrinsic, because in an important sense *LCS*, like all properties that agree with some intrinsic property in all compound worlds, satisfies the platitude.

So at this point appeal to disjunctive and non-disjunctive properties is needed. Intuitively, intrinsic properties are not only capable of being instantiated in all possible combinations with other intrinsic properties, they are capable of being so instantiated in *the same way* in all these possible combinations. We need to distinguish between the disjunctive and the non-disjunctive properties in order to say which properties are instantiated the same way in all these different combinations.

It might be thought at this stage that we could just adopt Langton and Lewis's definition of the disjunctive properties. If that definition worked, we could say the basic intrinsic properties are the non-disjunctive properties that are in *I*-sets, then define duplication and intrinsicness as they do in terms of basic intrinsics. The definition does not, it seems, work as it stands because it does not show that *LCS* is disjunctive. This will be easier to follow if we name all the components of *LCS*, as follows:

C = *being cubical*

L = *being lonely*

M = *being simple*

H = *being spherical*

$LCS = (C \ \& \ \neg(L \ \& \ M)) \ \lor \ (L \ \& \ M \ \& \ H)$

Let us agree that *LCS* is not a natural property, if naturalness is an on/off state, or is very unnatural, if naturalness comes in degrees. On Langton and Lewis's first definition, it is disjunctive if it is a disjunction of conjunctions of natural properties. This seems unlikely: $\neg(L \ \& \ M)$ is not a natural property. This is the property of *being in a compound world*, hardly a natural property. Similarly, $C \ \& \ \neg(L \ \& \ M)$, *being a cube in a compound world*, is hardly natural either. We could insist that these properties are natural, but at this point Yablo's complaint, that clear facts like the extrinsicness of *LCS* are being made to rest on rather obscure facts, like the putative naturalness of *being in a compound world*, returns to haunt us. (I assume, for the sake of the argument, that $L \ \& \ M \ \& \ H$ is a natural property, though this assumption could be easily questioned.) On the second definition, *LCS* is disjunctive if it is much less natural than $\neg(L \ \& \ M)$, or than $C \ \& \ \neg(L$

& *M*). Again, it seems unlikely that this is the case. These properties seem rather unnatural. I have defined enough terms that we can state in the lexicon of this paper just what ¬(*L* & *M*) amounts to, i.e. *being in a compound world*, but the apparent simplicity of this definition should not make us think that the properties are natural. It is true in natural languages that predicates that are easy to express are often natural, but this fact does not extend across to the technical language that is employed here.

The way out is to change the definition of disjunctive properties. A property is disjunctive, intuitively, if it can be instantiated in two quite different ways. Most properties of the form: $(N_1$ & $U_1)$ v $(N_2$ & $U_2)$, where N_1 and N_2 pick out distinct (relatively) natural properties, and U_1 and U_2 pick out distinct (relatively) unnatural properties that are independent of N_1 and N_2, will be like this. If we name this predicate *F*, there will be two quite different types of *F*s: those that are N_1 and those that are N_2. Note that this will be true no matter how unnatural U_1 and U_2 are; provided some *F*s are N_1, and some are N_2, there will be these two ways to be *F*. So I suggest we amend Langton and Lewis's definition of disjunctiveness as follows:

> A property *F* is disjunctive iff it can be expressed as a disjunction of conjunctions, i.e.:
>
> $(A_{11}$ & ... & $A_{1n})$ v ... v $(A_{k1}$ & ... & $A_{km})$
>
> and in each disjunct, at least one of the conjuncts is much more natural than *F*.

On this definition it is clear that *LCS* is disjunctive, since it is much less natural than *being cubical* and than *being spherical*, and in its expression above, *being cubical* is one of the conjuncts in the first disjunct, and *being spherical* is one of the conjuncts in the second disjunct. These kinds of comparisons of naturalness do not seem contentious, or any less obvious than the conclusions about extrinsicness we use them to generate. Further, the new definition of disjunctiveness is not meant to be an *ad hoc* fix. Rather this requirement that only one conjunct in each disjunct need be much more natural than *F* seems to follow directly from the reason we introduced the concept of disjunctiveness to begin with. For each *F* that satisfies the combinatorial principle (either independence of accompaniment in Langton and Lewis's theory, or being in an *I*-set in my theory), we wanted to know whether it only does this because there are two or more ways to be an *F*. If *F* satisfies the definition of disjunctiveness I offer here, it seems there are two or more ways to be an *F*, so the fact that it can be in an *I*-set should not lead us to believe it is intrinsic.

Using this definition of disjunctiveness, we can say that the basic intrinsic properties are those that are neither disjunctive nor the negation of a disjunctive property, and are in at least one *I*-set, then say duplicates are things that share all basic intrinsic properties, and finally that intrinsic properties are properties shared by all duplicates. There are two reasons for thinking that this definition might well work. First, as we have seen, it handles a wide range of hard cases. More importantly, the way that the hard cases were falling gave us reason to suspect that the only extrinsic properties that will be in *I*-sets are properties like *LCS*: properties that agree with some intrinsic property in all compound worlds. It is reasonably clear that these properties will be disjunctive according to the above definition. To see this, let F be the extrinsic property in an *I*-set, and let G be the intrinsic property it agrees with in all compound worlds. Then for some J, F can be expressed as $(G \ \& \ \neg(L \ \& \ M)) \vee (L \ \& \ M \ \& \ J)$, and it will presumably be much less natural than G, probably much less natural than J, and almost certainly much less natural than *being simple*, our L. So if these are the only kind of extrinsic properties in *I*-sets, our definition is correct.

Indeed, if these are the only kinds of extrinsic properties in *I*-sets, we may not even need to worry about which properties should count as disjunctive. Say that a property F *blocks* another property G iff both F and G are in *I*-sets, but there is no *I*-set containing both F and G. If F and G were both intrinsic, then there would be an *I*-set they are both in, such as say *SI*, so the fact that there is no such *I*-set shows that one of them is extrinsic. Note that *LCS* blocks *being cubical*. To prove this, assume *LCS* and *being cubical* are in an *I*-set, say I_k. By two applications of (B), *LCS and not cubical* is in I_k. This property is instantiated in some possible worlds: it is instantiated by all lonely spheres. So by (T) there should be a world containing two things that satisfy *LCS and not cubical*. But only lonely, simple spheres satisfy this property, so there is no world where two things satisfy it, contradicting our assumption that *LCS* and *being cubical* can be in the same *I*-set. The proof here seems perfectly general: if G is intrinsic and F differs from G only in which things in simple worlds satisfy it, and G is in an *I*-set, then F will block G. Blocking, as defined, is symmetric, so the fact that F blocks G is no evidence that F is extrinsic, as opposed to G. Still, if G is much more natural than F, then in all probability the reason F blocks G is that they agree about all cases in compound worlds, and disagree just about the simple worlds. In that case, it seems that F is extrinsic, and G is intrinsic. So I think the following conjecture has merit: F is intrinsic iff it is in an *I*-set and does not block any property much more natural than itself. If the conjecture works, the only kind of naturalness comparisons we need to make will be between properties like *LCS* and properties like *being cubical*. Again, I think these kinds of comparisons should be fairly uncontentious.

6 Back to Basics?

Most of the work in my theory is done by the concept of *I*-sets. It might be wondered whether we can do without them. In particular, it might be thought that the new definition of disjunctivenes I offer in §5 will be enough to rescue Langton and Lewis's theory from the objections I have been fretting about. Indeed, the new definition of disjunctiveness *does* suffice for responding to Yablo's objection. However, it will not do on its own, and I think it will end up being essential to define intrinsicness in terms of *I*-sets.

Yablo notes that a property like *being the only red thing* is independent of accompaniment, and that the way Langton and Lewis suggest showing it is disjunctive is by expressing its negation as *being red and accompanied by a red thing, or not being red*. Yablo criticises the claim that the first of these disjuncts really is a natural property. Above I agreed that this was a good objection. However, on the new definition of disjunctiveness, it is beside the point.

To show that *not being the only red thing* is disjunctive, we need only express it as a disjunction of conjunctions such that at least one conjunct in each disjunct is much more natural than it is. We have the disjunctive expansion of *not being the only red thing*, and the first disjunct is *being red and accompanied by a red thing*. Now this disjunct as a whole may not be particularly natural, but the first conjunct, *being red*, is much more natural than *not being the only red thing*. So all we need to show is that one of the conjuncts in the second disjunct is much more natural than the whole disjunction. Since the second disjunct has only one conjunct, this means we have to show *not being red* is much more natural than *not being the only red thing*. However, there seems to be no simple way to show this. It is just entirely unclear how natural properties like *not being red* should seem to be. My guess (for what it is worth) is that like most properties that can be expressed by negations of English predicates, it is very unnatural. Certainly it is very unnatural if we suppose, as seems fair in *this* context, that F is only a natural property if all the things that are F resemble each other in some important way. The class of things that are not red is as heterogeneous a class as you can hope to find; blue berries, green leaves, silver Beetles, colourless gases and immaterial souls all find their way in. It is true that in "New Work for a Theory of Universals," David Lewis provides two importantly distinct criteria for naturalness. One is the resemblance criterion just mentioned. The other is that F is only perfectly natural if it is fundamental. It might be thought that when we look at this criterion, it does turn out that *not being red* is much more fundamental than *being the only red thing*. Even if this is the case, it is not clear that it does help, or more importantly, that it *should* help. The problem Langton and Lewis were trying to handle is that *not being the only red thing* satisfies a particular combinatorial principle (independence of accompaniment), but only, they say, because there are two different ways of instantiating that property: *not being red* and *being accompanied by a red thing*. The problem is that *not being red* is not a way to instantiate a property, because it is not a way that something could be. It seems very intuitive that 'ways things could be', in this sense, are resemblance properties: they are properties that make for resemblance amongst their instantiators. And even if we can defend the claim that *not being red* is a fundamental property, the fact that it is not a resemblance property seems to undercut Langton and Lewis's case here.

The new definition of disjunctiveness does not provide a defender of Langton and Lewis's theory with a response to Yablo's criticism. On the new definition of disjunctiveness, we do not have to show that *being red and accompanied by a red thing* is more natural than *not being the only red thing* in order to show that the latter is disjunctive. However, in order to show that *not being the only red thing* is disjunctive, we still need to show that *not being red* is a moderately natural property, and this does not seem to be true.

7 Conclusion

There are four major differences between the analysis of intrinsic properties provided here and the one provided by Langton and Lewis. Three of these are reflected in the difference between the combinatorial principle they use, independence of accompaniment, and the combinatorial principle I use, membership in an I-set. All properties that are in I-sets are independent of accompaniment, but they also have a few other nice features. First, membership in an I-set guarantees not just independence of whether there are other things, but independence of what other types of things there are. This is the independence principle encoded in condition (T) on I-sets. Second, membership in an I-set guarantees independence of where the other things are. This is the principle encoded in condition (S). Third, the mereological principle (M) has no parallel in Langton and Lewis's theory.

The effect of these extra three restrictions is that I have to make many fewer appeals to naturalness than do Langton and Lewis. The fourth difference between their theory and mine is in the role naturalness considerations play in determining which properties are intrinsic. In §5 I offer two ways of finishing the analysis using naturalness. The first is in the new definition of disjunctiveness; with this definition in hand we can finish the story just as Langton and Lewis suggest. The second is in terms of blocking: F is intrinsic iff it is in an I-set and does not block any property that it is much less natural than. Both ways are designed to deal with a quite specific problem: properties that differ only in which things instantiate them in simple worlds have the same combinatorial features, so a definition of intrinsicness in terms of combinatorial features (as is Langton and Lewis's, and as is mine) will not be able to distinguish them. Still, both solutions seem likely to provide the same answer in all the hard cases: the right answer.

References

Armstrong, D. M. (1989). *A Combinatorial Theory of Possibility.* Cambridge: Cambridge University Press.
Langton, Rae and David Lewis (1998). "Defining 'Intrinsic'". *Philosophy and Phenomenological Research* 58: pp. 333–45.
Lewis, David (1983a). "Extrinsic Properties". *Philosophical Studies* 44: pp. 197–200.
Lewis, David (1983b). "New Work for a Theory of Universals". *Australasian Journal of Philosophy* 61: pp. 343–77.
Lewis, David (1986). *On the Plurality of Worlds.* Oxford: Blackwell.
Marshall, Dan and Josh Parsons (2001). "Langton and Lewis on 'Intrinsic'". *Philosophy and Phenomenological Research* 63: pp. 347–52.
Sider, Theodore (forthcoming). "Maximality and Intrinsic Properties". *Philosophy and Phenomenological Research* 63: pp. 357–64.
Taylor, Barry (1993). "On Natural Properties in Metaphysics". *Mind* 102: pp. 81–100.
Yablo, Stephen (1999). "Intrinsicness". *Philosophical Topics* 26: pp. 479–505.

David Denby
Essence and Intrinsicality

Abstract: In the first half of this paper, I argue that essential properties are intrinsic and that this permits a modal analysis of essence that is immune to the sort of objections raised by Fine (1994). In the second half, I argue that intrinsic properties collectively have a certain structure and that this accounts for some observations about essences: that things are essentially determinate; that things often have properties within a certain range essentially; and that the essential properties of things are their core properties.

I

According to Kit Fine (1994), "a property of an object is essential if it must have the property to be what it is; otherwise, the property is accidental" (p. 1).[1] One might attempt to analyze this in modal terms, i.e. in terms of quantification over worlds:

[M]   x has F *essentially* iff x has F at every world.[2]

Often, of course, quantifiers are restricted. Some restrictions on [M]'s world-quantifier vary with context, allowing that x has F essentially in some contexts but not in others; others don't, e.g., a restriction to worlds where x exists. (This restriction is required if contingent things are to have any essential properties at all. Contingent things don't have any properties at every world because they don't exist at every world, and existing is a prerequisite for having properties.)[3]

Fine rejects [M]. For any necessary truth P, the property *being such that P* is one everything has at every world. So, by [M], it is one everything has essentially. But, intuitively, *being such that there are infinitely many primes* or *being such that modus ponens is valid* are not among the essential properties of most things. Primes and logic have nothing to do with what makes me the object I am, for instance. Indeed, since facts about identity and diversity are necessary, and ev-

---

[1] Fine (1995b, p. 53). He is following a long tradition. See, e.g., Aristotle (*Metaphysics:* 1029b14): "the essence of a thing is what it is said to be in respect of itself".
[2] [M] is roughly what Fine (1994) calls the "categorical approach". He also discusses two more complicated conditional variants of [M], which I'll ignore here.
[3] Henceforth, I will suppress this restriction. When I say that something is true of x at every world, I will mean it is true of x at every world *at which x exists*.

erything is either identical to or distinct from everything, [M] entails that everything is involved in the essence of everything. Surely not! Surely, it is not part of my essence to be distinct from the Eiffel Tower or from some speck of dust on Mars, or from the number 15—these things are just irrelevant to what makes me the object that I am. Restrictions on [M]'s world-quantifier only make matters worse. If the worlds are restricted to those where P is the case, then [M] entails that *being such that P* is one of x's essential properties, whatever P says. Fine points out that a restriction to worlds where x exists means that existing becomes an essential property of everything, which doesn't sound very plausible (except perhaps for God).[4]

He concludes that modal analyses of essence are doomed. In fact, he doubts the viability of any analysis; he thinks we should take essence as primitive.[5] He even urges that we turn the tables on [M] and analyze modality in terms of the essences of things:

> We should view metaphysical necessity as a special case of essence...[E]ach class of objects...will give rise to its own domain of necessary truths, the truths that flow from the nature of the object in question. The metaphysically necessary truths can then be identified with the propositions that are true in virtue of the nature of all objects whatever. (1994, p. 9)

From this perspective, [M]'s modal approach fails because each class of objects "...makes its own contribution to the totality of necessary truths; and one can hardly expect to determine from the totality itself what the contributions were" (1994, p. 9).

II

However, taking essence as primitive is itself problematic. For one thing, it doesn't really seem basic enough to make an attractive primitive. When we say that x has F essentially, usually we don't just mean that x couldn't survive the

---

4 Though see Zalta (2006) for whom even ordinary concrete objects exist essentially (but are only contingently concrete).

5 Strictly, he proposes explaining essences in terms of "real definitions", but a real definition is characterized, a la Aristotle, only as "...the formula of the essence" (*Metaphysics*, 1031a12), which is tantamount to taking essence as primitive. Anyway, the notion of definition is obscure, especially if things and not just words are supposed to have definitions. A further worry is that things (or at least words) often have more than one definition, threatening to render (complete) essences non-unique.

loss of F. Usually, we mean that x couldn't survive any variation in the kind of property to which F belongs. If something is essentially red, then it couldn't survive not being red, but not simply because it couldn't survive having redness deleted from its property-profile. Nothing could survive that. That would leave it without any color, and presumably no colored thing could survive becoming uncolored. Indeed, it would leave it with a gappy property-profile, and nothing at all could be like that. Surely everything is essentially determinate. Everything must have a full complement of properties; it must be complete. Things *change* their features; they don't simply lose them. Something loses redness by gaining some other color instead. And it is that change we usually intend to rule out when we say that x is essentially red. We don't mean it couldn't be uncolored, we mean it couldn't be one of the other colors—blue or green or yellow or . . . It couldn't survive any such *variation* in its color. Similarly, Socrates is essentially human not just because he couldn't survive failing to belong to a species—no living thing could do that—but because he couldn't survive belonging to a *different* species; he couldn't be a dog or a marigold or a unicorn. His height, mass or color might vary, but not his species. *Mutatis mutandis*, for almost all quotidian essential properties.[6] Gold has atomic number 79 essentially because pieces of gold cannot vary in the atomic numbers of their atoms, even if they might change in other ways. The table is essentially wooden because it cannot vary in its constituent material, even if it might vary in color or age or shape. And so on. Essence, in short, involves invariance. But that would seem to make essence a poor primitive. How could invariance be conceptually basic? Invariance presupposes a dimension—color, species, atomic number, constituent material—along which there might have been variation, but there isn't.

For another thing, the notion of an essence seems rather too foggy to make a promising primitive. For a start, it is unclear which kinds of properties could be essential to things. Is every qualitative property eligible? The obvious place to start is with the determinate, natural properties. These are the properties on which so much else supervenes; they determine what the world is like. But they are dubious candidates. Could anything really be essentially *exactly* 17.3 kg in mass, not a jot more or less? That would be a very fragile thing indeed. Could anything really be essentially just one determinate shape? Or essentially a certain exact shade of red?[7] And what about haecceities, properties of the form, *being so-and-so*, e.g., *being Socrates*? Are they eligible to be essential? *Being Soc-*

---

6 I discuss some exceptions below.
7 Similarly for determinate natural relations: could any pair of things be essentially precisely one meter apart, no more, no less?

rates is a property that Socrates must have if he is to be the object he is, but in some ways it doesn't seem to be a very good candidate for being an essential property either. Only he could have it, yet we usually want to allow that distinct things, e.g., Socrates and his twin-Earth doppelganger, might share a complete essence, that they might be "essentially the same". Moreover, we usually think of the essential properties of a thing as its "central" or "core" properties in some sense, but haecceities don't seem to be central or core properties in any sense.[8] Haecceities are unrelated to all other interesting features of things, such as their qualitative natures, their powers, and their causal relations to other things. Socrates and his doppelganger could be exactly alike in all their interesting features, even extrinsic ones if the universe is suitably symmetrical, despite differing haecceitistically. What about Boolean consequences of essential properties? Are they eligible to be essential properties? Socrates has the property *being human* essentially, but does he also thereby have the property *being human or famous* essentially?[9] It is also unclear which kinds of things have essences. Fine wants to root all necessities in essences, so, since there are necessary truths about every kind of thing, presumably for him, every kind of thing had better have an essence. But why? Why couldn't there be protean things that have all their properties accidentally? Things usually have some of their properties accidentally, why not all of them? There are few properties that I couldn't do without, determinate, qualitative ones at least. I could have been a little taller or shorter, a little more or less massive, and so on. Finally, it is even unclear whether our talk of the essences of things is really rooted in the natures of the things themselves or merely reflects restrictions evoked by the conversational context. Perhaps essentialism is a wholly linguistic phenomenon.[10]

In short, the notion of an essence is neither conceptually basic nor clear enough to make a very promising primitive. Anyway, could an analysis of modality in terms of the essences of things really succeed? There seem to be many necessary truths that are not rooted in the essences of things, at least not actual things.[11] It is a necessary truth that had Hamlet existed, he would have been human, but there is nothing, no Hamlet, whose essence makes it so. Presumably

---

[8] Gorman (2005), for instance, characterizes essentialism as expressing "...the intuition that some features of a thing are more central and important than others are" (p. 2).
[9] Fine (1995b, p. 57) distinguishes properties that are "constitutively essential" like *being a man* from those that are mere logical consequences of them, e.g., *being a man or a mountain*. He grants, however, that it is not obvious how to formulate the distinction precisely. See also Gorman (2005, p. 5).
[10] The *locus classicus* of such a view is Quine (1960, p. 199). See also Lewis (1986, pp. 248–63).
[11] Cameron makes this point (2010, §2).

unicorns are essentially equine, but not in virtue of the essence of any existing thing. One might respond by accepting that essences, including individual essences like Hamlet's, exist uninstantiated, but not everyone would.

III

I think we should give the modal approach a second look.[12] In this section, I explore a simple fix to [M]: require that essential properties be *intrinsic*:

[M*]   x has F essentially iff x has F at every world *and F is intrinsic.*

Roughly, a property is intrinsic iff its instantiation is insensitive to the state or nature of anything other than its instances; otherwise, it is extrinsic.[13] Whether something is red, or 3 kg, or round is a matter of how it itself is, regardless of anything else. So redness, *being 3 kg*, and roundness are intrinsic properties. A useful test is that an intrinsic property cannot vary among duplicates.[14] By contrast, whether something is alone in the universe, or coexists with something red, or is a meter from the wall does depend on how other things are, so *being alone, coexisting with something red*, and *being a meter from the wall* are extrinsic properties. (Some extrinsic properties contain an intrinsic admixture. For a thing to instantiate *being the only red thing* not only must everything else be non-red, an extrinsic matter, but it itself must be red, which is an intrinsic matter. For simplicity I'll ignore these properties and pretend that every extrinsic property is purely extrinsic, i.e. entirely insensitive to the intrinsic nature of its instances, like, e.g., *membership in the singleton of Socrates* and *being a meter from the wall*. This simplification is harmless as long as impurely extrinsic properties all factor into a purely extrinsic property on the one hand and an intrinsic property on the other, which I think they do, though I won't argue for that here.[15])

---

12 I'm not the only one—see also Della Rocca (1996), Gorman (2005), Zalta (2006), and Correia (2007).
13 Perhaps properties aren't intrinsic or extrinsic *simpliciter*, but intrinsic to some things and extrinsic to others (Dunn (1990, p. 183); Francescotti (1999, pp. 591–2)). Perhaps, e.g., the property *being such that there are chairs* is intrinsic to my chair, but extrinsic to me. I will ignore this complication. It has no bearing on what follows. (Actually, I'm not convinced. Chairs might have chairhood intrinsically, and necessarily, if something has chairhood, it also has *being such that there are chairs*, but why think that necessary consequences of intrinsic properties are in general intrinsic? It is not plausible that *being human or popular* is intrinsic to me even though *being human* is.)
14 Lewis (1986, pp. 61–3).
15 See Denby (2010).

By excluding extrinsic properties, [M*] disqualifies properties that involve things other than their instances from being essential. It thereby avoids Fine-style counterexamples, all of which do drag in other things—primes, argument forms, the Eiffel Tower, specks of dust, etc. Moreover, classifying essences as intrinsic seems natural. What makes an object the object it is surely has to do with *its* features; what other things are like is just irrelevant.[16] Indeed, extrinsic properties, at least the qualitative ones, seem all ultimately to concern not just what other things are like, but what other things are like *intrinsically*.[17] For a thing to have an extrinsic property, something else—another thing, the whole of the rest of the world, a pair (or triple, or...) or a plurality of things—must be a certain way intrinsically.[18] Something is alone iff the rest of the world is empty. Something is a meter from the wall iff the pair of it and the wall has the intrinsic property of having members a meter apart. Something is one of many iff a certain plurality has the intrinsic feature of being numerous. (Qualitative) extrinsic properties, it seems, are grounded ultimately in intrinsic properties of other things—reflected light that requires a light source. How could it really be that x is F by virtue of y's being F*, and y is F* by virtue of z's being F**, and so on ad infinitum, where F, F*, F**,... are all (qualitative) extrinsic properties? That seems to be a good reason to think they are not essential to it.

Intrinsicality is a relatively clear notion.[19] And classifying essences as intrinsic dispels some of the fog surrounding essences. Are Boolean consequences of essential properties also essential? It depends on whether the compound is intrinsic. Socrates has both *being human* and *being rational* essentially: he has both properties in all worlds and both properties are intrinsic. He also has their conjunction, *being human and rational*, essentially, for he has it at every world and since the conjunction of intrinsic properties is intrinsic, it is also intrinsic. But he does not have *being human or famous* essentially: it is one he has at every world, but the involvement of fame renders it extrinsic. Does restricting

---

16 See Della Rocca (1996), Gorman (2005), Zalta (2006), and Correia (2007) for other ways to analyze Fine-style counterexamples' failure to be fully "about" their instances.

17 Below, I discuss whether some non-qualitative properties—haecceities, membership in various sets—are also grounded in the intrinsic features of other things. I will ignore others that depend on the non-existence rather than the intrinsic properties of other things, e.g., *being a world* (something is a world iff nothing other than it exists). They don't seem to undermine the intuitions I am trying to elicit here.

18 By 'something else' here I mean something not identical to it, so even if a pair (or plurality, or...) involves a thing, it counts as something else.

19 In (Denby 2006, 2010) I argue that it can be characterized precisely in quasi-logical terms. Not everyone agrees (Marshall 2009), and not everyone agrees that it is clear (Dennett 1988). But it does at least seem clearer than the notion of an essence.

the world-quantifier in [M*] to worlds where x exists entail that everything exists essentially? Only if existence is an intrinsic property. If, for instance, it is a second-order property and this means that it is not intrinsic (to the things that exist), then nothing exists essentially. [M*], of course, is neutral on the nature of existence. But leaving the question of whether anything exists essentially as a substantial metaphysical issue having to do with the nature of existence is how it should be.[20] At least it is an improvement on [M]. What is objectionable about something existing essentially is that existence should belong to its *nature*, not that the thing should exist at every world where it exists.[21]

IV

There are some natural worries about proposing to analyze essence in terms of intrinsicality. For one, is it circular? I don't think so, but I won't explore the issue. The intrinsic/extrinsic division among a thing's properties concerns which of them characterize it alone and which are sensitive to its environment, whereas the essential/accidental division concerns which it could lack and which it couldn't. On the face of it, these seem to be quite different ideas. And clearly things have intrinsic properties that are not essential to them—mine include my particular color, mass, shape, and height.[22]

One might also worry that abstract and grounded entities have some extrinsic properties essentially, in violation of [M*]. Sets, for instance, are defined by their membership; it is what makes them the very entities that they are. So a set containing Socrates does so essentially. But *contains Socrates* is an extrinsic property. Presumably, whether a set contains Socrates doesn't have anything to do with its intrinsic properties, whatever they might be. How could a set—or anything else—*intrinsically* involve something distinct from itself? So sets have some extrinsic properties essentially, and [M*] is false. *Mutatis mutandis*

---

[20] Here it might matter whether intrinsicality is a relative or absolute notion (see fn. 13). One might want to allow that some things have existence intrinsically and others don't.

[21] Classifying essences as intrinsic also clarifies the other issues I mentioned above—Are all qualitative determinate properties eligible to be essences? Does everything have some properties essentially? Is the source of essentialism metaphysical or merely linguistic?—though I postpone discussion until section VI.

[22] Some philosophers have indeed appealed to essences in analyzing intrinsicality (Francescotti 1999, Witmer, Butchard, and Trogdon 2005), but it is not clear these appeals are ineliminable. I have argued (Denby 2006, 2010) that intrinsicality is analyzable in terms of relations among *properties*, albeit modal ones. These relations presuppose nothing about the essences of their instances.

for grounded entities generally: if x is grounded in y, then *being grounded in y* is an extrinsic property that is essential to x.

The best response to this worry, I think, is to deny that sets have their members essentially. This might sound like a non-starter, but it is hard to see what good reason there really is for supposing that they do. Of course, this is not to deny that it is a necessary truth that Socrates' singleton, "{Socrates}", contains Socrates[23], but that doesn't show that it has *contains Socrates* essentially. It is a necessary truth that Socrates is such that modus ponens is valid, but he does not have *being such that modus ponens is valid* essentially. That was Fine's original objection to [M]—it fails to distinguish a thing's essential properties from among those it has necessarily. It seems arbitrary just to ignore the distinction in the case of sets (and other grounded entities).

Neither set theory itself nor any of its theoretical deployments seems to require that {Socrates} have *contains Socrates* essentially. They require only that, for any things, there be a unique set having exactly those things as members, and, presumably, that this be the case at every world.[24] This shows that nothing that doesn't contain Socrates could qualify as his singleton, but nothing follows about the essence of the singleton itself. At every world, Socrates' dog belongs to Socrates, but it is not of the essence of any dog to belong to Socrates; it is just that if they part ways, the dog no longer qualifies as his. Indeed, the utility of set theory does not even seem to require that {Socrates} be the same entity at every world—perhaps a different entity plays the {Socrates}-role at different worlds. But even if it is the same entity, it still doesn't follow that it has *contains Socrates* essentially. One and the same entity is Socrates at every world and he has *being a member of {Socrates}* at every world, yet, as Fine points out, it is implausible to suppose that *being a member of {Socrates}* is essential to Socrates— what makes Socrates the very thing he is surely has nothing to do with set theory.

Nor does the epistemology of sets seem to require that {Socrates} have *contains Socrates* essentially. It is true that we know very little that is distinctive about {Socrates} except that it contains (only) Socrates, but sets are mind-independent entities, so it is hard to see how anything about their essences could follow from epistemological facts, let alone from our ignorance about sets! We know very little that is distinctive about Jonah except that he was swallowed by a whale, but presumably this was not part of his essence. Indeed, if anything,

---

23 That is, at every world at which it exists, {Socrates} contains Socrates. Recall that I am suppressing the restriction to worlds where the subjects exist.
24 Ignoring the usual restrictions required to avoid paradox.

epistemological considerations undermine claims to know about the essences of sets. Sets are abstract, so any putative knowledge of their essences was not gained by causal acquaintance with them. Nor was it gained on the basis of intuitions about the nature of properties like *contains Socrates*. Such properties are non-qualitative and non-natural, which would seem to preclude intuitive insight into them.

Nor does semantics require that {Socrates} have *contains Socrates* essentially. It is true that the reference of '{Socrates}' depends on the reference of 'Socrates', but sets are language-independent entities, so it is hard to see how anything about their essences could follow from mere semantic facts. We often refer to things via their accidental properties—the thing by the wall, the father of the bride. Granted, unlike things by the wall and fathers, '{Socrates}' can be referred to in only one way, viz. via Socrates. But how could the impoverishment of our semantic resources reveal anything about the essences of any language-independent things referred to?

Most seriously, there does not even seem to be anything about the metaphysics of sets (or their members) that requires that sets have their members essentially. It is true that {Socrates} exists only if Socrates exists, but Socrates exists only if {Socrates} exists too—they exist at the same worlds—yet, as we have just seen, it is implausible to suppose that *being a member of {Socrates}* is essential to Socrates. It is true that {Socrates} unlike Socrates is *abstract*, but quite what abstraction amounts to is notoriously obscure.[25] If *being abstract* is intrinsic, then it is hard to see how it can have any bearing on whether an extrinsic property like *containing Socrates* is essential to {Socrates}. But even if *being abstract* is extrinsic—perhaps it is a matter of being abstracted *from* something: its origin or source or ground—it is still hard to see how anything about the essence of {Socrates} should follow. Plausibly, blueness is abstracted from blue things, but nothing obviously follows about the essence of blueness. In particular, *being instantiated by the sky* (or by any other actually blue things) does not seem to be essential to blueness—blueness exists at worlds that have only alien blue particulars, and even worlds without any blue particulars at all if Platonists are right. Either way, the fact that sets are abstract does not seem to show that *contains Socrates* is essential to {Socrates}.

Perhaps one thinks, with Fine, that necessary truths must all be grounded somehow in the essences of things. Then the necessary truth that {Socrates} contains Socrates must be grounded in the essence of something. But it is not grounded in the essence of Socrates, so it is tempting to suppose that it must

---

25 See Lewis (1986, pp. 81–6).

be grounded in the essence of {Socrates} instead. However, there is a third, more natural option: it is grounded in the essence of the *pair* of {Socrates} and Socrates. Pairs, sums, and pluralities have essences too; they'd better if all necessary truths are grounded in essences because they too are the subject of necessary truths. And their essences do not seem in general to reduce to the essences of their members. My essential properties, e. g., do not reduce to the essential properties of the fundamental particles of which I am composed (considered separately); at the least, the particles' arrangements matter too. Now, the pair of {Socrates} and Socrates has the property that its first member contains its second, and it has this property at every world. Although this property does not reduce to the intrinsic properties either of {Socrates} or of Socrates considered separately—otherwise, Socrates' doppelganger would be a member of Socrates' singleton—it does seem to be an intrinsic feature of the pair; it doesn't seem to depend on anything other than {Socrates} and Socrates and their interrelations. So [M*] classifies this property as essential to the pair. So [M*] can allow that the necessary truth that Socrates' singleton contains Socrates is grounded in the essence of something, just not in the essence either of {Socrates} or of Socrates. Instead, it is grounded in the essence of their pair.

One might point out that {Socrates} is postulated or posited, whereas Socrates is discovered. But to postulate or posit something that is mind- and language-independent is not to generate or produce it. Rather, it is to claim that it was there all along, playing the role we hope something is there to play: containing Socrates.

In sum, neither set theory, epistemology, semantics, nor even metaphysics obviously compels us to think that a set really has its membership essentially. They require only that it be a necessary truth that it does. And that can be attributed to the essences of pairs of sets and their members, if needs be. There are epistemic and semantic asymmetries between sets and their members: our grasp of and reference to {Socrates} must go via Socrates, but not vice versa. Perhaps that is why it seems natural to say that sets have their members essentially: their membership provides our only access to them. However, a metaphysical asymmetry remains elusive. Sets are posited as abstract correlates of things—one for each collection of things. But neither their abstractness nor the fact that they are posited shows that {Socrates} contains Socrates essentially. And the correlation is symmetrical: sets exist iff their members do. I conclude that even if properties like *contains Socrates* are extrinsic, they do not force us to abandon [M*] because they don't seem to be essential to their instances. *Mutatis mutandis*, for the defining properties of other grounded entities.

Finally, one might worry that [M*] misclassifies haecceities, properties of the form *being so-and-so*, e.g., *being Socrates*.[26] Intrinsic properties cannot vary among duplicates, but haecceities can—Socrates instantiates *being Socrates*, but his twin-earth doppelganger does not. So haecceities are not intrinsic, and so, according to [M*], they are not essential. But, the objection runs, surely haecceities are essential properties *par excellence*—if anything makes Socrates the object he is, it is that he has the property *being Socrates*.

One response would be simply to add a clause to [M*] to accommodate haecceities: F is essential to x iff x has F at every world and either F is intrinsic *or F is the property of being x*. However, this would be ad hoc and inelegant. Another response would be to recharacterize intrinsic properties so that haecceities qualify. After all, characterizing them as those that cannot vary among duplicates automatically excludes haecceities simply because haecceities are nonqualitative: 'duplicate' here means *qualitative* duplicate. But, one might argue, the real test should be whether the property is sensitive to anything other than its instances, regardless of whether it is qualitative. And by that test, haecceities seem to qualify—surely *being Socrates* is sensitive only to Socrates. However, this response seems flawed. Contrary to initial appearances, haecceities *do* involve other things, albeit implicitly and generically; they fail even this test. Intuitively, if having a certain property—qualitative or not—is an intrinsic matter, then so is lacking that property; if x's being F is a matter only of how x is, then so is x's lacking F. So if *being Socrates* were intrinsic, then *being distinct from Socrates* would be intrinsic too, since to have *being distinct from Socrates* just is to lack *being Socrates*. But *being distinct from Socrates* surely does involve something other than its instances, viz. Socrates; it seems to be an extrinsic property *par excellence*. Anyway, it can't be intrinsic if *being Socrates* is, for, since something has *being Socrates* iff the rest of the world has *being distinct from Socrates*, that would mean that having *being Socrates* constrains the rest of the world *intrinsically*, and surely only an extrinsic property could do that—intrinsic properties vary independently among distinct things. So *being Socrates* is not intrinsic, not just because it is non-qualitative but because it is "uniqueness-entailing"—if x has it, everything else lacks it—and so implicitly it does involve other things after all.[27]

---

26 Haecceitistic or non-qualitative properties are those tied to a specific individual, e.g., *being near Socrates* and *liking Paris*. I use 'haecceity' for haecceistic properties whose instantiation is a matter of being identical to a specific individual, e.g., *being Socrates*.

27 Whence the necessity, if Fine is right that all necessities are grounded in essences? It is of the essence of any pair <x, x> that its members be identical. And this is intrinsic to the pair—any duplicate of the pair would also have to have identical members. Even if x* is a distinct

Instead of amending [M*] or our characterization of intrinsicality to allow that haecceities are essential, I think we should just bite the bullet and deny that they really are. After all, classifying haecceities as essential would drain essences of some of their interest. Haecceities are non-qualitative, non-natural, and they exist iff certain things—their mandatory and only instances—also exist. They don't correspond to similarities; they don't figure in the laws of nature; and it is hard to see how we can have intuitive insight into them. And their only theoretical role is to distinguish qualitatively identical possibilities.[28] If [M*] proves to be plausible and illuminating in other respects, it would be a shame to abandon it on the grounds that it misclassifies such uninteresting properties as haecceities. That leaves us with the task of explaining why we are tempted to classify them—incorrectly—as essential. I speculate that this is because they are properties their instances have necessarily, but unlike other properties a thing has necessarily but not essentially, e. g. *being such that there are infinitely many primes*, they seem to involve their instances alone. That is, they seem essential precisely because they are necessary properties that seem intrinsic. However, since they are uniqueness-entailing, really they do involve things other than their instances, though this is not obvious because they do so implicitly and generically.

In sum, [M*] doesn't seem circular, and its classification of certain properties of sets and haecceitistic properties as non-essential is defensible enough to make further exploration of [M*] worthwhile. There is more to say, especially on haecceities, but I want to turn next to some observations about intrinsic properties. These turn out to illuminate some interesting general observations about essences.

V

Intrinsic properties are posited, primarily, to account for similarities. However, we cannot simply say that things are similar iff they share a property, perhaps as a common (non-spatial) part. Sharing a property is an all-or-nothing matter: things can't half-share a property. Similarity, by contrast, is a matter of degree: my blue pen is quite similar to my black pencil, and it would be even more sim-

---

duplicate of x, the pair <x, x*> would not be a duplicate of <x, x>, at least if x and x* are physical objects—the members of <x, x*> are some distance apart but the members of <x, x> aren't, for instance.

28 And perhaps they are not needed even there. See Lewis (1986, pp. 220–48).

ilar to it if it were black too. And my pen and my pencil are more similar to one another than either is to my shoe.

A second suggestion: things are similar to degree N iff they share N properties. The idea here is that degrees of similarity reflect the numbers of common properties: the more properties things have in common, the more similar they are. My pen and my pencil share more properties than my pen and my shoe and that's why they are more similar. But this suggestion won't do either. Some properties make for greater similarity and so should count for more than others. Sharing exactly the same shade of red makes for more similarity than merely sharing reddishness, which, in turn, makes for more similarity than sharing *being either red or blue*, which makes for almost no similarity at all.

Suggestion three: things are similar to degree N iff the weighted sum of the properties they share = N. Suppose we assign scores to properties that reflect how much similarity they confer on their instances. A specific shade of red would get a higher score than reddishness, which would get a higher score than *being either red or blue*. Summing these scores for all shared properties would give a measure of overall similarity among things that reflects the properties' unequal contributions. This allows a role for context to play in determining similarity. Perhaps some contexts demand that a lot of weight be given to sameness of mass, while others demand that it barely count at all. However, if similarity is determined by summing, double-counting must be avoided, regardless of context. So disjunctive and other compound properties should get zero weight whatever the context. If things are both F, then no extra similarity is conferred by the fact that they are both also either F or G. And if one is F but not G, and the other is G but not F, then the fact that they are both either F or G is no similarity at all. Intuitively, unspecific properties, e.g., *being reddish*, *being about 10 kg*, should also get zero weight, regardless of context.[29] A thing has an unspecific property only by virtue of its specific properties; an unspecific property is not an *additional* way for something to be. A thing can be reddish only by virtue of being some specific shade; it can be about 10 kg only by having a specific mass; and so on. How could unspecific properties generate new similarities that weren't already present at the level of the specific properties on which they supervene? Surely, it is the specific properties of things that fix their natures and so the facts about similarities. Negative properties should get zero weight or, at best, nearly zero weight: *being non-green* makes for barely any similarity, especially if the green is some highly specific shade.

---

29 Lewis suggests (1986, p. 61) that unspecific properties just are disjunctive properties anyway.

However, even this third suggestion is inadequate. First, things might be very similar despite sharing no specific properties at all. Perhaps one thing is 10 kg, red, and square, whereas the other is not quite 10 kg but 10.1 kg, not quite red but pink, and not quite square but slightly rounded. Indeed, they might be almost perfect duplicates without sharing a single specific property. They would share many less specific properties—*being reddish-pink, being about 10 kg, being roughly square*—but, to repeat, these should be given no weight. Similarities must be accounted for at the level of the specific properties, and at that level there is no sharing of properties at all. Second, given that properties vary in the similarity they confer on their instances, things might be quite dissimilar even though they share nearly all their properties. Two paintings might be exactly alike in every respect except color—perhaps one is entirely blue and the other entirely red. Yet this single difference might count for a lot. In certain contexts—aesthetic ones perhaps—the property-weighting evoked might mean that the pictures are about as dissimilar as can be. Third, things might be similar to different degrees without differing at all in the number of properties they share or in the weightings of those properties. *Ceteris paribus*, a red thing is more similar to a pink thing than it is to a blue thing, but not because of any difference in the numbers of shared properties or their weightings. Colors are alternatives; things that differ in color differ in *which* properties they have, not in *how many* they have. And, in most contexts, no color is more weighty than any other. Suggestion 3 is powerless to account for any of this.[30]

In sum, similarity is a matter of degree, so it cannot be a matter of sharing properties. Perhaps if it were a matter of degree only at the gross level of overall similarity, it might be a matter of how many properties, suitably weighted, are shared. But it isn't. It is a matter of degree even at the level of particular respects of similarity—color-similarity, mass-similarity, length-similarity, etc.—where the relevant properties are equally weighted alternatives. And there is no hope of capturing this in terms of a count of shared properties, even a weighted count, because there can be similarity without any sharing, sharing without any similarity, and differences in similarity without any differences in the number of shared properties or their weights. Similarity seems to be a matter of *which* properties things have—which determinate masses, lengths, charges, shapes, and so on—not *how many* properties they share.

---

[30] There is nothing special about colors. Similarity is still a matter of degree even at the level of the most fundamental properties. Things could be more or less similar in mass, e.g., even if they differ in no other way.

An alternative to modeling similarity in terms of sharing properties is suggested by several observations. Focus on the specific, non-compound, intrinsic properties. Notice first that these seem to divide up into families of contraries, e.g., the colors (specific shades of redness, blueness, yellowness...), the masses (*being 3 kg, being 100 kg, being 1245.76 kg*), the shapes (roundness, squareness,...), etc. Notice also that each family encodes a distance relation among its members, defining the "space" for that family. The structure of this space varies from family to family: the structure of the color-space is captured in the color-wheel; the mass-space, length-space, and the spaces of many other quantities have the structure of the positive reals; the structure of the shape-space is determined both by the number of sides and the ratios of their lengths; and so on. Notice third that every family is inherently *quasi-global:* roughly, everything instantiates some member of every family (in fact, a unique member, given that the members are contraries). It is not that some things are colored, some are massive, others are shaped, with perhaps some overlap among the three groups. Rather, the domain of every family is the same and it includes everything: *everything* has some color, some mass, and some shape. I say "roughly" for two reasons. First, the families seem to be global only within an ontological category or other broad domain: physical things might all have some color, mass, shape, etc., but abstract things don't; living things all belong to some species, but inanimate things don't. Second, even within a category, the families aren't straightforwardly global. Electrons, e.g., are physical things but, unlike tables and chairs and other physical things, they have no color at all. And, unlike electrons, tables and chairs do not have dimensions precise to the nearest Planck length. However, it does seem that everything at least overlaps or is overlapped by something that instantiates some member of every family—fundamental particles might not have any color, but their fusions do; tables might not have very precise dimensions, but their parts do.[31] (One might still object. According to our best theories, photons lack any (rest) mass, despite having an energy, frequency, speed, etc., which shows that the mass family is not global. I disagree: photons have zero (rest) mass, which is quite different from being massless.[32] If a thing lacks mass, then its momentum and the effects of a force on it are ill-defined; not so for something with zero mass. And a physical object that lacked a well-defined momentum or responses to forces would be a dubious thing indeed. Photons might have zero mass, but they don't lack mass altogether.) Anyway, I will

---

[31] Of course, this raises a number of questions. What about lone particles afloat in space? How could the fusion of some things be less precise than they are? I address these questions elsewhere (Denby MS).
[32] *Pace* Bricker (forthcoming, 2013).

suppress these two qualifications from now on. When I use 'global', I'll presuppose that we are sticking to one ontological category or broad domain, and we are counting things as falling in the domain of a family if their parts or fusions do. I don't think anything turns on this simplification.

Properties that are unspecific or Boolean compounds of other properties or extrinsic do not in general belong to unique, quasi-global families of contraries under a distance relation. Some unspecific properties in the same family, e.g., *being reddish* and *being bluish*, are not contraries—purple things are both reddish and bluish. Some compound properties, e.g., *being 10 kg and round*, have a foot in more than one family. Some extrinsic properties, e.g., *being a sibling*, lack contraries altogether, while others, e.g., being a meter from the wall, belong just as naturally to families of non-contraries, e.g., the *being-a-meter-from-x* family, as to families of contraries, e.g., the *being-x-meters-from-the-wall* family. However, intuitively, all such properties ultimately supervene on the specific, non-compound, intrinsic properties (of their instances or of other things); it is to the latter we should look to account for similarities. And these all do seem to belong to such families.

These observations, though rough, suggest a different model of similarity. Each specific, non-compound, intrinsic property belongs to a unique family of contraries under a distance relation. These families constitute "dimensions" of similarity—color-similarity, mass-similarity, shape-similarity, and so on. Similarity between things on a given dimension is determined by the distance between the properties within that family's space that the things instantiate: for any family F, the closer these properties are in the F-space, the more F-similar their instances are. If things instantiate the very same F, then they are perfectly F-similar. If they instantiate very distant Fs, then they are very F-dissimilar. Distance is undefined for properties belonging to different families—one thing being blue and another being 10 kg, or one thing being positively charged and another being round makes for neither similarity nor dissimilarity. Similarities among things might vary with different dimensions. Two things might be very similar in color and shape (one is red, the other pink; one is octagonal, the other nonagonal), but very dissimilar in mass and charge (one is 10^{-34} kg, the other 10^{34} kg; one is positive, the other negative). And various dimensions of similarity might differ in how important they are in determining overall similarity. So each family could be assigned a score to reflect this.[33] Again, the scores might be context-sen-

---

[33] Perhaps the story is a bit more complicated. Rather than a fixed score for each family—one for color, one for mass, one for charge, etc.—perhaps there is a function that assigns different scores to different distances within the same family. Maybe instantiating nearby shades of red should count for more than instantiating nearby shades of blue.

sitive. And again, there will some acontextual constraints on the weighting to avoid double-counting similarities. Finally, we can say: x and y are similar to degree N iff the weighted sum for all property-families F, of the F-similarities/dissimilarities between x and y = N.³⁴

On this model, the fundamental entity is not the individual property, but the structured family of contraries, a quasi-global classification space. In effect, where the earlier suggestions look to *identities* between x's properties and y's properties, i.e. to shared properties, this suggestion looks to the *distances* between their properties, subsuming the case of a shared property as the limiting case of zero distance. Similarity is a matter of closeness within a sea of alternatives, not partial identity. It is still determined by which specific properties things instantiate, but it is a matter of degree even at the level of specific respects of similarity, obviating the need to resort to counting properties.

Even without filling in the details of this sketch—saying how to identify which properties are compounds or negative or unspecific, how to understand quasi-globality, how to add similarities and differences drawn from different dimensions, and so on—the picture is clear enough, I think, that we can profitably return now to essences. If essences really are intrinsic, as I claim, they too have this family-structure. And we can already see how this structure, sketchy though it is, accounts for certain observations about essences. In the next section, I discuss three such observations.

VI

The first is that everything is essentially *determinate*; everything essentially has a full complement of properties. It is just inconceivable that something should be ontologically incomplete. This determinacy has several aspects. One is that nothing can have a determinable property (*being colored, being massive, having a shape*) without also having one of its determinates (*being red, being 10 kg, roundness*). Another is that the determinates of a given determinable are exclusive. When a thing has a determinate color, mass, shape, etc., it is thereby determined whether or not it has any other determinate color, mass or shape: it doesn't. If it is red, it isn't blue or yellow or...; if it is round, it isn't square or triangular or .... A third is that determinables are exhaustive: their determinates exhaust the alternatives for their instances. Although something that is colored, massive, or shap-

---

34 This model covers only intrinsic similarity. A full account of similarity requires that we extend it to take extrinsic similarities into account.

ed usually could have all sorts of different determinate colors, masses, and shapes, it couldn't have *no* color, mass or shape; anything colored, massive, or shaped is essentially so.

The above model accounts for these three aspects of the essential determinacy of things straightforwardly. We need only identify the determinable properties with the properties that correspond to the families (to have a determinable property is just to instantiate one of the family-members) and the determinate properties with the family-members themselves. Then it is automatic that something instantiates a determinable iff it instantiates one of its determinates—the first aspect of determinacy. The fact that the family-members are contraries guarantees that determinates of the same determinable are exclusive. And the fact that the families are (quasi-)global guarantees that they are exhaustive. Moreover, it is not clear how to accommodate the essential determinacy of everything without thinking of determinables and their determinates along these lines, as constituting quasi-global classificational spaces. Identifying determinables with disjunctions or sums of determinate properties might account for the first aspect of determinacy, but not the others. The disjuncts of a disjunctive property are not in general exclusive or exhaustive: a thing might be blue or 10 kg, or both, or neither. Likewise for the parts of a complex property: perhaps *being a man* and *being unmarried* are the parts of the complex property of bachelorhood, but clearly some people—bachelors—are both male and unmarried, and other people—wives—are neither.[35]

This dispels some of the fog surrounding whether there could be protean things that instantiate all their properties accidentally. In one sense of 'protean', there couldn't be. Since the determinables are global or near enough, nothing could fail to instantiate every determinable. Everything is essentially colored, massive, shaped, and so on. However, there is another sense of 'protean' in which there might be. Nothing in this model precludes the possibility of things

---

[35] Are there other aspects of determinacy than these? One candidate is the fact that anything red must have a determinate shade of red, anything 3 meters in length to the nearest meter must be some determinate length, etc. Perhaps this is indeed another aspect of determinacy, but perhaps it is already covered. Perhaps it just reflects the fact that some determinables come in more and less fine-grained versions. There is the fine-grained color determinable that classifies things according to their specific shades and the coarse-grained color determinable that classifies things according to whether they are red, or blue, or yellow, or... There are various length determinables that classify things with different degrees of precision—to the nearest millimeter, to the nearest meter, and so on. (There are some interesting and delicate issues here. Macroscopic entities like tables and chairs have determinate dimensions, but they do not have dimensions to the nearest Planck length. See Denby MS.)

that could instantiate any determinate at all from each family, something that could be any shape, or any mass, or any color, in any combination.

A second observation about essences that the family-structure of intrinsicality helps account for is that often a thing doesn't have a particular determinate property essentially, but rather some determinate property or other within a certain *range*. There are all sorts of shapes I could have, but probably I couldn't be perfectly round or a straight line; I could have a greater or smaller mass, but probably I couldn't have zero mass or infinite mass or even a mass of 200 trillion kg. Sometimes things do have particular determinates essentially—it is essential to all pieces of gold that their constituents have atomic number 79, no more, no less—but "range-essences" seem to be more common. Very few colored things couldn't be at least a slightly different shade. Very few massive things have their exact masses essentially. Some variation is usually possible. Quite how much seems to depend on the things involved. Perhaps there could be something so fragile that for every family, there is one particular determinate property in that family that the thing has to instantiate. Its essence ranges as narrowly as possible. At the other extreme, perhaps there could be a protean thing whose essence ranges as widely as possible, that could instantiate any particular determinate property at all, or even any combination of them. Most things lie somewhere between these extremes: I couldn't vary at all in my species, I could vary somewhat in mass, and I could vary a lot in color.

The above model of intrinsic properties can accommodate range-essences straightforwardly in terms of the distance relations that define the spaces of the various property-families. I could only have those shapes or masses that are within a certain distance of those I actually have—*being perfectly round* and *being infinite in mass* are probably too far away. Where a particular determinate is essential, any distance is too far; this is simply the limiting case, a range of one. Moreover, without a distance relation among properties, it is hard to see how to make sense of range-essences. Are they just disjunctive properties that things have essentially? Is it that x has a length between 1.9 m and 2.1 m essentially, say, iff it has the disjunctive property, *being 1.9 m or,..., or 2.1 m* essentially, where there is a disjunct for each determinate length property in the range from 1.9 m to 2.1 m? Not in general. The "disjunction" would often be infinite and so ungraspable, which range-essences clearly are not. Moreover, sharing a range-essence, at least if the range is not too wide, implies similarity, whereas instantiating a disjunctive property generally does not: if x is black and y is white, they share *being either black or white* but they are not similar. Are range-essences just unspecific properties that things have essentially? Is it that x has a length between 1.9 m and 2.1 m essentially iff it has the unspecific property, *being about 2 m long* essentially? I don't think so. Unspecific properties are not independent ways to be—nothing could have an unspecific length or shape or color. Rather, something has an unspecific length *by virtue of* having some specific length; it is not an additional feature of it. To attempt to make sense of a range of specific properties in terms of an unspecific property would be to put the cart before the horse.

This dispels some of the fog surrounding which qualitative properties are eligible to be essential. As I remarked above, most determinate, natural properties, e.g., *being exactly 17.3 kg, being perfectly circular*, seem poor candidates—how could anything really be so fragile? On the other hand, as we have just seen, unspecific or non-natural features of things like *being quite massive* or *being grue* or *being round or square* also seem poor candidates. They are instantiated only in virtue of determinate, natural properties, and it is at that level that we should look for essences. Viewing essences through the lens of intrinsicality and its family-structure resolves the difficulty: what a thing has essentially is not usually some particular determinate natural property or some unspecific, imperfectly natural property, but some natural, determinate property within a certain range. And presumably most determinate natural properties are eligible to be in a range of properties that a thing has essentially.

A third observation is that the essential properties of a thing constitute its *core* or *central* properties. This is a traditional metaphor, but it is opaque. It doesn't seem to mean the thing's most *salient* properties, those that contribute most to similarities. Often accidental features, e.g., its determinate mass, charge, or color, matter more. Sometimes even extrinsic features matter most for similarity. Conversely, in many contexts, some essential properties contribute little or nothing to similarity. It could well be essential to me that I have something close to the genes that I actually have, yet in most contexts that is not a very salient feature of me. Nor does it seem to mean its most *fundamental* properties, those on which its other properties supervene. My features supervene on the intrinsic properties of and interrelations among the fundamental particles that compose me. But it is not essential to me that I be composed of particles having these features. I could survive all sorts of changes in my constituent particles (though not all, of course): countless rearrangements, swaps, slight increases in mass, etc. Conversely, many of the properties that are essential to me, e.g., my humanity and my various functional and organizational properties, are not fundamental. Nor does it seem to mean the most *explanatory* properties.[36] In fact, essential proper-

---

36 *Contra* Copi (1954) and Gorman (2005, p. 2).

ties have a limited explanatory role. Presumably, they do not explain their instances' accidental properties, not fully at least, since what makes a property accidental is that it can vary independently of any essential properties and so cannot be explained by them. Nor do they explain causally, though they might play an auxiliary role in causal explanations. Causation is a contingent relation, involving other things. Causal explanations for why a thing is as it is feature its accidental and extrinsic properties. The only explanatory role that seems to require a thing's essential properties is grounding its other necessary properties. Anyway, why should there be any connection between explanation and essence at all? *Prima facie*, explanation is a matter of *sufficient* conditions for why a thing exists and is the way it is, whereas essences are a matter of *necessary* conditions for its survival. These just seem to be different ideas.[37]

So what *does* it mean to say that the essential properties of a thing constitute its core or central properties? Again, attention to the family-structure of intrinsic properties suggests an answer. Notice that painting a bar of gold would change its color but little else about it; its mass, malleability, etc. would be unaffected. But changing the number of protons in its constituent atoms would have a huge effect; its chemistry would change radically. In fact, doing so would wreak such havoc on the bar's overall intrinsic property-profile that it wouldn't survive; not so, with changing its color. This suggests another sense in which a thing's essential properties might be its core properties: their loss would bring too much intrinsic change in its wake for the thing to survive. But how are we to make sense of change as a matter of degree? It is here that it helps to think of the property-unit as a quasi-global family of contraries under a distance relation rather than the individual property. If a thing loses some determinate property F belonging to one family, it often also changes in which determinates belonging to *other* families it instantiates. And it does so to varying degrees. Perhaps, losing F will utterly transform its mass and charge, only slightly affect its color, and not affect its atomic number at all. Suppose then that for every property-family, we have some measure of how much the loss of F will affect which determinate property of that family the thing instantiates. Perhaps losing F will decrease its mass by 75%, reverse its charge, and alter its color by one shade. And suppose we also have some way to weight the families affected according to how important they are (in the context). Then the weighted sum of all such changes provides a measure of the total change that the thing would suffer if it were to

---

[37] There are, of course, other worries about appealing to explanation: it is a notoriously obscure notion, and may be interest-relative, which would render essences unacceptably subjective.

lose F. Now, a thing can usually survive only so much change. So we can say that F is a *central* or *core* property of x iff the total change in x's intrinsic nature that would result from losing F exceeds x's threshold of survivable change.[38] And it is not clear that this too-much-intrinsic-change-to-survive interpretation is available without appealing to something like the family-structure I have argued is characteristic of intrinsic properties. How much something has changed is a matter of how similar overall it is after the change to how it was before. And, as we have already seen, overall similarity cannot be captured by any (weighted) count of properties. It seems to require a distance relation among them.

This dispels some more of the fog surrounding our talk of essences. We can now see how essences could be rooted in things themselves not just in context-evoked quantifier-restrictions. Although the threshold of survivable change and the weights assigned to the various families might well be contextually relativized, how sensitive various property-families are to the loss of a given property, i.e., how central that property is, is a context-independent feature of the world. Scientific laws relating families—volume, temperature, and pressure; force and acceleration; atomic number and chemistry; etc.—thus contribute to our understanding of essences by capturing the covariance of property-families.

VII

The essential properties of a thing are connected with its identity: its existence is impossible without them. But that's not all. Its essential properties must be features of *it*; properties involving other things—objects near and far, the rest of the world, sets or pluralities to which it belongs—are not eligible to belong to *its* essence. Essential properties are intrinsic. Recognizing this saves the modal analysis of essence from Fine-style objections. Although it does mean that things do not have their haecceities essentially, and, more alarmingly, that sets do not have their members essentially, these are defensible consequences. And classifying essential properties as intrinsic proves illuminating. Intrinsic properties constitute quasi-global families of contraries under a distance relation and this accounts for various observations about essences, e.g., that everything is essentially determinate, and that things often have range-essences. It also enables a more promising interpretation of the sense in which a thing's essential properties are

---

[38] Presumably, we need only consider *intrinsic* families. Losing F might well affect the extrinsic properties of x, but as I argued above, that is ultimately a matter of the intrinsic features of *other* things, and so is irrelevant to the identity and survival of x itself.

its core properties than that they are somehow always more salient or fundamental or explanatory, viz. that their loss would bring too much overall change in its wake for the thing to survive.

References

Bricker, P. (forthcoming). "Truthmaking: With and Without Counterpart Theory". In B. Loewer and J. Schaffer (eds.), *The Blackwell Companion to David Lewis*. Oxford: Blackwell.
Cameron, R. (2010). "The Grounds of Necessity". *Philosophy Compass* 5: pp. 348–358.
Copi, I. (1954). "Essence and Accident". *Journal of Philosophy* 51: pp. 706–719.
Contessa, G. (2010). "Modal Truthmakers and Two Varieties of Actualism". *Synthese* 174: pp. 341–353.
Correia, F. (2007). "(Finean) Essence and (Priorean) Modality". *Dialectica* 61: pp. 63–84.
Della Rocca, M. (1996). "Recent Work on Essentialism, Parts 1 & 2". *Philosophical Books* 37: pp. 1–13, 81–89
Denby, D. A. (2006). "The Distinction between Intrinsic and Extrinsic Properties". *Mind* 115: pp. 1–17.
Denby, D. A. "Parts and Wholes as Alternatives: Another Answer to the Special Composition Question". Unpublished Manuscript.
Dennett, D. (1988). "Quining Qualia". In A. J. Marcel and E. Bisiach (eds.), *Consciousness in Contemporary Science* (pp. 42–77). New York: Oxford University Press.
Dunn, J. M. (1990). "Relevant Predication 2: Intrinsic Properties and Internal Relations". *Philosophical Studies* 60: pp. 177–206.
Fine, K. (1994). "Essence and Modality". *Philosophical Perspectives* 8: pp. 1–16.
Fine, K. (1995a). "The Logic of Essence". *Journal of Philosophical Logic* 24: pp. 241–273.
Fine, K. (1995b). "Senses of Essence". In W. Sinnott-Armstrong, D. Raffman, and N. Asher (eds.), *Modality, Morality, and Belief: Essays in Honour of Ruth Barcan Marcus* (pp. 53–73). Cambridge: Cambridge University Press.
Fine, K. (2002). "The Varieties of Necessity". In T.S. Gendler and J. Hawthorne (eds.), *Conceivability and Possibility* (pp. 253–282). Oxford: Oxford University Press.
Fine, K. (2005). *Modality and Tense: Philosophical Papers*. Oxford: Oxford University Press.
Fine, K. (2007). "Response to Fabrice Correia". *Dialectica* 61: pp. 85–88.
Francescotti, R. (1999). "How to Define Intrinsic Properties". *Nous* 33: pp. 590–609.
Gorman, M. (2005). "The Essential and the Accidental". *Ratio* 18: pp. 276–289.
Lewis, D. K. (1968). "Counterpart Theory and Quantified Modal Logic". *Journal of Philosophy* 65: pp. 113–126.
Lewis, D. K. (1986). *On the Plurality of Worlds*. Oxford: Basil Blackwell.
Marshall, D. (2009). "Can 'Intrinsic' Be Defined Using Only Broadly Logical Notions?" *Philosophy and Phenomenological Research* 78: pp. 646–672.
Quine, W. V. O. (1960). *Word and Object*. Cambridge, MA: MIT Press.
Witmer, D. G, Butchard, W., and Trogdon, K. (2005). "Intrinsicality without Naturalness". *Philosophical and Phenomenological Research* 70: pp. 326–350.
Zalta, E. (2006). "Essence and Modality". *Mind* 115: pp. 659–694.

D. Gene Witmer
A Simple Theory of Intrinsicality

An intrinsic property is one that the bearer has in virtue of the way it is and not in virtue of the way other things are or how they are related to it.

This simple formula is normally adequate to convey the notion intended by classifying a property as "intrinsic." In this paper I offer a theory of intrinsicality meant to match the simplicity of this initial characterization. More precisely, the theory will make its link to the above formula evident; if correct, it explains why that formula is normally adequate to convey the notion in question. It will also explain why other characterizations frequently used for the same purpose are suited for doing so, though the theory's connection to the above formula will be the most obvious.

The paper is divided into two parts. In the first, I focus on what we may think of as standard "orienting characterizations" that we use to fix ideas—characterizations like the one with which I opened the paper. Such characterizations may seem theory enough; if they succeed in directing us to the notion in question, what more do we want? Here, I explain what more a theory ought to tell us and examine the several characterizations in some detail. That examination provides constraints and motivations that guide the positive proposal here defended.

The second part introduces and develops that proposal. According to what I dub "the Simple Theory," our understanding of intrinsicality depends on our prior understanding of *grounding*, where grounding is a metaphysical relation whereby something less fundamental is linked to something more fundamental on which it depends.[1] More precisely, the proposal makes use of the claim that an individual has one property in virtue of having another. In my view, this notion is understood sufficiently for use in theory building, though I refer the reader to other work for a defense of this claim (Witmer et al. 2005; Rosen 2010).

The Simple Theory is not unlike the theory of intrinsicality I offered in Witmer et al. (2005); it differs in a number of substantial ways, however, discussion of which I reserve to a note.[2] It is also very similar to a brief proposal made by Gi-

---

[1] For a recent anthology of papers focused on this notion, see Correia and Schnieder (2012).
[2] There are two especially significant differences to which I draw attention.

First, the "Strong Independence Definition" given in 2005 made the local notion of intrinsicality more basic than the global notion; that is, it *first* defined what it is for an individual to have a property in an intrinsic fashion on a particular occasion and *then* defined what it is for a property itself to be intrinsic. The Simple Theory takes the reverse route; see. §2.5.

deon Rosen (2010), though the main ideas of this paper were developed independently.[3]

1 Orienting Characterizations

1.1 Getting a fix on the notion

How is it that we get a handle on the concept of an intrinsic property in the first place? I began with a simple formulation: an intrinsic property is one that the bearer has in virtue of the way it is and not in virtue of the way other things are or how they are related to it. This may be described as an "orienting characterization," as it is the sort of thing that is said by way of orienting us so as to fix on what is presumably a single notion of intrinsicality.

Of course, there are many such characterizations. Here are several that I take to be representative.

(A) "Intuitively, a property is *intrinsic* just in case a thing's having it (at a time) depends only on what that thing is like (at that time), and not on what any wholly distinct contingent object (or wholly distinct time) is like." (Vallentyne 1997, p. 209)

Second, the Simple Theory, unlike the 2005 theory, makes no use of the notion of independence of accompaniment. I take this as a virtue of the theory for two reasons. First, there may be ways in which the requirement is too strong; I note some potential problems in §2.3. Second, the theory of intrinsicality may play an important role in explaining certain modal facts, and if so, it should not presuppose them. I have in mind the possibility of explaining what may be called "Hume's Dictum," the thesis, as Jessica Wilson puts it, that 'there are no metaphysically necessary connections between distinct, *intrinsically typed*, entities" (emphasis added) (Wilson 2010, p. 595). I expect that some refinement of this is correct and important, and a correct theory of intrinsicality should help explain this fact. If independence of accompaniment were built into the definition of intrinsicality, such an explanation would be likely doomed to circularity. The Simple Theory, I believe, offers some promise of a noncircular explanation.

3 Rosen's proposal is only briefly given as an illustration of the potential utility of grounding as a theoretical tool. (Needless to say, I am in agreement with him on this.) Here is Rosen's proposal:

F is an intrinsic property iff, as a matter of necessity, for all x:

If x is F in virtue of $\phi(y)$—where $\phi(y)$ is a fact containing y as a constituent—then y is a part of x; and

If x is not-F in virtue of $\phi(y)$, then y is part of x.

There are a number of significant differences between Rosen's proposal and the Simple Theory here developed, but the two theories are obviously very close in spirit.

(B) "*You* know what an intrinsic property is: it's a property that a thing has (or lacks) regardless of what may be going on outside of itself. To be intrinsic is to possess the second-order feature of stability-under-variation-in-the-outside-world." (Yablo 1999, p. 33)

(C) "Metaphysically, an intrinsic property of an object is a property that the object has by virtue of itself, depending on no other thing." (Dunn 1990, p. 178)

(D) "A thing has its intrinsic properties in virtue of the way that thing itself, and nothing else, is." (Lewis 1983, p. 197)[4]

(E) "An intrinsic property is a property that is internal in the sense that whether an object has it depends entirely upon what the object is like in itself." (Francescotti 1999, p. 590)

(F) "A sentence or statement or proposition that ascribes intrinsic properties to something is entirely about that thing; whereas an ascription of extrinsic properties to something is not entirely about that thing." (Lewis 1983, p. 197)

(G) "If something has an intrinsic property, then so does any perfect duplicate of that thing; whereas duplicates situated in different surroundings will differ in their extrinsic properties." (Lewis 1983, p. 197)

With all of these characterizations of intrinsicality on hand, just what do we need a theory for?

1.2 The point of a theory of intrinsicality

For one, it would be best to have a single, canonical characterization. It is not obvious that all of these are equivalent, to say the least. Nor is it clear that all of them are even *true*. All that is clear is that such characterizations apparently succeed in directing our attention to a presumably single notion of intrinsicality.

---

[4] Quotations (D), (F) and (G) are all taken from the very same paragraph in David Lewis, "Extrinsic Properties" (1983). It has been suggested (Weatherson and Marshall 2013) that the three statements from that single paragraph indicate three distinct notions. This seems unlikely given their occurrence in the very same paragraph. In any case, this ambiguity thesis is unnecessary; as I hope to show here, the Simple Theory can in fact make sense of all of the several different characterizations as directing our attention to a single notion.

Second, we may want a theory that reflects our understanding of the distinction, so that it amounts to a conceptual analysis. If so, then, while such an analysis will presumably link up in important ways to the various characterizations, it will also privilege some characterization as reflecting how it is we grasp the distinction between intrinsic and extrinsic properties, a characterization that is fit to play a normative role that we would intuitively certify as correct.

Third, we may want a theory that spells out the conditions under which a property is intrinsic where those conditions are specified using some restricted, somehow privileged vocabulary. Here is how Dan Marshall describes this goal, focusing on "broadly logical notions":

> It would be good if we could define 'intrinsic' using notions that are better understood, and less closely related to the notion of an intrinsic property, than notions like 'a thing having a property wholly in virtue of how it is'. This could be achieved if we could define 'intrinsic' using only broadly logical notions, where broadly logical notions are those notions that can be expressed using the following vocabulary: the logical vocabulary of first order predicate logic; the predicates 'is a possible world', 'is a set', 'exists', '=', '∈', 'is a proper part of', 'instantiates' and 'is a property'; and the modal operators 'possibly', 'necessarily' and 'at'. (Marshall 2009, pp. 647–648)

The idea here is that the restricted vocabulary is, at least in contrast to that used in the orienting characterizations, better understood. Perhaps so, though I should hasten to caution that matters of philosophical fashion likely have a pernicious influence on what gets counted as clearly understood and what does not. Be that as it may, it is not obvious that the best response to such a situation is to *avoid* using the less well understood vocabulary as opposed to taking on the task of *better* understanding the vocabulary that seems central to our grasp of the target notion in the first place. Insisting on keeping to familiar ground is unhappily reminiscent of the proverbial fellow who looks for his lost keys near the street lamp, even though he felt them drop from his hands when he was in deep shadow, explaining his choice by pointing out that, after all, the light is better there.

While Marshall aptly describes one goal one might have in developing a theory of intrinsicality, I should note that he does not think that it can be accomplished; the quotation is taken from his paper (2009) arguing that it is *not* possible to define "intrinsic" in broadly logical terms. My comments may be taken as aiming to show that this result need not be seen as an unhappy one.

Of these three possible motivations for a theory of intrinsicality, I share just the first two. The primary goal is to provide an account of the concept; more precisely, the goal is an account that makes explicit the conditions we intuitively take as normative for identifying a property as intrinsic or not. The orienting characterizations may manage to direct our attention to the concept, and hence to the conditions we take as normative in this way, but they don't succeed in making those conditions explicit in a way that matches our intuitive judgments.

As a preliminary to developing a positive theory, we should examine these characterizations more carefully. In doing so, we will both uncover key intuitive constraints on the notion of intrinsicality and see just how the explicit statements in (A)–(F) are lacking.

1.3 An examination

Let us start with (A) and (B) together. Both focus on the idea that if something has an intrinsic property, its having that property is independent of what other things—those that are "outside" of it or are wholly distinct from it—are like.[5] On one very straightforward reading of this independence idea—emphasized by Stephen Yablo in (B) with the "stability under variation" phrase—for a property F to be intrinsic is just for it to be possible for something to have F and be in any otherwise possible environment. As is well-known, this account implies that *no* property is intrinsic, since one of those otherwise possible environments is, of course, one in which individuals have the property of being unaccompanied by anything with F. And it is not possible for there to be something with F in *that* environment.

This unhappy result can be avoided if we add one further constraint, namely, that the otherwise possible environments be characterized solely by relations between individuals in that environment and their intrinsic properties. But that, of course, leans on an understanding of "intrinsic" to characterize the relevant independence.

Such circularity can be avoided, however, if we understand the talk of dependence in (A) in a more robust fashion. Consider the property of being spherical—an apparently intrinsic property. Does being spherical depend on what the surrounding environment is like? The case for saying it does is that a certain situation is not possible, namely, one in which something is a sphere in an environment in which other things have the property of being unaccompanied by anything spherical.

---

5 There is an excellent question about which things, exactly, are to be counted as appropriately "outside" the individual that bears the property in question, but I suppress it for now and address it when developing the positive proposal; see §2.4.

There is a straightforward sense of "depends" in which the impossibility of that situation indeed shows that being spherical depends on what the surrounding environment is like. We might think of this as a purely functional (as in *mathematical*) notion of dependence. But there is a robust sense of "depends" such that the impossibility of the above situation does nothing to show that being spherical depends on the surrounding environment. Indeed, a very natural thing to say is that the situation is impossible because the property of being unaccompanied by anything spherical depends on the property of being spherical and *not* vice versa.

The operative notion of dependence is plainly related to grounding: what grounds the instantiation of the property of being unaccompanied by anything spherical is a fact about the property of being spherical. Reading (A) as relying only on the functional, purely modal notion of dependence is plainly to misconstrue it, especially as reading it that way raises the obvious problem of needing to limit the possible environments to those characterized intrinsically.

As noted above, I take it that we have a sufficient grip on the notion of grounding that it is acceptable to use in a theory of intrinsicality. If that assumption is false, then the prospects for a theory of intrinsicality seem rather dim, as the orienting characterizations seem to appeal to grounding as a matter of course, whether they appeal to talk of "dependence," one property's being had "by virtue of" another, or some other locution. In light of this it seems an inevitable part of any good theory of the concept.

Such appeal to grounding certainly shows up in (C), where we are told that an intrinsic property is one the object has "by virtue of itself." As I read this, "by virtue of itself" is equivalent to saying that the property is had "by virtue of *how* it is*." There is another reading available, perhaps, namely, "by virtue of *what* it is," and the distinction is quite significant. Talk of "what it is" is often talk of the essence of a thing, that which (as we say) makes it what it is. So if we say that something has a property in virtue of what it is, then that property is, presumably, part of the essence of that thing. Intrinsic properties are not the same as essential properties, of course, though the link just noted here may explain the occasional conflation.

So let us return to the main thread: an intrinsic property is one the bearer has by virtue of *how* it is. This, by itself, is clearly not sufficient for being intrinsic. Suppose that Amy is a sister—a clear-cut case of an extrinsic property. Does she have this property by virtue of how she is? Yes. She has that property in virtue of being both female and a sibling. In saying she has *those* properties (being female and being a sibling) we are, of course, describing *how she is*. It won't help to stress that we're interested in how she *herself* is; it's not as if we made an error in attributing those properties to *her*, as if we should have attributed them to some other individual.

The point should make it plain that the second part of (C) is no redundant add-on. Recall the formulation: an intrinsic property is a property "that the object has by virtue of itself, *depending on no other thing.*" The "depending on no other thing" is crucial. Intuitively, that rules out the case of sisterhood from being intrinsic. Her being a sister depends on how she is, yes—since it depends on her being a sibling. But that, in turn, depends on how some other things are, namely, her parents and whether they have had another child.

As with (A), the "depending on no other thing" clause may be read in either a purely modal fashion or in a way that implies a grounding claim. If we take it as the former, we will run into the same problem as before—every property F will depend on there not being an individual with the property of being unaccompanied by something with F. But if we take it the latter way, the resulting reading of (C) is virtually the same as (D): a thing has its intrinsic properties in virtue of the way it is, and it does not have its intrinsic properties in virtue of the way any other thing is. This is also the formulation with which I opened the paper, and it is, I think, the characterization that comes closest to being an adequate theory of intrinsicality.

Moving on to (E), we see a somewhat different locution appear: whether an object has an intrinsic property "depends entirely upon what the object is like *in itself.*" "In itself" is dangerously close to "intrinsically." But there may be a hint of another reading here: what something is like in itself is, we might say, what it is like even if all the other things relating to it were stripped away. "In itself" might be, in other words, akin to "on its own." On this reading, the idea might be that if F is intrinsic, then when something has F, it could have it even if it were entirely on its own in the world. This, of course, is the idea behind the proposal (usually attributed to Kim 1983) that an intrinsic property is one that is compatible with *loneliness*—that is, the property of being the only contingent thing that exists—and the subsequent suggestion (Langton and Lewis 1998) that an intrinsic property must be *independent of accompaniment* in the sense that all four of the following cases are possible: something lonely has the property; something lonely lacks it; something accompanied has it; and something accompanied lacks it.

This strategy is described by Brian Weatherson and Dan Marshall (2013) as a "combinatorial" approach. It may be seen as a successor to the idea that intrinsic properties are had independently of *how* other things are, substituting for it instead the idea that they are had independently of *whether* other things are. That very contrast, though, should make us pause. Issues about the existence conditions of individuals may run interference with issues about the intrinsicality of properties. Suppose, for instance, that no individual is capable of existing unaccompanied. If being intrinsic requires being independent of accompaniment, then in that case no property is intrinsic. But this hardly seems the right result, especially if the reason no individuals can exist unaccompanied has nothing to do with the nature of any of the properties thereby ruled out as not intrinsic.

With the last two characterizations, two further elements are introduced. With (F), the key notion is that of *aboutness*. A sentence (or proposition) that ascribes an intrinsic property to something "is entirely about that thing," in contrast to those ascribing extrinsic properties. Notably, this characterization doesn't even hint at a modal formulation in terms of independence. What it suggests, rather, is a focus on explanation, or more precisely, an explanation in terms of *truth-making:* for it is natural to say that what a sentence is *about* are those (non-representational) things involved in *making* the sentence true or false.

The apparent divergence of (F) from the other characterizations is, then, somewhat superficial. If aboutness is to be understood in terms of truth-making, we have again an appeal to grounding, since truth-making is a *species* of grounding: a truth-maker for a sentence or proposition is something that grounds the fact that the sentence or proposition is true. For this reason, I see (F) as not indicating any substantive independent constraint on intrinsicality. Its aptness as a way of orienting us to the notion is plausibly a side effect, so to speak, of the more important facts about what properties are grounded by what other properties.

Finally, in (G) another new notion is introduced: that of a perfect duplicate. For any x and y, if x and y are perfect duplicates, then any intrinsic property had by x is also had by y, and vice versa. This is only true, however, if duplication is understood as limited to the replication of intrinsic properties. A perfect duplicate of a dollar bill in this sense need not share all of its properties, since it may be, of course, a counterfeit, and hence lack an important extrinsic property. How, then, does (G) help orient us to the notion of intrinsicality? Presumably it does so by pointing to one important way in which we want to use the notion, namely, by using it to *determine* an interesting notion of a duplicate. This doesn't rule out much by way of candidate intrinsic properties, perhaps, but it does do this much: properties that are incapable of being multiply instantiated are not intrinsic.

There are several examples of such properties that are also plainly to be counted as extrinsic. Consider being the happiest person in the world, being the only cat ever to receive a tail transplant, and the like. There is, however, one sort of property incapable of multiple instantiation that seems not appropriately classified as extrinsic. I have in mind such properties as being William Shakespeare, or being Rudolf Carnap—in general, properties that may be expressed with "being _____ ," where the blank is filled in with the proper name of some individual. Call any such property an *identity property*.[6] Identity properties are a species of *impure* properties, that is, those the expression of which requires the use of proper names. While identity properties cannot be multiply instantiated, this is not generally true of impure properties. The property of being a student of Rudolf Carnap is, for example, instantiated by many lucky individuals.

So far as (G) guides our understanding of intrinsicality, then, identity properties are excluded from being intrinsic. But this may seem puzzling. While the other properties mentioned (such as being the only cat ever to receive a tail transplant) are, in keeping with (G), intuitively classified as extrinsic, it is hardly intuitive to say that being William Shakespeare is an *extrinsic* property. Surely, one may think, Shakespeare's having of that property is a function of just how he is, alone, without anything else being relevant.

One reaction to this puzzle is to propose that there is more than one notion of intrinsicality at work in the characterizations (A) through (G). Brian Weatherson and Dan Marshall pursue this idea, in fact suggesting that there are three different notions at work (2013). That is one option, but it is best to avoid positing such ambiguities if possible.

We can avoid doing so if we can make it plausible that the notions of intrinsicality and extrinsicality range over only a limited domain of properties, so that some properties, those outside the domain, are properly classified as neither intrinsic nor extrinsic. If there is independent motivation to think that identity properties are among those not to be classified as either, then we can exclude identity properties and endorse (G) without having to say that they are extrinsic. The Simple Theory will in fact do this, as we'll see in §2.3.

2 The Simple Theory

2.1 The main idea

As I've indicated, I think the characterization in (D) is the most useful for developing a clear theory of intrinsicality. There are two conditions set out in that

---

[6] These might also be called *haecceities* or *haecceitistic* properties, but I am sticking with the easier label. Note that there is no commitment here to the idea that a property is an identity property whenever it is necessarily attached to just a single individual. More precisely, I allow that P may be a property such that there is a particular individual x where, necessarily, something has P if and only if that thing is identical with x, yet P is not itself an identity property.

characterization: a positive one (an intrinsic property is had in virtue of the way the bearer is) and a negative one (an intrinsic property is *not* had in virtue of the way any other things are). Formalizing slightly, we have:

(1) For any property F, F is intrinsic if and only if
necessarily, for any x, if x has F, then (i) x has F in virtue of how x is and (ii) for any y ≠ x, it is not the case that x has F in virtue of how y is.

In reviewing the characterizations earlier we saw that the positive condition is hardly sufficient for being intrinsic. If Amy is a sister, she has that property in virtue of how she is, but being a sister is clearly not an intrinsic property. We need the negative condition to rule that property out. She does have the property of being a sister in virtue of how something else is; for example, her having that property is grounded (in part) by, say, her mother's having given birth to Basil, her brother.

The main idea of the Simple Theory is that by leaning on this negative condition, we can do nearly all the work we need to do to specify just when a property is intrinsic. The positive condition plays an important role, but that role is less straightforward.

To develop the theory, I will focus on four issues, adjusting the account at each stage. First, there is an immediate problem with (1) due to those extrinsic properties whose instantiation depends on the *absence* of certain individuals. The solution to this invokes what I call a "twofold approach," one that builds into the analysis of "F is intrinsic" requirements on both F and the property corresponding to its negation, not-F.[7]

Second, there are puzzles about the positive condition in light of properties that cannot be said to be instantiated in virtue of how their bearers are, yet which are not instantiated in virtue of how other things are, either. I explain how to handle such cases and what to make of the prominence of the usual positive characterization.

Third, I address the usually neglected question of what, exactly, should be counted as the "other things" that must not play a grounding role for the possession of intrinsic properties. It is clear that an intrinsic property may be had in virtue of some feature of an individual not strictly identical with the bearer; the usual strategy is to allow that the properties of the bearer's *parts* may be rel-

---

[7] More precisely, the negation should be understood as follows. I take property names to be canonically formed from predicate expressions. So, "the property of being F" corresponds to the predicate expression "is F." The negation of "x is F" is what corresponds to "it is not the case that x is F." I will make use of less careful expressions, such as using plain "F" for the property of being F; in that case, "not-F" should be understood in an analogous fashion.

evant, but this is, in my view, insufficiently general. The proposed account allows us to make sense of a wider variety of cases.

Finally, there is a well-recognized distinction between local and global notions of intrinsicality, and a good test of a theory is to ask how it explains and relates the two notions. I defend the Simple Theory by showing how on that theory the global notion may be taken as more fundamental, the local notion being defined in terms of the global notion.

Before we begin, I want to make one stipulation and confess to one presumption. First, in using the locution "in virtue of," I mean the same thing that is sometimes expressed as "partly in virtue of." I take this to be the customary meaning of "in virtue of," in contrast to "solely in virtue of" or "entirely in virtue of." On this way of talking, Amy is a sister in virtue of being female, though she is also a sister in virtue of being a sibling. The grounding conditions need not be sufficient for the conditions grounded.[8]

Second, I presume an abundant view of properties. For any meaningful (one-place) predicate, the corresponding property name is assumed to correspond to a property unless we have special reason to think it does not—e.g., in the case of predicates for which the assumption leads to paradox. Such a presumption is common in discussions of intrinsicality, and one motivation for this is plain. Those less liberal about properties are apt to appeal to intrinsicality as a way of trimming the class of alleged properties to the class of genuine ones, but if we're trying to explain intrinsicality in the first place, we can hardly suppose such trimming already to have been done.

For most of the discussion I will limit my attention to properties properly so-called, leaving aside many-place relations. This is just for ease of exposition. When I sum up the theory (§2.6), I will briefly go over how multiple-place relations may be accommodated and classified as intrinsic or not.

---

[8] It is worth noting here that the crucial negative condition *needs* to be read in this way. A property can fail to be intrinsic even if it is not instantiated *entirely* in virtue of things other than the bearer. We might reserve the term "purely extrinsic" to mean those properties that are instantiated solely in virtue of how things outside the bearer are. ("Cambridge changes" might be defined in terms of the gain or loss of a purely extrinsic property in this sense.) Plain "extrinsic" seems mostly to be used to include both those and what we might call "partly extrinsic" properties.

2.2 Absences and a two-fold approach

The property of being a lonely red thing is plainly not an intrinsic property. But (1) classifies it as such.

Consider an arbitrary instantiation of being a lonely red thing. This will be an individual—call her Rhoda—who is both red and the only contingent thing in existence. Now, we can ask two questions about Rhoda and her being a lonely red thing. First, the positive condition: does Rhoda have this property in virtue of how she is? The answer seems clearly *Yes*. She is a lonely red thing at least partly in virtue of being the exact shade of red she is. Second, the negative condition: is there any individual other than Rhoda such that Rhoda is a lonely red thing in virtue of some way that other individual is? Clearly not: she is the only individual, after all.[9] So, we've shown that for any arbitrary instantiation of this property, the two conditions are met, and being a lonely red thing turns out to be intrinsic according to (1).

There is a straightforward fix: for any property to be intrinsic it must be the case that its negation is also intrinsic. This is what I am calling a "twofold approach": the analysis of "F is intrinsic" includes requirements on both F and its negation not-F. In other words, if a property is intrinsic, that tells us something both about cases in which something instantiates it *and* about cases when something fails to instantiate it, viz. has its negation.

Such an approach is in keeping with the usual orienting characterizations, which occasionally stress that intrinsic properties are ones had *or lacked* in virtue of how the thing itself is; see (B) and (E) for examples. And in general it is uncontroversial that the set of intrinsic properties is closed under negation.[10] Adjusting (1) to a twofold approach, we get (2):

(2) For any property F, F is intrinsic if and only if

(a) necessarily, for any x, if x has F, then (i) x has F in virtue of how x is and (ii) for any y ≠ x, it is not the case that x has F in virtue of how y is; and

(b) necessarily, for any x, if x has not-F, then (i) x has not-F in virtue of how x is and (ii) for any y ≠ x, it is not the case that x has not-F in virtue of how y is.

---

9 Well, she is the only contingent individual aside from her own parts; noncontingent individuals and the bearer's own parts don't seem to count here. More on this in §2.3 and §2.4.
10 For example, in his proposed account of intrinsicality, Brian Weatherson (2001) makes this claim, along with other closure principles, key to the positive account.

On this formulation, the property of being a lonely red thing turns out to be extrinsic. The negation of being a lonely red thing is the property of being either not-lonely or not-red. There is a possible case in which something has that property in virtue of being not-lonely; and in that case there is some individual other than the bearer such that the bearer is not-lonely in virtue of that other thing's being a certain way, namely, that other thing's accompanying the bearer.

The idea that the status of a property as intrinsic is to be determined in part by considering its negation is reflected in those combinatorial approaches that require an intrinsic property to be independent of accompaniment, since, of course, they impose conditions regarding possible instances of the property's negation. The Simple Theory does *not* require that intrinsic properties be independent of accompaniment, though its twofold character is, I think, a different response to the same felt need.

2.3 Making sense of the positive condition

What I'm calling "the positive condition" is the requirement that the individual in question have the property in virtue of how that individual is. I stressed earlier that the negative condition—that the individual not have the property in virtue of how other things are—is needed because the positive condition is not sufficient. But the positive condition is worse than that; at least, on one reading, it makes the theory too strong, ruling out properties that ought to be allowed as intrinsic.

Consider the condition (a)(i) of (2): x has F in virtue of how x is. A natural way to read this is as saying:

There is some G such that x has G and x has F in virtue of having G.

Call this the "straightforward reading" of the positive condition. On the straightforward reading, no property that is fundamental can count as intrinsic, where a fundamental property is one such that its instantiation is never grounded in anything more basic. It is arguably a general truth that no property is instantiated in virtue of itself, since grounding carries explanatory import, and it is no explanation to say that an individual has F because it has F.

So if F is fundamental, then on the straightforward reading, F cannot satisfy the positive condition and cannot count as intrinsic. This is surely the wrong result. Nonetheless, it is hard to deny that an intrinsic property is one had by virtue of how the bearer itself is. There is something at least appropriate for using that statement in characterizing intrinsicality. What might this amount to if the straightforward reading is abandoned?

I suggest that the aptness of the phrase derives from the contrasts to which it points. More precisely, I suggest that when we say

An intrinsic property is one had by virtue of how the bearer is,

we can be best understood as saying

An intrinsic property is one such that whether or not something has it is determined by facts about *how* the thing is, in contrast to *other* kinds of facts about the thing.

Call this the "contrastive reading." Its significance depends on what those other kinds of facts might be; so what are they? There are two contrasts that seem salient. First, consider a statement about an individual that tells us *which thing* or *who* that individual is as opposed to *how* it is. If I say that a particular individual is William Shakespeare, I am saying who it is, but it hardly seems right to say that I am describing *how* he is. Importantly, I am not describing how anyone else is, either; I am not describing *how* anything is at all. Plausibly, then, in attributing an identity property to an individual, one does not describe how that individual is.

The other contrast to which the positive characterization may draw our attention is that between saying how something is and saying *what* it is, or perhaps what *kind* of thing it is. If I aim to say what an individual is by describing it as, say, a cat, I am likely trying to describe in part the essence of that individual—to say something about what it is to be that thing. This second contrast does not (as the first does) indicate any special class of properties as irrelevant to one of the two projects (saying how something is vs. saying what it is). After all, a single property might be mentioned both in saying *how* an individual is and in saying *what* it is, even while those two claims are distinct. This second contrast, then, does not require any restriction of the properties to be considered as candidates for being intrinsic.

Let us return to the first contrast and the division of properties it suggests. It will be convenient to have some labels. While it would be a gross category mistake to say that a property is literally descriptive in the ordinary sense of the term, I will stipulate a technical sense as follows:

A property F is *descriptive* if and only if necessarily, a true ascription of F to an individual is a description of how that individual is.

A property is *nondescriptive* if and only if it is not descriptive.[11]

---

[11] What if a property is such that its expression makes ineliminable use of expressions of both

If we consider again some of the orienting characterizations, we have reason to think that the intrinsic/extrinsic distinction is supposed to be drawn among the descriptive properties, while nondescriptive properties are set aside as not being candidates for either label. Consider our first one again:

(A) Intuitively, a property is intrinsic just in case a thing's having it (at a time) depends only on what that thing is like (at that time), and not on what any wholly distinct contingent object (or wholly distinct time) is like.

Note the use of "what that thing is like." Talk of *what an object is like* is not infrequently used to exclude from consideration certain properties as irrelevant. If I tell you that the object behind Door #3 is identical with itself, you may complain that I am not telling you anything about what it is like, anything about *how it is*. Since talk of *what an object is like* indicates that the properties at issue are descriptive, it is plausible that the intrinsic/extrinsic distinction is drawn among descriptive properties only, setting aside as irrelevant nondescriptive properties.

Happily, this result makes sense of the puzzle we noted in considering the last of the orienting characterizations invoking duplicates. There, we noted that identity properties such as being William Shakespeare cannot be shared among duplicates simply because they cannot be multiply instantiated, yet they are not intuitively extrinsic. The answer to the puzzle is that they are nondescriptive properties and for that reason neither intrinsic nor extrinsic.

Supposing, then, that the contrastive reading of the positive condition is correct and that the key contrast is between descriptive and nondescriptive properties, we can *drop* the first "positive condition" in our analysis in favor of restricting the initial quantification to descriptive properties. Given this restriction, we should add an explicit analysis of extrinsicality to abide by the same restriction. Finally, we can introduce the straightforward reading of "in virtue of how it is" for the negative condition, since the negative condition (unlike the positive condition) *can* be met by both fundamental and non-fundamental properties. The result is (3) and (4):

(3) For any descriptive property F, F is intrinsic if and only if

---

descriptive and nondescriptive properties? In that case, we might call it nondescriptive without fear of missing out on some descriptive properties, since the descriptive elements of such can stand on their own.

(a) necessarily, for any x, if x has F, then for any y ≠ x and property G, it is not the case that x has F in virtue of y's having G; and

(b) necessarily, for any x, if x has not-F, then for any y ≠ x and property G, it is not the case that x has not-F in virtue of y's having G.

(4) For any descriptive property F, F is extrinsic if and only if F is not intrinsic.

A good question here is whether there are any nondescriptive properties other than the identity properties that should be excluded from consideration. Above, I used the example of being self-identical; and indeed it seems that if I say that an object is self-identical, I am not describing how it is. The fact that it's true to say that Shakespeare, for example, is self-identical is due entirely to facts *about the nature of identity generally* and not at all about *how Shakespeare is*. Nor is it really about *how* identity *itself* (the abstract relation) is. Or so it seems to me. What is important, however, is not so much the status of that property in particular but how it interacts with judgements about intrinsicality. Insofar as one thinks that the truth of "Shakespeare is self-identical" does *not* reflect on how he is, one will be inclined, I suggest, to think that being self-identical is neither intrinsic nor extrinsic. If one thinks that being self-identical is obviously intrinsic, one likely thinks of it as descriptive as well.

What other properties might be likewise irrelevant to how their bearers are? Consider the property of being such that 2+2=4. I submit that whether we take this to be descriptive turns on what we think about mathematical talk generally. If we adopt a frank mathematical realism according to which there are objects such as 2 and 4, then the fact that I am such that 2+2=4 is indeed grounded in how something else is—namely, in how those mathematical objects are. If, on the other hand, we reject such realism and take the truth of the mathematical statement to be a very different sort of beast, where, say, there are no entities that make such statements true, then we are likely to take this as a *non*descriptive property.

The example of being such that 2+2=4 fits into a general category of property of special interest. Say that a property F is *indiscriminately necessary* if and only if necessarily, for any individual x, x has F. It is tempting to think that our notion of intrinsicality is designed for properties that are only contingently instantiated and hence that indiscriminately necessary properties may be set aside just as nondescriptive ones are on the current proposal. After all, it is a common thought that, when F is indiscriminately necessary, the claim that a particular individual has F is (apart from its implication that the individual exists) empty of content. In earlier work I wanted to set aside indiscriminately necessary properties as not relevant, but I now think that I was misdiagnosing the felt impulse (see Witmer et al. 2005, pp. 347–349). What should be set aside as such are nondescriptive properties, not indiscriminately necessary properties. How many of the latter are ultimately to be set aside as nondescriptive will depend on just how one understands the nature of those properties, and I take no stand on such in this paper.

2.4 The "other things"

The main idea of the Simple Theory is to lean on the negative condition: an intrinsic property is one that is not had in virtue of properties of things other than the bearer. Thus far, I have been treating this distinction—between the bearer and the other things—as nothing more or less than a lack of identity. But this was a temporary measure, as it is clear that the "other things" need to be understood in a less exhaustive fashion. There are examples in which an individual has an intrinsic property in virtue of how some distinct individual is but where that distinct individual is closely related to the bearer of the property in a way that makes this distinctness benign.

Consider a simple example. Suppose that being red is an intrinsic property and a particular shirt is red; now take a patch of that shirt that is also red. Plausibly, the shirt itself is red in virtue of that patch's being red. The patch is not identical with the shirt, of course, so if the "other things" that are not to play a grounding role in the intrinsic property's instantiation include a thing's parts, being red will turn out not to be intrinsic after all. And that is the wrong result.

This is a well-recognized point, and it is standard in theories of intrinsicality to limit the "other things" to those that are not only distinct from the bearer but also *wholly* distinct in the sense of having no parts in common with the bearer (e.g., Francescotti 1999; Trogdon 2009; Weatherson and Marshall 2013). While this is a move in the right direction, it does not go far enough. There is also a sense in which it goes too far. I take the latter point first.

Suppose we restrict the negative condition so that what is required for intrinsicality is just that property (and its negation) never be grounded in any properties of an individual wholly distinct from the bearer of the property. The resulting conditions are too weak. Consider an ordinary physical object O with a proper part O_p. Given the definition of "wholly distinct," O and O_p are not wholly distinct. Now suppose O_p has some property F in virtue of O's having some property G. For example, O_p could have the property of being part of a hammer-shaped object, where O is a hammer. Is the property of being part of a hammer-shaped object intrinsic? I take it intuition is clear here in denying it that status. After all, in this case the possession of F depends on how things are, as we might put, "outside" of its bearer.

It is easy to fix this problem. The "other individuals" should not include parts of the bearer, but they *should* include objects *of which the bearer is a part*. The quantification in the negative conditions, then, might be adjusted to

for any y such that y ≠ x and y is not a part of x.

So far, so good. But the appeal to *parts* is insufficiently general. There may be ways in which one individual is "made up of" some other individuals without those being *parts* of the former—perhaps because the individuals in question aren't located in space and time, or aren't so located in any way that makes the "parts" talk straightforward. Here's an example.[12]

Suppose the philosophy majors at a particular institution form a student organization deemed the "Philosophy Club," and at a certain point in its history, nearly every member of the Philosophy Club is a student inclined to describe herself as "pre-law," as nearly every member hopes to go to law school. At that time, then, the Philosophy Club has the property of being dominated by would-be law students. Let Basil be a would-be law student who is a member of the Philosophy Club. It seems clearly that the Club's possession of the property of being dominated by would-be law students is grounded in part in Basil's being a would-be law student.

Now, is the property of being dominated by would-be law students an intrinsic property? Perhaps not, but it seems clear that the grounding of this property in Basil's being a would-be law student doesn't suffice to bar it from that status. Yet Basil is presumably not to be reckoned a *part* of the Philosophy Club. He's a member, not a part. Nonetheless, he stands in a relation to the Club that is relevantly similar to the relation a part may stand to a whole. The Philosophy Club is, as we may put it, *ontologically dependent* on its members, including Basil. The Club exists in virtue of the existence of those members. (Not solely in virtue of their existence, of course; but their existence does indeed partly ground the existence of the Club.)

For another example, consider Socrates and the singleton set {Socrates}. The latter has the property of having a philosopher as a member; it has this in virtue of Socrates' being a philosopher. Since a set is ontologically dependent on its

---

[12] My thinking about the need to accommodate examples such as these was motivated by correspondence with Dan Marshall.

members, this is no threat to the intrinsicality of having a philosopher as a member.[13]

Let us generalize and define ontological dependence as follows:

For any x and y, x is ontologically dependent on y if and only if x exists (at least partly) in virtue of the fact that y exists.

Plausibly, whenever x has y as a part, x is *also* ontologically dependent on y, but the reverse is not true: the notion of ontological dependence is broader than that of a part. It is similar, however, in that if a property is grounded by a property of some individual that is distinct from the bearer yet is such that the bearer is ontologically dependent on it, that fact plausibly does not threaten the property's intrinsicality.

Given this revision of the notion of the "other things" that must not be involved in grounding an intrinsic property, our analysis (3) becomes (5):

(5) For any descriptive property F, F is intrinsic if and only if

   (a) necessarily, for any x, if x has F, then for any property G and any individual y such that y ≠ x and x is not ontologically dependent on y, it is not the case that x has F in virtue of y's having G; and

   (b) necessarily, for any x, if x has not-F, then for any property G and any individual y such that y ≠ x and x is not ontologically dependent on y, it is not the case that x has not-F in virtue of y's having G.

Grounding is here invoked twice over: in the statement of the crucial negative condition that the property in question is not grounded in how things other than the bearer are and in the explanation of which "other things" are at issue. I take this result to be congenial given how often orienting characterizations make use of grounding talk. In the next section, we'll see one more way in which grounding is given work to do.

2.5 Local and global notions

Consider the property of being cubical or within five feet of a sphere. The property itself is not intrinsic, but in a particular case, it may be instantiated in an

---

[13] Marshall (forthcoming) addresses this sort of case and makes a claim that just surprises me. He claims that the property of having a member (as applied to sets) is extrinsic, not intrinsic. This seems to me just false, and if we keep in view the fact that a set is ontologically dependent on its members, the contrary judgement should seem plausible.

intrinsic fashion. Suppose Clara is a cube that is not within five feet of a sphere. The way Clara has the property—on this particular occasion, at least—is solely a matter of how she is, not a matter of how other things are. So she has it intrinsically, even if the property itself is not intrinsic. The local notion of intrinsicality is that expressed by saying that Clara has that property in an intrinsic fashion; the global notion is that which classifies properties themselves as intrinsic. How are the local and global notions related?

A natural reaction to such cases is to propose that we define the local notion first, and then define the global notion using the biconditional (6):

(6) For any property F, F is intrinsic if and only if necessarily for any x, if x has F, x has F in an intrinsic fashion.[14]

Call this the "local-first" strategy. Insofar as (6) seems an obvious truth, one may be tempted to insist on a local-first strategy as a means of vindicating it. The Simple Theory, however, does not take a local-first strategy. While it does imply that whether a property is intrinsic depends on what conditions are met by possible instances of it, those conditions do not suggest a sensible way of defining the local notion.

Consider those conditions spelled out as (5)(a) and (5)(b). Suppose we want to use them to define "x has F in an intrinsic fashion." The conditions regarding instances of not-F won't be relevant, of course, so an attempt to define the local notion using (5) gets us (7):

(7) For any descriptive property F and any individual x, x has F in an intrinsic fashion if and only if for any property G and any individual y such that y ≠ x and x is not ontologically dependent on y, it is not the case that x has F in virtue of y's having G.

This definition of the local notion is plainly inadequate. Recall Rhoda, the lonely red thing we discussed in §2.2. According to (7), she has the property of being a lonely red thing in an intrinsic fashion. After all, there are no other individuals the properties of which could ground her having that property. This sort of problem is exactly why I introduced a twofold approach in the first place.

The local/global distinction raises two questions for the Simple Theory. First, just how is the local notion to be understood? Since the Simple Theory defines the global notion first, we should complete the theory by showing how the local notion can be defined in terms of the global notion. The local notion is

---

14 Such a local-first approach using that biconditional was key to the definition in Witmer et al. (2005).

clearly *available*; the example of Clara the cube's having the disjunctive property in an intrinsic fashion is quite compelling, as are others. So some analysis is needed. Second, can the appealing biconditional (6) be vindicated given that analysis? If so, whatever pressure that biconditional may put on us to take a local-first approach is removed.

There is in fact a straightforward way to understand what we are getting at when we say that an extrinsic property is nonetheless had in an intrinsic fashion. In the case of Clara, she has that disjunctive property solely in virtue of having one of its disjuncts—being cubical—where that disjunct is itself an intrinsic property. Here, the crucial notion is that of one property had *solely* in virtue of another. Having a property (partly) in virtue of having an intrinsic property is plainly not sufficient for the first one to be had in an intrinsic fashion. After all, many properties will be instantiated both in virtue of some intrinsic aspects and in virtue of some extrinsic aspects; for example, the property of being cubical and within five feet of a sphere will always be instantiated at least partly in virtue of having an intrinsic property, but there is no temptation to say that it is always had in an intrinsic fashion.

Generally, then, to have an extrinsic property in an intrinsic fashion is just to have that extrinsic property solely in virtue of some intrinsic property one has. To have an intrinsic property in an intrinsic fashion might be defined as a kind of default case: if the property is intrinsic, it's trivially had in an intrinsic fashion. My suggestion, then, is to define the local notion thus:

(8) For any individual x and property P, x has P in an intrinsic fashion if and only if either P is intrinsic or there is some P* such that P* is intrinsic and x has P solely in virtue of having P*.

To have a property in an extrinsic fashion is then defined simply as (9):

(9) For any individual x and property P, x has P in an extrinsic fashion if and only if P is extrinsic and it is not the case that x has P in an intrinsic fashion.

What of our second question about the biconditional (6) linking the local and global notions? Do our definitions vindicate the claim that a property is intrinsic if and only if every possible instance of it is a case in which it is had in an intrinsic fashion? The left-to-right direction of (6) is easy. Given definition (8), if a property F is intrinsic, it is trivial that anything that has it has it in an intrinsic fashion. The right-to-left direction is less straightforward. Could it happen that a property that is necessarily had in an intrinsic fashion is nonetheless itself extrinsic?

Arguably not. Here is the argument. Suppose that F is such that, necessarily, whenever some x has F, x has F in an intrinsic fashion. This implies that if F is not itself intrinsic, then for any instance of F, the individual x has some intrinsic property I such that x has F *solely* in virtue of I. Let $\{I_1, I_2, ...I_z\}$ be the set of every intrinsic property such that F is possibly instantiated solely in virtue of having that property. That set then exhausts all the ways in which F might be instantiated.

To show that F itself is intrinsic, we need to show that the two negative conditions—one for possible instances of F and the other for possible instances of not-F—are satisfied. Consider the first. Are there any possible instances in which an individual has F in virtue of how some other thing is? If so, it would have to be an instance in which the individual also had F solely in virtue of some intrinsic property in $\{I_1, I_2, ...I_z\}$. But given that this instance is grounded *solely* in the instantiation of that member of $\{I_1, I_2, ...I_z\}$, and given that those intrinsic properties had by the individual are of course not themselves grounded in how any other individuals are, we can conclude in none of these cases is F grounded in how other things are. The first condition is satisfied.

Consider the second condition concerning possible instances of not-F. Plausibly, if $I_1, I_2, ... I_z$ are all the ways in which something could have F, then if something lacks F, it lacks F in virtue of lacking one of those properties—or, equivalently, in virtue of possessing the conjunction of their negations. So, for any x, if x has not-F, it has not-F in virtue of having neither I_1, nor I_2, nor I_3, ... nor I_z—the conjunction of the negations in $\{I_1, I_2, ...I_z\}$.

Each member of $\{I_1, I_2, ... I_z\}$ is intrinsic. Since the Simple Theory as set out in (5) implies that the negation of any intrinsic property is itself intrinsic, each member of $\{\text{not-}I_1, \text{not-}I_2, ... \text{not-}I_z\}$ is intrinsic. The conjunction of any number of intrinsic properties will itself be intrinsic, since an individual will have a conjunctive property solely in virtue of having each conjunct. So, the property of having neither I_1, nor I_2, nor I_3, ... nor I_z is intrinsic. We established above that any instance of not-F is had solely in virtue of having neither I_1, nor I_2, nor I_3, ... nor I_z. It follows that it's necessarily the case, for any x such that x has not-F, that x has not-F solely in virtue of some intrinsic property. This is sufficient to show that it is never the case that x has not-F in virtue of how other individuals are; the same proof given for the positive case applies. Hence, (5)(b) is satisfied.

Our analysis of the local notion in terms of the global notion, then, vindicates the plausible biconditional (6) without requiring us to take a local-first approach.

2.6 The theory in summary

Let us sum up the Simple Theory and illustrate it with some applications. Our formulations (5) and (6) give the theory:

> For any descriptive property F, F is intrinsic if and only if
>
> (a) necessarily, for any x, if x has F, then for any property G and any individual y such that y ≠ x and x is not ontologically dependent on y, it is not the case that x has F in virtue of y's having G; and
>
> (b) necessarily, for any x, if x has not-F, then for any property G and any individual y such that y ≠ x and x is not ontologically dependent on y, it is not the case that x has not-F in virtue of y's having G.
>
> For any descriptive property F, F is extrinsic if and only if F is not intrinsic.

As it stands, the Simple Theory only classifies properties—that is, one-place attributes—as intrinsic or extrinsic, but arguably the same distinction can apply to many-place relations as well. Brian Weatherson and Dan Marshall helpfully provide a relevant platitude:

> An n-place intrinsic relation is an n-place relation that n things stand in in virtue of how they are and how they are related to each other, as opposed to how they are related to things outside of them, and how things outside of them are. (Weatherson and Marshall 2013)

How is the Simple Theory to be generalized to all attributes, both one-place and many-place? Suppose an attribute A is being evaluated for intrinsicality. Consider a possible tuple T_A that exemplifies A and ask: is T_A's exemplification of A grounded in the attributes of any ordered sets of individuals outside T_A? Again, we must take care with how the "other things" are to be understood. A tuple T_O will be distinct from T_A if and only if either their cardinalities differ or there is some i such that the ith member of T_A ≠ the ith member of T_O. In addition, however, to be appropriately other, it must also be the case that T_O does not help constitute T_A; it must not be the case that T_A exists (at least partly) in virtue of the existence of T_O. The theory is then straightforwardly reworded for greater generality:

> For any descriptive attribute A, A is intrinsic if and only if:

(a) Necessarily, for any tuple T_A, if T_A exemplifies A, then for any attribute B and any tuple (of whatever cardinality) T_O such that $T_A \neq T_O$ and T_A is not ontologically dependent on T_O, it is not the case that T_A exemplifies A in virtue of T_O's exemplifying B.

(b) Necessarily, for any tuple T_A, if T_A exemplifies not-A, then for any attribute B and any tuple (of whatever cardinality) T_O such that $T_A \neq T_O$ and T_A is not ontologically dependent on T_O, it is not the case that T_A exemplifies not-A in virtue of T_O's exemplifying B.

For any descriptive attribute A, A is extrinsic if and only if A is not intrinsic.

Now that the theory is on the table, much more can, and should, be said by way of evaluating it. However, given space limits, I here confine my remarks to a few comments in support of the theory and an examination of a handful of cases.

Instead of just setting out the Simple Theory at the outset, I chose in this paper to develop it in stages only after a look at several orienting characterizations. The point was to exhibit how the theory thus developed is well-founded in our intuitive grip on the notion. In examining those characterizations, I took pains to note how they related to each other, and in particular related them to (D), here repeated:

(D) A thing has its intrinsic properties in virtue of the way that thing itself, and nothing else, is.

This claim is enshrined in the Simple Theory as the central claim. Characterizations such as (F) and (G) that seem to introduce other elements can be seen, as I argued, as deriving from the basic idea in (D).

A crucial test for a theory of intrinsicality is, of course, whether it classifies particular examples in the way it should. In developing the theory above I have often resorted to this test, but I will here review a handful of examples, including both some already mentioned and others not touched on yet in this paper.

Identity properties, such as being William Shakespeare, are classified as neither intrinsic nor extrinsic. It is true that one might want to say Shakespeare has this property in virtue of *who* he is—but that, I take it, is not the same as having it in virtue of *how* he is, and only the latter is relevant to intrinsicality. However, the structural similarity here between saying that a property is grounded in who someone is (or which thing it is) and saying that a property is grounded in how something is explains the temptation to count identity properties as intrinsic. The same kind of similarity explains the conflation of being intrinsic with being essential, as the intrinsic is grounded in *how* something is and the essential in *what* something is, or *what kind* of thing it is.

What about what we might call *distinctness properties*, such as the property of being *distinct* from William Shakespeare? This, too, I think, is nondescriptive. It tells us something about which thing the individual is by telling us what thing it isn't, but nothing about how it is.

Identity and distinctness properties are impure properties, and both are set aside as not being candidates for the intrinsic or extrinsic designation. But not all impure properties are set aside as nondescriptive. The property of being a student of Rudolf Carnap is plausibly descriptive and extrinsic. Quine has it in virtue of how something else is; his possession of that property is grounded in Carnap's having the property of having taught Quine.

Many impure properties will be extrinsic. Are any intrinsic? Here, examples are less easy to come by, but here is one. The property of *being a set with Shakespeare as one's sole member* is, I think, intrinsic. The set has that property in virtue of Shakespeare's being its member, but the set is itself ontologically dependent on Shakespeare, so this grounding in a distinct thing's features is not the kind of grounding that threatens its status as intrinsic. Note, too, that the negation of this property is intrinsic. The negation is the property of being either not a set or a set with something other than Shakespeare as a member. Not being a set is presumably intrinsic. If something is not a set, that is hardly a function of how other things are. If something is a set that has something other than Shakespeare as a member, that feature is grounded in the features of its members—and hence grounded in the features of things on which it is ontologically dependent.

Indiscriminately necessary properties such as being self-identical and being such that 2+2=4 do not receive a uniform classification. Being self-identical is arguably not descriptive and hence neither intrinsic nor extrinsic. Being such that 2+2=4 may be intrinsic if there are no facts about entities that make it true that 2+2=4, but it won't be if it's true in virtue of how mathematical objects are. Our difficulties in classifying these can be explained as due to our difficulties in understanding the relevant ontology in the first place.

What about what Ted Sider calls *border-sensitive* properties? A property is border-sensitive in this sense if and only if "whether it is instantiated by an object depends on what is going on, intrinsically, outside that object at its borders" (Sider 2001, p. 358). To take one of his examples, consider a solid cube of gold; within that cube there is a quantity of gold that takes up the space of a sphere, yet that gold is not itself a sphere. To be a sphere requires that it have a border with an appropriate shape. Intuitively, such border-sensitivity rules out intrinsicality. The Simple Theory captures this in a straightforward way. In the case of being a sphere, there are possible cases of not being a sphere that are grounded in how other things are. Sider's own example makes this plain. Let George be the quantity of gold that is embedded in a larger gold cube. George has the property of being not a sphere in virtue of how something else is, namely, the surrounding gold; that gold has the feature of being gold and surrounding George, and this helps make George not a sphere.

What of the property of *being an intrinsic duplicate of Shakespeare?* This is extrinsic. There is a possible case in which an individual distinct from Shakespeare (and not ontologically dependent on him) has that property by virtue of the way Shakespeare is. What, however, of the distinct property of being an intrinsic duplicate of Shakespeare *as he actually is?* The same point holds, I believe, though in this case it is worth pointing out that this extrinsic property will be necessarily coextensive with some intrinsic property, namely, the one determined by conjoining all the intrinsic properties of Shakespeare as he actually is (at a given time, of course—I am abstracting away from time for simplicity here).

A few others: what of the property of *attending to something* (Hawthorne 2001, p. 399)? This counts as extrinsic because there is a possible case in which an individual (say, Amy) attends to a distinct individual (say, Basil, who is another person and not something on which Amy ontologically depends). In that case, Amy has the property of attending to something in virtue of a property had by Basil, namely, being the target of Amy's attention. Recall that "in virtue of" here is not the same as "solely in virtue of": Amy's having the property of attending to something is never had solely in virtue of how other things are; but so long as one possible case is partly grounded in some other thing's being a certain way, the property is extrinsic.

What of the property of *being one of at most 17 cubes?* This is plainly extrinsic. The twofold approach to intrinsicality gives a happy result; the negation is the property of being either not a cube *or* a cube accompanied by more than 16 distinct cubes. There is a possible case in which this disjunctive property is grounded in how some other thing is, say, when the bearer is accompanied by 50 other cubes. In that case, the property is grounded by one of those other individuals' being a cube.

This is just a smattering of cases for consideration. So far as I have found, there are no cases that pose a clear counterexample to the Simple Theory.[15]

---

[15] I say that I have found no cases that pose a *clear* counterexample, but there is a kind of property that at least raises questions about just how to apply the theory. I have in mind any intuitively extrinsic property that is either uninstantiable or has a negation that is uninstantiable. Consider the modal conditions (a) and (b): if the property at issue is one such that either it or its negation is not possibly instantiated, one or both of those conditions will be, at least on one standard reading, vacuously satisfied. That reading results in an inappropriate classification of such properties.

This alone doesn't give me much confidence that the theory is correct—after all, we all know how hard it is to anticipate all potential counterexamples. The fact that the theory is developed by close attention to the orienting characterizations, on the other hand, gives me reason to think that something close to it, at least, is correct.[16]

---

[16] Here are two examples that show this. First: the property of being both a brother and not a brother. Since nothing could have it, the conditional (a) is true, and since nothing could have its negation, the conditional (b) is true as well. Yet we are hardly going to be happy with declaring the property of being both a brother and not a brother an intrinsic property. Insofar as we are inclined to classify it, it seems extrinsic. Second: the property of being not a creature of God— that is, being something that is not created by God. This plainly cries out for classification as extrinsic—yet the conditions are again met. Since God does not exist, and hence could not exist (assuming his essence includes necessary existence), everything necessarily has this property. Further, since God could not exist, there are no instances of the property grounded in features of God. No other "outside" entity seems relevant, so condition (a) is met. Consider the negation: being a creature of God. Since God could not exist, nothing could have the negation, and condition (b) is vacuously satisfied.

We can avoid these unhappy results if we read (a) and (b) in such a way that allows for counterpossibles to be substantively true or false. Suppose that something were, *per impossibile*, to have the property of being a brother and not a brother. In that case, it would have that property (partly) in virtue of being a brother, and hence (partly) in virtue of how something else is. Similarly, if something were, again *per impossibile*, a creature of God, it would have that property in virtue of God's being a certain way, namely, having created him.

If we are unwilling to allow counterpossibles with nontrivial truth-values, of course, the examples must be handled in some other way. They are rather peculiar examples, of course, and it is not unreasonable to expect that a suitable treatment may be had, perhaps one guided, in fact, by the way in which the nontrivial counterpossible readings appear to churn out the right results.

16 Thanks to Dan Marshall for some correspondence related to these issues. His forthcoming paper, "Intrinsicality and Grounding," is an attack on the theory suggested by Rosen 2010 that is rather similar to this. The Simple Theory is, I think, immune to the objections there posed, though I lack space here to engage in that battle.

References

Correia, Fabrice and Benjamin Schnieder (eds.) (2012). *Metaphysical Grounding: Understanding the Structure of Reality.* Cambridge: Cambridge University Press.
Dunn, J. Michael (1990). "Relevant Predication 2: Intrinsic Properties and Internal Relations." *Philosophical Studies* 60(3): pp. 177–206.
Francescotti, Robert (1999) How to Define Intrinsic Properties." *Noûs* 33(4): pp. 590–609.
Hawthorne, John (2001). "Intrinsic Properties and Natural Relations." *Philosophy and Phenomenological Research* 63(2): pp. 399–403.
Kim, Jaegwon (1982). "Psychophysical Supervenience." *Philosophical Studies* 41(1): pp. 51–70.
Langton, Rae and David Lewis (1998). "Defining 'Intrinsic'." *Philosophy and Phenomenological Research* 58(2): pp. 333–345.
Lewis, David (1983). "Extrinsic Properties." *Philosophical Studies* 44(2): pp. 197–200.
Marshall, Dan (2009). "Can 'Intrinsic' Be Defined Using Only Broadly Logical Notions?." *Philosophy and Phenomenological Research* 78(3): pp. 646–672.
Marshall, Dan (forthcoming). "Intrinsicality and Grounding." *Philosophy and Phenomenological Research.*
Rosen, Gideon (2010). "Metaphysical Dependence: Grounding and Reduction." In B. Hale and A. Hoffmann (eds.): *Modality: Metaphysics, Logic, and Epistemology.* Oxford: Oxford University Press.
Sider, Theodore (2001). "Maximality and Intrinsic Properties." *Philosophy and Phenomenological Research* 63(2): pp. 357–364.
Trogdon, Kelly (2009). "Monism and Intrinsicality." *Australasian Journal of Philosophy* 87(1): pp. 127–148.
Vallentyne, Peter (1997). "Intrinsic Properties Defined." *Philosophical Studies* 88(2): pp. 209–219.
Weatherson, Brian (2001). "Intrinsic Properties and Combinatorial Principles." *Philosophy and Phenomenological Research* 63(2): pp. 365–380.
Weatherson, Brian and Dan Marshall (2013). "Intrinsic vs. Extrinsic Properties." In E.N. Zalta (ed.), *The Stanford Encyclopedia of Philosophy,* http://plato.stanford.edu/archives/spr2013/entries/intrinsic-extrinsic/.
Wilson, Jessica (2010). "What Is Hume's Dictum, and Why Believe It?" *Philosophy and Phenomenological Research* 80(3): pp. 595–637.
Witmer, D. Gene, William Butchard, and Kelly Trogdon (2005). "Intrinsicality without Naturalness." *Philosophy and Phenomenological Research* 70(2): pp. 326–350.
Yablo, Stephen (1999). "Intrinsicness." *Philosophical Topics* 26(1–2): pp. 479–505. (Reprinted in Yablo (2010). *Things: Papers on Objects, Events, and Properties.* Oxford: Oxford University Press.)

Carrie Figdor
What's the Use of an Intrinsic Property?[1]

Introduction

Philosophical work on the intrinsic/extrinsic distinction is typically motivated not only by its intrinsic interest, but by citing its uses in other areas of philosophy. This roster standardly includes, among others, uses in metaethics, regarding intrinsic moral value; philosophy of mind, regarding the supervenience of mental properties on physical properties; philosophy of science, regarding causal efficacy; and metaphysics, regarding real change. But how the analytical work that follows the list helps to illuminate the items on it is rarely explicitly addressed.[2] Presumably, the proposed analyses are ready to be called upon whenever participants in these other debates need further clarification of what is meant by 'intrinsic' or 'extrinsic'. I will argue, however, that it is not clear that these analyses can do any work at all, and that in the specific case of intrinsic value this assumption is clearly false. Ellis (2002, p. 51) once complained that philosophers "have not succeeded in explicating a concept [of intrinsic] that is of much relevance to the theory or practice of science." I suspect they have not provided an analysis of much relevance to anyone. It is not that standard analyses draw a distinction without a difference, but that the distinction they draw may make no difference.

I'll begin by clarifying what I call standard I/E analyses before examining why they do nothing to illuminate core metaethical debates, such as that over moral value. The core problem is that the analyses are committed to an assumption that is inconsistent with the nature of many properties, of which *having value* is an important example. This assumption cannot be given up without leaving the standard view unmotivated; while if it is kept and defended, what is left is rendered unfit for duty. In effect, standard accounts face the problem of being either irrelevant or impotent.

---

[1] Many thanks to Robert Francescotti and Vera Hoffmann-Kolss for helpful comments on earlier drafts and discussion of the issues raised in this paper.
[2] An exception is Hoffmann-Kolss (2010), who examines the role of the distinction in supervenience. Among non-metaphysicians, metaphysical work on the I/E distinction has been explicitly called upon by Barcelo Aspeitia (2011) in his defense of internalist justification in epistemology; notably, he employs a localist analysis (Figdor 2008, described below). I focus here on metaethics, although my arguments should pressure those defending standard I/E accounts to demonstrate that their analyses can actually do the work they are supposed to be able to do.

1 The Standard I/E Distinction

The platitudes used to characterize the I/E distinction of interest here involve claims about a thing having a property in itself, or in and of itself, or by its intrinsic nature—in short, in some way that is not dependent on other things or what they or the world that the thing is in is like.[3] The platitudes may be stated somewhat more formally in both global and local terms as a first step towards analysis:

>   Global: F is an intrinsic property iff necessarily, any x that is F is F in virtue of the way x itself, and nothing else, is.
>
>   Local: x has F intrinsically iff x has F in virtue of how x itself, and nothing else, is. (Weatherson and Marshall 2013) [4]

What I call the *standard* I/E distinction is a *global* distinction. With the exception of Figdor (2008), those who have published on the topic focus on defining a global rather than a local distinction.[5] Here I largely set aside the question of

---

[3] Examples from across the decades include: "Intuitively, a property P is an intrinsic property of an object x just in case x's having P does not depend on the features of x's environment, but only on what x is like in itself" (Francescotti 2012, p. 91); "*You* know what an intrinsic property is: it's a property that a thing has (or lacks) regardless of what may be going on outside of itself" (Yablo 1999, p. 479); and "The intrinsic properties of something depend only on that thing; whereas the extrinsic properties of something may depend, wholly or partly, on something else" (Lewis 1983, p. 197). Weatherson and Marshall (2013) call this the "interior/exterior" notion, in contrast with a duplication preservation notion and a local/non-local notion in which (necessarily, for any F), an ascription of F to a thing is entirely about that thing and its parts and not at all about other things. (This use of 'local' is not to be confused with a localist view—explained below—of, say, their local/non-local notion.)

[4] Globalist views are often not clearly or consistently distinguished from localist ones. For example, W&M begin their section on analyses of the I/E distinction as follows: "It is at least initially appealing to think that, if an object has a property in an intrinsic fashion, then it has it independently of the way the rest of the world is. The rest of the world could disappear, and the object might still have that property." This sounds like a prelude to local analyses, but only global analyses follow.

[5] The localist analysis I provided in Figdor (2008) was as follows:

(I-ly*) x has F intrinsically $=_{df.}$ x has F, and (i) x's having F is compatible, in the relevant set of possible worlds, with x's having A_R and with x's having $\sim A_R$, or (ii) x has G intrinsically, and x's having G explains x's having F.

(E-ly*) x has F extrinsically $=_{df.}$ x has F, and (i) x's having F is not compatible, in the relevant set of possible worlds, with x's having A_R or else x's having $\sim A_R$; or (ii) x has G extrinsically, and x's having G explains x's having F.

A_R is "relevantly accompanied", where relevance is relative to the context of use of the claim

how these two distinctions are related to focus on the question of whether we need a global distinction to begin with.[6] We do want a distinction, but it's not at all clear that a global distinction is what we want. I'll begin by characterizing global and local distinctions, and then use a widely known, if not wholly embraced, contender for an adequate global distinction to press my case.

A global distinction is a distinction between kinds of properties, akin to the physical/mental and natural-kind/artifact-kind distinctions: it is a 2nd-order distinction that partitions properties.[7] Universally accepted, if not logically necessary, features of global I/E distinctions can be gleaned from the literature by considering how recalcitrant instances are treated.

First, it is typically assumed that the Law of Excluded Middle (LEM) holds in the sense that, for any property F, F is either intrinsic or extrinsic. Global analyses usually provide conditions for a property to be intrinsic, and what's not intrinsic is *ipso facto* classified as extrinsic; there is no "neither" category if a property does not meet the conditions for intrinsicality. (Vallentyne 1997, p. 209 provides a typical expression of LEM in this context: "A property is extrinsic just in case it is not intrinsic.") That said, since some do argue for exempting certain kinds of properties from the domain of application of the I/E distinction, LEM in this context holds for any property F that belongs to any class of properties to which the I/E distinction applies. For example, if the I/E distinction applies only to purely qualitative properties—to a first approximation, those picked out by predicates that lack reference to particular individuals, places or times—any non-purely-qualitative property is *ipso facto* in the "neither" category; but the purely qualitative ones are either intrinsic or extrinsic. These and other do-

---

about intrinsicness or extrinsicness. These criteria do not rule out the case where x can have F in a way that satisfies I-ly* and in a way that satisfies E-ly* at the same time. (I provide detail in the text below.)

6 A local distinction can ground a global distinction in various ways. If a property is had intrinsically (with logical or conceptual necessity) by all possible individuals that can have it, then the property may be classified as intrinsic. But a property could also be classified as intrinsic iff a weighted majority of its instances are had intrinsically, or if most instances are had intrinsically and it is a basic physical property, or whatever.

7 For simplicity, I'll assume properties are universals that are instantiated by individuals, although presumably the I/E distinction is neutral regarding various theories of properties, including realist, nominalist or conceptualist views (see also Marshall 2012, p. 532, who identifies properties as sets of pairs of things and worlds). The discussion in the text can be adjusted accordingly. So, for example, if properties are tropes rather than universals, a global I/E distinction would hold (by LEM, discussed below) that all 1st-order resemblance classes of tropes fall into one of two 2nd-order resemblance classes (the intrinsic class or the extrinsic class), while a local distinction would claim that tropes in the same 1st-order resemblance class may fall in distinct 2nd-order resemblance classes.

main restrictions effectively make the standard I/E distinction 3rd (or higher)-order.

Second, intrinsicality and extrinsicality are exclusive in that a property cannot be both intrinsic and extrinsic. For example, if F is intrinsic, and an instance intuitively has F extrinsically, the recalcitrant instance is treated as a putative counterexample to which the response that the property F is both intrinsic and extrinsic is not an option. (A recalcitrant instance is just a case where a given standard analysis renders a verdict on a property, e.g., it is intrinsic, and an individual intuitively seems to have the property the other way, e.g., extrinsically.) I will discuss exclusivity further below. Note that LEM does not rule out the "both" option; LEM forbids a property F to be put in the (non-existent) middle but leaves open that F could be put on both sides of the distinction.

Third, the global distinction is primary or prescriptive in that the property classification dictates how its instances should be had: if F is intrinsic, then any instance of F *should* be had intrinsically, such that any instance of F that intuitively is not had intrinsically is *ipso facto* a putative counterexample.[8] Weatherson (2001) may be taken to express the primacy commitment when he writes: "[I]f F is intrinsic, then whether some particular thing is F is independent of the way the rest of the world is" (pp. 365–6). One cannot derive an 'ought' from an 'is', but the fact that recalcitrant instances are typically treated as counterexamples to a given analysis shows that a normative element is already built into this 'is'.

These three features—LEM, exclusivity, and primacy—structure current debate as global analyses are proposed, assessed, criticized and defended. The basic structure is as follows. First, a global analysis will classify a property F as intrinsic.[9] If it does, then by primacy all its instances should be had intrinsically. When instances are found that intuitively do not follow suit, they are putative counterexamples to the analysis. By exclusivity, reclassifying F as both in-

---

[8] Note that primacy currently holds for intrinsic properties; if a property is classified as extrinsic it is permissible for it to be had intrinsically (e.g., *is square or accompanied* had by a square). But primacy need not and did not always apply to the intrinsics. By Kim's (1982) definition, a property is intrinsic if it is possible for it to be had without other contingent things existing, and extrinsic if necessarily it could only be had with other contingent things existing. In this case primacy applies to the extrinsics. Either way, primacy is or encapsulates a normative standard by which intuitive judgments of how a property F is had in a particular case can show (at least *prima facie*) that a given analysis's classification of F is wrong.

[9] Alternatively, a global analysis is proposed that classifies previously problematic (as well as unproblematic) properties intuitively correctly. A new property F is found that satisfies the analysis but which has an instance that intuitively has F in the "wrong" way; primacy kicks in and debate proceeds as in the text.

trinsic and extrinsic is not an option. This leaves LEM as the only commitment that can be, and often is, fiddled with—that is, the domain of application is shrunk so that LEM still applies, albeit within a more restricted domain. The only other alternative seems to be to minimize the counterexample as a non-disfiguring flaw.[10]

A local distinction is an account of the cases. It is a 1st-order distinction, between the ways in which individuals have properties. A local I/E distinction partitions how individuals have properties into having them intrinsically or extrinsically. The I/E localist is in good company, for other local distinctions include the essential/accidental, internal/external and necessary/contingent distinctions: a property had intrinsically by one individual (which is then an intrinsic property *of that individual*) may be had extrinsically by, and hence be an extrinsic property of, another individual, just as *being a mathematician* is an essential property of one individual (Andrew Wylie) and an accidental property of another (Paul Krugman). Moreover, the same individual can have the property at the same time both intrinsically and extrinsically, such that the property is both an intrinsic and an extrinsic property of that individual. As I will discuss below, *has value* and *is good* are properties that an individual can have both intrinsically and extrinsically at the same time.

Localists of any variety are motivated by the fact that the vast majority of properties have instances that will fall on both sides of any global distinction. In this specific case, localists judge the intrinsicality of each instance, not the intrinsicality of the property. The local distinction is considered fundamental, but this is not the same as primacy. If an instance of F is had intrinsically by an individual, this does not imply that other instances *should* be had intrinsically just because this one is. A legitimate global notion can be developed, but it needs motivation.[11]

---

[10] The role of "our" intuitions in this debate cannot be overemphasized. As a typical example, Trogdon (2009, p. 137), following Witmer, Butchard, and Trogdon (2005), claims that the reason "we all" find *being cubical and lonely or non-cubical and accompanied* intuitively non-intrinsic is because it can be had by individuals in virtue of intuitively non-intrinsic properties. But many of us may have no intuitions about it, or have conflicting intuitions, or may not agree that such intuitions track the truth. Thus, while Witmer, Butchard, and Trogdon (hereafter, "WTB") state that "while we don't want to say that every property can be classified a priori as intrinsic or not, ..." (2005, p. 330), globalists do give the impression of doing just this given their use of intuitive classificatory judgments that are assumed to be both reliable and universal as the sole source of evidence for or against global accounts.

[11] For example, Francescotti (1999) proceeds by developing a global notion from a local one. All his effort is put into developing the local notion; an intrinsic property *simpliciter* is just one in which it is necessary that any item that has F has F intrinsically. He describes (pp. 591–2) the

While LEM, exclusivity and primacy are not logically required of global analyses, giving up any one of them undermines the motivation for pursuing a globalist approach. For example, it is a standard criticism of particular global analyses that responses to counterexamples that constitute fiddling with the domain of application of LEM ("fiddling with LEM," for short) tend to introduce further notions themselves in need of analysis (and also appear *ad hoc*). The debate over property naturalness exemplifies this criticism.[12] From the current perspective, however, the problem is that for each putative counterexample that is taken to represent a class of properties to which the analysis does not apply, the global I/E distinction divides an ever smaller domain (and will often become an even higher-order distinction), without a principled limit to this process. Since the utility of any global distinction varies inversely with its scope, the motivation for drawing one depends heavily on dealing with putative counterexamples in some way other than by fiddling with LEM. And since so many properties have instances that will be recalcitrant to a global analysis, the problem facing global analyses is to maintain their ability to do any work at all.

But for the globalist giving up primacy and exclusivity are not viable options either. Without primacy, there is no reason to treat recalcitrant cases as counterexamples; it becomes unclear why one needs to classify the property F if one has a localist account of x's having F, especially if F can be had intrinsically or extrinsically. Exclusivity also seems constitutive of extant global accounts in that the "both" option (a property that is both intrinsic and extrinsic) appears incoherent, and is not simply ignored; I will underscore this point in the next two sections. It is a swift slide into irrelevance for a global distinction once the "both" option is live. Moreover, if a property F can be both, then given a recalcitrant instance of F there seems to be no principled way to choose between reclassifying F as "both" or maintaining the original classification and dealing with the problem some other way. It becomes too easy to shield an analysis from counterexamples.

---

local/global distinction in terms of a property being had intrinsically by an individual vs. a property being intrinsic as a kind or *simpliciter*, using *co-exists with the number 21* as an example of a property that is not intrinsic *simpliciter* because it is had intrinsically by the number 21 and had extrinsically by anything else.

12 The problem of hyperintensionality for Lewis's duplication-based account (Eddon 2011) also relies on exclusivity and primacy, and the responses Eddon considers (and counters) include fiddling with LEM and minimizing the flaw. The problem of hyperintensionality (for Lewis) is that (a) if one individuates properties in terms of sets of possible individuals, and (b) if one holds that duplicates are worldbound individuals, then one will not be able to distinguish intrinsic from extrinsic necessary properties or intrinsic from extrinsic identity properties.

Despite these problems, one might maintain that the original motivations still underscore the need for a global distinction. What I will show, however, is that globalists face a dilemma: if they give up the commitments, the global distinction lacks motivation vis-à-vis a local distinction; but if they keep those commitments, the global distinction can't do the work it's supposed to do. Either way, how a given global analysis deals with recalcitrant instances is not the critical issue; it is whether any global analysis is worth the trouble.

2 A Specific Standard Account and Exclusivity Illustrated

There is no "received" standard analysis, but Langton and Lewis (1998) command a fair number of partial adherents for at least providing a necessary condition for intrinsicality in the form of an independence of accompaniment criterion (described below). The Langton and Lewis (L & L) account has been defended by others via development (WBT 2005) or modification (Weatherson 2001), and is intended by L&L to buttress Lewis's earlier (1983, 1986) duplication-based accounts. But even among those preferring alternative analyses, L&L's independence criterion (IC) generally has not been the target of criticism (e.g., Vallentyne 1997 provides an account of the having or lacking of a property in a way that is independent of the presence or absence of other objects or times, but elaborated in terms of world-time-contractions). Rather, their additional criterion of property naturalness, introduced to exclude disjunctive properties from the class of basic intrinsics, has been far more widely criticized (e.g., Hawthorne 2001, Sider 2001, Marshall and Parsons 2001).[13] It is fair to say that their independence criterion, as a way of capturing at least part of what it is for a property to be had "in and of itself," enjoys widespread tacit acceptance if not explicit support.

In what follows I will target IC, not naturalness, by showing how exclusivity is built into IC and how damaging this commitment is to the ability of a standard distinction to do the work it is supposed to do. Generally speaking, any analysis

---

13 IC is regarded (including by L&L) as not sufficient because disjunctive properties can satisfy it even though individuals can have them in ways that are intuitively non-intrinsic. The property *being cubical and lonely or non-cubical and accompanied* will satisfy IC, yet for many this property is intuitively not intrinsic. Exclusivity and primacy both play roles in this criticism, while L&L's restriction of basic intrinsics to natural properties (which are non-disjunctive) is a way of fiddling with LEM.

that excludes the possibility of the instantiation of a property by a thing, both in itself and in relation to other things at the same time, will have the same problem. Since other global analyses are *prima facie* committed to exclusivity, if not as explicitly as in IC, I leave it to their champions to show how their accounts avoid the globalist's dilemma.

IC formalizes what it is to be independent of accompaniment by another contingently existing thing: a property P is intrinsic only if it is independent of accompaniment, and extrinsic otherwise.[14] There is no "neither" option except implicitly in the form of excluded kinds of properties, such as non-natural properties; and there is no "both" option. In fact, there *can't* be a "both" option. Independence of accompaniment is determined by whether, for any property P, all four of the following cases are logically or conceptually or metaphysically possible: (1) an individual has P and is accompanied by another contingently existing thing (A), (2) an individual has P and is lonely (which is defined as the negation of accompaniment, ~A), (3) an individual lacks P and has A, and (4) an individual lacks P and has ~A. Assuming classical logic, it is not logically possible for an individual to have (P & ~A) and (P & A) at the same time.

One reason a localist finds IC problematic is because it requires all four cases to be considered in assessing independence. When we assess whether an individual has a property intrinsically, we will want to consider whether it would still have the property even if it were alone in the universe (or relevantly alone), but how other individuals might have the property is beside the point. A cube will have *being cubical and lonely or non-cubical and accompanied* if it is lonely and will lack this property if accompanied, but what might be the case with non-cubes or other cubes (that are not its counterparts) is not relevant to assessing whether this cube has it intrinsically.[15] A localist assessment of independence will require that the same individual (or its counterparts) be considered in the two relevant cases—here, (1) and (2)—and will ignore the other two as irrelevant.[16]

---

14 As just stated, IC is a modification of the Simple Independence Criterion (from WBT 2005), which includes an 'iff'. IC (or SIC) was motivated by the fact that Kim's (1982) analysis resulted in classifying the property *being lonely* (~A) as intrinsic, when Lewis (1983) and everyone since intuitively thinks it is extrinsic. (I will question this below.)

15 I include reference to (Lewisian) counterparts so as to remain neutral regarding the metaphysics of modality. Localists, like globalists, need some interpretation or other of the semantics of modal statements.

16 This is why WBT's (2005) modification of L&L remains a global distinction: it avoids their natural-property condition, but adopts (all of) IC as a necessary condition. On their view an intrinsic property is one that satisfies IC either directly or else indirectly if one has it by virtue of having another property that satisfies IC. Thus, WBT's to "have F in an intrinsic fashion" is not

But the deeper problem with IC stems from its interpretation of the relation between being accompanied and being lonely. These are of course technical terms. 'Accompaniment' refers to the property of being accompanied by other contingent objects, and 'loneliness' is defined as the negation of accompaniment. But self-accompaniment (or reflexive accompaniment) and other-accompaniment are compatible, not contradictory. One can be (and usually is) self-accompanied and other-accompanied at the same time. Thus any property that can be had both ways at the same time by the same individual cannot be assessed for intrinsicality using IC.[17] Any analysis that treats being lonely and being accompanied as exclusive, formally or not, faces the same issue.

Properties that can be had intrinsically and extrinsically at the same time by the same individuals are neither rare nor weird; recalcitrant instances of them cannot be minimized as non-disfiguring flaws. To borrow Hawthorne's (2001) example, the property *is attending*—the "existential derivative" of the relation *attending to something or other*—is "flexible" (as Hawthorne puts it): a thing can have this property by either self-attending or other-attending. Notably, Hawthorne uses the example against L&L's naturalness condition; that it meets IC is "beyond dispute." But he also adds (in fn.1) that "I assume we do not want to relativize matters so that we count the existential derivative [*is attending*] an intrinsic property of Jones (who is attending to his leg) but not of me (who is attending to the table)." This assumption is true only if "we" are globalists. And if Jones is attending to his leg and to Hawthorne at the same time, "we" also presumably do not want to say that this property is both intrinsic and extrinsic. Yet if the very same property can be had self-reflexively and other-relationally by the same thing at the same time, then *is attending* cannot be assessed for intrinsicality at all, since then it can be had by a single individual in a way that is logically consistent with its being the only thing and logically inconsistent with its being the only thing at the same time.

If we call properties that can be classified using IC *exclusive-disjunctive* properties, then the problem is that many properties are not exclusive-disjunctive. Exclusive-disjunctive properties in general are those that can be partitioned by their logical independence of a pair of logical contradictories. In the case of the I/E distinction, the relevant contradictories are accompaniment and loneliness. At best, then, the standard I/E distinction must really just be about a

---

the same as Figdor's (2008) "having F intrinsically." For WBT, to have a property in an intrinsic fashion is either to have a property F that satisfies IC or to have another property that satisfies IC and in virtue of which one has F.

17 Of course, IC's four cases will be satisfied by this property, so it will be classified as extrinsic anyway.

very special subclass of properties—a subclass which with each recalcitrant case threatens to get smaller all the time.

Size might not matter if no important properties were left out of the standard distinction's domain of application. Unfortunately for the globalist, this is not the case.

3 The Standard I/E Distinction and Metaethics

While the 'in itself' locution and the term 'intrinsic' appear regularly in metaethical discussions, not all are germaine to the I/E distinction (global or local) discussed above. In particular, the distinctions between final vs. instrumental value and non-derivative vs. derivative value involve uses of 'intrinsic' that are not the ones I/E analyses try to capture. Relevant debates concern such questions as in virtue of what things have value, and what explains their having the value they have, and the relation between having value and being valued (Dorsey 2012). Does final value (value as an end, or for its own sake) supervene on intrinsic properties, as Moore (1903) held, or can something—a rare stamp, for example—have final value without its value supervening on its intrinsic properties, as Korsgaard (1983), Kagan (1998) and others hold? Does having value depend on being valued, as subjectivists claim (see, e.g., Kagan 1998, p. 281 and fn. 4)? These are the sorts of issues where the standard I/E distinction ought to provide illumination, if any.

Instead, it introduces confusion. Moore originated, or at least established as the received view, the connection between intrinsic value and the I/E distinction that justifies the inclusion of metaethics on the utility list.[18] In "The Conception of Intrinsic Value" Moore (1922, p. 260) states that "[t]o say that a kind of value is intrinsic means merely that the question of whether a thing possesses it, and the degree to which it possesses it, depends solely on the intrinsic nature of the thing in question." In *Principia Ethica* (1903: Ch. VI, §112), he describes the method of determining what is intrinsically good by considering "what things are such that, if they existed by themselves, in absolute isolation, we should yet judge their existence to be good; …" The Moorean position may be put by saying

---

[18] Fletcher (2008) argues that Moore newly identified intrinsic value with intrinsic nature, essentialism, and final value; Mill, for example, appears to have used the term (to the extent he used it at all) to distinguish between value as an end (final value) vs. value as a means (instrumental value). If "Mooreanism" is the set of theses in which intrinsic value is identified with final value, held with necessity, and dependent solely on intrinsic properties of bearers (Fletcher 2008, p. 531), only the third thesis matters here.

that, for Moore, intrinsic value is a kind of value such that when it is possessed by something, it possesses it solely in virtue of its intrinsic properties, and its intrinsic properties are the properties the thing would continue to have even if it were alone in the universe (Bradley 2006). This is the view Korsgaard, Kagan and others argue against.[19]

All this should sound very familiar—and yet globalists should immediately start feeling queasy. Any standard I/E analysis that does not classify *being lonely* as an extrinsic property is deemed flawed. It was because *being lonely* (defined as above) came out as intrinsic on Kim's original (1982) proposal that it was jettisoned; L&L was its immediate successor, but every other global analysis follows suit or is deemed flawed. So given the universally accepted globalist classification of *being lonely*, Moore must be interpreted as saying that intrinsic value is value that depends on an extrinsic property. By any charitable reading of Moore, this is implausible. So either *being lonely* as defined is not an adequate rendering of Moore's intended uses of 'being alone in the universe' or 'in itself', or *being lonely* is improperly classified as extrinsic (or both).

What about typical metaethical properties? These include *having value* and *being good*. Do standard I/E analyses help illuminate debates about value and goodness? The short answer is that they can't, because these are not exclusive-disjunctive properties.

For a Moorean, something has final value when it possesses its value in virtue of its intrinsic properties. (This use of 'intrinsic' is ambiguous between a localist and globalist reading.) But properties a thing could have while alone in the universe include properties it can also have non-reflexively. *Having value* is such a property. Suppose (*pace* Moore) an item's *having value* entails the existence of a minded creature that has a pro-attitude towards the item—that is, it depends on *being valued* (what Kagan calls the "radical subjectivist" view). Then *having value* could include self-valuing and other-valuing cases. Those who think *having value* depends on *being valued* do not rule out the case where the valued is also the valuer. So a thing could have value in such a way that it would still have value while alone in the universe in either the Moorean way or in the subjectivist way (by valuing itself). In both cases the thing can also *have value* at the same time for reasons that do not depend on its being alone or that are consistent with its being accompanied. It can have value both intrinsically and extrinsically, and

---

[19] These platitudes, like the ones in metaphysics, can be understood in global or local terms. However, as Feldman (1998) notes, the intrinsically good as "good in virtue of its intrinsic nature" is distinguishable from the intrinsically good as "that which would still be good even if it existed in complete isolation." To simplify matters here, I adopt his (1998, p. 349) interpretation of 'intrinsic nature' as 'the set of intrinsic properties'.

so *having value* will be both an intrinsic and an extrinsic property of that individual.

The point may be emphasized by seeing how *having value* can be had intrinsically and had extrinsically by the same item at the same time on the specific localist view I have defended (see fn. 4). Suppose F = has value and G = being valued. x can have F intrinsically in two ways. First, it can have F in a way that is compatible with x's not being accompanied by other valuers and with x's being so accompanied (because the existence of other valuers is irrelevant to its having value). That's a Moorean view. Second, it could have F intrinsically by having G in one of the two ways in which x could have G—namely, by valuing itself—and thus by having G in a way that is compatible with x's not being accompanied by other valuers and with being so accompanied (since these other valuers are not relevant), and by adding that x's having G explains x's having F. That's a subjectivist view. But x could also have F extrinsically—although not to Moore—by having F in a way that is not compatible with x's not being accompanied by other valuers or with its being (only) self-accompanied; this is perhaps the typical sort of case subjectivists have in mind when they claim that a thing has value by being valued and the valuers are others, not x itself. Finally, one way for x to have F in both ways at the same time (which Mooreans will deny is a proper way of understanding value) would be for it to have G in both ways at the same time—that is, given a subjectivist theory, in the case in which x both values itself and is valued by others simultaneously, and in which both ways are relevant to its having value. The localist position does not preclude any of these (or presumably other) metaethical possibilities, as one might expect of any adequate way of analyzing the intrinsic/extrinsic distinction. But it is difficult for any globalist analysis to exhibit the metaphysical flexibility that allows for the logical space of metaethical positions without precluding one position or another. One solution would be to give up exclusivity for F or for G, but this solution opens the floodgates to too-easy deflection of putative counterexamples to a given global analysis.

What about *being good*? It is difficult to see how any global analysis can account not only for the fact that we think some things are intrinsically good and others are extrinsically good, but that the same thing can be good in itself and good in relation to other things at the same time. (This is not to be confused with the final/instrumental distinction.) Consider Frankena's (1973, pp. 87–8) long list of intrinsic goods, which includes love. The same person can, at the same time, be loved by loving herself and by being loved by others. The same can be said for *being right* in the sense in which acts are right or wrong. An act can be right for multiple reasons at the same time, some of which wholly depend on the act alone and some of which depend on external factors. The property of *being a morally relevant feature* is similarly problematic. In short, metaethicists might well ignore the dictates of any standard I/E analysis when it comes to classifying *having value, being good* and *being right*. As noted above, fiddling with LEM to rule out non-exclusive-disjunctive properties will protect the standard I/E analysis, but this move will leave core metaethical properties out of its domain of application.

The above problems press on the standard analyses' commitment to exclusivity, which appears most explicitly in L&L's independence criterion. But one can also press from the commitment to primacy. For example, if *having value* is classified as an intrinsic property by a global analysis, then by primacy any individual *should* have it intrinsically if it has it at all. If this is right, then it seems that all it takes to win the metaethical debate is to point to this global analysis, note that some things, intuitively, have value extrinsically, and conclude that Moore must be wrong about *having value*.

Similarly, the standard I/E distinction runs roughshod over the metaethical debate regarding particularism. Particularists such as Dancy (1983) argue that whether a feature is good- or bad-making depends on contextual factors. For example, a Shakespeare play and a public execution can both be *well-performed* and thus *cause pleasure* in audiences, but in virtue of the latter feature the play is good but the execution is bad. It follows that while *being good* may be grounded in the same features, we cannot generalize from the presence of these features in one case to the claim that anything with these features will also be good (or, more generally, have the same moral valence that the given case exhibits).[20] So it is not merely that *being good* seems to be a property that cannot be classified by any global analysis because things can have this property based on multiple non-exclusive grounds at the same time. It also seems that important nuances of metaethical discussion are lost if the property of *being good* must be classified one way or the other when based on these grounds.

A usual response to the particularist intuition about crowd-pleasing executions (e.g. Lippert-Rasmussen 1999) is to draw a distinction, such as between *causes pleasure by way of making a crowd pleased* vs. *causes pleasure by way*

---

[20] Dancy (1983, p. 531) partly characterizes his targets, whom he calls pluralists, as follows: "Pluralists generally assume that if a property tells in favor of an action being a duty, then it will tell in favor of any action that bears it." This is similar in spirit to the commitment to primacy that partly characterizes global analyses. Indeed, Dancy raises an objection to pluralists structurally similar to the exclusive-disjunctive problem for globalists: if acts of type ϕ are to be promoted while acts of type ψ are to be avoided, "when we have an act which, as is possible, is both ϕ and ψ, something has to give."

of making a billionaire lose a bet and donate a huge sum to charity. Drawing distinctions yields more fine-grained properties. Similarly, a defender of the standard analysis might respond that *having value* subdivides into *having self-value* and *having other-value*. But this splitting response does not resolve the issue. For any (presumably principled) way of determining when the splitting stops, at that point the globalist will face the same problem. There is no obvious place at which only exclusive-disjunctive properties are left standing, and if such a place were found it would likely be such that the vast majority of properties of interest will not be in it. When we individuate properties so finely that it becomes the rule, and not the exception, that only one individual can have the property in question, we have reached a point where one might as well just be a localist.[21]

Conclusion

The idea of a property being had by something "in itself" has motivated a variety of ways of precisifying the I/E distinction—as independence from accompaniment by other contingent objects, as not including relations to other contingent objects, and so on. The fact that the vast majority of properties have instances that will be recalcitrant on any global analysis has not to date been regarded as a fundamental flaw of the globalist approach. The attitude is that these are counterexamples to particular analyses and the globalist approach is fundamentally sound. Perhaps adding the fact that, for many properties, the same individual can have the same property at the same time in different ways without this being a contradiction will cause some to question this fundamental soundness. But the fact that critical moral properties are of this type should lay to rest the idea that global analyses are worth the trouble even if all counterexamples can be dealt with. A global analysis that covers only exclusive-disjunctive properties, either explicitly by adopting IC or in a more subtle way, will fail to be of much interest to anyone.

How did standard I/E analyses go so far off the rails? No doubt there are many contributing factors. But among them must be the "intuitive" judgment

---

[21] It is taken for granted in this literature that any well-formed predicate corresponds to a property (*being such that X* and *being R or Q* are typical property-generating formulas); this alone allows for generating as fine-grained properties as one might want. But only an individuation scheme in which every property has just one instance will protect the globalist from the problem. This is an implausible view of properties, as it abandons the purposes for which we want properties to begin with.

that *being lonely* is just like *being accompanied* in that it also depends on how the world is, yet can also be adequately defined as its contradictory. We have not gotten the differences in their dependence on the world sorted out. One can uphold the intuitive judgment, but negation is too blunt an instrument to capture the differences we want. As Danto (1964) pointed out, with *Brillo Box* Warhol was trying to not not-represent, but this is not equivalent to trying to represent. So, too, with being alone in the universe. This is not the logical contradictory of being accompanied, but a way of being whose contrast is imperfectly captured by a negation sign. Moreover, this violation of classical logic reflects the success of natural languages in dealing with a nuanced world. In general, the globalist perspective requires us to fundamentally misconstrue the nature of many properties and the utility of our concepts for characterizing a world of complex cases.

This is not the place to defend an alternative local account. However, I think Moore's (1922, p. 263 and elsewhere) reference to "intrinsic nature" suggests a fruitful way to proceed. Korsgaard (1983, p. 175) explains Moore's view as being that intrinsic goodness "is dependent only on the thing's intrinsic nature and is just as constant: so long as the thing remains what it is it has the same value: and the value is the same, of course, for everyone and so also objective." I suggest that these references to a thing's nature are what we are trying to get at when we say that something has a property intrinsically, or that a property is intrinsic to, or is an intrinsic property of an individual. It has the property by its nature, and elements of a thing's nature are picked out by the fact that they are cross-contextually robust (but not thereby essential). From this perspective, independence of accompaniment (however ultimately defined) is a symptom of the distinction, not a core part of it. Obviously, the nature of "nature" must be illuminated in some other way than by identifying a thing's nature with the set of its intrinsic properties (*pace* fn. 19 above) or with the set of properties shared by duplicates, as one might also explicate the notion (see, e.g. Francescotti 1999, p. 591, although he does not support the duplication-based approach). But since there are already distinct ways of understanding a thing's nature, the challenge is to develop a notion that is compatible with the localist perspective. That account must await another opportunity.

References

Barcelo Aspeitia, Axel Arturo (2011). "An Insubstantial Externalism." *The Journal of Philosophy* 108(10): pp. 576–582.
Bradley, Ben (2006). "Two Concepts of Intrinsic Value." *Ethical Theory and Moral Practice* 9 (2): pp. 111–130.
Dancy, Jonathan (1983). "Ethical Particularism and Morally Relevant Properties." *Mind* New Series 92(368): pp. 530–547.
Danto, Arthur (1964). "The Artworld." *The Journal of Philosophy* 61 (19): pp. 571–584.
Denby, David (2006). "The Distinction between Intrinsic and Extrinsic Properties." *Mind* 115 (457): pp. 1–17.
Dorsey, Dale (2012). "Intrinsic Value and the Supervenience Principle." *Philosophical Studies* 157(2): pp. 267–285.
Eddon, Maya (2011). "Intrinsicality and Hyperintensionality." *Philosophy and Phenomenological Research* 82(2): pp. 314–336.
Ellis, Brian (2002). *The Philosophy of Nature: A Guide to the New Essentialism.* Quebec and Chesham: McGill-Queen's University Press and Acumen Press.
Feldman, Fred (1998). "Hyperventilating About Intrinsic Value." *The Journal of Ethics* 2(4): pp. 339–354.
Figdor, Carrie (2008). "Intrinsically/Extrinsically." *The Journal of Philosophy* 105(11): pp. 691–718.
Fletcher, Guy (2008). "Mill, Moore, and Intrinsic Value." *Social Theory and Practice* 34(4): pp. 517–532.
Francescotti, Robert (1999). "How to Define Intrinsic Properties." *Nous* 33(4): pp. 590–609.
Francescotti, R. (2012). "Understanding the Intrinsic/Extrinsic Distinction." *Metascience* 21(1): pp. 91–94.
Frankena, William F. (1973). *Ethics.* Englewood Cliffs, NJ: Prentice-Hall.
Hawthorne, John (2001). "Intrinsic Properties and Natural Relations." *Philosophy and Phenomenological Research* 63(2): pp. 399–403.
Hoffmann-Kolss, Vera (2010). *The Metaphysics of Extrinsic Properties.* Frankfurt: Ontos-Verlag.
Humberstone, I. L. (1996). "Intrinsic/Extrinsic." *Synthese* 108(2): pp. 205–267.
Jensen, Karsten Klint and Kasper Lippert-Rasmussen (2005). "Understanding Particularism." *Theoria* 71(2): pp. 118–137.
Kagan, Shelly (1998). Rethinking Intrinsic Value." *The Journal of Ethics* 2(4): pp. 277–297.
Kim, Jaegwon (1982). "Psychophysical Supervenience." *Philosophical Studies* 41(1): pp. 51–70.
Korsgaard, Christine M. (1983). "Two Distinctions in Goodness." *The Philosophical Review* 92 (2): pp. 169–195.
Langton, Rae and David Lewis (1998). "Defining 'Intrinsic'." *Philosophy and Phenomenological Research* 58(2): pp. 333–345.
Lewis, David (1983). "Extrinsic Properties." *Philosophical Studies* 44(2): pp. 197–200.
Lewis, David (1986). *On the Plurality of Worlds.* Oxford: Blackwell.
Lewis, David (2001). "Redefining 'Intrinsic'." *Philosophy and Phenomenological Research* 63 (2): pp. 381–398.
Lippert-Rasmussen, Kasper (1999). "On Denying a Significant Version of the Constancy Assumption." *Theoria* 65(2/3): pp. 90–113.

Marshall, Dan (2012). "Analyses of Intrinsicality In Terms of Naturalness." *Philosophy Compass* 7(8): pp. 531–542.

Marshall, Dan and Josh Parsons (2001). "Langton and Lewis on "Intrinsic." *Philosophy and Phenomenological Research* 63(2): pp. 347–351.

Moore, G. E. (1903). *Principia Ethica* (Cambridge: Cambridge University Press). Cited here from http://fair-use.org/g-e-moore/principia-ethica.

Moore, G. E. (1922). "The Conception of Intrinsic Value." *Philosophical Studies* (London: Routledge and Kegan Paul).

Rabinowicz, Wlodek and Toni Ronnow-Rasmussen (2000). "A Distinction in Value: Intrinsic and For Its Own Sake." *Proceedings of the Aristotelian Society* 100(1): pp. 33–51.

Trogdon, Kelly (2009). "Monism and Intrinsicality." *Australasian Journal of Philosophy* 87(1): pp. 127–148.

Sider, Ted (2001). "Maximality and Intrinsic Properties." *Philosophy and Phenomenological Research* 63(2): pp. 357–364.

Vallentyne, Peter (1997). "Intrinsic Properties Defined." *Philosophical Studies* 88(2): pp. 209–219.

Weatherson, Brian (2001). "Intrinsic Properties and Combinatorial Principles." *Philosophy and Phenomenological Research*, 63(2): pp. 365–380.

Weatherson, Brian and Dan Marshall (2013). "Intrinsic vs. Extrinsic Properties." In E. Zalta (ed.), *The Stanford Encyclopedia of Philosophy* (*Spring 2013 edition*), http://plato.stanford.edu/archives/spr2013/entries/intrinsic-extrinsic/

Witmer, Gene D., William Butchard and Kelly Trogdon (2005). "Intrinsicality without Naturalness." *Philosophy and Phenomenological Research* 70(2): pp. 326–350.

Yablo, Stephen (1999). "Intrinsicness." *Philosophical Topics* 26(1–2): pp. 479–505.

Zimmerman, Michael J. (2010). "Intrinsic Value." In E. Zalta (ed.), *The Stanford Encyclopedia of Philosophy* (*Winter 2010 edition*), http://plato.stanford.edu/archives/win2010/entries/value-intrinsic-extrinsic/

Vera Hoffmann-Kolss
Is the Intrinsic/Extrinsic Distinction Hyperintensional?

Several authors have recently claimed that the distinction between intrinsic and extrinsic properties is hyperintensional, i.e., that there are cointensional properties P and Q, such that P is intrinsic, while Q is extrinsic. In this paper, I aim to defend the classical view that whenever P and Q are cointensional properties, then P and Q are either both intrinsic or both extrinsic. I first argue that the standard characterization of the intrinsic/extrinsic distinction involves dependence claims: intrinsic properties are those properties whose instantiation by x only depends on what x is like in itself, whereas extrinsic properties are those properties whose instantiation by x may also depend on what other individuals are like. I then consider a number of examples supposed to show that the intrinsic/extrinsic distinction is hyperintensional and argue that none of them succeeds if the dependence characterization of the distinction is taken seriously.

1 Introduction

A property is intrinsic iff its instantiation by some individual only depends on what the individual itself is like, not on its environment. A property is extrinsic iff it is not intrinsic, i.e., iff its instantiation by some individual depends, at least partially, on the individual's surroundings. Accordingly, *being red* or *having a mass of 3 kg* are intrinsic properties, while the properties of *having children* or *being accompanied by something red* are extrinsic.

Giving a definition of the intrinsic/extrinsic distinction has turned out to be one of the most controversial and difficult tasks in contemporary metaphysics. Most definitions of 'intrinsic' implicitly or explicitly presuppose that the intrinsic/extrinsic distinction is not hyperintensional. Thus, any cointensional properties P and Q, i.e., any properties P and Q which have the same extension in all possible worlds, are either both intrinsic or both extrinsic. For instance, if intrinsic properties are defined as those properties which cannot differ between duplicate individuals, as prominently suggested by Langton and Lewis (1998, pp. 336–7), it is not possible for cointensional properties to fall on different sides of the intrinsic/extrinsic divide. For whenever P is classified as intrinsic, according to this account, whereas Q is classified as extrinsic, then P and Q differ in their instantiation conditions. But if P and Q were cointensional, they would not differ in their instantiation conditions and, hence, could not fall on different sides of the intrinsic/extrinsic divide (for a similar argument see Eddon 2011, p. 318).

The non-hyperintensionality of the intrinsic/extrinsic distinction has long been the received view in the debate on this metaphysically important distinction. Recently, several authors have argued, however, that the distinction between intrinsic and extrinsic properties is hyperintensional. Their strategy typically consists in finding pairs of cointensional properties, one of which is uncontroversially intrinsic, whereas the other is uncontroversially extrinsic. Finding one such pair of properties is considered sufficient for showing that the intrinsic/extrinsic distinction is hyperintensional—and that classical accounts which presuppose that the distinction is non-hyperintensional are inadequate.

Currently, there seems to be a general tendency to acknowledge the hyperintensional character of the intrinsic/extrinsic distinction. It can be shown, however, that the pertinent examples of cointensional properties putatively falling on different sides of the intrinsic/extrinsic divide are far less uncontroversial than is commonly assumed. In this paper, I therefore aim to defend the classical view that the intrinsic/extrinsic distinction is non-hyperintensional. Since the classification of properties as intrinsic and as extrinsic crucially depends on our intuitive characterization of the distinction, I begin by investigating the intuitions underlying the debate on the notions of intrinsicness and extrinsicness (section 2). I argue that intuitive characterizations of the intrinsic/extrinsic distinction typically involve the dependence claims introduced at the beginning of this section: the instantiation of an intrinsic property by x is always independent of the environment of x, while the instantiation of an extrinsic property by x may, at least partially, depend on x's surroundings. Then, I consider four attempts to show that the intrinsic/extrinsic distinction is hyperintensional and argue that if the dependence characterization of the intrinsic/extrinsic distinction is taken seriously, none of them succeeds (section 3). I conclude by briefly discussing a possible objection to my argument (section 4).

Before considering the intuitions underlying philosophical accounts of intrinsicness, it should be noted that the debate on whether the intrinsic/extrinsic distinction is hyperintensional regards only what is often called the *global* version of this distinction. According to the global version of the intrinsic/extrinsic distinction, properties are classified as intrinsic or as extrinsic *simpliciter*, independently of the individuals instantiating them. However, there is also a local version of the distinction, which does not classify properties *simpliciter*, but classifies ways in which properties are had by individuals (see Dunn 1990, p. 183; Humberstone 1996, pp. 227–8; Figdor 2008, p. 692). For instance, the disjunctive property of *being red or accompanied* is usually considered globally extrinsic. Nonetheless, this property is had intrinsically by every red individual. Since it is moreover had extrinsically by every accompanied individual and since an individual can be both red and accompanied, this implies that *being red or accompanied* can be had both intrinsically and extrinsically by the very same individual.

One might think that if properties can be had both intrinsically and extrinsically by the very same individual, this already implies the hyperintensionality of the intrinsic/extrinsic distinction. However, this is not the case. The observation that the property of *being red or accompanied* can be had intrinsically and extrinsically by the same individual does not imply that *being red or accompanied* is cointensional with some globally intrinsic property. Accordingly, even though there are individuals that are both red and accompanied, it need not be the case that there is a globally intrinsic property P, which is instantiated by all and only those individuals that are red or accompanied (or both). The claim that the global version of the intrinsic/extrinsic distinction is hyperintensional requires independent justification. In what follows, I will discuss whether such justification can be given.

2 The Dependence Characterization of the Intrinsic/Extrinsic Distinction

Philosophical investigations are often concerned with notions taken from everyday contexts—such as causation, knowledge, person, virtue, consciousness or explanation. Obviously, we have a rather clear pre-philosophical intuitive understanding of such notions, and philosophical theories have to be in accordance with these intuitions. However, there are also notions whose philosophical use differs from the way in which they are used in everyday contexts. The notion of being essential to something is a case in point. If we say that a good educational system is essential to a country's prosperity and wealth, what we mean by this in everyday discourse is that a good educational system is highly important if a country is to have a prospering economy. But there is also a philosophical use of the term 'being essential to x', which is considerably narrower and more technical than this everyday use: according to this philosophical understanding of the term, a property is essential to x, or essentially had by x, iff x has this property in every possible world where it exists.

The notions of intrinsicness and extrinsicness belong to this second type of philosophically important notions. While the terms 'intrinsic' and 'extrinsic' exist in natural language, the distinction between intrinsic and extrinsic properties as used in philosophical discourse is more specific than the notions of intrinsicness and extrinsicness occurring in everyday contexts. This is part of the reason why the intrinsic/extrinsic distinction is so hard to define.

Typically, the process of providing a philosophical analysis of the intrinsic/extrinsic distinction is structurally analogous to the practice of hypothesis testing in the empirical sciences. A general definition is proposed, specifying necessary and sufficient conditions which a property has to fulfill in order to be classified as intrinsic (or as extrinsic as the case may be). This analysis is then evaluated in the light of our intuitive understanding of the intrinsic/extrinsic distinction. If there turn out to be recalcitrant "data", i.e., intuitions about single cases which contradict the proposed analysis, the definition is modified or replaced by a new account. The problem is, however, that even though in some cases, we have rather clear intuitions concerning what counts as an intrinsic property and what counts as an extrinsic property, there are other cases which are intuitively controversial. There is, for instance, no intuitive agreement on whether the property of *not being identical to David Lewis* is intrinsic or extrinsic. One can plausibly hold that this property is intrinsic because the property of *being identical to David Lewis* is intrinsic and the class of intrinsic properties is closed under negation. However, it can also be argued that it is extrinsic since an individual's having it depends on its standing in a certain relation to a distinct individual (see Marshall 2012, p. 536). One may even hold that there are two notions of intrinsicness, one notion, according to which identity properties (including negations of identity properties) come out intrinsic, and a different notion, according to which identity properties are extrinsic (for a view along these lines, see Vallentyne 1997, p. 215). Clearly, our understanding of the natural language terms 'intrinsic' and 'extrinsic' is not specific enough to be a reliable guide when it comes to classifying such cases.

In this respect, the notions of intrinsicness and extrinsicness are different from everyday notions such as causation or knowledge. Philosophical accounts of notions such as causation or knowledge do not usually start with an explicit description of the intuitions they are supposed to capture. Our intuitive account of such notions is assumed to implicitly follow from the way they are used in everyday contexts. By contrast, almost all philosophical accounts of the intrinsic/extrinsic distinction start with an explicit non-formal characterization of the notion of intrinsicness. This characterization specifies the intuition which formal definitions of the intrinsic/extrinsic distinction are supposed to match. It should be noted, however, that the intuitive adequacy of a proposed definition of intrinsicness will always be relative to the intuitive characterization which it is supposed to capture. I will argue that according to one intuitive characterization predominant in the current literature, the intrinsic/extrinsic distinction is not hyperintensional. The characterization I have in mind is expressed in the following —remarkably similar—quotes:

> The intrinsic properties of something depend only on that thing; whereas the extrinsic properties of something may depend, wholly or partly, on something else. (Lewis 1983, p. 197)

> Intuitively, a property is intrinsic just in case a thing's having it ... depends only on what that thing is like ..., and not on what any wholly distinct object ... is like. (Vallentyne 1997, p. 209)

> An intrinsic property is a property that is *internal* in the sense that whether an object has it depends entirely upon what the object is like *in itself*. (Francescotti 1999, p. 590; author's emphasis)

> *You* know what an intrinsic property is: it's a property that a thing has (or lacks) regardless of what may be going on outside of itself. (Yablo 1999, p. 479; author's emphasis)

> The notion of an intrinsic property plainly has something to do with the notion of *independence:* an intrinsic property is one had in a way that is independent of how things are outside the individual in question. (Witmer, Butchard and Trogdon 2005, p. 327; authors' emphasis)

> Intuitively, an intrinsic property is a property that characterizes something as it is in itself. What intrinsic properties something has in no way depends on what other things exist ... or how it is related to them. (Skow 2007, p. 111)

Accordingly, the intrinsic/extrinsic distinction is characterized in terms of dependence claims: an intrinsic property is one whose instantiation by an individual entirely depends on what the individual itself is like, not on its environment. Slightly more formally put, a property P is classified as intrinsic, according to this intuitive criterion, iff for any individual x, whether or not x has P only depends on what x is like and not on the environment of x. Since a property is extrinsic iff it is not intrinsic, a property P is extrinsic iff there is an individual x, such that whether or not x has P not only depends on what x is like, but also on the environment of x. I will call this the *dependence characterization* of the intrinsic/extrinsic distinction.

The dependence characterization is closely related to the distinction between real or genuine change and mere Cambridge change. Real change is often characterized as change of intrinsic properties, whereas an object undergoes mere Cambridge change iff some of its extrinsic properties, but none of its intrinsic properties change (see Vallentyne 1997, p. 209; Denby 2006, p. 1). Accordingly, an individual x undergoes real change iff x loses or acquires some intrinsic property. Moreover, if a property P is such that for any individual x, the only way of changing whether x has or lacks P is to make x undergo real change, then P should be classified as intrinsic.[1] For if the only way of changing whether x has P is to make x undergo real change, i.e., to change what x is like in itself, then whether or not x has P only depends on what x is like in itself, and it follows directly from the dependence characterization that P is intrinsic. I will argue in the next section that if the dependence characterization and the related intuitions about real change and mere Cambridge change are taken at face value, arguments purported to show that the intrinsic/extrinsic distinction is hyperintensional are problematic.

3 Why the Intrinsic/Extrinsic Distinction is Not Hyperintensional

As pointed out above, the intrinsic/extrinsic distinction is hyperintensional iff there is a pair of cointensional properties P and Q, such that P is intrinsic, while Q is extrinsic. In this section, I discuss and reject four attempts to find such a pair of properties.

(a) Cointensional properties in a Lewisian framework

The most elaborate argument to the effect that the intrinsic/extrinsic distinction is hyperintensional has been given by Eddon (2011). Eddon argues that in a Lewisian framework, according to which individuals are worldbound, it follows immediately that the intrinsic/extrinsic distinction comes out hyperintensional. For it is plausible to assume that properties of the form *being a*, e.g., *being David Lewis*, are intrinsic: whether or not x has this property depends neither on what other individuals are like nor on x's relations to other individuals. Moreover, it is plausible to assume that disjunctions of such properties, i.e., properties of the form *being a_1 or being a_2 or being a_3 ...*, where a_1, a_2, a_3, ... are individuals, are intrinsic as well. The reasoning is precisely the same as for the property

---

[1] One might object that defining real change in terms of intrinsicness and intrinsicness in terms of real change is viciously circular. It should be noted, however, that the purpose of this section is not to provide non-circular definitions of these notions, but to describe intuitive platitudes underlying the debate on the intrinsic/extrinsic distinction. All I claim here is that the dependence characterization and its relation to the distinction between real change and mere Cambridge change belong to the standard inventory of intuitions that have to be taken into account when discussing features of the intrinsic/extrinsic distinction.

of *being David Lewis:* whether or not x has the property of *being a_1 or being a_2 or being a_3* ... only depends on whether x is identical to one of the individuals a_1, a_2, a_3, ..., not on how x is related to other individuals.

However, given that individuals are worldbound, each extrinsic property P is cointensional with some property of the form *being a_1 or being a_2 or being a_3* ..., where a_1, a_2, a_3, ... are all those and only those individuals which instantiate P in some possible world. It follows that each extrinsic property is cointensional with some intrinsic property, hence, that there are cointensional properties falling on different sides of the intrinsic/extrinsic divide (see Eddon 2011, p. 330).

This argument crucially hinges upon the assumption that individuals are worldbound. However, if this assumption is taken for granted, it can be argued along analogous lines that other metaphysical distinctions between properties are hyperintensional as well. To see this, suppose that the X/non-X distinction is a metaphysically relevant distinction between classes of first-order properties. Further suppose that properties of the form *being a_1 or being a_2 or being a_3* ... are always assigned to the category of X-properties. Then there will always be a non-X-property which is cointensional with some X-property, i.e., there will be cointensional properties falling on different sides of the X/non-X divide.

For instance, if properties of the form *being a_1 or being a_2 or being a_3* ... are categorical (as one may plausibly assume), each dispositional property will be cointensional with some categorical property. If properties of the form *being a_1 or being a_2 or being a_3* ... are classified as non-qualitative, each qualitative property will be cointensional with some non-qualitative property. If properties of the form *being a_1 or being a_2 or being a_3* ... are classified as non-relational, each relational property will be cointensional with some non-relational property. And so on.

In general, if individuals are worldbound, any metaphysically relevant distinction between first-order properties which assigns properties of the form *being a_1 or being a_2 or being a_3* ... to the same category will be hyperintensional. But then Eddon's line of reasoning seems to be a *reductio ad absurdum* of the assumption that individuals are worldbound, rather than a serious argument showing that the intrinsic/extrinsic distinction is hyperintensional. If the assumption of worldbound individuals leads to the conclusion that all metaphysically relevant X/non-X distinctions are hyperintensional, independently of how the distinctions are defined, and that it is not even possible to define a non-hyperintensional categorization of properties (unless we assume that properties of the form *being a_1 or being a_2 or being a_3* ... may belong to different categories), we had better give up on worldbound individuals.

(b) Cointensional properties in a non-Lewisian framework

However, arguments supposed to show that the intrinsic/extrinsic distinction is hyperintensional are not committed to assuming that individuals are worldbound. Eddon puts forward alternative examples which do not rely on this assumption. She points out that even if David Lewis exists at several possible worlds, the intrinsic property of *being David Lewis* is cointensional with some disjunctive property of the form *having such-and-such-features-and-so-and-so-relations to other things_(w_1) or having such-and-such-features-and-so-and-so-relations to other things_(w_2) or having such-and-such-features-and-so-and-so-relations to other things_(w_3) or* ..., i.e., a property providing a complex description of characteristics uniquely instantiated by David Lewis in those possible worlds in which he exists. According to Eddon, properties of this form are "uncontroversially extrinsic" (Eddon 2011, p. 334, fn. 31). But this implies that there are extrinsic properties which are cointensional with intrinsic properties.

Moreover, she argues that under the assumption of worldbound individuals, intrinsic properties of the form *being a* are cointensional with extrinsic properties of the form *being a and being located at w*, where *w* is the world at which *a* is located (see Eddon 2011, p. 330). This argument can plausibly be modified in order to cover cases where *a* is not worldbound: simply take the disjunction of all properties of the form *being a and being located at w_i*, where the w_i are all and only those possible worlds at which *a* is located. If complex properties of this form are considered extrinsic, this provides further evidence that there are cointensional properties falling on different sides of the intrinsic/extrinsic divide.

One way of avoiding this conclusion would be to reject the intuition that properties such as *being a* (of which *being David Lewis* is an example) are intrinsic. A motivation for doing so could be to save the duplication-based account of the intrinsic/extrinsic distinction à la Langton and Lewis from counterexamples. Since distinct individuals can be qualitative duplicates, qualitative duplicates can differ concerning properties of the form *being a*. Consequently, such properties have to be classified as extrinsic, according to this account.[2]

As pointed out above, intuitions concerning the intrinsic/extrinsic distinction may diverge. However, I agree with Eddon that identity properties of the form *being David Lewis* are intrinsic. One cannot plausibly maintain that whether

---

[2] It should be noted, however, that Langton and Lewis do not classify properties such as *being a* as extrinsic, but restrict their analysis to purely qualitative properties (see Langton and Lewis 1998, pp. 334–5; for a critical discussion of this strategy see Eddon 2011, pp. 319–22).

or not *x* is identical with David Lewis depends on what *other* individuals are like or on the relations in which *x* stands to other individuals. Thus, if the dependence intuition concerning the intrinsic/extrinsic distinction is taken seriously, properties of the form *being a* should be classified as intrinsic.

However, the claim that properties of the form *having such-and-such-features-and-so-and-so-relations to other things_(w_1)* or *having such-and-such-features-and-so-and-so-relations to other things_(w_2)* or *having such-and-such-features-and-so-and-so-relations to other things_(w_3)* or … and properties of the form *being a and located at w_1 or being a and located at w_2 or being a and located at w_3 or* … are extrinsic is less uncontroversial than Eddon assumes.

To see this, consider first properties of the form *being a and located at w_i*. According to Eddon, such properties are extrinsic (see Eddon 2011, p. 330). This is also in accordance with the dependence characterization. It is possible to change *x*'s having this property by moving *x* to a different possible world, i.e., by changing the environment of *x* without changing what *x* is like in itself. Therefore, whether or not *x* has such a property partially depends on the environment of *x*, i.e., on whether *x* inhabits w_i. An immediate objection to this line of reasoning could be that properties of the form *having P at w_i* (of which *being a and located at w_i* is an example) are a special case. One may plausibly assume that unless explicitly specified otherwise, 'has P' is elliptical for 'has P at the actual world', and that the property of *having P* is not just cointensional but identical with the property of *having P at the actual world*. But then classifying properties of the form *having P at w_i* as extrinsic *per se* has the absurd consequence that each property of the form *having P* is identical to some extrinsic property and has to be classified as extrinsic as well. This is reason enough to reject the claim that properties of the form *having P at w_i* should be classified as extrinsic.[3]

However, even if one rejects this line of reasoning and follows Eddon in classifying properties of the form *being a and located at w_i* as extrinsic, this does not imply that disjunctions of such properties, notably the disjunctive property of *being a and located at w_1 or being a and located at w_2 or being a and located at w_3 or* …, which is cointensional with *being a*, are extrinsic as well. By analogy, consider the disjunctive property of *being either cubical and accompanied or cubical and lonely*, i.e., (cubical & accompanied) ∨ (cubical & lonely). Many philosophers consider this a paradigmatic case of a property which is intrinsic despite containing extrinsic properties as logical parts. Since the conjunctive properties of *being cubical and accompanied* and *being cubical and lonely* are typically clas-

---

3 This has been pointed out to me by Robert Francescotti.

sified as extrinsic, this is moreover taken as evidence that the class of extrinsic properties is not closed under disjunction.[4]

That properties such as *being either cubical and accompanied or cubical and lonely*, which are logically equivalent to intrinsic properties, should be classified as intrinsic is well-supported by the dependence characterization of the intrinsic/extrinsic distinction. Whether or not x instantiates this property only depends on whether x is cubical. The only way of changing whether or not x instantiates this property consists in changing x's shape, i.e., making x undergo real change. According to the considerations at the end of section 2, this should be intuitive reason enough to conclude that x's having this property only depends on what x is like in itself, and not on what other individuals are like.

Now consider the property of *being either cubical and located at w or cubical and not located at w*, i.e. (*cubical & located at w*) ∨ (*cubical & not located at w*). Given that this property and the property of *being either cubical and accompanied or cubical and lonely* are structurally alike, it is plausible to argue that if the latter is intrinsic, so is the former. Again, this is in accordance with the dependence intuition: whether or not x instantiates *being either cubical and located at w or cubical and not located at w* only depends on whether x is cubical, not on the properties of other individuals or the relations in which x stands to them.

But then, analogous considerations hold for properties containing more disjuncts. If $w_1, w_2, w_3, ...$ are exactly those worlds in which a exists, then whether or not x has the complex property of *being a and located at w_1 or being a and located at w_2 or being a and located at w_3 or ...* does not depend on which world x inhabits, but only on whether x is identical to a. Thus, the only way in which x can lose this property is by ceasing to be identical with a, and the only way in which x can acquire this property is by becoming identical with a. But then, x can only lose or acquire this property by changing identity, i.e., by undergoing real change.

One might object that changing identity is a weird concept and that x can only lose or acquire the property of *being a* by ceasing to exist or coming into existence, while ceasing to exist or coming into existence is not a change concerning what x is like in itself, but does not count as undergoing change at all. However, then it could be argued along analogous lines that properties of the form *being a* should not be classified as intrinsic either and the whole argument to the effect that the *intrinsic* property of *being a* is cointensional with some extrinsic property would not get off the ground. Accordingly, the fact that *being a* and *being a and located at w_1 or being a and located at w_2 or being a and located*

---

[4] The most prominent proponent of this view is Lewis: see his 1983, pp. 199–200.

at w_3 or ... are cointensional does not imply that the intrinsic/extrinsic distinction is hyperintensional—the two properties are both intrinsic.

How about the property of *having such-and-such-features-and-so-and-so-relations to other things_(w_1)* or *having such-and-such-features-and-so-and-so-relations to other things_(w_2)* or *having such-and-such-features-and-so-and-so-relations to other things_(w_3)* or ... ? *Prima facie* this property is extrinsic: whether or not an individual has it depends on the world it inhabits and on the relations in which it stands to other individuals in this world. Yet again, this intuition is not supported by the dependence characterization of the intrinsic/extrinsic distinction. Given that this property is uniquely had by David Lewis, whether or not x instantiates it only depends on whether x is identical with David Lewis, not on which properties other individuals have or on the relations obtaining between x and other individuals. Again, the only way in which x may lose or acquire this property is by ceasing to exist or coming into existence, i.e., by undergoing real change. Thus, *being David Lewis* and *having such-and-such-features-and-so-and-so-relations to other things_(w_1)* or *having such-and-such-features-and-so-and-so-relations to other things_(w_2)* or *having such-and-such-features-and-so-and-so-relations to other things_(w_3)* or ... are both intrinsic, according to the dependence and change intuitions about intrinsicness specified in section 2. It follows that the examples provided by Eddon do not show that there are cointensional properties falling on different sides of the intrinsic/extrinsic divide and, hence, do not show that the intrinsic/extrinsic distinction is hyperintensional.

(c) Properties involving comparisons with concrete individuals

There is a rather strong intuition that properties involving comparisons with concrete individuals are extrinsic. The property of *having the same height as the Eiffel Tower*, for instance, qualifies as extrinsic according to the dependence characterization of extrinsicness. Whether or not a building has this property not only depends on its own height, but also on the height of the Eiffel Tower. Likewise, the property of *having the same height as the Eiffel Tower at the actual world* seems to be extrinsic. Whether or not a building has the same height as the Eiffel Tower at the actual world seems to partially depend on the height of the Eiffel Tower at the actual world. However, given that the Eiffel Tower is 324 m high at the actual world, the latter property is cointensional with the intrinsic property of *being*

324 m high.[5] It might, hence, be concluded that even if the examples discussed in the previous two sections fail, this example clearly shows that there are cointensional properties falling on different sides of the intrinsic/extrinsic divide.

Yet again, it is far from clear that *having the same height as the Eiffel Tower at the actual world* comes out extrinsic, according to the dependence criterion. To see this, consider the property of *having the same height as the Eiffel Tower* (without explicit reference to a particular possible world) for comparison. The claim that an individual x has this property is usually understood as the claim that x inhabits a certain possible world w and has the same height as the Eiffel Tower in w. Then *having the same height as the Eiffel Tower* is an extrinsic property. For instance, if the Eiffel Tower is 324 m high in w and x is also 324 m high in w, then x instantiates *having the same height as the Eiffel Tower* in w. However, if x is 324 m high and inhabits a different world w^* in which the Eiffel Tower happens to be 325 m high, x does not instantiate *having the same height as the Eiffel Tower* in w^*. Thus, whether x has the same height as the Eiffel Tower depends not only on x's height, i.e., on what x is like in itself, but also on whether x inhabits w or w^* (and on the height of the Eiffel Tower in w and w^*).

It should be noted, however, that the observation that *having the same height as the Eiffel Tower* is extrinsic does not show that the intrinsic/extrinsic distinction is hyperintensional. *Having the same height as the Eiffel Tower* is not cointensional with the intrinsic property of *being 324 m high*. As the previous argument shows, it is possible that there is a building which is 324 m high and, hence, has the latter property, while lacking the property of *having the same height as the Eiffel Tower*.

The property of *having the same height as the Eiffel Tower at the actual world* is different though. Any 324 m high individual x has this property independently of whether x inhabits a possible world in which the Eiffel Tower is 325 m, 500 m or 3 m high, even independently of whether x coexists with the Eiffel Tower at all. Accordingly, x can only lose or acquire the property of *having the same height as the Eiffel Tower at the actual world* if x changes in height, i.e., if x undergoes real change. But then once again, the dependence and change intuitions about intrinsicness specified in section 2 imply that *having the same height as the Eiffel Tower at the actual world* should be classified as intrinsic.

---

5 For ease of exposition, I ignore complications which arise from the fact that the Eiffel Tower may have different heights at different times. In order to accommodate changes over time, one could replace the property of *having the same height as the Eiffel Tower at the actual world* with the property of *having the same height as the Eiffel Tower at the actual world **at time t*** and re-run the argument given in this section without having to make any substantial changes.

It follows that the intuition that *having the same height as the Eiffel Tower* (without reference to a particular world) is extrinsic must not be conflated with the intuition that the property of *having the same height as the Eiffel Tower **at the actual world*** is extrinsic. The latter has to be classified as intrinsic, according to the dependence characterization, and the fact that *having the same height as the Eiffel Tower at the actual world* is cointensional with *being 324 m high* does not show that the intrinsic/extrinsic is hyperintensional.

It should be obvious that analogous considerations hold for other properties involving comparisons with concrete individuals. *Prima facie*, there is a strong intuition that properties such as *being an intrinsic qualitative duplicate of David Lewis* are extrinsic (see, e.g., Francescotti 1999, p. 593). If this property is taken to refer to the qualitative intrinsic properties had by David Lewis at the actual world, it is cointensional with the conjunction of the intrinsic qualitative properties which David Lewis has at the actual world. Since conjunctions of intrinsic qualitative properties are intrinsic, it follows that *being an intrinsic qualitative duplicate of David Lewis* is cointensional with an intrinsic property. However, it should now be clear why this does not show that the intrinsic/extrinsic distinction is hyperintensional. *Being an intrinsic qualitative duplicate of David Lewis* is instantiated by any *x* instantiating the combination of intrinsic qualitative properties which David Lewis actually has, independently of the world which *x* inhabits and of whether or not *x* coexists with David Lewis. No individual can lose or acquire this property without losing or acquiring some intrinsic qualitative property, i.e., without undergoing real change. Thus, first appearances to the contrary, this property comes out intrinsic according to the dependence characterization, and the example does not show that the intrinsic/extrinsic distinction is hyperintensional.

(d) Universally essential properties

A still different class of properties which calls the non-hyperintensionality of the intrinsic/extrinsic distinction into question is the class of necessary or universally essential properties, i.e., properties which are instantiated by every possible individual. It can be argued that properties such as *being self-identical* or *being either cubical or non-cubical* are intrinsic properties, whereas *being such that there possibly exists something greater in mass* or *being such that 2+3=5* are extrinsic. Nonetheless, all these properties are cointensional. Moreover, the intrinsic property of *being cubical* is cointensional with the conjunctive property of *being cubical and such that 2+3=5*, which is plausibly extrinsic if *being such that 2+3=5* is extrinsic.

Whether universally essential properties are intrinsic or extrinsic is one of the most controversial issues in the debate on the intrinsic/extrinsic distinction. A number of authors claim that *being such that 2+3=5* is an intrinsic property since changes in the environment of x cannot have any implications on x's having or lacking this property. In this sense, x's being such that 2+3=5 is independent of the environment of x. Of course, analogous considerations hold for other universally essential properties. This view is defended by Vallentyne:

> ...if there are universally essential properties, it is not a mistake to classify them as intrinsic ... For a universally essential property is such that either it, or its negation, is "metaphysically glued" to every single object. ... Consequently, in an important sense, there is no dependence (since there is no room for variation) on what the rest of the world is like. (1997, p. 217)

Francescotti embraces exactly the opposite view:

> ... when it comes to essential relations to distinct individuals, rather than saying there is no dependence on what the rest of the world is like because there is no room for variation, it seems more accurate to say that because there is no room for variation, there is a dependence on what the rest of the world is like, and a dependence of the strongest possible sort —i.e., a necessary dependence. (1999, p. 597; see also Francescotti 2012, p. 93)

Each of these views is endorsed by other authors as well. (For an argument supporting the claim that universally essential properties are intrinsic see, e.g., Langton and Lewis 1998, p. 340; for an argument supporting the opposite claim see, e.g., Eddon 2011, pp. 317–8.) Universally essential properties are a special case since it is unclear how the question of whether these properties are intrinsic or extrinsic should be settled (see also Hoffmann-Kolss 2010, p. 22). The quotes from Vallentyne and Francescotti show that even among proponents of the dependence characterization, there is no intuitive agreement on whether essential properties should be classified as intrinsic or as extrinsic.

What does this imply for the question of whether the intrinsic/extrinsic distinction is hyperintensional? Given that the classification of universally essential properties is so controversial, these properties do not represent a clear case of cointensional properties falling on different sides of the intrinsic/extrinsic divide. This does not mean that it is impossible to devise an intuitive characterization of the intrinsic/extrinsic distinction which would clearly imply that some universally essential properties are intrinsic, whereas others are extrinsic, and that, consequently, the intrinsic/extrinsic distinction is hyperintensional. However, this characterization would have to be different from the dependence characterization. As long as intrinsic and extrinsic properties are defined in terms of dependence claims, the hyperintensional character of the intrinsic/extrinsic distinction cannot be uncontroversially established by considering universally essential properties.

4 Concluding Remarks

Proponents of the view that the intrinsic/extrinsic distinction is hyperintensional typically adduce examples of cointensional properties falling on different sides of the intrinsic/extrinsic divide in order to support their claim. Which properties are to be classified as intrinsic or as extrinsic is decided on an intuitive basis. However, given that the distinction between intrinsic and extrinsic properties is not part of everyday discourse, there are no reliable pre-philosophical intuitions concerning which properties qualify as intrinsic and which properties qualify as extrinsic. Therefore, analyses of the intrinsic/extrinsic distinction always start with a more or less intuitive characterization of the distinction at issue. Whether a property is intrinsic or extrinsic then has to be decided in view of this intuitive characterization.

I have argued that if the intrinsic/extrinsic distinction is characterized in terms of the dependence and change intuitions described in section 2, then the distinction is not hyperintensional, contrary to what a number of authors assume.[6] This does not show that it is impossible to characterize the distinction in a different way which implies that there are cointensional properties falling on different sides of the intrinsic/extrinsic divide. One such possibility might be to characterize the intrinsic/extrinsic distinction in terms of *in-virtue-of* claims rather than dependence considerations. Such characterizations have been proposed by several authors:

> A thing has its intrinsic properties in virtue of the way that thing itself, and nothing else, is. (Lewis 1983, p. 197)

> We have some of our properties purely in virtue of the way we are. ... We have other properties in virtue of the way we interact with the world. ... The former are the intrinsic properties, the latter are the extrinsic properties. (Weatherson and Marshall 2013)

One disadvantage of characterizing the intrinsic/extrinsic distinction along these lines is that the *in-virtue-of* relation may be less well understood than the notions

---

[6] In particular, it should be noted that Eddon seems to acknowledge the dependence characterization as a suitable way of analyzing the intrinsic/extrinsic distinction (see Eddon 2011, p. 315, fn. 2).

of dependence and change.⁷ The challenge would, hence, consist in providing an illuminating definition of the *in-virtue-of* relation employed in this context, which would lead to the conclusion that the intrinsic/extrinsic distinction comes out hyperintensional. The previous argument does not show that such a definition cannot be given. All that has been shown is that the dependence characterization of the intrinsic/extrinsic distinction does not warrant the existence of cointensional properties falling on different sides of the intrinsic/extrinsic divide.

Therefore, the conclusion of my argument is modest. Currently, the standard intuitive characterization of the intrinsic/extrinsic distinction is based on dependence relations. I have argued that if we accept this standard characterization, arguments supposed to show the hyperintensional character of the intrinsic/extrinsic distinction are problematic. In order to show that the intrinsic/extrinsic distinction is hyperintensional, one would have to (1) provide an alternative intuitive characterization of the intrinsic/extrinsic distinction which is clearly distinct from the dependence characterization, (2) argue that this characterization captures the notions of intrinsicness and extrinsicness employed in philosophical contexts as well as the dependence characterization does, and (3) show that if properties are classified according to this alternative characterization, the intrinsic/extrinsic distinction is hyperintensional. Whether such a characterization can be found will have to be subject to further investigation.⁸

---

7 This holds in particular if your first language is not English. A non-representative survey among native German philosophers clearly showed that there is no unanimous way of translating the term 'in virtue of' into German, whereas this problem does not arise for the terms 'dependence' and 'change'.
8 I would like to thank Carrie Figdor and Robert Francescotti for helpful comments on earlier drafts of this paper.

References

Denby, D. A. (2006). "The Distinction between Intrinsic and Extrinsic Properties". *Mind* 115 (457): pp. 1–17.

Dunn, J. M. (1990). "Relevant Predication 2: Intrinsic Properties and Internal Relations". *Philosophical Studies* 60(3): pp. 177–206.

Eddon, M. (2011). "Intrinsicality and Hyperintensionality". *Philosophy and Phenomenological Research* 82(2): pp. 314–336.

Figdor, C. (2008). "Intrinsically/Extrinsically". *Journal of Philosophy* 105(11): pp. 691–718.

Francescotti, R. M. (1999). "How to Define Intrinsic Properties". *Noûs* 33(4): pp. 590–609.

Francescotti, R. M. (2012). "Understanding the Intrinsic/Extrinsic Distinction". *Metascience* 21 (1): pp. 91–94.

Hoffmann-Kolss, V. (2010). *The Metaphysics of Extrinsic Properties.* Frankfurt: ontos verlag.

Humberstone, I. L. (1996). "Intrinsic/Extrinsic". *Synthese* 108(2): pp. 205–267.

Langton, R. and Lewis, D. (1998). "Defining 'Intrinsic'". *Philosophy and Phenomenological Research* 58(2): pp. 333–345.

Lewis, D. (1983). "Extrinsic Properties". *Philosophical Studies* 44(2): pp. 197–200.

Marshall, D. (2012). "Analyses of Intrinsicality in Terms of Naturalness". *Philosophy Compass* 7(8): pp. 531–542.

Skow, B. (2007). "Are Shapes Intrinsic?". *Philosophical Studies* 133(1): pp. 111–130.

Vallentyne, P. (1997). "Intrinsic Properties Defined". *Philosophical Studies* 88(2): pp. 209–219.

Weatherson, B. and Marshall, D. (2013). "Intrinsic vs. Extrinsic Properties". In E. N. Zalta (ed.), *The Stanford Encyclopedia of Philosophy,* http://plato.stanford.edu/archives/spr2013/entries/intrinsic-extrinsic/.

Witmer, D. G., Butchard, W. and Trogdon, K. (2005). "Intrinsicality without Naturalness". *Philosophy and Phenomenological Research* 70(2): pp. 326–350.

Yablo, S. (1999). "Intrinsicness". *Philosophical Topics* 26(1–2): pp. 479–505.

Robert Francescotti
Intrinsic/Extrinsic: A Relational Account Defended

> A sentence or statement or proposition that ascribes intrinsic properties to something is entirely about that thing ... A thing has its intrinsic properties in virtue of the way that thing itself, and nothing else, is ... The intrinsic properties of something depend only on that thing ... If something has an intrinsic property, then so does any perfect duplicate of that thing ... (Lewis 1983a, p. 197)

I once offered a definition that was meant to capture the notion expressed by the intuitive descriptions in this quote from Lewis.[1] The basic idea is that F is an intrinsic property of an item x just in case x's having F consists entirely in x's having certain *internal* properties, where an internal property is one whose instantiation does not consist in one's relation to any distinct items (items other than oneself and one's proper parts). I still think that this relational analysis is largely correct, and here I wish to provide additional support for it and defend it against some objections that have been raised. In the process I aim to make the account somewhat more precise, especially by contrasting it with a *grounding* approach to defining the intrinsic/extrinsic distinction.

1 In Favor of a Hyperintensional Account

Consider those properties that must be exemplified by any item that exists. Following Weatherson and Marshall (2013), let's call them "indiscriminately necessary" properties. *Being self-identical* is an indiscriminately necessary property. Unlike the property of being identical with Dennett, being self-identical is a property that cannot go unexemplified by anything. In addition to being indiscriminately necessary, the property of being self-identical also seems to be intrinsic; having this property does not seem to be a matter of how an item relates to anything distinct from itself. While this one seems intrinsic, some indiscriminately necessary properties (INPs) appear to be extrinsic. Assuming that numbers exist and exist necessarily, the property of *coexisting with the number 9* is an INP. Given realism about numbers, our coexisting with 9 consists in our relation to something distinct from ourselves, which seems to make it an extrinsic feature of you and me.

---

[1] See Francescotti (1999).

It is well-known that some popular definitions of intrinsicality have the consequence that all INPs are intrinsic. These include the duplication accounts of Lewis (in 1983b and 1986[2]) and Langton and Lewis (1998).[3] Since the INPs of any item are shared by each of its duplicates, these accounts entail that all INPs are intrinsic. Vallentyne's contraction view also entails that all INPs are intrinsic, since removing from x's world as much as possible while x remains leaves x with all of its INPs intact.[4] Since coexisting with 9 (or any other number) certainly seems to be an extrinsic feature of each of us, the consequence that all INPs are intrinsic is a count against these analyses.

However, some have argued that no INPs' being extrinsic is not as implausible as it might seem. Sider mentions that an INP of some object "does not depend in any natural sense on what other objects are like, since this property is necessarily had by every object" (1996, p. 11). Consider, for example, *being such that either Socrates is wise or not wise*. Despite the reference to Socrates, Sider notes that having this property "doesn't imply any dependence on Socrates, since the property is, of necessity, universally instantiated" (p. 11). Hoffmann-Kolss (2010) mentions that she will exclude INPs from the scope of her discussion, citing the property of *being such that 2 + 3 = 5* and claiming that "whether or not an individual x has a non-contingent property of this kind neither depends on what x is like, nor on the environment of x, but rather on the logical structure of the *property itself*" (p. 22). Vallentyne focuses on arguably essential properties of the form *having thus-and-such origin* (e.g., some specific date or zygote), and contends that it is not so implausible to regard these properties as intrinsic since they are "metaphysically glued" to each of their bearers, and therefore, "in an important sense, there is no dependence since there is no room for variation on what the rest of the world is like" (1997, p. 217). And Harris defends the view that all INPs are intrinsic by appealing to the principle that "[i]f *being a concrete object* is intrinsic, so, too, is every property that necessarily follows from *being a concrete object*" (2010, p. 472).

---

[2] See especially 1983b, pp. 355–8 and 1986, pp. 61–3.
[3] The account of Langton and Lewis is based on the notion of a property being *independent of accompaniment* (independent of accompaniment by distinct concrete objects). What they call "basic intrinsic" properties as those that are independent of accompaniment, not disjunctive properties, and not negations of disjunctive properties. They define objects as duplicates just in case they share the same basic intrinsic properties, and then define an intrinsic property as one that can never differ between duplicates.
[4] Vallentyne proposes that a property P is intrinsic just in case for any world w, object x, and time t, if x is P in w at t, then x is P at t in each x-t contraction of w, and likewise for the negation of P (i.e., if x is not-P in w at t, it is not-P at each x-t contraction of w).

These defenses are not entirely convincing. Recall *being such that either Socrates is wise or not wise*. It seems that this property *does* depend on the existence of Socrates, for if Socrates did not exist, then neither disjunct would be true, in which case, the disjunction itself would not be true. Our *being such that 2 + 3 = 5* also depends on the way the rest of the world is, assuming that numbers exist. Note, also, that these properties qualify as *mere Cambridge* properties of each of us,[5] and therefore seem to count as extrinsic in the strongest possible sense. Regarding Vallentyne's point that having a particular origin is metaphysically glued to each of us: rather than proving intrinsicality, the metaphysical glue means that we are essentially related to distinct objects, which suggests not that these features are intrinsic, but rather that some of our essential features are extrinsic. And rather than saying that there is no dependence on what the rest of the world is like since there is no room for variation, it seems more appropriate to say that since there is no room for variation, there is extreme dependence on what the rest of the world is like.[6] Also, it's not clear why we should agree with Harris that if being a concrete object is intrinsic, then so is every property that necessarily follows from being a concrete object. Suppose that F is an intrinsic feature of x and that having F necessitates having G. Should we then expect that G is an intrinsic feature of x? We should—only if x's exemplifying G has solely to do with x's exemplifying F. This is not the case when G is *being accompanied by 9* and F is *being a concrete object*. In this case, the former does not have solely to do with the latter since the truth of the former depends on the existence of numbers. In fact, the former seems to have little if anything to do with latter, since for any object x, if numbers exist, then x is accompanied by 9 whether or not x is concrete.

As Eddon (2011) reports, "our intuitions about intrinsicality are fine-grained," such that "cointensive properties may intuitively diverge with respect to their intrinsicality" (p. 318). That is, our intuitions about intrinsicality seem to entail that

(HI)   there are necessarily coextensive properties, F and G, such that F is intrinsic and G is extrinsic

(where 'HI' stands for 'hyperintensional'). If a property F of x is had by all possible duplicates of x, then any property necessarily coextensive with F is had by all possible duplicates of x. So duplication accounts entail that all INPs are the same in terms of intrinsically (all intrinsic); they therefore entail that HI is false.

---

5 I say "each of us" to exclude Socrates himself, and the numbers 2, 3 and 5.
6 I make this point in my 1999, p. 597.

Since our intuitions about intrinsicality are hyperintensional, as Eddon shows, duplication accounts yield counter-intuitive results in the case of certain INPs.

In addition to HI, there is the related hyperintensionality thesis:

(HI_L) there are necessarily coextensive properties, F and G, such that possibly, there are individuals x and y, and x has F intrinsically while y has G extrinsically.

While HI mentions *properties* being intrinsic or extrinsic, HI_L refers to *individuals having properties* intrinsically or extrinsically. This distinction between "global" and "local" intrinsicality (as Humberstone calls it[7]) is well-known. Dunn (1990) mentions the difference between "*being an intrinsic property* (as a kind), and *intrinsically being a property of a given individual* (as a specific happening)." For example, "if an individual *a* intrinsically has the property of being square (*a* is square by virtue of itself alone), then *a* also intrinsically has the property of being square-or-accompanied (*a* is square-or-accompanied by virtue of itself alone)" (p. 183); however, being square-or-accompanied is had extrinsically by an accompanied circular object. So, we see, the same property can be had intrinsicality by one item and extrinsically by another. Humberstone (1996, p. 228) gives the example of *being either made of tin or adjacent to something made of tin*, a property which is exemplified intrinsically by tin objects but extrinsically by nearby tinless items.

Some INPs illustrate HI_L. Being accompanied by the number 9 is an extrinsic property of each of us, but it seems to be intrinsic to the number 9 itself. The non-INPs mentioned by Dunn and Humberstone also qualify as instances of HI_L. Since any property is necessarily coextensive with itself, any time a property can be instantiated both intrinsically and extrinsically, there is an F that can be instantiated intrinsically and a necessarily coextensive G (which is F) that can be instantiated extrinsically. So the mixed-cases mentioned in the previous paragraph seem to establish the truth of HI_L. And as Figdor (2008) reveals, these mixed cases include more than just philosophers' designer properties. Many less contrived properties can be used to support HI_L. Figdor has us consider the property of being witty, which Falstaff has in and of himself, and which Prince Hal has extrinsically since he is witty only in the presence of other witty people. She also mentions, among other examples, the property of being valuable, which might be exemplified by some things in virtue of what they are like in themselves, and by other things in virtue of their relational features (e.g., their consequences). In fact, if one item can be valuable intrinsically

---

[7] See Humberstone (1996, pp. 227–8).

while another item is valuable extrinsically, then as Figdor (2014)[8] describes, it is also possible that the *same item* has value intrinsically (due to its internal properties) and extrinsically (e. g., because it is valued by others) at the very *same time*. This is an uncontrived, ultra-mixed case—the same property had by the same individual at the same time both intrinsically and extrinsically.[9] In his recent defense of the hyperintensionality of intrinsicality, Bader (2013) also mentions cases in which a property is possessed by an individual both intrinsically and extrinsically.[10]

Given the plausibility of HI and HI_L, one might like to know which account of intrinsicality best accommodates both.[11] One natural way to honor both is with an appeal to the notion of *grounding*. The grounding approach is discussed in the following sections, along with the non-grounding view that I favor.

2 The Grounding Approach

Talk of grounding is meant to capture the intuitive idea of one fact *consisting in* or holding *in virtue of* another fact. Examples of grounding talk include the claim that moral facts obtain in virtue of non-moral facts, that facts about mentality consist in nothing more than physical facts, and that dispositional facts are grounded in categorical properties.[12]

---

[8] See Figdor's paper, "What's the Value of an Intrinsic Property?", which she wrote for this collection.
[9] The possibility of these ultra-mixed cases is suggested by Figdor's 2008 discussion. Talk of having properties intrinsically, she claims, indicates independence from contextually relevant counterfactual circumstances, and which counterfactual circumstances are relevant and when depends on our explanatory purposes, as she describes in detail. If this explanatory account is correct, then there is reason to suspect that depending on our explanatory purposes, property F might count as one that x has intrinsically at t or as one that x has extrinsically at t.
[10] The mixed cases make it tempting to regard the local notion of intrinsicality as more fundamental than the global notion, as Figdor (2008, 2014) and Bader (2013) make clear. Although see Witmer (2014), in this anthology, for an intriguing defense of the claim that the global notion is in fact the more basic.
[11] One might argue that despite the evidence to the contrary (offered by Eddon, Figdor, and Bader), a hyperintensional approach should actually be rejected. See Hoffmann-Kolss' "Is the Intrinsic/Extrinsic Distinction Hyperintensional?," in this collection, for a strong defense of the view that the notion of intrinsicality is *not* hyperintensional. I do not deny that a decent case can be made against the hyperintensionality claim. However, what I wish to focus on here is what definition of 'intrinsic' we should accept assuming that we do wish to honor HI and HI_L.
[12] For a list that includes these and other examples of grounding talk, see Correia (2010, p. 251).

Many who defend the notion of grounding as a valuable philosophical concept have tried to explain what they consider some of its most distinctive logical features in an effort to make the notion less than unacceptably obscure.[13] One feature often considered crucial to grounding is *necessitation*; it is claimed that one fact is grounded in another only if the latter necessitates the former. In general, "If [p] is grounded in [q], then q entails p," and when grounding is understood as a type of metaphysical dependence, the "facts that ground [p] together ensure as a matter of metaphysical necessity that [p] obtains" (Rosen 2010, p. 118). Another logical feature commonly cited in discussions of grounding is *asymmetry*. It is thought that if one set of facts is grounded in another, then the latter is not grounded in the former. The appeal to asymmetry honors the idea that the ground is more fundamental than the facts that are grounded. Because the ground is thought of as more fundamental, *irreflexivity* has also been considered definitive of grounding since no fact can be more fundamental than itself. *Transitivity* is also mentioned in discussions of grounding since it is tempting to think that if (for example) a moral fact is grounded in a behavioral fact and the behavioral fact is grounded in a microphysical fact, then the moral fact is grounded in the microphysical fact.[14]

To illustrate the potential usefulness of the notion of grounding, Rosen gives examples of how the notion might help solve various metaphysical issues, including its potential use in analyzing intrinsicality. On "one intuitive gloss," Rosen notes, "a property F is intrinsic iff whether or not X is F depends entirely on how things stand with X and its parts, and not on X's relations to things distinct from X" (2010, p. 112). This intuitive characterization of intrinsicality, Rosen claims, can be made explicit as follows:

> F is an intrinsic property iff, as a matter of necessity, for all x:
> If x is F in virtue of ϕ(y)—where ϕ(y) is a fact containing y as a constituent—then y is part of x; and
> If x is not-F in virtue of ϕ(y), then y is part of x. (p. 112)

Like grounding accounts generally, this one is hyperintensional.[15] Being accompanied by the number 9 is grounded in the fact that 9 exists, and this fact has the number 9 as a constituent, a constituent that obviously is not a part of you or me. So being accompanied by 9 is plausibly classified as one of our extrinsic

---

[13] Rosen (2010) provides a helpful description of the logical and structural features characteristic of grounding.
[14] Although, Schaffer (2012) offers counter-examples to the transitivity of grounding.
[15] I say "like grounding accounts generally" since the notion of grounding itself is hyperintensional.

properties. On the other hand, being self-identical is classified as intrinsic, since for any x, x's being self-identical is grounded in the fact that x = x, and x trivially is a part of x. Both features are INPs, but on Rosen's account only one of them is intrinsic.

When applied locally, Rosen's account also correctly classifies non-INP mixed cases. *Being accompanied by Fido* is an extrinsic property of us but it's exemplified intrinsically by Fido since our being accompanied by Fido has a constituent that is distinct from us, but Fido's being accompanied by Fido does not have any constituent distinct from Fido. *Being either made of tin or adjacent to something made of tin* is an intrinsic feature of tin object x on the local version of Rosen's account since x has this property in virtue of the fact that it is made of tin and this fact does not contain any object that is not part of x. But any tinless object that has the disjunctive property has it extrinsically since it has it in virtue of the fact that it is adjacent to something made of tin, a fact which contains something that is not part of the tinless object.

By honoring HI and HI_L, Rosen's definition yields the intuitively correct result in these cases and each of the others mentioned earlier. Another version of the grounding approach that provides the same plausible results is the grounding definition Witmer develops in "A Simple Theory of Intrinsicality," written for this collection. On this view, F is an intrinsic property of x just in case its presence or absence is grounded only in facts that are "parts" of x (where the notion of x's spatial parts is replaced by Witmer with the notion of that on which x is *ontologically dependent*).[16]

---

[16] Witmer, Butchard, and Trogdon (2005) offer a grounding account that retains the idea of Langton and Lewis that intrinsic properties are *independent of accompaniment*. They propose: "Property P is intrinsic iff, for any possible individual x, if x has P, x has P in an intrinsic fashion," where "x has P in an intrinsic fashion iff (i) P is independent of accompaniment and (ii) for any property Q, if x has P in virtue of having Q, Q is also independent of accompaniment" (p. 333). With the phrase 'in virtue of' they seem to be utilizing the notion of grounding, for they claim that with their account "we are directed to look at the bottom-level properties that *ground* the others" (p. 340; their emphasis). And with the appeal to grounding, their definition improves on the Langton-Lewis account at least by allowing that in some cases "two properties which are necessarily coextensive can yet differ in whether they are intrinsic" (p. 334). However, although the account is hyperintensional, by requiring independence from accompaniment as a necessary condition for intrinsicality, the account is arguably not hyperintensional enough, and in particular, it does not classify *any* INP as intrinsic. (They defend this consequence by noting that while an INP does not depend on anything outside the individual, "it doesn't depend on anything *inside* the individual either—it is simply independent of everything" (p. 348). However, for any x, *being self-identical* does seem to depend, and depend entirely, on x itself.)

However, there are other ways to accommodate HI and HI_L, ways that do not rely on the notion of grounding. Late in the next section, I mention one such way.

3 A Relational Approach

On a relational account of the intrinsic/extrinsic distinction,

(R) whether F is extrinsic or intrinsic (or had extrinsically or intrinsically) is a matter of whether having F depends on relations to distinct items.[17]

One possible way to understand the phrase 'depends on' in R is in terms of the necessary biconditional. On this view F is extrinsic (or had extrinsically) just in case there is a relation such that, *necessarily*, an object has F *if and only if* it bears that relation to a distinct thing, and otherwise F is intrinsic (had intrinsically). However, biconditionals, even necessary biconditionals, are not hyperintensional. So if we want a relational account that's compatible with HI and HI_L, we need to rely on something other than biconditionality.[18]

We might understand the dependence relation mentioned in R in terms of grounding, and then we would have a grounding account that is also relational. It seems that Rosen's proposal is exactly of this sort; recall his intuitive characterization—"a property F is intrinsic iff whether or not X is F depends entirely on how things stand with X and its parts, and not on X's relations to things distinct from X" (2010, p. 112). A *grounding-relational* account of the intrinsic/extrinsic distinction is any account that takes the form:

(R_G) whether F is extrinsic or intrinsic (or had extrinsically or intrinsically) is a matter of whether having F is grounded in relations to distinct items.[19]

Instead of relying on the notion of grounding, one can honor HI and HI_L by appealing to *identity*, with a relational view of the form:

---

[17] Again, y is *distinct* from x iff y is not identical with x or any of x's proper parts.
[18] Hoffmann-Kolss' (2010) relational account, like my own, is based on the idea that one's intrinsic properties are those that do not consist in one's relations to distinct objects. But by construing the notion of *consisting in* at work here in terms of necessary biconditionals, her account entails that (HI) and (HI_L) are false.
[19] A grounding approach does not need to rely on the notion of relationality; e.g., the grounding account of Witmer, Butchard, and Trogdon (2005) relies, instead, on the notion of being independent of accompaniment.

(R₁)   whether F is extrinsic or intrinsic (or had extrinsically or intrinsically) is a matter of whether having F *is* (*identical with, the very same as*) being suitably related to distinct items.

My 1999 account is an instance of R. The proposal was that

(R*)   F is an intrinsic property of item x =$_{df}$ x has F, and there are internal properties I₁,..., Iₙ had by x, such that x's having F consists in x's having I₁,..., Iₙ,

where an *internal* property is one that is *not d-relational*, and where d-relations are relations one bears to distinct items.[20] The "consists in" relation mentioned in R* could be understood in terms of grounding, and in that case the definition would be an instance of R$_G$. But I chose, instead, to view the "consists in" relation, in this context, as *identity*. I claimed that for the purpose of R*, "the event or state, x's having F, consists in the event or state, x's having G, just in case *x's having F is the very same event or state as x's having G*" (p. 599). The result is

(R₁*)   F is an intrinsic property of item x =$_{df}$ x has F, and there are internal (non-d-relational) properties I₁,..., Iₙ had by x, such that x's having F *is the same as* x's having I₁,..., Iₙ.[21]

According to R₁*, being self-identical is an intrinsic property of x since there is an internal, non-d-relational property, I, where I is *being identical with x* and x's being self-identical is same event or state as x's being identical with x. The necessarily coextensive property, *being accompanied by the number 9*, is classified as an extrinsic property of you and me since our having this property is nothing more or less than our bearing the right relation (the coexisting relation)

---

[20] Borrowing from Khamara's (1988) characterization of different types of relational properties, I mentioned different types of d-relational properties. F is a positive, existential, impure d-relational property of an item x just in case there is a relation R, and an item y, such that x's having F consists in x's bearing R to y, and y is distinct from x. F is a positive, existential, pure d-relational property of x just in case there is a relation R, and a class of items C, such that x's having F consists in there being some member of C to which x bears R, and at least one member of C to which x bears R is distinct from x. And as Humberstone reminds us (1996, p. 212), an existential relational property has a universal counterpart. A positive universal d-relational property of x is such that there is a relation R, and a class of items C, such that x's having F consists in x's bearing R to every member of C, and there is a possible member of C that is distinct from x. There are also the negative counterparts of each of these positive d-relational properties. And variations on any of these can be used to describe other types of d-relationality; e.g., with relations that are more than two-place.

[21] The identity construal is also meant to apply to the phrase 'consists in' that figures in the descriptions of the various d-relational properties.

to a distinct item (the number 9). Thus, with R_I^* we allow the truth of HI. R_I^* also allows mixed cases where the same property can be had intrinsically and also extrinsically, which entails HI_L. *Being either square or accompanied* is an intrinsic feature of the lonely square, according to R_I^*, because the lonely square's having the disjunctive property is nothing other than its being square, which is an internal (non-d-relational) property. However, the accompanied circle has the property extrinsically since its being *square or accompanied* is simply its being accompanied, which is d-relational. The ultra-mixed cases described by Figdor (2008, 2014) are also allowed by R_I^*. It might be that at the very same time x has value intrinsically and also extrinsically—where there is some internal property I and some d-relational property D, such that x's intrinsic instantiation of value is its having I, and x's extrinsic instantiation of value is its having D.

R_I^* is compatible with HI and HI_L. But so is a grounding approach (including grounding views of the relational variety, R_G). So for those who wish to honor HI and HI_L, the question is: which is preferable—R_I^* or an account of intrinsicality that appeals to grounding? Maybe the correct answer is "neither": maybe some altogether different approach is the best way to hyperintensionally define the intrinsic/extrinsic distinction. However, here I focus on the choice between R_I^* and a grounding account.

4 Grounding or Identity?

Recall Rosen's proposal that F is an intrinsic property just in case, necessarily, for any x, (i) if x is F in virtue of $\phi(y)$, then y is part of x; and (ii) if x is not-F in virtue of $\phi(y)$, then y is part of x. In his discussion of this view, Marshall (2013, sec. 2) mentions a worry about fundamental properties. Given that no fact can ground itself, if a fact is fundamental, then it is not grounded. By the phrase, 'in virtue of', Rosen has the grounding relation in mind. So for any x and F such that x's having F is a fundamental fact and x's lacking F is also fundamental, the two conditionals, (i) and (ii), in Rosen's definition are vacuously true. Thus, on Rosen's account, any property whose presence or absence is a fundamental fact is intrinsic. However, we might wish to allow extrinsic properties whose presence or absence is fundamental; at least, a definition of 'intrinsic' should not rule out this possibility.

We can avoid the result that all properties whose presence or absence is fundamental are intrinsic properties by adding, prior to (i) and (ii), the condition that if x is F (or not-F), then x's being F (or not-F) is grounded, i.e., that there is some fact $\phi(y)$ in virtue of which x is F (or not-F). Of course, then we get the even more implausible result that whenever either x is F or x is not-F is fundamental, F is not an intrinsic property. A major worry, then, for grounding accounts is how to express the grounding intuition in a way that yields plausible results in the case of fundamental facts.[22]

R_I^*, on the other hand, has no problem correctly classifying fundamental facts about the presence or absence of intrinsic properties. Suppose that x contains y as a proper part, and that this is a wholly fundamental fact, not grounded in anything more basic. Then according to R_I^* *containing y as a proper part* is an intrinsic feature of x, despite its fundamentality, since *containing y as a proper part* is an internal (non-d-relational) feature of x. R_I^* also allows that some fundamental facts are facts about the presence or absence of extrinsic properties. Suppose it is a primitive fact that atom x is to the left of atom y. R^*_1 correctly classifies *being to the left of y* as extrinsic despite its fundamentality since x's having this property is its bearing the *left of* relation to the distinct object y.

Marshall mentions that a grounding theorist might try to avoid the result that all fundamental properties are intrinsic with the following revision of Rosen's proposal:

> F is an intrinsic property just in case, necessarily, for any x, (i) if x is F in virtue of, *or is identical with*, $\phi(y)$, then y is part of x; and (ii) if x is not-F in virtue of, *or is identical with*, $\phi(y)$, then y is part of x.[23]

With this account, fundamental facts of the form 'x is F' and 'x is not-F' are not prevented from being extrinsic. Suppose that for some x, x's being F (not-F) is identical with $\phi(y)$. If y is distinct from x, then F (not-F) is extrinsic, according to G*, even if x's being F (not-F) is fundamental and therefore ungrounded.

Yet, Marshall (2013, sec. 3) notes, there is another major objection to a grounding analysis of intrinsicality, one which threatens the revision as well as Rosen's original. It seems possible for x's having some intrinsic property to be grounded in facts about items that are not parts of x. Marshall has us consider the singleton set, {Obama}. The fact that {Obama} exists is grounded in the fact that Obama exists. But Obama himself is not literally a *part* of any set since sets are abstract objects. It would seem to follow that {Obama}'s existence is ground-

---

[22] The account of Witmer, Trogdon, and Butchard (2005) allows that some fundamental properties are intrinsic and some are not. Yet, despite their appeal to grounding, the independence from accompaniment component gives the implausible result that all INPs are extrinsic (as mentioned in note 16).

[23] This is my phrasing, not Marshall's. Incidently, Marshall points out that this account like the original can be reformulated so as not to presuppose a Russellian view of facts (a view on which facts are structured entities with individuals and properties as constituents). As Marshall notes, the account can be rephrased to mention facts *concerning* rather than *containing* an individual y.

ed in a fact concerning that which is not a part of {Obama}. Marshall concludes that on Rosen's account, existing ends up being an extrinsic property of {Obama}, clearly an undesirable result since existence would seem to be intrinsic to all things that exist.

One might argue that this case is not a threat to Rosen's proposal or the revised version since the notion of parthood utilized in a definition of intrinsicality can be, and should be, liberal enough to include more than just spatial parts. Temporal segments should also be included so that, for example, the property of containing many minutes may be considered an intrinsic property of an hour; and the temporal parts that perdurantists speak of certainly count as genuine parts, assuming they exist. Set membership should arguably also be considered a type of parthood. And if so, then the existence of {Obama} being grounded in the existence of Obama need not be considered a threat.[24]

Still, it seems there are possible cases in which facts about the intrinsic properties of an individual are grounded in facts about things that are not among what plausibly count as it *parts*. One might believe, for example, that the totality of contingent beings depends for its existence on some necessary being, where the dependence is such that the existence of the latter grounds the existence of the former. While this belief may be false, it is a belief one can consistently endorse while also holding that contingent beings have intrinsic properties. Suppose, for example, that an object x is comprised of gold. Being comprised of gold would seem to be one of x's intrinsic properties even if x would not have been made of gold and would not have even existed if not for the presence of some distinct being. If one were to acquire the belief that there is a supreme being on which all contingencies ultimately depend (including the existence of the gold object and its having the properties it has), it seems one wouldn't thereby need to deny that some of its properties are intrinsic. So it seems possible for the instantiation of an intrinsic property to depend in some intimate way, and a way that might be labeled "grounding," on facts about distinct items. And if so, then a definition of intrinsicality should not prevent intrinsic properties from ultimately being grounded in facts about distinct items.[25]

---

24 Marshall mentions that one can employ a broadened notion of a *part* (the notion of a *"generalised part"*), which includes the membership relation. However, he worries that for the definition to remain compatible with a variety of different metaphysical theories, there is no telling how much the notion of a generalized part will need to include, making a satisfactory version of the grounding account difficult if not impossible to achieve.

25 Trogdon (2009) illustrates this point with the help of *priority monism*. On this view, facts about the world as a whole ground the facts about the world's proper parts. While many may find this view implausible, the worry remains: if priority monism were true, then on a grounding

Perhaps a plausible grounding analysis can be developed so as to allow properties to be intrinsic despite their grounding in facts about distinct items; although, this remains to be seen. Note, however, that R_I^* easily allows intrinsic properties to depend in some intimate way, and a way that might be called "grounding," on relations to distinct items. According to R_I^*, existing is an intrinsic property of singleton {Obama} simply because there is an internal (non-d-relational) property I, where I is the property of existing, and {Obama}'s existing is the very same as {Obama}'s having I. Granted, {Obama}'s existing depends in some significant sense on Obama existing, but {Obama}'s existing is not the same state of affairs as Obama's existing. {Obama}'s existing is its possession of an internal property, not its possession of the apparently d-relational property of being such that Obama exists. So, with R_I^*, even assuming that Obama is not considered *part* of {Obama}, existing counts as an intrinsic property of {Obama}. Or suppose there is a god, and this god is the ultimate source of all contingencies—that on which all contingencies depend. Being comprised of gold would still be an intrinsic feature of object x, according to R_I^*, since x's having this property is its having the internal property of containing large amounts of Au. Whether there is a distinct being on which x's containing large amounts of Au depends does not change the fact that being comprised of gold (containing large amounts of Au) is not itself a d-relational feature. It seems, then, that R_I^* can allow that F is intrinsic to x even if x's being F is grounded in facts about how x relates to distinct things.

There is another reason to prefer R_I^* to a grounding view. The notion of an intrinsic property does not itself imply anything about whether the intuitive notion of grounding, as described in the literature, is a relation that actually ob-

---

account of intrinsicality, none of the properties of any proper parts of the world would be intrinsic, for each property would be instantiated by the parts in virtue of their relation to the whole world.

To make priority monism consistent with a grounding view, Trogdon (2009) modifies the original Witmer, Butchard and Trogdon (2005) account by distinguishing between *intra-* and *inter-*level grounding (being instantiated *intra-virtue-of* vs. *inter-virtue-of*). He proposes that "x has P in an intrinsic fashion just in case (i) P is independent of accompaniment; and (ii) for any individual y and property Q, if x has P intra-virtue-of y's having Q, then Q is either fundamental or independent of accompaniment" (2009, p. 143). Since properties of the proper parts of the world are had *inter*-virtue-of properties of the whole, they are not precluded from being intrinsic with this new view. There is, however, the worry that by specifying only intra-level grounding in condition (ii), the revised definition gives the result that all properties that are *inter*-level grounded are classified as intrinsic so long as they are independent of accompaniment. Skiles (2009) describes an extrinsic property that seems to satisfy (i) and (ii) by being independent of accompaniment and grounded in relations that cross mereological levels. However, see Trogdon's (2010) reply to Skiles' objection.

tains. It is a matter of controversy whether talk of grounding should be embraced or viewed with suspicion, and it is a matter of controversy even for those who take the intrinsic/extrinsic distinction seriously. It seems, then, that a definition of intrinsicality should remain neutral on whether grounding is actually a real phenomenon. To its credit, R_I^* does remain neutral on this issue. R_I^* tells us that what makes F an intrinsic property of x is that there is an internal, non-d-relational property (or set of such properties) I, such that x's having F is x's having I. That there is this identity leaves it completely open whether x's having F, i.e., x's having I, is itself grounded in some more fundamental fact, or whether talk of grounding ever describes anything that actually obtains.

So there are some reasons to prefer R_I^* to a grounding account. I wish to provide further support for R_I^* by answering some objections to the definition that have been raised.

5 Objections to R_I^*

a. Weatherson and Marshall (2013, sec. 2.1) present a general worry for relational accounts of intrinsicality, a worry that applies to R_I^* in particular. They mention the property, *not being within a mile of a rhododendron*, and note that a non-rhododendron all alone in the world can have this property without its bearing a relation to any non-part. Since the lonely non-rhododendron's having this property does not consist in any relation to a non-part, the worry is that a relational account yields the implausible result that the lonely non-rhododendron has the property intrinsically.

On some possible relational accounts, for F to be an extrinsic feature of x, there must exist a distinct item y such that x's having F consists in x's bearing the right relation or relations to y. But a relational account need not, and should not, have this requirement. A property that consists in a relation one bears to a distinct item qualifies as extrinsic since it is a property that one has in virtue of what the rest of the world is like. The negation of such a property requires that there is no distinct item to which one is related in that way. So the negation is also a matter of what the rest of the world is like, and therefore should also be considered extrinsic. It seems, then, that what a relational account should entail is that if F is an extrinsic feature of x, then x's having F consists in *either* x's bearing a certain relation to a distinct thing *or* x's not bearing that relation to a distinct thing. And a relational account will entail this disjunction so long as the relations to distinct items that make for extrinsicality are taken to include *negative* as well as positive d-relations. Being within a mile of a rhododendron is a positive (existential, pure) d-relational property of x; to be within a mile of a rhododendron is for there to be a member of the class of rhododendrons which is distinct from x and to which x bears the *within a mile of* relation. The negation of this positive d-relational property is *not being within a mile of a rhododendron*, and x's having this negative d-relational property consists in there being *no member of the class of rhododendrons* to which x bears the *within a mile of* relation. The lonely non-rhododendron has this negative d-relational property. So by including negative d-relations in the class of d-relations that yield extrinsicality, proponents of a relational account can ensure that *not being within a mile of a rhododendron* counts as an extrinsic feature of the lonely non-rhododendron.

b. Weatherson and Marshall (2013, sec. 3.5) claim that my definition is incompatible with certain accounts of property-identity. Consider, for example, a coarse-grained view according to which, (i) all necessarily co-extensive properties are identical. Each property is necessarily co-extensive with a d-relational property; e.g., any property F is necessarily co-extensive with being *either (F and lonely) or (F and accompanied)*. So given (i), each property is identical with a d-relational property. Add R_I^* and we get the result that all properties are had extrinsically. But, surely, a definition of 'intrinsic' should not itself prevent properties being had intrinsically. So the objection is: if R_I^* is to allow that some properties are sometimes had intrinsically, as it should, then it cannot allow the truth of (i), which is a problem since a definition of 'intrinsic' should remain neutral on how finely or coarsely properties are to be individuated.

Granted, a definition of 'intrinsic' should remain neutral on how finely or coarsely we should individuate properties. However, R_I^* is perfectly compatible with (i). We can consistently accept R_I^* along with (i) simply by allowing that no properties are ever had intrinsically. This consequence may be considered implausible, but it's not clear that whatever implausibility it has is any threat to R_I^*. For, as Weatherson and Marshall concede, if we wish to avoid the result that there is no intrinsicality, then rather than rejecting R_I^*, we can easily reject the coarse-grained view of property-identity instead. And in favor of this latter option note that with *any* definition of intrinsicality, (i) yields the implausible view that every F is in every case extrinsic (given that the necessarily coextensive *being either F and lonely or F and accompanied* is always had extrinsically). So, in response to Weatherson and Marshall, there are two points to stress: R_I^* is neutral regarding (i) since R_I^* is consistent with the view that no properties are had intrinsically, and while this consequence may be implausible, its implausibility arguably counts more against (i) than against R_1^*.[26]

---

[26] Weatherson and Marshall (2013, sec. 3.5) contend that my definition is also incompatible

c. For the purpose of my definition, I understood the 'consists in' that figures in R* above in terms of identity. The proposal was that "the event or state, x's having F, consists in the event or state, x's having G, just in case *x's having F is the very same event or state as x's having G*" (1999, p. 599). Hoffmann-Kolss (2010, pp. 91–2) worries that with the absence of detail about what makes events or states identical, my definition, R_I^*, does not sufficiently elucidate the notion of intrinsicality, and for all we can tell from the scant details provided, the definition might very well give implausible results. As Hoffmann-Kolss indicates, for all I say about event- or state-identity, my definition allows, for example, that for any arbitrary chosen property F and any object x,

(iii) *x's having F is the same event/state as x's having F and having the same pure properties as every qualitatively identical y.*[27]

However, it would seem that if (iii) is true, then all properties are d-relational (since *having the same pure properties as every qualitatively identical y* is a universal d-relational property). So if (iii) is true, then there is no internal property I such that x's has F is x's having I. So by adding (iii) to R_I^* we get the result that no properties are intrinsic or had intrinsically. The worry, then, is that in the absence of details about event/state-identity, details which might entail that (iii) is false, R_I^* threatens to preclude all intrinsicality.

---

with certain fine-grained accounts of property-identity. Consider the view that (ii) properties are structured entities whose structure matches the syntactic structure of the predicates that express them. Given (ii), the property of *being accompanied* is not identical with the d-relational property of *being such that there is a contingently existing x which one is distinct from and co-exists with* given the difference in syntactic structure, and it seems that if (ii) were true, then *being accompanied* would not be identical with any d-relational property. So the worry is that with R_I^*, *being accompanied* is falsely classified as intrinsic. It would seem, then, that to give the right results, R_I^* cannot allow the truth of (ii).

Granted, an account of intrinsicality, relational or otherwise, should not force us to reject (ii). And R_I^* does not force us to reject it. In fact, we can easily endorse (ii) along with R_I^*, and all without conceding that *being accompanied* is intrinsic—simply by insisting that *being accompanied* is syntactically equivalent to a d-relational property since it, itself, is d-relational.

27 As Hoffmann-Kolss puts it, "Francescotti does not specify a theory of identity of events which excludes a trivialization of his criterion. For suppose that *P* is an arbitrary property of *x*'s, that *R* is the relation in which *x* stands to *y* iff *x* has *P* and *y* has exactly the same qualitative properties as *x* and that **C** consists of all individuals that have the same qualitative properties as *x*. Then in the same vein as one can argue that being taller than every red-headed person in the world is a universal d-relational property of *x*'s, because *x*'s having it is the same event as *x*'s standing in the taller than relation to all red-headed persons in the world, one can argue that *x*'s instantiating *P* consists in *x*'s standing in *R* to all members of **C**, viz. to all individuals having the same qualitative properties as *x*" (2010, pp. 91–2).

It is true that for all I say about event/state-identity, (iii) is true. There might be good reason to reject (iii), but even so, it seems that the falsity of (iii) does not follow from the notion of intrinsicality itself. The notion of an intrinsic property is compatible with a variety of different views about the identity of events or states, and it seems compatible even with ones that entail (iii). It is true that given (iii), R_I^* yields the result that there are no intrinsic properties and no properties had intrinsically. Yet, while this result certainly seems false, it is not clear that a definition of 'intrinsic' should entail that it is false, since the presence of intrinsicality, while presumably true, does not seem to be a conceptual truth. It is arguable, then, that as a definition of 'intrinsic' R_I^* should not include an account of event- or state-identity that prevents (iii) from being true.

In fact, despite the silence regarding event/state-identity, what I did propose is probably not quite neutral enough. It's arguable that any definition of 'intrinsic' should remain silent on the nature of event-identity and the identity of states of affairs, facts, property-instances, occurrences, and episodes. A definition of intrinsicality should also remain neutral on the ontological status of, and even the existence of, any one of these types of entity. The nature of facts, events, states of affairs, and the rest are matters of great debate, and the notion of an intrinsic property does not in itself provide any answer to these controversial issues. To remain neutral on the nature of such items, we might adopt a suggestion made by Harris (2010). Rather than interpreting 'consists in' in R* above as talk about event- or state-identity, or as talk about the sameness of property-instances, or sameness of occurrences, or of facts, Harris proposes that we interpret 'consists in' in the relational account simply as 'the same as' or 'identical with' and leave it at that. That is why R_I^* was phrased as claiming that x's having F *is the same as* x's having internal properties, $I_1, ..., I_n$. How the true nature of the items that are the same is best construed is left entirely open.

d. A definition of intrinsicality should also remain neutral on whether properties are universals or tropes. However, if properties are universals, then they are distinct from the objects that exemplify them, and in that case for any property F, x's exemplifying F consists in a relation (the exemplification relation) that x bears to a distinct item (the universal, F-ness). So it seems that if properties are universals (which a definition of 'intrinsic' should allow), then with R_I^* all properties are always had extrinsically.

One might attempt to avoid this problem by restricting the d-relations that yield extrinsicality to d-relations to *particulars*. Then F-ness being distinct from x would not be enough to make F an extrinsic feature of x. However, this maneuver avoids the problem only by presupposing that properties are not particulars —a controversial claim which the notion of intrinsicality does not itself imply. So rather than restricting the d-relations that yield extrinsicality to d-relations to particulars, I suggested instead that "the question 'Is F an intrinsic property of x?' should be interpreted as 'Does x's having F consist in a relation that x bears to a distinct item, *other than F itself?*'" (1999, p. 603). When we ask whether F is an intrinsic feature of an object, the answer our definition gives should not rely on any general view about the nature of properties (e.g., whether they are distinct from particulars) or how objects have them (e.g., by exemplifying universals or by containing tropes). There is good reason, then, to view the d-relations definitive of extrinsicality as relations other than mere exemplification.

However, Harris mentions a different and difficult problem that remains. "Abstract particulars are no less problematic than universals: no measurement would be intrinsic if a relation to an abstract particular were to qualify as a d-relation" (Harris 2010, p. 471). Consider *being 4 meters wide* or *having a mass of 1 kilo*. These properties seem to be intrinsic. But the worry is that, assuming numbers exist, these properties count as extrinsic according to $R_I{}^*$ (and other versions of R) since an object's having them is a matter of its being related to distinct particulars.

To solve this "measurement" problem, Harris recommends restricting the d-relations that yield extrinsicality to those one bears to *concrete* items. That way we avoid having to say that x's relation to the number 4 makes being 4 meters wide extrinsic. (The exemplification problem is also solved with Harris' restriction since the property F to which x relates is not concrete—either because properties are universals or because they are tropes, which are commonly viewed as abstract particulars.)

Restricting the d-relations that make properties extrinsic to those one bears to concrete items certainly is an attractive way to avoid the measurement problem. Unfortunately, with this restriction we face another difficulty. In some cases, a d-relation to an abstract item appears to be extrinsic. The property of *coexisting with the number 9* seems extrinsic, and so does the property of *being such that sets exist*.[28]

But without a restriction on the d-relations that yield extrinsic properties, how can an advocate of the relational approach solve the measurement problem? We use the predicate 'is 4 meters wide' to denote the property of being 4 meters wide, but we might use the more cumbersome '*has a meter width measurement equal to 4*' instead. Doesn't the availability of this paraphrase make it clear that an object x's being 4 meters wide is the same as its *having a meter*

---

[28] That's why Harris, as mentioned in section 1, attempts to defend the counter-intuitive claim that these properties are intrinsic.

width measurement equal to 4? I don't think so. It seems that one can consistently deny that numbers exist while also accepting the truth of various measurement claims; anti-realism about numbers does not commit one to denying that objects have a certain width, length, weight, and other measurable features. So, it seems, it can be true that some object x is 4 meters wide even if there are no numbers. And if there were no numbers, then

(i) x's being 4 meters wide

would *not* consist in

(ii) x's bearing the *having a meter width measurement equal to* relation to the number 4.

But suppose that numbers do exist. Wouldn't it then be that (i) consists in (ii)? On many plausible construals of 'consists in', it would be true that (i) consists in (ii). One might even find it appropriate to say that (i) is grounded in (ii). However, even if (i) consists in (ii), in some strong sense of the phrase, there is still a difference between (i) and (ii). (i) does not require the existence of numbers; as was mentioned, an anti-realist about numbers need not deny the truth of measurement claims. But (ii) does require the existence of numbers; being related to the number 4 obviously requires the existence of the number 4. So what's required for (i) is not the same as what's required for (ii). It is arguable, then, that (i) is not identical with (ii) even if numbers do exist. And if this is right, then even though (ii) is identical with x's instantiation of a d-relational property, we can plausibly deny that this is true of (i). So with the emphasis on identity in R_I^* (in place of 'consists in' in R^* or the appeal to grounding in R_G), it seems we can avoid the result that being 4 meters wide is an extrinsic feature of x. So even if we allow that d-relations to abstract particulars yield extrinsicality, there is a plausible reason available, for proponents of R_I^*, to deny that all measurement claims describe the instantiation of extrinsic properties. (But note: it does not seem wise to add to our definition of 'intrinsic' a clause guaranteeing that at least some measurement claims describe intrinsic properties. A definition of 'intrinsic' should not itself entail that this is true; the definition in itself should not guarantee that any properties are had intrinsically.)

6 Concluding Remarks

We have seen that INPs are problematic for accounts of intrinsicality that do not hyperintensionally distinguish the intrinsic from the extrinsic. Another type of property that is known to be problematic for many of these same accounts is the *non-qualitative* ("impure") variety. A duplication based account, for instance, implausibly classifies haecceitistic identity properties (properties of the form, *is identical with x*) as extrinsic since these properties are not shared by any duplicate of an object other than the object itself. With Langton and Lewis (1998, p. 335), one might avoid the result that these identity properties are extrinsic by restricting the duplication account to qualitative properties (pure rather than impure properties)—and perhaps defending this restriction by arguing that the word 'intrinsic' is ambiguous between the qualitative sense and the non-qualitative sense.[29] However, against the idea that there is a distinct qualitative notion of intrinsicality, Eddon claims that the qualitative notion merely picks out a proper subset of the set of intrinsic properties: "an 'intrinsic qualitative property' is simply an intrinsic property that is also qualitative" (2011, p. 323, fn. 22). This seems exactly right. It is most plausible to think that qualitative intrinsic properties comprise merely a subset of the class of intrinsic properties, and that they are intrinsic in the very same sense (whatever that might be) that non-qualitative intrinsic properties are intrinsic. A relational account nicely accommodates this intuition. On a relational account, qualitative intrinsic properties are intrinsic in the very same sense as the non-qualitative ones, by being instantiated in virtue of having internal/non-d-relational properties. The difference between the two groups is simply whether those internal properties are qualitative.

Recall the quote from Lewis at the start of this essay. One intuitive characterization of intrinsicality he mentions is the idea that a sentence or statement ascribing an intrinsic property to something is entirely about the thing itself. There is also the quite similar (and arguably the same) idea that a thing has its intrinsic properties in virtue of the way that thing itself and nothing else is, the intrinsic properties of something depending only on the thing itself.[30] Relational approach R (and R_i^* in particular) clearly captures these aspects of the notion of intrinsicality; if x's having F is a matter of its internal, non-d-relational proper-

---

[29] Sider contends that there is a qualitative sense of 'intrinsic' and this is the sense which duplication accounts are meant to capture. "As I see it, we have a notion of the *qualitative* intrinsic properties, which are had in virtue of the *way* objects are" (1996, p. 4). Vallentyne also identifies a qualitative sense of the word, which he calls the "narrow" sense. A property is intrinsic in the broad sense "just in case having it is appropriately independent of the existence of other objects," whereas a property is intrinsic in the narrow sense "just in case it is intrinsic in the broad sense *and is a qualitative property*" (1997, p. 215).

[30] Although Weatherson and Marshall (2013, sec. 2) question whether the former "locality" construal is the same as the latter interpretation.

ties, then and only then is x's having F solely a matter of what x itself is like, entirely about x itself, and not a matter of what the world distinct from x is like.

The duplication description, however, stands out as expressing something a bit different. As Lewis put it, "[i]f something has an intrinsic property, then so does any perfect duplicate of that thing" (1983a, p. 111). That's what G. E. Moore said about intrinsic value: if something possesses it to any degree, then "anything *exactly like* it, must, under all circumstances, possess it in exactly the same degree" (1922, p. 261). The duplication description does capture something crucial to the notion of an intrinsic property. If intrinsic properties are those something has "in itself," then it would seem that no matter what environmental differences there are, so long as two objects are duplicates, they will have all the same intrinsic properties. Of course, whether duplication tracks intrinsicality depends on the type of duplication. If we include the duplication of impure identity properties (of the form *being identical with x*), then necessarily for any x, only x is a duplicate of x, in which case, the duplication definition yields the implausible result that all of x's properties are intrinsic. On the other hand, if duplicates are supposed to be those that share all the same qualitative properties, then the problem is that *being identical with x* is not classified as intrinsic. A relational approach helps make sense of what duplication has to do with intrinsicality. According to R_I^*, it is the duplication of one's internal properties that ensures the duplication of one's intrinsic properties and that is because the duplication of internal properties is what preserves those features of an object that are not had in virtue of what the rest of the world is like.

R_I^* nicely captures the common intuitive descriptions of intrinsicality in the quote from Lewis. R_I^* also handles well-known objections to other accounts of intrinsicality. Unlike the famous account of Langton and Lewis, R_I^* can correctly classify disjunctive properties without the contentious notion of naturalness, it correctly classifies properties of the form *being such that there is an F*, and it correctly classifies border-sensitive properties, such as being a rock.[31] There are other ac-

---

[31] The first of these three objections has be raised by many, including Yablo (1999), Marshall and Parsons (2001), and Witmer et al. (2005). The second is presented by Marshall and Parsons (2001). And Sider (2001) raises the objection regarding border-sensitive properties. It should not be hard to see how R_I^*, with its hyperintensionality, allows that some disjunctive properties can be had intrinsically and also had extrinsically. *Being the only F* is correctly classified as extrinsic by R_I^* since x's being the only F is, in part, x's having the negative d-relational property of there not being any distinct Fs ("in part" given that x's being the only F requires x not containing any Fs as proper parts and also implies that x is F). And given that being a rock requires not being enclosed within a larger rock, x's being a rock is also (in part) the possession of a negative d-relational property.

counts that avoid these objections,[32] but unlike R_I^* many of these fail to accommodate the apparent hyperintensionality of the intrinsic/extrinsic distinction and also incorrectly classify non-qualitative properties. Like R_I^*, a grounding account, such as Rosen's (2010) and Witmer's (2014), avoids each of these problems. However, as shown in section 3 (with great help from Marshall's 2013 discussion), it seems that intrinsic properties might be grounded in facts about distinct objects. As was also mentioned in section 3, it is arguable that a definition of 'intrinsic' should remain neutral on whether grounding talk describes a phenomenon that actually obtains. For these reasons, R_I^* is preferable.

---

[32] Weatherson's (2001) combinational view, for example, was explicitly introduced as a way to avoid these three objections.

References

Bader, Ralf M. (2013). "Towards a Hyperintensional Theory of Intrinsicality." *The Journal of Philosophy* 110(10): pp. 525–563.
Correia, Fabrice (2010). "Grounding and Truth-Functions." *Logique et Analyse* 53 (211): pp. 251–279.
Dunn, J. Michael (1990). "Relevant Predication 2: Intrinsic Properties and Internal Relations." *Philosophical Studies* 60(3): pp. 177–206.
Eddon, Maya (2011). "Intrinsicality and Hyperintensionality." *Philosophy and Phenomenological Research* 82(2): pp. 314–336.
Figdor, Carrie (2008). "Intrinsically/Extrinsically." *The Journal of Philosophy* 105(11): pp. 691–718.
Figdor, Carrie (2014). "What's the Use of an Intrinsic Property?" In R. Francescotti (ed.), *Companion to Intrinsic Properties*. Berlin: De Gruyter.
Francescotti, Robert (1999). "How to Define Intrinsic Properties." *Noûs* 33(4): pp. 590–609.
Harris, Roger (2010). "How to Define Extrinsic Properties." *Axiomathes* 20(4): pp. 461–478.
Hoffmann-Kolss, Vera (2010). *The Metaphysics of Extrinsic Properties*. Frankfurt: Ontos-Verlag.
Hoffmann-Kolss, Vera (2014). "Is the Intrinsic/Extrinsic Distinction Hyperintentional?" In R. Francescotti (ed.), *Companion to Intrinsic Properties*. Berlin: De Gruyter.
Humberstone, I. Lloyd (1996). "Intrinsic/Extrinsic." *Synthese* 108(2): pp. 205–267.
Khamara, E. J. (1988). "Indiscernibles and the Absolute Theory of Space and Time." *Studia Leibnitiana* 20(2): pp. 140–159.
Langton, Rae and David Lewis. (1998). "Defining 'Intrinsic'." *Philosophy and Phenomenological Research* 58(2): pp. 333–345.
Lewis, David (1983a). "Extrinsic Properties." *Philosophical Studies* 44(2): pp. 197–200.
Lewis, David (1983b). "New Work for a Theory of Universals." *Australasian Journal of Philosophy* 61(4): pp. 343–377.
Lewis, David (1986). *On the Plurality of Worlds*. Oxford: Blackwell.
Marshall, Dan (2013). "Intrinsicality and Grounding." *Philosophy and Phenomenological Research*. Early view: published online, 3 July 2103.
Marshall, D. and J. Parsons (2001). "Langton and Lewis on 'Intrinsic'." *Philosophy and Phenomenological Research* 63(2): pp. 347–351.
Moore, G. E. (1922). *Philosophical Studies*. London: Routledge and Kegan Paul.
Rosen, Gideon (2010). "Metaphysical Dependence: Grounding and Reduction." In B. Hale and A. Hoffmann (eds.), *Modality: Metaphysics, Logic, and Epistemology* (pp. 109–136). Oxford: Oxford University Press.
Schaffer, Jonathan (2012). "Grounding, Transitivity, and Contrastivity." In F. Correia and B. Schnieder (eds.), *Metaphysical Grounding: Understanding the Structure of Reality* (pp. 122–138). Cambridge: Cambridge University Press.
Sider, Theodore (1996). "Intrinsic Properties." *Philosophical Studies* 83(1): pp. 1–27.
Sider, Theodore (2001). "Maximality and Intrinsic Properties." *Philosophy and Phenomenological Research* 63(2): pp. 357–364
Skiles, Alexander (2009). "Trogdon on Monism and Intrinsicality." *Australasian Journal of Philosophy* 87(1): pp. 149–154.
Trogdon, Kelly (2009). "Monism and Instrinsicality." *Australasian Journal of Philosophy* 87(1): pp. 127–148.

Trogdon, Kelly (2010). "Intrinsicality for Monists (and Pluralists)." *Australasian Journal of Philosophy* 88(3): pp. 555–558.

Vallentyne, Peter (1997). "Intrinsic Properties Defined." *Philosophical Studies* 88(2): pp. 209–219.

Weatherson, Brian (2001). "Intrinsic Properties and Combinatorial Principles." *Philosophy and Phenomenological Research* 63(2): pp. 365–380.

Weatherson, Brian and Dan Marshall (2013). "Intrinsic vs. Extrinsic Properties." In E. N. Zalta (ed.), *The Stanford Encyclopedia of Philosophy* (Spring 2013 edition). http://plato.stanford.edu/archives/spr2013/entries/intrinsic-extrinsic/

Witmer, D. Gene (2014). "A Simple Theory of Intrinsicality." In R. Francescotti (ed.), *Companion to Intrinsic Properties*. Berlin: De Gruyter.

Witmer, D. Gene, Willaim Butchard, and Kelly Trogdon (2005). "Intrinsicality without Naturalness." *Philosophical and Phenomenological Research* 70(2): pp. 326–350.

Yablo, Stephen (1999). "Intrinsicness." *Philosophical Topics* 26(1–2): pp. 479–505.

Dan Marshall
Yablo's Account of Intrinsicality[1]

1 Introduction

An intrinsic property is roughly a property something has in virtue of how it is, as opposed to how it is related to other things. More carefully, the property of being F is intrinsic iff, necessarily, for any x that is F, x is F in virtue of how it is, as opposed to how it is related to wholly distinct things or how wholly distinct things are.[2] An extrinsic property, on the other hand, is any property that is not intrinsic. An example of an extrinsic property is the property of being an uncle. The property of being an uncle is extrinsic since, necessarily, any uncle is an uncle at least partly in virtue of how he is related to people wholly distinct from him. Examples of intrinsic properties are more controversial. It is widely held, however, that both the property of being cubical and the property of being made of tin are examples of intrinsic properties.[3]

As Stephen Yablo has pointed out, there are several simple principles connecting intrinsicality with parthood, including (1–3).[4]

1. If u is part of v, then u cannot intrinsically change without v intrinsically changing.

2. If u is part of v, then u and v have a region of intrinsic match.

3. If u is properly part of v, then u and v have intrinsic differences.

---

[1] Thanks to Josh Parsons for helpful discussions on an early version of the material in this paper in 2000. Thanks also to Robert Francescotti, Michael Johnson, Alex Skiles and Stephen Yablo for helpful comments on the paper in 2013.
[2] Two things are wholly distinct iff they have no parts in common. Similar intuitive characterisations of intrinsicality in the literature include: "We distinguish intrinsic properties, which things have in virtue of the way they themselves are, from extrinsic properties, which they have in virtue of their relations or lack of relations to other things" (Lewis, 1986, p. 61); "[A]n intrinsic property of an object is a property that the object has by virtue of itself, depending on no other thing" (Dunn, 1990, p. 178); "[T]he idea of an intrinsic property is the idea of a property a thing has in and of itself" (Humberstone, 1996, p. 229); and "[A]n intrinsic property is one an object has in virtue of itself alone" (Eddon, 2011, p. 315).
[3] Philosophers who have held that *being cubical* is intrinsic include Lewis (1986, pp. 200–1) and Sider (2001). For reasons to think that *being cubical* is not intrinsic, see Bricker (1993) and Skow (2007).
[4] See Yablo (1999, p. 481).

Yablo claims that these principles can be turned into an attractive analysis of intrinsicality. The account of intrinsicality he provides promises to analyse intrinsicality by appealing only to familiar and well understood notions such as logical, modal and mereological notions, and without appealing to contentious notions such as perfect naturalness or metaphysical grounding. His account also promises to establish that intrinsicality is not a fundamental aspect of reality, but is instead analysable in terms of more fundamental logical, modal and mereological properties, relations and operators.

Unfortunately, as I will argue, these promises can't be kept since Yablo's account of intrinsicality fails. I will also argue that, while his account can be modified so that it does a better job at analysing intrinsicality than many other accounts in the literature, these modifications are also unsuccessful. I will conclude that it is likely that any account of intrinsicality in the spirit of Yablo's account will be similarly unsuccessful.[5]

Yablo gives two different versions of his account of intrinsicality. One of these versions requires concrete realism about possible worlds, where concrete realism is the thesis that there are possible worlds and that possible worlds are concrete.[6] I will call this version of his account the concretist version of his account. In section 2, I will discuss this version of his account and argue that both it and a number of modifications of it are unsuccessful. The other version of his account of intrinsicality is intended to be compatible with any theory of possible worlds and I will call this version the neutral version of his account. In section 3, I will discuss this version of his account and argue that it and a number of modifications of it are also unsuccessful.

In the first paragraph of this paper I provided a standard intuitive characterisation of what it is for a property to be intrinsic. The purpose of this characterisation was to provide an intuitive grasp of the notion of intrinsicality philosophers like Yablo are trying to give a more satisfactory account of. Yablo doesn't give the above characterisation, but instead provides an alternative characterisation, which he presumably takes to be at least materially equivalent. Be-

---

[5] As Yablo acknowledges, his account is similar in some respects to the account given by Vallentyne 1997. Some of the objections raised in this paper against Yablo's account and its modifications also apply to Vallentyne's account. I discuss Vallentyne's account in Marshall (2013).

[6] Concrete realists will also typically have a view about what kinds of possible worlds there are. Lewis, for example, holds that every qualitative way a possible world could be is a way some possible world is. As a result, since it is possible for there to be a possible world containing blue swans, talking donkeys and flying pigs, Lewis holds that there is a possible world containing these things. Lewis also endorses certain recombination principles that specify what kinds of other worlds exist given facts about the actual world. (See Lewis 1986, sec. 1.8.)

fore proceeding to the next section, I will first argue that Yablo's alternative characterisation is unsatisfactory since it is incompatible with certain popular metaphysical views. As a result of this incompatibility, I will appeal to the characterisation of intrinsicality given above when evaluating various attempts to analyse intrinsicality in the next two sections, rather than Yablo's alternative.

In intuitively characterising intrinsicality, Yablo writes:[7]

> *You* know what an intrinsic property is: it's a property that a thing has (or lacks) regardless of what may be going on outside of itself. To be intrinsic is to possess the second-order feature of stability-under-variation-in-the-outside-world. (1999, p. 479, author's emphasis)

As Yablo points out, one problem with this characterisation is that it is circular.[8] He writes:

> "Variation in the outside world" has got to mean "variation in what the outside world is like *intrinsically.*" Otherwise every property G is extrinsic; for a thing cannot be G unless the objects outside of it are *accompanied* by a G. (1999, p. 479, author's emphasis)

Yablo's characterisation, however, faces a more serious problem than simply being circular. His characterisation seems to amount to the following:

1. For any property p, p is intrinsic iff, necessarily, for any x: i) if x has p, then no possible alteration to how the world outside of x is intrinsically can ensure that x loses p; and ii) if x lacks p, then no possible alteration to how the world outside of x is intrinsically can ensure that x gains p.

The problem with (1) is that it is plausibly incompatible with a number of popular metaphysical views that hold that there are necessary connections between wholly distinct things. For example, as I will argue below, (1) is incompatible with the popular view of sets that holds that, necessarily, each thing x has a singleton set $\{x\}$ that is wholly distinct from it and is such that, necessarily, x exists

---

[7] Weatherson 2001 and Witmer et al. 2005, perhaps influenced by Yablo, have both given characterisations similar to Yablo's. Weatherson's characterisation is: "It is a platitude that a property F is intrinsic iff whether an object is F does not depend on the way the rest of the word is" (Weatherson 2001, p. 369). Witmer et al.'s is "[A]n intrinsic property is one that is had in a way that is independent of how things are outside the individual in question" (Witmer et al. 2005, p. 327). Both these characterisations face the same difficulty that Yablo's characterisation faces.

[8] It is plausible that the intuitive characterisation of intrinsicality I give is also circular. (See Marshall 2012, p. 531.)

iff {x} exists. Similar arguments can be given that (1) is also incompatible with other theories that posit necessary connections between wholly distinct things.

The argument that (1) is incompatible with the above theory of sets is the following: Suppose the above theory of sets is true. Suppose also that an object x has an intrinsic property p such that, necessarily, anything having p exists. Given the above theory of sets, x has a singleton set {x} that is outside of x and whose nonexistence would ensure the nonexistence of x. Since an alteration in what exists outside of x is an alteration in how the world outside of x is intrinsically, and since {x} is outside of x, an alteration in whether {x} exists is an alteration in how the world outside of x is intrinsically.[9] Hence, since an alteration in whether {x} exists is an alteration in how the world outside of x is intrinsically, since the nonexistence of {x} would ensure the nonexistence of x, and since the nonexistence of x would ensure that x fails to have p, it follows that an alteration in how the world outside of x is intrinsically can ensure that x loses p. Hence (1) falsely classifies p as extrinsic. This establishes the incompatibility of Yablo's intuitive characterisation with the above theory of sets.[10]

2 The concretist version of Yablo's account

The concretist version of Yablo's account of intrinsicality not only requires concrete realism about possible worlds. It also requires a certain version of concrete realism, which is a modification of Lewis's concretist theory of possible worlds. In this section I will first describe this modified version of Lewis's theory of pos-

---

[9] Yablo agrees that an alteration in what exists outside of an object is an alteration in how the world outside of that object is intrinsically. He writes, for example, that "*one* good way to arrange for intrinsic variation in the world outside of x is to *expand it*: add something new". (See Yablo, 1999, p. 482.)

[10] This argument relies on 'ensure' in (1) having its necessitarian reading, according to which x ensures that ϕ iff x necessitates that ϕ. (1) only captures what Yablo actually means by his characterisation if 'ensure' has this necessitarian reading. A defender of Yablo's characterisation, however, might claim that, if it is to characterise intrinsicality in a way that is compatible with theories such as the above theory of sets, the characterisation should be understood differently. One option is to understand 'x ensures that ϕ' as 'x metaphysically grounds the state of affairs that ϕ'. (For the notion of metaphysical grounding, see Rosen 2010.) This option, however, doesn't work, since, given the above theory of sets, the existence of x plausibly metaphysically grounds the existence of {x}. As a result, an alteration to how things intrinsically are outside of {x} that results in the nonexistence of x will metaphysically ground the nonexistence of {x}, and hence will presumably also ground the failure of {x} to have the property p. As a result, p will be falsely classified as extrinsic under the grounding reading of (1).

sible worlds. I will then describe the concretist version of Yablo's account of intrinsicality, before arguing that both it, and a number of attempts to fix it, fail.

According to Lewis's theory of possible worlds, possible worlds are not abstract entities such as properties, sets or numbers. Instead, possible worlds are concrete entities of a kind with the world that contains us and all our surroundings.[11] Possible worlds can therefore contain familiar things such as birds, mountains and planets as parts. They can also contain more exotic things not found in the world we live in, such as blue swans, talking donkeys and flying pigs.

Lewis endorses the standard Leibnizian schema (Pos) connecting possibility to possible worlds, although his interpretation of it differs from that of typical abstractionists about possible worlds.

(Pos)   Possibly φ iff, for some possible world w, at w, φ.

Philosophers who hold that possible worlds are abstract typically use 'at w, φ' to mean 'According to w, φ' or 'Necessarily, if w obtains then φ'. Lewis, in contrast, uses 'at' so that it works in the same way as 'in' does in sentences like 'In Australia, every swan is black'. Since Lewis thinks that 'in Australia' works mainly by restricting quantification within its scope, he thinks 'at w' works in this way as well. Lewis writes:[12]

---

11 Lewis has reservations about the term 'concrete', which he thinks is both ambiguous and unclear on at least some of its disambiguations. (See Lewis 1986, sec 1.7.) As a result of this, instead of saying that possible worlds are concrete, he prefers to say that possible worlds "are of a kind with this world of ours" (1986, p. 81).

12 Despite what this quote suggests, Lewis holds that, when 'at w' restricts the domain of a quantifier, it does not normally restrict it to include only parts of w. Instead, he thinks that the restricted domain in such cases also includes all of the numbers and some but not all of the sets (1983, p. 40). This allows Lewis, for example, to hold that, in relatively normal contexts, 'Possibly, there are no numbers' is false.

Two other components of Lewis's account of 'at' are the following. First, Lewis thinks that 'In Australia' and 'at w' may fail to restrict all the quantification within their scope. He gives the example of the sentence 'In Australia, there is a yacht faster than any other', which is true on a natural reading iff there is a yacht *in Australia* that is faster than any other yacht *without restriction*. Given Lewis also thinks that this sentence can also be used to say that there is a yacht *in Australia* that is faster than any other yacht *in Australia*, Lewis is committed to holding that many sentences containing 'at w' are ambiguous or context dependent. This view of 'at' however, raises problems in interpreting Lewis. For example, given his account of 'at' is correct, we face the problem of determining which readings of the instances of (Pos) are the readings under which he endorses those instances. In this paper I will largely ignore this complication and assume Lewis endorses the simpler account of 'at' according to which it always restricts all quantification within its scope.

> In Australia, all swans are black—all swans are indeed black, if we ignore everything not in Australia; quantifying only over things in Australia, all swans are black. At some strange world *W*, all swans are blue—all swans are indeed blue, if we ignore everything not part of the world *W*; quantifying only over things that are part of *W*, all swans are blue. (1986, p. 5)

As well as restricting explicit quantification, Lewis also holds that 'in Australia', and hence 'at *w*' on his use, can restrict implicit quantification. He writes:

> ['In Australia' and 'at *W*'] influence the interpretation of expressions that are not explicitly quantificational, but that reveal implicit quantification under analysis: definite descriptions and singular terms definable by them, class abstracts and plurals, superlatives, etc. An example: it is the case at world *W* that nine numbers the solar planets iff nine numbers those solar planets that are part of *W*. Another example: words like 'invent' and 'discover' are implicitly superlative, hence implicitly quantificational; they imply doing something *first*, before *anyone* else did. So the inventor of bifocals at *W* is the one who is part of *W* and thought of bifocals before anyone else who is part of *W* did. (1986, pp. 5–6, author's emphasis)

Lewis holds that possible worlds do not overlap: that is, he holds that nothing is part of more than one possible world.[13] As Yablo points out, however, Lewis is not overly hostile to overlap among worlds. Rather, he is hostile towards there being something that intrinsically differs between worlds it is part of, where *x*

Secondly, Lewis thinks that both 'in Australia' and 'at *w*' can "restrict" proper names. He writes: "In Australia, and likewise at a possible world where the counterparts of British cities are strangely rearranged, Cardiff is a suburb of Newcastle—there are various places of those names, and we banish ambiguity by restricting our attention to the proper domain. Here I am supposing that the way we bestow names attaches them not only to this-worldly things, but also to other-worldly counterparts thereof. That is how the other-worldly Cardiffs and Newcastles bear those names in our this-worldly language. In the same way, the solar planets at *W* are those that orbit the star Sol of the world *W*, a counterpart of the Sol of this world." (1986, p. 6)

As a result of this, Lewis in *On the Plurality of Worlds* doesn't think that (Pos) needs to be augmented with his 1968 counterpart theory to handle sentences containing proper names. Contra what Lewis suggests, however, it is not obvious that the account of possibility that results from this account of 'at' is compatible with his counterpart theory. Nor is it clear precisely what the resulting account is. For example, given *a* has two counterparts that are parts of *w*, one of which is made of tin, and one of which is not made of tin, it is not clear what the truth value of 'At *w*, *a* is made of tin' is supposed to be on Lewis's account. I will assume in this paper that, on his account, if *a* is part of *w*, then 'At *w*, *a* is *F*' is true iff '*a* is *F*' is true with all of its explicit and implicit quantification suitably restricted.

13 More carefully, Lewis holds that nothing is part of more than one possible world given his provisional view that there are no universals. He thinks that, if there are universals, then they are parts of multiple worlds. See Lewis (1983, p. 40 and 1986, p. 2).

intrinsically differs between w_1 and w_2 iff there is a predicate F expressing an intrinsic property such that ⌜at w_1, Fx⌝ is true while ⌜at w_2, Fx⌝ is false, where 'w_1', 'w_2' and 'x' refer to w_1, w_2 and x, respectively.

Lewis's argument against there being something that intrinsically differs between different worlds it is part of may be presented as follows. Consider the intrinsic property of having five fingers.[14] Suppose x is part of two possible worlds w_1 and w_2. Given this, and given Lewis's account of 'at', 'At w_1, x has five fingers' is true iff w_1 contains five of x's fingers, while 'At w_2, x does not have five fingers' is true iff w_2 does not contain five of x's fingers. It follows that these sentences cannot be both true, since if they were both true x would be part of w_2 even though w_2 wouldn't contain all of x's fingers, which is impossible since x's fingers are parts of x. Hence, if x is part of worlds w_1 and w_2, 'At w_1, x has five fingers' is true iff 'At w_2, x has five fingers' is true. Lewis thinks this argument can be generalised to show that, provided F expresses an intrinsic property, if x is part of worlds w_1 and w_2, then ⌜at w_1, Fx⌝ is true iff ⌜at w_2, Fx⌝ is true. If this is the case, then things can't intrinsically differ between different worlds they are part of.[15]

It is important to note that this argument does not extend to predicates that express extrinsic properties. Given Lewis's account of 'at', and given x is part of a world w, 'At w, x is the tallest man', for example, is true iff x is the tallest man that is part of w. Since x might be the tallest man who is part of w_1 while not being the tallest man who is part of w_2, there is no problem with 'At w_1, x is the tallest man' being true while 'At w_2, x is the tallest man' is false. As far as Lewis's argument goes, then, there is nothing to rule out ⌜at w_1, Fx⌝ and ⌜at w_2, Fx⌝ differing in truth value when F expresses an extrinsic property and x is part of worlds w_1 and w_2. Lewis's argument therefore doesn't rule out a thing extrinsically differing between worlds it is part of.

Lewis ends up ruling out overlap for what he describes as "less weighty" reasons. He writes:

> Overlap spoils the easiest account of how worlds are unified by interrelation: namely, the mereological analogue of the definition of equivalence classes. (1986, p. 209)

While he claims that "[t]he complication is unwelcome", he thinks that "it's nothing worse" (p. 209). Lewis, then, thinks he has no decisive reason to reject

---

[14] I am assuming that the property of having five fingers is the property of having five fingers as parts. Given this assumption, non-physical souls, for example, presumably can't have fingers.
[15] For Lewis' version of this argument, see his (1986, pp. 199–200).

overlap, provided things don't intrinsically differ between the different worlds they are part of.

Yablo thinks that concrete realists should lift Lewis's ban on overlap provided Lewis's ban on things intrinsically differing between the worlds they are part of is kept in place. In particular, Yablo seems to think that concrete realists should hold that every concrete object is a possible world.[16] A major advantage of modifying Lewis's theory of possible worlds in this way, Yablo claims, is that it allows the following analysis of intrinsicality, where '≤' symbolises 'is a part of', '$\underline{F}$' refers to the property expressed by the predicate 'F', and 'at' is used in the same way 'in' is in sentences like 'In Australia, every swan is black':[17]

---

[16] Yablo doesn't say why concrete realists should modify Lewis's theory of possible worlds in the way he suggests. One reason Yablo might give for concrete realists to adopt his suggested modification is that, given intrinsicality can be analysed on his modification but not on Lewis's original version of concrete realism, the modified version has more explanatory power, and hence is more likely to be true. Yablo's suggested modification to concrete realism, however, is not without its problems, and these problems might outweigh any added explanatory power the modification might provide. One such problem is that it is hard to make sense of actuality given overlap. See, for example, (Sider 2003, pp. 195–6) and (Bricker 2008, p. 124).

[17] The formulation of Yablo's account given in (2) differs from Yablo's own formulation, which is given by (A) (Yablo, 1999, p. 485).

(A) G is intrinsic iff: for all $x < w < w'$, x has G in w iff x has G in w'.

I have replaced Yablo's 'iff' with '$=_{df}$', where '$\phi =_{df} \psi$' symbolises 'For it to be the case that ϕ is for it to be the case that ψ', since I am assuming that an analysis of the notion of an intrinsic property must be either a sentence of the form 'For any p, p is an intrinsic property $=_{df} \varphi(p)$' or a schema of the form '$\underline{F}$ is an intrinsic property $=_{df} \varphi(F)$'. I have also used '≤' rather than '<' to symbolise 'is a part of', and I have stuck with Lewis's 'at' rather than 'in', despite the fact that Lewis thinks these are effectively synonymous on their relevant uses. (As I am using 'part', each thing is a part of itself.)

Another difference between (2) and (A) is more substantive. (A) is incompatible with Lewis's view that, if something x were to be part of two worlds w_1 and w_2, then, for any intrinsic or extrinsic property p, it couldn't be the case that x has p at w_1 but does not have p at w_2. Lewis writes, for example, that things have their properties simpliciter and that what properties they have "cannot vary from world to world" (Lewis 1986, p. 201). Given this aspect of Lewis's view, (A) falsely classifies all properties as intrinsic. (2), on the other hand, is compatible with this aspect of Lewis's view.

I have emphasised Lewis's account of how 'at' functions when it is used in the same way as 'in' in 'In Australia, every swan is black' since it is a well known account that is typically assumed to be true in discussions of concrete realism. In recent personal correspondence, however, Yablo has indicated that, when writing "Intrinsicness" he didn't endorse Lewis's account of 'at' when used in this way, and may have instead endorsed a counterfactual account according to which, on the relevant use, 'at w, φ' is true iff 'Had w been the whole of reality it would have been the case that φ'. The argument given in the main text against Lewis's account of how 'at w' works on this use applies just as well to this alternative counterfactual account.

2. F is intrinsic $=_{df}$ for any x, and for any possible worlds w_1 and w_2 such that $x \leq w_1 \leq w_2$, (at w_1, Fx) iff (at w_2, Fx).

An example of a property (2) correctly classifies as intrinsic, given Lewis's account of 'at' and Yablo's modification of Lewis's theory of possible worlds, is the property of having five fingers. As argued above, given Lewis's account of 'at', if x is part of w_1 and w_2, 'At w_1, x has five fingers' is true iff 'At w_2, x has five fingers' is true. It follows from this that (2) correctly classifies the property of having five fingers as intrinsic. An example of a property (2) correctly classifies as extrinsic, given Lewis's account of 'at' and Yablo's modification of Lewis's theory of possible worlds, is the property of being the tallest man. Given Yablo's modified version of Lewis's theory of possible worlds, every concrete object is a possible world. Since I am the tallest man in my apartment, but I am not the tallest man in my city, it follows that, on Lewis's account of 'at', 'At my apartment, I am the tallest man' is true while 'At my city, I am the tallest man' is false. As a

---

Yablo's alternative account of 'at' motivates the modification of Yablo's account discussed in footnote 21.

It is important to note that Yablo only endorses (A) relative to the simplifying assumption that there are no distinct coinciding entities, where x and y coincide iff they have the same parts. Yablo actually thinks this simplifying assumption is false. He thinks that, while there are no distinct coinciding entities at the bottom level of matter, there are distinct coinciding entities when we count higher level entities that are constituted by entities at the bottom level. He also thinks that these constituted entities stand in necessary connections with other wholly distinct concrete entities, and that the existence of these necessary connections renders (A) false due to the existence of essential extrinsic properties such as *being descended from some particular zygote Z*. (See Yablo 1999, p. 486.) As a result, Yablo replaces (A) with two much more complicated accounts which correspond, he thinks, to two different notions of intrinsicality. These two accounts (modified along the lines of (2)) are given by (B) and (C), where (B) is meant to analyse a notion of intrinsicality that can be instantiated by both categorical and non-categorical properties, while (C) is meant to analyse a notion of intrinsicality that can only be instantiated by categorical properties. (See Yablo 1999, p. 493.)

(B) F is intrinsic $=_{df}$ for any x, and for any possible worlds w_1 and w_2 such that $x \leq w_1 \leq w_2$: (at w, Fx) iff, for *some* x' that is coincident to x, (at w_2, Fx').

(C) F is intrinsic $=_{df}$ for any x, and for any possible worlds w_1 and w_2 such that $x \leq w_1 \leq w_2$: (at w_1, Fx) iff, for *any* x' that is coincident to x, (at w_2, Fx').

I don't find Yablo's rationale for adopting (B) and (C) given the existence of distinct coincident entities convincing. To avoid complicating the discussion, however, I will simply assume that there are no distinct coincident entities (as well as no non-bottom level entities and no wholly distinct concrete entities which are necessarily connected to each other). Given (2) fails given this simplifying assumption, then (B) and (C) will also fail with or without this assumption.

result, given Yablo's modified version of Lewis's theory of possible worlds, (2) correctly classifies the property of being the tallest man as extrinsic.

The right hand side of (2) does not contain any expressions expressing controversial metaphysical notions such as perfect naturalness or metaphysical grounding. Instead, it contains expressions expressing parthood and logical notions such as universal quantification and material equivalence. It also contains the expression 'at' which as it is used in (2) is synonymous with the natural language expression 'in' as it occurs in 'In Australia, every swan is black'. Since it might be thought that we have a good understanding of 'in' as it occurs in this sentence due to our ordinary competence with English, it might be thought that we have a similarly good understanding of 'at' as it occurs in (2). As a result of this, it might be thought that Yablo is justified in claiming that we have a good understanding of the right hand side of (2), and hence justified in claiming that (2), if true, provides a significant clarification of the notion of intrinsicality. If (2) is true, Yablo might also be thought to be justified in claiming that (2) establishes that intrinsicality is not a fundamental aspect of reality, but is instead analysable in terms of more fundamental logical and mereological notions. I will now argue, however, that (2) fails to be true in a rather spectacular way. Yablo's account fails since it fails to classify paradigmatic extrinsic properties, such as the property of being an uncle, as extrinsic.

Consider the sentence (3), where Kelly is an uncle who is in the relevant classroom, although none of his nephews and nieces are in this classroom.

3. In the classroom, Kelly is an uncle.

While (3) sounds like an odd sentence, it can be argued to be true as follows: (3) is equivalent to 'Kelly is an uncle in the classroom', which in turn is equivalent to 'Kelly is an uncle who is in the classroom'. Since Kelly is an uncle who is in the classroom, (3) is therefore true.[18]

---

[18] Michael Johnson has suggested to me an explanation of the oddness of (3) along the following lines. The fronting of 'in the classroom' in (3) typically focuses it. As a result, (3) typically implicates that the instances of 'In a, Kelly is an uncle' potentially differ in truth value. Since this implication is false, it is typically inappropriate to utter (3), and it is this fact that accounts for the oddness of the sentence. The fact that this explanation is compatible with the truth of (3) provides further support for the claim that (3) is indeed true.

It is worth noting that two similar accounts of the oddness of (3), which are incompatible with the truth of (3), don't offer any help to Yablo's account. On the first account, due to the focusing of 'in the classroom', (3) typically *presupposes* that the instances of 'In a, Kelly is an uncle' potentially differ in truth value, while on the second account, (3) typically *entails* that the instances of 'In a, Kelly is an uncle' potentially differ in truth value. Since this presupposition and entailment is false, the first account entails that (3) typically lacks a truth value, while the

Further support for the truth of (3) can be obtained by considering the following possible dialogue. Suppose A asks B whether there are any uncles in the classroom, perhaps because the topic of the day is family relationships and it would be helpful if there was at least one uncle who was in the classroom. B might truthfully respond to A's question by saying that there is an uncle in the classroom, namely Kelly. This truthful response would entail that Kelly is an uncle in the classroom, or more flamboyantly, that, in the classroom, Kelly is an uncle. It would therefore entail the truth of (3).

A similar argument can be given that (4) is also true, where Susan is in the relevant classroom but is not an uncle.[19]

4. In the classroom, Susan is not an uncle.

The truth of (3) and (4) raises the following problem for Yablo's account (2). If (3) is true, then 'At w, x is an uncle' is presumably true whenever 'at' is used in the way 'in' is used in sentences like (3) and 'In Australia, all swans are black', and when 'x' refers to something that is an uncle that is part of what 'w' refers to. Similarly, if (4) is true, then 'At w, x is not an uncle' is presumably true whenever 'at' is used in this way and 'x' refers to something that is not an uncle and is part of what 'w' refers to. Hence, if (3) and (4) are true, it is plausibly the case that, if x is part of w, then (x is an uncle iff at w, x is an uncle). Hence if (3) and (4) are true it is plausible that (5) is true.

5. For any x, and for any possible worlds w_1 and w_2 such that $x \leq w_1 \leq w_2$, (at w_1, x is an uncle) iff (at w_2, x is an uncle).

If (5) is true, however, (2) classifies the property of being an uncle as intrinsic, when it is in fact extrinsic. Yablo's account (2) therefore fails.[20]

---

second account entails that (3) is typically false. More generally, the first account entails that every instance of 'In a, x is an uncle' typically lacks a truth value, while the second account entails that every instance of 'In a, x is an uncle' is typically false. It follows from this that, on both accounts, relative to contexts in which instances of 'In a, x is an uncle' sound odd, (2) will fail to classify *being an uncle* as extrinsic.

19 That (4) is true is also a consequence of Lewis's account of 'at'.
20 Yablo might respond to the above problem by claiming that, while (3) has a reading on which it is true, it also has a reading on which it is false, and it is the latter reading that is relevant for his account. However, (3) seems to have no such reading. Or at least, it doesn't appear to have a reading on which instances of 'In w, x is an uncle' differ in truth value, as is required by Yablo's account. (See footnote 18.) Note also that, even if (2) does happen to have a difficult to access reading on which it is true, it might fail to provide an analysis of intrinsicality in terms of

As well as showing that (2) fails, the above argument shows that Lewis's account of how 'at' works on his use also fails. In particular, the argument shows there are cases where, contra to Lewis's account, 'in' in natural language, and hence 'at' on Lewis's use, cannot restrict all quantification within its scope. In light of this failure, a natural way to try to fix Yablo's account is to replace 'at' with an operator expression that does restrict all quantification within its scope. In particular, we might modify Yablo's account by replacing 'at' with the operator expression 'Rest', where 'Rest' is stipulated to function so that ⌜$\text{Rest}_w(\varphi)$⌝ expresses the state of affairs that results from restricting all the quantification in the state of affairs expressed by φ to parts of the referent of 'w'.[21] The result of this modification is (6).

---

familiar and well understood notions, since such a difficult to access reading might involve unfamiliar and not well understood notions.

21 A state of affairs is a way things are or a way things fail to be. Yablo has suggested to me an alternative modification of (2) under which 'at' is stipulated to function in (2) so that 'at w, φ' is true iff 'Had it been that w was the whole of reality, it would have been that φ' is true. A problem with this modification is posed by sentences such as 'Had it been that Dan was the whole of reality, it would have been that Dan was 6 feet tall'. Given I am 6 feet tall, and given that the property of being 6 feet tall is intrinsic, this sentence needs to be true for the modified account to be true. This sentence, however, might be thought to be false or lacking a truth value in the same way that 'Had there been only one electron then Freddie would have existed' is plausibly false or lacks a truth value, where Freddie is an electron. (The latter sentence is plausibly false or lacks a truth value since there is no reason to think that it would have been Freddie that was the only existing electron rather than some other electron.)

This problem with Yablo's suggestion can be avoided by instead stipulating 'at' to work so that 'at w, φ' is true iff 'Had w been the whole of reality, and w was as similar as possible to how it actually is, then it would have been the case that φ' is true, where the relevant sense of similarity is the unique most discerning overall objective notion of similarity. This second modification of (2), however, faces the problem that, given numbers necessarily exist and necessarily aren't parts of what are in fact concreta, and given the standard Stalnaker/Lewis account of counterfactuals according to which all counterfactuals with necessarily false antecedents are true, each instance of 'Had w been the whole of reality and w was as similar as possible to how it actually is, then it would have been the case that φ' is true when 'w' refers to any concrete object. As a result, given all possible worlds are concrete, this modification of (2) will falsely classify any intrinsic property that fails to be instantiated by something as extrinsic.

In light of this last problem, we might turn to a third modification of (2) under which 'at w, φ' is stipulated to be true iff 'Had w been the whole of reality apart from necessarily existing things, and w and the necessarily existing things were as similar as possible to how they actually are, then it would have been the case that φ'. This third characterisation, while superior to the first two modifications, still faces problems. For example, it falsely classifies the following properties as intrinsic: *being such that there is a number* (given numbers necessarily exist), *being 1 m away from Mars and Venus* (given there is nothing 1 m away from Mars and Venus), and *being such that there are no Platonic universals* (given there are no Platonic universals). This third modifi-

6. F is intrinsic $=_{df}$ for any x, and for any possible worlds w_1 and w_2 such that $x \leq w_1 \leq w_2$, $\text{Rest}_{w_1}(Fx)$ iff $\text{Rest}_{w_2}(Fx)$.

One problem with (6) is that the notion of an operator that restricts all quantification in what it applies to stands in urgent need of explanation. An attractive explanation of this notion can be given in terms of perfect naturalness, where: i) a perfectly natural property is a simple, or fundamental property; ii) a perfectly natural relation is a simple, or fundamental, relation; and iii) a perfectly natural operator is a simple, or fundamental, operator. (See Lewis 1986, pp. 59–60 and Sider 2011.) Suppose φ is any sentence expressing a state of affairs p. Let ψ be a sentence expressing p which contains names and variables, together with predicates and operator expressions that express perfectly natural properties, relations and operators. Finally, for any u, let ψ_u be a sentence obtained from ψ by replacing each quantifier expression in ψ with the restriction of that quantifier expression to the parts of u. So, for example, if ψ contains the existential quantifier expression '$\exists x \ldots$', then ψ_u will instead contain '$\exists x(x \leq u \wedge \ldots)$', and if ψ contains the universal quantifier expression '$\forall x \ldots$', then ψ_u will instead contain '$\forall x(x \leq u \supset \ldots)$'. Given this setting up, the action of 'Rest_u' on the sentence φ can then be defined by (7).

7. $\text{Rest}_u(\varphi) =_{df} \psi_u$.

While this is an attractive account of 'Rest', Yablo can't appeal to it without appealing to the notion of perfect naturalness, which is a notion he wishes to avoid. Without some such explanation, however, it is not clear whether 'Rest' can be understood sufficiently well for (6) to be successful.

(6) faces a further problem if there are entities, such as numbers or sets, that aren't parts of any possible worlds. For example, given numbers aren't part of any possible worlds, for any x, and for any possible world w, it is not the case that x is such that there is a number that is part of w, and hence it is not the case that $\text{Rest}_w(x$ is such that there is a number). As a result, given numbers aren't parts of any possible worlds, (6) falsely classifies the extrinsic property of being such that there is a number as intrinsic.

Given mereological universalism, the second problem for (6) can be easily avoided by replacing (6) with (8).[22]

---

cation might also face difficulties due to general problems for concrete realism concerning what modal claims concrete realists can endorse. (See Marshall MS.)

[22] Mereological universalism is the thesis that, for any xs, there is a fusion of the xs; where y is a fusion of the xs iff: i) each of the xs is part of y, and ii) each part of y overlaps one of the xs. If

8. F is intrinsic $=_{df}$ for any x, y and z such that $x \leq y \leq z$, $\text{Rest}_y(Fx)$ iff $\text{Rest}_z(Fx)$.

(8) correctly classifies the property of being such that there is a number as extrinsic given mereological universalism, since, while it is not the case that $\text{Rest}_x(x$ is such that there is a number) if x is a concrete object, it is the case that $\text{Rest}_y(x$ is such that there is a number) if y contains both x and a number as parts.

While (8) successfully classifies *being such that there is a number* as extrinsic given mereological universalism, it fails to correctly classify extrinsic properties that aren't quantificational, such as the property of being 1 m away from Yablo.[23] Since this property is not quantificational, for any w, Rest_w (x is 1 m away from Yablo) iff x is 1 m away from Yablo. This has the consequence that (8) falsely classifies *being 1 m away from Yablo* as intrinsic.

We might try to fix this problem by making a further modification to Yablo's account. There is an intuitive distinction between *non-qualitative* states of affairs that *haecceistically concern* particular entities, and *qualitative*, or general, states of affairs that do not haecceistically concern any particular entities. Examples of non-qualitative states of affairs include the state of affairs of Gillard being prime minister and the state of affairs of Obama being next to Yablo. Examples of qualitative states of affairs, on the other hand, include the state of affairs of there being a prime minister and the state of affairs of every emerald being green. Given we grant this distinction between qualitative and non-qualitative states of affairs, we should also grant the notion of a state of affairs haecceistically concerning certain particular entities, so that, for example, the state of affairs of Gillard being prime minister haecceistically concerns Gillard, while the state of affairs of Obama being next to Yablo haeccesitically concerns both Obama and Yablo.[24] Given this notion of a state of affairs haeccesitically concerning some

---

mereological universalism is false, we can replace (8) with (D), where Rest_S is defined to work so that '$\text{Rest}_S(\varphi)$' is true iff φ is true when all the quantification in the state of affairs expressed by φ is restricted to range over the members of S.

(D) F is intrinsic $=_{df}$ for any x, and for any sets S_1 and S_2 such that all the parts of x are members of S_1 and such that S_1 is a subset of S_2, $\text{Rest}_{S_1}(Fx)$ iff $\text{Rest}_{S_2}(Fx)$.

23 If *being 1 m away from* is quantificational, then replace it with a relation that isn't quantificational.

24 The notion of a state of affairs s haecceistically concerning an entity can arguably be characterised in terms of perfect naturalness as follows: s haecceistically concerns x iff, for any sentence ψ expressing p that contains only names and variables, together with predicates and operator expressions expressing perfectly natural properties, relations and operators, ψ contains a name referring to x.

particular entities, we can define a new operator expression 'Rest*' by (9), where φ abbreviates 'the state of affairs of it being the case that φ'.

9. $\text{Rest}^*_w(\varphi) =_{df} (\text{Rest}_w(\varphi)$ and, for any x, if φ haeccesitically concerns x then $x \leq w$).

We can then replace 'Rest' with 'Rest*' in (8) to obtain (10).

10. F is intrinsic $=_{df}$ for any x, y and z such that $x \leq y \leq z$, $\text{Rest}^*_y(Fx)$ iff $\text{Rest}^*_z(Fx)$.

Given there is something wholly distinct from Yablo that is 1 m away from Yablo, (10) correctly classifies the property of being 1 m away from Yablo as extrinsic. To see why, suppose x is both wholly distinct from Yablo and 1 m away from him. Then, given the definition of 'Rest*', $\text{Rest}^*_w(x$ is 1 m away from Yablo) iff (x is 1 m away from Yablo, and x and Yablo are both part of w). Since x is wholly distinct from Yablo, it is not the case that $\text{Rest}^*_x(x$ is 1 m away from Yablo). Since x and Yablo are both parts of the universe, however, $\text{Rest}^*_{\text{the universe}}(x$ is 1 m away from Yablo). Hence (10) correctly classifies the property of being 1 m away from Yablo as extrinsic.

While (10) correctly classifies *being 1 m away from Yablo* as extrinsic if there is something wholly distinct from Yablo that is 1 m away from him, it does not correctly classify it as extrinsic if there is no such entity. To use another example, consider the non-quantificational property of being a point sized object 1 m away from both Venus and Mars. Since Venus and Mars are more than 2 m apart, there is nothing point sized that is 1 m away from both of them. It follows that, for any x and for any w, it is not the case that $\text{Rest}^*_w(x$ is a point sized object 1 m away from both Venus and Mars). As a result, (10) falsely classifies the extrinsic property of being a point sized object that is 1 m away from Venus and Mars as intrinsic.

This last problem is difficult to solve. As far as I can see, there is no natural way of modifying (10) so that it correctly classifies non-instantiated non-quantificational extrinsic properties such as *being 1 m away from both Venus and Mars*. The best response a defender of a Yablo style account can give, I think, is to restrict the scope of their account so that it only applies to qualitative properties.[25] This response avoids the above problem since the above problem only arises for

---

25 A qualitative property is a property that does not haecceistically concern any particular entities. Examples of qualitative properties include *being cubical* and *being next to a tin*. Examples of non-qualitative properties include *being Obama* and *being next to Gillard*.

non-qualitative properties. A defender who adopts this response replaces (10) with (11).

11. F is a qualitative intrinsic property $=_{df}$ for any x, y and z such that $x \leq y \leq z$, $\text{Rest}_y^*(Fx)$ iff $\text{Rest}_z^*(Fx)$.

Given (11) is successful, such a defender might attempt to use the notion of a qualitative intrinsic property to then give a separate analysis of the notion of an intrinsic property simpliciter.

Unfortunately, however, this defence of a Yablo style account can't work, since (11) also fails. In particular, (11) fails to correctly classify certain qualitative extrinsic properties that concern properties that fail to be instantiated. Suppose, for example, that, just as Lewis believes, there are no Platonic universals. Then (11) falsely classifies the qualitative extrinsic property of being such that there are no Platonic universals as intrinsic. It does this, since, for any w and for any x that is part of w, $\text{Rest}_w^*(x$ is such that there are no Platonic universals). I can see no way of modifying (11) so as to avoid this problem. As a result, it does not seem possible to modify Yablo's concretist account of intrinsicality so that it is successful. In the next section I will argue that the same is true for the neutral version of Yablo's account.

3 The neutral version of Yablo's account

Unlike the concretist version of Yablo's account, the neutral version of his account does not require concrete realism and is meant to be able to be endorsed by both philosophers who think possible worlds are abstract entities and philosophers who don't think there are any possible worlds at all. Yablo formulates this version of his account using the indexed modal operator expressions introduced by Christopher Peacocke and Graeme Forbes.[26] Given the simplifying assumption that a S5 modal logic is valid (which entails, for example, that true identity claims are necessarily true), the neutral version of Yablo's account can be stated by (12).[27]

---

[26] See Peacocke (1978, pp. 485–7) and especially Forbes (1985, sec. 4.5).
[27] I am following Yablo in using $\ulcorner A_i^{x,y} \urcorner$ to abbreviate $\ulcorner A_i^x A_i^y \urcorner$. I am also assuming, as in footnote 17, that there are no coincident entities. Without these assumptions, Yablo's account for the more general notion of intrinsicality which allows for non-categorical intrinsic properties, is given by (E), where '$\approx$' symbolises 'coincidence'. (See Yablo 1999, p. 502.)

(E) F is intrinsic $=_{df} \Box_1 \forall u \forall p [(p \leq u) \supset \forall x [(x \approx p) \supset \Box_2 \forall v \forall q [(q \leq v) \supset \forall y [(y \approx q) \supset (A_1^{p,u} A_2^{q,v} (p = q \leq u \leq v) \supset (A_1^x Fx \equiv A_2^y Fy))]]]]$.

12. F is intrinsic $=_{df} \Box_1 \forall u \forall x [x \le u \supset \Box_2 \forall v [x \le v \supset [A_1^{x,u} A_2^v (x \le u \le v) \supset (A_1^x Fx \equiv A_2^x Fx)]]]$.

Given the existence of abstract possible worlds and the possible worlds account of the indexed modal operators Peacocke and Forbes provide, (12) can be rewritten as (13), where '$(u$ at $w_1 \le v$ at $w_2)$' symbolises 'u at w_1 is part of v at w_2', 'at w, φ' symbolises 'Necessarily, if w obtains then φ', and 'w_1' and 'w_2' are variables ranging over abstract possible worlds.[28]

13. F is intrinsic $=_{df} \forall w_1 [\text{at } w_1, \forall u \forall x [x \le u \supset \text{at } w_2, \forall v [x \le v \supset [(x \text{ at } w_1 \le u \text{ at } w_1 \le v \text{ at } w_2) \supset ((\text{at } w_1, Fx) \equiv (\text{at } w_2, Fx))]]]]$.

(13) requires abstract realism about possible worlds. It is not clear whether concrete realists and anti-realists about possible worlds can provide an alternative satisfactory explanation of what the indexed modal operator expressions mean that is compatible with their metaphysical views.[29] Putting aside the issue of whether concrete realists and anti- realists about possible worlds can understand the indexed modal operator expressions of Peacocke and Forbes, I will now consider whether (13) is successful given abstract realism about possible worlds. If, as I will argue, (13) fails given abstract realism, (13) plausibly fails regardless of which theory of possible worlds is true.

Given the simplest quantified S5 modal logic (according to which, for example, modal operator expressions and quantifier expressions commute), and given (14) (which connects transworld parthood with parthood simpliciter), the right

---

Given the assumption that S5 modal logic is valid and that there are no distinct coincident entities, (E) is true iff (12) is true.

28 (12) can be translated as (13) by using the following elementary translation principles, where '$\leftrightarrow_T$' symbolises 'is translated by', 'φ' is a schematic letter that can be replaced by any formula, and 'S' is a schematic letter that can be replaced by any complex or simple expression that renders the resulting expression containing it and its object well-formed and does not involve a clash of variables: i) '$S[A_1^x A_1^u A_2^v (x \le u \le v)]$' $\leftrightarrow_T$ '$S(x$ at $w_1 \le u$ at $w_1 \le v$ at $w_2)$'; ii) '$S(A_1^x Fx)$' $\leftrightarrow_T$ '$S(\text{at } w_1, Fx)$'; iii) '$S(A_2^x Fx)$' $\leftrightarrow_T$ '$S(\text{at } w_2, Fx)$'; iv) '$S(\Box_2 \varphi)$' $\leftrightarrow_T$ '$S(\forall w_2(\text{at } w_2, \varphi))$'; and v) '$S(\Box_1 \varphi)$' $\leftrightarrow_T$ '$S(\forall w_1(\text{at } w_1, \varphi))$'. These principles are based on the account of the indexed modal operator expressions given by Forbes (1985, sec. 4.5).

29 Concrete realists face a problem in explaining the indexed actuality operators that is similar to the well known problem they face in analysing the simple non-indexed actuality operator. (See Hazen 1979, and Fara and Williamson 2005.) Forbes is an anti-realist about possible worlds. While Forbes endorses the meaning equivalence of (12) and (13), he regards (12) as explaining the meaning of (13) rather than (13) explaining the meaning of (12). (See Forbes 1985, sec. 4.5.) This allows him to claim that he can use sentences like (13) in a non-standard way that does not entail the existence of possible worlds.

hand side of (13) is necessarily equivalent to the right hand side of the simpler (15).[30]

> 14. For any u and v, and for any possible world w: (u at w is part of v at w) iff (at w, u is part of v).

> 15. F is intrinsic $=_{df} \forall x \forall u \forall v \forall w_1 \forall w_2[((\text{at } w_1, x \le u) \wedge (\text{at } w_2, x \le v) \wedge (u \text{ at } w_1 \le v \text{ at } w_2)) \supset ((\text{at } w_1, Fx) \equiv (\text{at } w_2, Fx))]$.

Given this, we can for simplicity replace (13) with (15). If, as I will argue, (15) fails given the above simplifying assumptions, (13) plausibly also fails.

Given 'at w, φ' symbolises 'Necessarily, if w obtains then φ', it is not obvious what it is for something at one world to be part of a thing at another world. I will argue that on any reasonable interpretation of what this could mean, (15) is either circular, false, or both circular and false.

One natural suggestion for what 'u at w_1 is part of v at w_2' could mean is given by (16).

> 16. (u at w_1 is part of v at w_2) $=_{df}$ for any z, if (at w_1, z is part of u) then (at w_2, z is part of v).

Unfortunately, this suggestion renders (15) false. To see why, suppose F expresses an intrinsic property p such that, for some x, and for some possible worlds w_1 and w_2: i) x exists at both w_1 and w_2; ii) x has the same parts at both w_1 and w_2; iii) 'at w_1, Fx' is true; and iv) 'at w_2, Fx' is false. (An example of such a property might be the property of being cubical.) Let $u = x$, and let v be such that: v) at w_2, x is part of v. Then: vi) at w_1, x is part of u. Since x has the same parts at w_1 and w_2, and x is part of v at w_2, all the parts of x at w_1 are parts of v at w_2. Given suggestion (16), it follows that: vii) $u(=x)$ at w_1 is part of v at w_2. It then follows from (iii), (iv), (v), (vi) and (vii) that (15) falsely classifies p as extrinsic.

A second way we might try to understand 'u at w_1 is part of v at w_2' is given by (17).

> 17. (u at w_1 is part of v at w_2) $=_{df}$ i) at w_2, u is part of v; and ii) for any intrinsic property p, u has p at w_1 iff u has p at w_2.

(17) does a much better job of rendering (15) true. For example, given (17), (15) is not shown to be false by the case just described. The reason for this is that there is no reason to think that $u(=x)$ at w_1 is part of v at w_2 in this case given (17), since in this case x at w_1 is not a part of x at w_2 according to (17). (17), however, renders (15) circular: if we need to use the concept of intrinsicality to explain 'u

---

[30] See Menzel (2008) for the simplest quantified S5 modal logic.

at w_1 is part of v at w_2', then we can't use (15) to give a non-circular analysis of intrinsicality.

The third and final suggestion I will consider is motivated by an example discussed by Yablo which might be thought to shed light on the notion of transworld parthood he has in mind. Yablo discusses a picnic that would have been shorter than it actually was had everything gone out of existence at some point after the picnic had begun and before it had finished.[31] Call the picnic that actually occurred k, and call the world at which everything goes out of existence w. Yablo claims that the picnic k is identical to the shortened picnic at w. He also claims that k at w is a proper part of k at the actual world.[32] This claim of Yablo's suggests that the notion of transworld parthood Yablo is employing in his account of intrinsicality is one that renders this claim about the picnic true. But is there any reasonable reading of 'proper part' under which this claim about the picnic is true?

One possibility is the first suggested meaning of transworld parthood given by (16). On this suggestion, u at w_1 might be defined to be a proper part of v at w_2 iff every part of u at w_1 is a part of v at w_2, but not every part of v at w_2 is a part of u at w_1. Given this interpretation of transworld parthood, Yablo's claim about the picnic appears to be true. However, as argued above, this interpretation of transworld parthood renders (15) false.[33]

Another possibility is (18), where x at w_1 is a duplicate of y at w_2 iff, for any qualitative intrinsic property p, y has p at w_1 iff z has p at w_2.

18. (u at w_1 is part of v at w_2) $=_{df}$ for some z, i) z is part of v at w_2, and ii) u at w_1 is a duplicate of z at w_2.

Given (18), u at w_1 might be defined to be a proper part of v at w_2 iff, for some z, i) z is a proper part of v at w_2, and ii) u at w_1 is a duplicate of z at w_2. This interpretation of transworld parthood seems to render Yablo's claim about the picnic true, and it also seems to capture what Yablo meant by transworld parthood in his example. Like the above interpretation, however, it fails to render (15) true. Suppose, for example, that x has an intrinsic property p at w_1 but not at w_2, while y has p at w_2 but not at w_1. Suppose also that: i) u is the fusion of x and y at both w_1 and w_2; ii) u at w_1 is a duplicate of u at w_2; and iii) at w_2, u is part of v. Then, given (18): iv) at w_1, x is part of u; v) at w_2, x is part of v; vi) u at w_1 is part of v at w_2; vii) 'at w_1, Fx' is true; and viii) 'at w_2, Fx' is false.

---

31 See Yablo (1999, p. 499).
32 Yablo seems to be assuming a four dimensional theory of space and time, according to which the picnic is a four dimensional object with temporal parts. I will also assume this here.
33 It also seems too weak to capture what Yablo means by transworld parthood in his example.

Hence, given (18), (15) falsely classifies *p* as extrinsic. (18) also renders (15) circular since it explains the meaning of transworld parthood in terms of intrinsicality.

All three suggestions as to how to interpret '*u* at w_1 is part of *v* at w_2' therefore fail. As a result, there does not appear to be any reasonable reading of this construction on which Yablo's account (15) is successful.

While (15) fails, we can give a better account of intrinsicality by employing the restricting operator expression 'Rest*' defined in section 2. The better account is given by (19).

19. *F* is intrinsic $=_{df}$ necessarily, for any *x*, necessarily $Rest^*_x(Fx)$ iff *Fx*.

This account is arguably in the spirit of Yablo's account, or at least it is in the spirit of the concretist version of his account. The account avoids the above problems facing (15). It also avoids many of the problems facing Yablo's original concretist account and its modifications, as well as many other accounts of intrinsicality in the literature. The account, for example, plausibly correctly classifies the property of being such that there is a number as extrinsic. It also appears not to have any particular problem in correctly classifying non-qualitative properties. For example, (19) plausibly correctly classifies both the property of being 1 m away from Yablo and the property of being a point sized object 1 m away from both Venus and Mars as extrinsic. It classifies the latter property as extrinsic, for example, since it might have been the case that there was a point sized object *x* that was 1 m away from both Venus and Mars (since Venus and Mars might have been very close to each other), and if this was the case then, even though it would have been the case that *x* was 1 m away from both Venus and Mars, it would not have been the case that $Rest^*_x(x$ is 1 m away from both Venus and Mars), since neither Venus nor Mars would be parts of *x*. The account also plausibly correctly classifies both the non-qualitative property of being Yablo and the non-qualitative property of having Yablo as a part as intrinsic.[34]

---

[34] Yablo claims that the property of being Yablo is extrinsic. His reason for thinking this appears to be that he thinks that part of what it is for something to be Yablo is for it to be descended from a certain zygote *Z*, where *Z* is wholly distinct from him. (See Yablo 1999, p. 486.) In other words, he seems to hold that there is some sentence φ such that (G) is true.

(G) For any *x*, (*x* = Yablo) $=_{df}$ *x* descended from *Z* and φ.

Given the truth of (G), (19) might classify *being Yablo* as extrinsic, given that the analysis of 'Rest' given in the main text in terms of perfect naturalness is modified so that ψ cannot contain any name that can be analysed in terms of names referring to other entities, variables, predicates expressing perfectly natural properties and relations, and operator expressions expressing perfectly natural operators. (Yablo holds that he is a non-bottom level entity who coincides with other entities and hence is an entity that doesn't satisfy the simplifying assumptions made in

As a result, unlike in the case of the modified concretist account given by (10), there is no need to provide a separate account of non-qualitative properties.

Despite this success, (19) faces two problems also faced by (10). First, (19) employs the operator expression 'Rest*' which stands in need of explanation, and doesn't seem able to be explained without appealing to notions like perfect naturalness which Yablo wishes to avoid. Second, and most decisively, (19) suffers the same qualitative counterexamples as (10) does. For example, given that necessarily there are no Platonic universals, (19) classifies the qualitative property of being such that there are no Platonic universals as intrinsic. It does this, since, necessarily, for any x, necessarily: i) x is such that there are no Platonic universals, and ii) $\text{Rest}^*_x(x$ is such that there are no Platonic universals).[35] Since the property of being such that there are no Platonic universals is extrinsic, it follows that (19) fails. While (19), then, correctly classifies a great number of properties and is more successful than many existing accounts of intrinsicality, it still fails. In light of this failure, it is likely that any account of intrinsicality in the spirit of Yablo's account will also fail.

References

Bricker, P. (1993). "The Fabric of Space: Intrinsic vs. Extrinsic Distance Relations". In P. French, T. E. Uehling, Jr., and H. K. Wettstein (eds.), *Midwest Studies in Philosophy XVIII: Philosophy of Science* (pp. 271–294). University of Notre Dame Press, South Bend, IN.

Bricker, P. (2008). "Concrete Possible Worlds". In T. Sider, J. Hawthorne and D. Zimmerman (eds.), *Contemporary Debates in Metaphysics* (pp. 111–134). Malden, MA: Blackwell Pub.

Dunn, J. M. (1990). "Relevant Predication 2: Intrinsic Properties and Internal Relations". *Philosophical Studies* 60(3): pp. 177–206.

Eddon, M. (2011). "Intrinsicality and Hyperintensionality". *Philosophy and Phenomenological Research* 82(2): pp. 314–336.

Fara, M. and Williamson, T. (2005). "Counterparts and Actuality". *Mind* 114: pp. 1–30.

Forbes, G. (1985). *The Metaphysics of Modality*. Oxford: Clarendon Press.

Hazen, A. (1979). "Counterpart-Theoretic Semantics for Modal Logic". *Journal of Philosophy* 76(6): pp. 319–338.

Humberstone, L. (1996). "Intrinsic/Extrinsic". *Synthese* 108(2): pp. 205–267.

Lewis, D. (1968). "Counterpart Theory and Quantified Modal Logic". *Journal of Philosophy* 65(5): pp. 113–126.

---

footnote 17. For each bottom level entity x, he thinks the property of being x is intrinsic. See Yablo 1999, p. 487.)

35 '$\text{Rest}^*_x(x$ is such that there are no Platonic universals)' is true since it is materially equivalent to 'x is part of x, and x is such that there are no Platonic universals that are part of x'.

Lewis, D. (1983). *Philosophical Papers, Volume 1*. Oxford: Oxford University Press.
Lewis, D. (1986). *On the Plurality of Worlds*. Oxford: Basil Blackwell.
Marshall, D. (2012). "Analyses of Intrinsicality in Terms of Naturalness". *Philosophy Compass* 7(8): pp. 531–542.
Marshall, D. (2013). "Analyses of Intrinsicality without Naturalness". *Philosophy Compass* 8(2): pp. 186–197.
Marshall, D. "A Puzzle for Modal Realism". Unpublished manuscript.
Menzel, C. (2012) "Actualism". In E. N. Zalta (ed.), *The Stanford Encyclopedia of Philosophy*. http://plato.stanford.edu/archives/fall2012/entries/actualism/
Peacocke, C. (1978). "Necessity and Truth Theories". *Journal of Philosophical Logic* 7(1): pp. 473–500.
Rosen, G. (2010). "Metaphysical Dependence: Grounding and Reduction". In B. Hale, and A. Hoffmann (eds.), *Modality: Metaphysics, Logic, and Epistemology* (pp. 109–36). Oxford University Press, Oxford.
Sider, T. (2001). *Four-Dimensionalism*. Clarendon, Oxford.
Sider, T. (2003). "Reductive Theories of Modality". In M. J. Loux, D. W. Zimmerman (eds.), *Oxford Handbook of Metaphysics* (pp. 180–208). Oxford University Press, Oxford.
Sider, T. (2011). *Writing the Book of the World*. Oxford University Press, Oxford.
Skow, B. (2007). "Are Shapes Intrinsic?". *Philosophical Studies* 133(1): pp. 111–130.
Vallentyne, P. (1997). "Intrinsic Properties Defined". *Philosophical Studies* 88(2): pp. 209–219.
Weatherson, B. (2001). Intrinsic Properties and Combinatorial Principles". *Philosophy and Phenomenological Research* 63(2): pp. 365–80.
Witmer, D. G., W. Butchard, and K. Trogdon (2005). "Intrinsicality without Naturalness". *Philosophy and Phenomenological Research* 70(2): pp. 326–350.
Yablo, S. (1999). "Intrinsicness". *Philosophical Topics* 26(1/2): pp. 479–505.

Alexander Skiles
Primitivism about Intrinsicality

Introduction

To many philosophers, a *reductive analysis* of intrinsicality—an account that comprehensively and non-circularly specifies, preferably in a compact schema, what intrinsicality *is* in metaphysically more fundamental terms—has appeared tantalizingly close. This optimistic attitude is perhaps most clearly displayed by the increasingly complicated attempts proposed in the continually growing literature on the nature of intrinsicality, and the increasingly sophisticated conceptual resources appealed to in order to state them. (For evidence, just flip through the pages of the book you're now holding.) One hope sustaining this attitude is to clarify intuitive judgments about intrinsicality that David Lewis says are "absurd" to dispense with altogether (1983, p. 197), and that Theodore Sider says are "as fit a foundation for philosophical theorizing as we can reasonably demand" (1993, p. 2). Another is to make more precise the multitude of distinctions, disputes, and arguments throughout philosophy that essentially rely upon at least some antecedent grasp of what intrinsicality is.[1] Thus the already substantial current literature cataloguing and evaluating reductive analyses of intrinsicality continues on, showing no signs of slowing (let alone stopping).

But, however nice it would be to possess a reductive analysis of intrinsicality, the faith that one is forthcoming—or even that one *exists*—seems increasingly difficult to square with the situation on the ground. As is well known, attempt after attempt to produce one has met with a broad array of recalcitrant cases and (in some cases) "no-go" results demonstrating that any attempt in the vicinity is bound to fail as well. (For evidence, just flip through the pages of the book you are now holding.) Yet there has been relatively scant discussion of why a reductive analysis should be assumed to be attainable, or even why taking intrinsicality to instead be *reductively unanalyzable* is to be avoided. When some philosophically central notion has revealed itself to be especially resistant to

---

[1] Humberstone (1996) and Weatherson and Marshall (2012) provide particularly extensive discussion of the central tasks that intrinsicality has served throughout philosophy. But not exhaustive (as they admit): we could also add recent discussions regarding the intrinsicality of consciousness (Merricks 1998), personal identity (Wasserman 2005; Williams 2013), a material object's geometrical features such as its shape (Skow 2007; Schaffer 2009a), and the features of fundamental microphysical systems (Ladyman and Ross 2007; Ney 2010) to the list.

reductive analysis, making peace with taking it as *primitive* has often been considered to be a live option. Why believe that intrinsicality is any different? Objections to the thesis that intrinsicality fails to succumb to reductive analysis have not been fully articulated or defended anywhere in the literature. Indeed, the thesis is rarely mentioned even as an option (let alone a live one). Nor has it been discussed what a viable account of intrinsicality along these lines could, or should, look like.[2]

The goal of this chapter is to explore the prospects of the view I shall call *primitivism about intrinsicality*, and offer a limited defense. A key component of this limited defense consists simply in clarifying what it could be, exactly, for intrinsicality to be "primitive". As we shall see, at least some *prima facie* decisive objections to primitivism seem less convincing once this has been done. Doing so is the task of section 1. In section 2, I then consider several arguments for primitivism about intrinsicality. And finally, in section 3, I consider several arguments against it.

1 What is primitivism about intrinsicality?

As I shall understand it, primitivism about intrinsicality is the conjunction of the following two theses about intrinsicality:

(PI-1)   There are at least some positive, mind-independent truths about which properties (or relations) are intrinsic to which things (or sequences thereof).[3]

---

[2] I am aware of only five discussions of these issues in the extant literature, all of them brief. The most extensive is due to Josh Parsons, who argues for "anti-reductionism about intrinsicality", which he characterizes as the twofold thesis that (*i*) intrinsicality is reductively unanalyzable, and in addition (*ii*) "[i]t is simply a brute fact about some properties that they are intrinsic (or, more nominalistically, about some pairs of objects that they are duplicates)" (2001, §2.23). The thesis I will be exploring in this paper endorses the first claim but not necessarily the second (see Sections 3.1 and 3.2 for more discussion). Maya Eddon concludes a critique of a wide array of attempts at reductive analysis by claiming that "we may discover that our intuitive notion of intrinsicality is not amenable to reduction", and then adding that "[w]hatever discomfort one may feel at the thought of taking intrinsic as primitive, it is worse to settle for an account that is false" (2010, p. 334). Lewis (1983), Sider (1993), and Francescotti (1999) round out the list of those who briefly mention taking intrinsicality as primitive, albeit as a last resort.
[3] A relation, R, is intrinsic to a sequence of things x1, x2, ... iff, roughly, it is intrinsic to x1, x2, ... that R is exemplified by them, in that specific order. I will suppress extension of what I say to relations, as well as to properties and relations collectively exemplified by two or more things, in what follows.

(PI-2) At least one notion of intrinsicality is reductively unanalyzable (i.e., *primitive*).

A *reductionist about intrinsicality* accepts (PI-1) yet rejects (PI-2). One might weaken (PI-2) slightly in order to classify as primitivists those who refuse the need to supply a reductive analysis when employing intrinsicality for some theoretical purpose. One might also classify as primitivists those who are doubtful (or perhaps simply agnostic) about the prospects of supplying one, yet who do not foreclose the possibility. Yet it would be most interesting to see how primitivism fares when considered at full strength, so I will commit the primitivist to (PI-2) here.[4]

With the restriction embedded in (PI-1) to positive, mind-independent truths about which properties are intrinsic to which things, I wish to contrast primitivism with two rival views. One is *eliminativism about intrinsicality*: the thesis that there are no truths about which properties are intrinsic to which things beyond, perhaps, various "negative" truths (such as that it is *not* intrinsic to the Eiffel Tower that it is made of iron, *not* intrinsic to my body that it is composite, and so forth). The eliminativist might maintain this as a (rather surprising) contingent matter of fact. More likely, the eliminativist will maintain this because she believes there to be something defective with the very concept of intrinsicality itself, or with the platitudes often used to convey what that concept is.[5] The eliminativist may well agree with the primitivist regarding (PI-2): believing that there are no positive facts about intrinsicality seems completely compatible with believing that intrinsicality is reductively unanalyzable. Nonetheless the two part ways with respect to (PI-1).

---

4 (PI-2) should also be understood to exclude possible (and as far as I am aware, undeveloped) views that take *highly implausible* construals of intrinsicality to be reductively unanalyzable, yet that take the most plausible construals of it to succumb to reductive analysis. Thanks to Robert Francescotti here.

5 Eliminativism is discussed even less frequently than primitivism, but the view is occasionally given voice. Daniel Dennett seems to express the view when he writes that "[i]f even such a brilliant theory-monger as David Lewis can try and fail, by his own admission, to define the extrinsic/intrinsic distinction coherently, we can begin to wonder if the concept deserves our further attention after all" (1988, p. 67). Another entry point into eliminativism hinted at in the literature is this. It is widely thought that a property is intrinsic to a thing only if it is exemplified "in virtue of" how that thing is, a feature that may "hyperintensionally" distinguish it from properties it is necessarily co-exemplified with (see Section 1.2; cf. Eddon 2011 and Bader 2013). Thus another kind of eliminativist may accept this thought while raising doubts about the coherence of the relevant, non-causal sense of "in virtue of" here (like those doubts expressed in Hofweber 2009 and Daly 2012) or about hyperintensional distinctions among properties (like those doubts discussed in Hawthorne 2009).

The other view primitivism is to be contrasted with is *non-objectivism about intrinsicality*. One version of such a view, *subjectivism about intrinsicality*, holds that whether a given property is intrinsic to a thing is ultimately grounded in facts about the subjective responses that tend to be elicited when confronted with this thing's exemplification of that property (whether empirically or on the basis of *a priori* reflection). Another version, *pragmatism about intrinsicality*, holds instead that facts about intrinsicality are ultimately grounded in facts of some kind about what our practical or epistemic interests happen to be at the moment.[6] Since I have no novel, informative account to offer here of what it is for a truth to be "mind-independent", I cannot give a more precise characterization here of the range of accounts I wish to exclude with (PI-1). Nonetheless this much is clear. Both the subjectivist and the pragmatist may well agree with the primitivist regarding (PI-2): believing that every fact about intrinsicality is ultimately grounded in facts either about our subjective responses or our interests is completely compatible with believing that intrinsicality is reductively unanalyzable. But presumably, any reasonably familiar conception of mind-independence would entail that if either view were correct, then truths about intrinsicality would fail to be mind-independent, which would in turn entail that the primitivist and the non-objectivist part ways with respect to (PI-1).[7]

The primitivist, then, states that there is at least one notion of intrinsicality that is reductively unanalyzable—and moreover, that at least some of these notions can be used to express positive truths about mind-independent reality. But before turning to what I mean by "reductively unanalyzable", what do I mean by a "notion"? The best way to convey what I mean is with an example. Take the predicate "is true" (as used in "The sentence 'Obama is a Democrat' is true") and the sentential connective "it is true that" (as used in "It is true that Obama is a Democrat"). I slice notions finely: this predicate and this sentential connective, although they both provide the means for expressing statements about truth, nonetheless express two different *notions* of truth. Suppose that these are the only two notions of truth. Then to claim that one takes truth to be reductively analyzable leaves open which of these two notions one takes to be primitive. One view takes the notion expressed by "is true" to be primitive, and reductively analyzes the notion expressed by "it is true that" in terms of

---

[6] Taylor (1993) defends such an account of naturalness, which he then uses in a reductive account of intrinsicality.

[7] The relevant sense of "ground" at issue here, along with my contention that facts about intrinsicality may ultimately be grounded in other facts even though intrinsicality itself is reductively unanalyzable, will play a significant role in what is to come. I will defer discussion of these matters to Sections 1.1, 3.2, and 3.3.

it; a second view says the opposite; and a third takes them to be reductively analyzable in terms of non-alethic notions rather than each other. As we shall see, primitivists about intrinsicality face a similar set of choices about which of the many notions of intrinsicality to take as primitive. And as we shall also see, which they choose has subtle (and often important) consequences for the tenability of the resulting view. I shall explore these in more depth in section 1.2.

1.1 What is it for a notion of intrinsicality to be *reductively unanalyzable?*

In a now classic article that helped initiate the contemporary literature on intrinsicality, Lewis (1983) presented two counterexamples to an attempt at reductive analysis originally proposed by Roderick Chisholm (1976) and further refined by Jaegwon Kim (1982). Chisholm's and Kim's accounts unpack what intrinsicality is in terms of notions that are purely modal and mereological. One way to attempt to reductively analyze what it is for a property to be intrinsic, or what Lloyd Humberstone (1996) has dubbed *global* intrinsicality, one which maintains the spirit of Chisholm's and Kim's own attempts, is the following:

(CKG) F is an intrinsic property iff: F is a property, and necessarily, if some x has F, then it is possible that (*i*) x has F and (*ii*) there is no contingent existent, y, that is not part of x (i.e., x is lonely).

A Chisholm-Kim style attempt to reductively analyze what it is for a property to be intrinsic to a particular thing (on some particular occasion)—what Humberstone calls *local* intrinsicality—goes like this:

(CKL) F is an intrinsic property of x iff: x has F, and it is possible that (*i*) x is F and (*ii*) x is lonely.[8]

My concern in the following subsection is neither with Lewis's specific counterexamples to accounts along these lines, nor with the many subsequent refinements that have been introduced in order to evade them. Rather, I want to ask what might be some of the necessary conditions for statements such as (CKG) and (CKL), when offered as reductive analyses, to be correct. What follows is

---

[8] On my view, facts about the having of a property are to be relativized (at least) to a time and possible world (perhaps with the exception of the having of properties of times and worlds themselves). A thing's properties, and indeed the intrinsicality status of a thing's properties, can vary (at least) from time to time and world to world. However, I will suppress this qualification throughout (but will revisit it in Section 2.2).

far short of a reductive analysis of reductive analysis, and some reductivists may disagree with what I take some of these necessary conditions to be (and perhaps even with whether they are saddled with providing what *I* call a "reductive analysis"). Yet what follows comports well enough with what primitivists and reductionists seem to take to be what is at stake.[9]

A notion of intrinsicality is reductively analyzable just in case there exists a reductive analysis, which one might think of as a type of proposition that (CKG) and (CKL) both purport to state. (Sometimes I will speak of the activity of producing sentences that purport to state reductive analyses as "reductively analyzing" a notion, although context will make clear which I have in mind.) Ignoring other notions of intrinsicality, it is sufficient for there to exist a reductive analysis of every notion of intrinsicality that (CKG) and (CKL) succeed at stating reductive analyses.[10] But what would it take for (CKG) and (CKL) to state reductive analyses? It is by now well known that it is necessary, but not sufficient, that each substitution instance of "F" and "x" in (CKG) and (CKL) must yield a pair of necessarily true sentences. For if this condition were sufficient, then reductively analyzing intrinsicality would be far too easy: "F is an intrinsic property" is necessarily equivalent in truth-value to "an omniscient being would know that F is an intrinsic property", "F has this property" (where "this" directly picks out the property of *being an intrinsic property* through a mental act of ostension), and simply "F is an intrinsic property", but none of these express reductive analyses. (Thus my use of "iff:" rather than "iff" to indicate that substitution instance of (CKG) and (CKL) are being considered as stating putative reductive analyses of intrinsicality rather than merely as necessitated biconditionals.) The hard task for a full-blown account of reductive analysis is to specify what more is required beyond necessary covariation in truth-value. However, I will assume that the following two conditions are at least necessary.

---

9 Although there is some literature on the nature of reductive analysis (and, more generally, of the nature and varieties of what I call *metaphysical analysis* in contrast to "conceptual analysis": see below), the issue has received relatively little direct attention in comparison to how often the concept crops up in first-order applications. Concepts similar in at least some respects to what I am calling "reductive metaphysical analysis" have been discussed recently by Fine (1994), King (1998; 2007), Dorr (2004; 2005; 2008; manuscript), Melia (2005), Rayo (2013), Schroeder (2005), and Wedgwood (2007), but there are rather stark differences separating how these authors articulate these concepts, and separating how I articulate the concept of metaphysical analysis here. Space prevents me from providing a full comparison, although I hope to do so in future work.

10 Some would say that (CKG) and (CKL) state reductive analyses even if they are *unsuccessful*. Those who choose to speak this way should insert "true" in front of every occurrence of "reductive analysis" throughout this chapter.

First, in order for (CKG) and (CKL) to state reductive analyses, there must in some sense be an *identification* between the "aspect of reality" that the analysandum sentence concerns and the "aspect of reality" that the analysans sentence concerns. This requirement—call it *the identification requirement*—is easiest to see when the notion targeted for reductive analysis is a property. For (CKG) to state a reductive analysis, for instance, it must say which property the higher-order property of *being an intrinsic property* really just *is*—or as Jeffrey King puts it, (CKG) cannot merely "[say] that the property in question is related to this or that property in certain ways" (1998, p. 177 fn. 26). And presumably, since *being an intrinsic property* is not identical to the property of *would be known to be an intrinsic property by an omniscient being*, the sentence "F is an intrinsic property iff: every omniscient being would know that F is an intrinsic property" does not state a reductive analysis, as one wants to say.[11]

Although the identification requirement is clear enough when a *property* is the targeted notion, it is difficult to state what it involves when some other kind of notion is involved without straying into controversial matters that I ultimately wish to stay neutral towards. To recall an earlier example, many would want to maintain that one can reductively analyze the notion expressed by the sentential connection "it is true that" without committing oneself to the further view that there is some *entity*—whether it be a property, or from another ontological category—that serves as a relatum for identification. But for sake of concreteness, and since the discussion to follow will largely not turn on such matters, I will work with my own views about them and construe the identification requirement as follows. Say that if a sentence, "p", is true, then it *picks out* an obtaining fact, which I symbolize as: [p]. Although I will assume that there are facts, I will not assume that the predicates, sentential connectives, or other expressions occurring in "p" pick out constituents of [p], or that [p] has any other kind of internal structure. However, I will assume that a necessary condition for a statement like (CKG) or (CKL) to express a reductive analysis is that for any uniform substitution of "x" and "F" with names of particular objects and particular properties, the resulting analysans sentence, if it is true, picks out the same fact as the resulting analysandum sentence.[12]

---

[11] Here and throughout, I am assuming that properties are "fine grained" (and not, e.g., individuated merely by sets of their actual and possible instances).

[12] This ontologically loaded way of construing the identification requirement must eventually face up to hard questions about the conditions under which "two" facts are identical. My own view is that there are no interesting principles of fact individuation that apply across all cases, but nonetheless this is no reason to deny that there might be interesting cases of fact identity. But if there *are*, presumably they will have to be fine-grained enough so that [a is intrinsically F]

Along with the identification requirement, I will also assume that for either (CKG) or (CKL) to succeed at reductive analysis, the embedded analysans sentence must in some sense express only notions that are "metaphysically more fundamental" than the notion targeted for reductive analysis expressed in the analysandum sentence. Spelling out this in full detail also leads us into vexed matters I wish to avoid, but I take this relative fundamentality requirement to have at least two upshots, both of which are compatible with a reductive analysis also satisfying the identification requirement.

The grounding constraint

The first upshot makes use of the concept of *metaphysical grounding:* the relationship by which one collection of facts is said to non-causally "wholly derive from", "hold wholly in virtue of", or be "wholly brought about by" another collection of facts. Since the concept has played such a prominent role in recent attempts at reductively analyzing intrinsicality, I will presuppose a basic familiarity with it here.[13]

To help get a feel for the grounding constraint, suppose (CKL) is true. Say that a sentence with the logical structure as an instance of (CKL), i.e. any sentence of the form "p iff: ($q_1 \wedge q_2$)", expresses an *instance of reductive analysis* just in case it is a true sentence that results from uniformly substituting "x" and "F" in (CKL) with names of objects and properties. Then for the case of (CKL), the grounding constraint is met only if for every instance of reductive analysis, two conditions are met: (*i*) the fact picked out by "p" is grounded in the collection of facts picked out by "q_1" and "q_2", and (*ii*) neither fact in this collection is itself grounded in facts, some of which are picked out by true sentences that express the notion of intrinsicality targeted for reductive analysis. So, for example, if (CKL) states a reductive analysis, then the fact that the property *being made of iron* is an intrinsic property of the Eiffel Tower is grounded in the collection consisting of just the following two facts, neither of which are grounded in collections of facts that include facts involving the relevant notion of intrin-

---

and [every omniscient being would know that a is intrinsically F] count as distinct, yet coarse-grained enough that uncontroversial instances of reductive analysis like [George Clooney is a bachelor] and [George Clooney is an adult unmarried male] are not distinct. For alternative conceptions of reductive analysis that are not ontologically loaded in this manner, see Dorr (manuscript) and Rayo (2013).

13 See Witmer *et al.* (2005), Rosen (2010), and Bader (2013) for general discussion of the relevant concept of grounding.

sicality: namely, [the Eiffel Tower has *being made of iron*] and [it is possible for the Eiffel Tower to both have *being made of iron* and to be lonely]. This constraint can be generalized in obvious ways to sentences that purport to state reductive analyses that differ from (CKL) in logical structure.[14]

The essence constraint

The second way in which the analysans sentence expresses "metaphysically more fundamental" notions makes use of the concept of the collection of true sentences about a notion's *essence:* those that all hold in virtue of the notion's nature or identity, and collectively constitute the smallest exhaustive characterization of *what* that notion is (as opposed to *how* it is).[15] Supposing that it is unique, let Σ be the collection of truths about some notion v_1, and say that some notion v_2 is a *constituent* of the essence of v_1 just in case it is expressed by a constituent of some sentence in Σ. (So, for instance, if Σ collects all truths about the essence of the set {Socrates}, and includes the sentence "Socrates is a member of {Socrates}", then "Socrates", "is a member of", and "{Socrates}" all express constituents of {Socrates}'s essence.) Then according to the essence constraint, if v_1 is reductively analyzable in terms of v_2, it follows that v_1 is *not* a constituent of the essence of v_2.

The essence constraint has at least two *prima facie* motivations. First, it is plausible to think that if v_1 is reductively analyzable in terms of v_2, then v_2 is *au-*

---

[14] The idea here would be to extend the grounding constraint based on general principles about how facts with a certain logical structure are grounded in facts of a different logical structure. So, for instance, one might say that if "*p* iff: (*q* ∨ *r*)" is an instance of some reductive analysis, then [*p*] is either grounded in [*q*] or grounded in [*r*]; if "*p* iff: ∃*x*Φ*x*" is an instance of some reductive analysis, then for any *a* which is such that the sentence "[Φ*a*]" is true, [*p*] is grounded in [Φ*a*]; if "*p* iff: ∀*x*Φ*x*" is an instance of some reductive analysis, then for every *a*, *b*, ... which is such that "[Φ*a*]", "[Φ*b*]", ... are true, [*p*] is grounded in a collection of facts that includes all of [Φ*a*], [Φ*b*], ...; and so on. Complications emerge, however, when considering analysans sentences in which the main connective is a sentential connective (such as "it is possible that" or "it will always be the case that"), since it is controversial whether such sentences are grounded at all, and if they are, what facts they are grounded in. Unfortunately I cannot explore these in detail here.

[15] For influential discussions of the relevant concept of essence, see Fine (1994; 1995) and Lowe (1998). Fine and Lowe focus solely on the concept of *objectual* essence, which figures into answers to questions like "what is it to be Socrates?". However, Correia (2006) has convincingly argued that there is also the concept of *generic* essence, which figures into answers to questions like "what is it for a proposition to be true?". Here, I primarily have Correia's concept of generic essence in mind, extended to sentences that need not have subject-predicate logical structure.

tomatically included in truths about what v_1 is: a collection of truths that fails to include "every bachelor is an unmarried male", for instance, would fail to include an important truth about the essential nature of the notion of bachelorhood. Yet some have argued that constituents of a notion's essence help to determine non-trivial *individuation conditions* for that notion, and moreover that a notion cannot help determine non-trivial individuation conditions for that which determines its own.[16] From the previous claims, the essence constraint directly follows. A second, more mundane motivation for the essence constraint is simply that it comports with how we intuitively reason about putative reductive analyses. For instance, those who claim to analyze what necessity and possibility are in terms of facts about "causal powers" (e. g., the causal power of a cube of sodium chloride to dissolve in water) will often immediately add that the proposed analysis is not reductive because they take the collection of truths about a causal power's essence to include truths about which effects they *would* or *could* produce across various actual and non-actual circumstances.[17]

One might add further constraints—for instance, requiring that the analysans sentence not just be a mere disjunction of all possible scenarios in which the analysandum sentence is satisfied, say—but only the previous two constraints will play a role in what follows. However, note that I have *not* assumed that a reductive analysis must satisfy any *cognitive* constraints: for instance, I do not assume that a reductive analysis must be informative, or that epistemic access to it either can or must be a priori, or that it state a conceptual truth (in any of the many senses of "conceptual truth" found in the literature). As I understand it, the reductionist about intrinsicality is only committed to the *metaphysical* analyzability of all notions of intrinsicality, while neutral about whether how it is *conceptually* represented in either thought or talk can be unpacked in other terms, and about how one could gain evidence that notions of intrinsically reduce in the manner proposed.

---

16 See Lowe (2012) for such an argument.
17 Sometimes this constraint is posed in a somewhat misleading fashion, though. For instance, Jonathan Jacobs writes that his account of modality in terms of causal powers is "non-reductive, for the properties (or the relations between them) are *intrinsically* modal" (2010, p. 233, my emphasis). The strict and literal reading of this constraint seems much too strong: if it is intrinsic to the relation between a thing and its parts that it is an intrinsic relation, it does not automatically follow that an account of what intrinsicality is in terms of parthood cannot be reductive. However, later Jacobs indicates that the intended reading is not in terms of intrinsicality, but rather in terms of essence, when he says that "[s]uch possibilities are […] metaphorically written into the nature of" a causal power and that "the precise nature of a powerful property is an a posteriori necessity" (p. 239).

1.2 *Which* notions of intrinsicality are reductively unanalyzable?

Even though primitivists all agree that at least some notion of intrinsicality is primitive, nonetheless there remains the question of which notions these *are*. Reductionists face a similar dispute: which notions of intrinsicality are not reductively analyzable *in terms of other notions of intrinsicality*, and thus serve as the "entry points" for the reductive account? Yet the question that faces the primitivist seems theoretically more pressing. An unwise choice of primitives may expressively impoverish the primitivist's account if they are too few or of the wrong kind; or it may render the primitivist's theory ideologically unparsimonious—it may ascribe *too much* to reality's ultimate structure beyond what is required—if there are instead too many, or if redundancies emerge. Rather than take on the general question of which notions the primitivist should take as primitive, in this section I will merely sketch out some options that deserve consideration, since how they differ will also have an impact on the prospects of primitivist accounts.

Which intrinsicality platitude(s) is the notion supposed to satisfy?

As Brian Weatherson and Dan Marshall (2012) note, one might distinguish between numerous non-equivalent varieties of intrinsicality, each roughly associated with a different platitude about intrinsicality. Thus one may distinguish properties had independently of outside forces (cf. Ellis 1991) or independently of the external environment more generally (cf. Figdor 2008); or properties that any pair of possible duplicates cannot differ with respect to (cf. Lewis 1983b); or properties had in virtue of the way that a thing is in and of itself (cf. Vallantyne 1997); or properties the ascription of which are only about a thing and its parts rather than its relations to other things (cf. Francescotti 1999). Now, one may take some or all of these as imperfect glosses on a single common primitive notion, or instead take some or all of these to express *distinct* notions of intrinsicality. If one goes the latter route, there is the option to take one or more of these notions of intrinsicality as primitive. Call a *pluralist* any primitivist who takes two or more of these platitudes about intrinsicality to each be associated with a (or, perhaps, more than one) notion of intrinsicality, and a *monist* any primitivist who rejects pluralism.

Local or global intrinsicality?

As we noted before, it is now common to distinguish the claim that the property *being less than a kilometer from the Eiffel Tower* is intrinsic to the Eiffel Tower (a seemingly true claim about *local* intrinsicality) from the non-equivalent claim that *being less than a kilometer* is an intrinsic property (a seemingly false claim about *global* intrinsicality, since a tourist climbing the Eiffel Tower may have this property, yet not intrinsically). It has become standard recently to take global intrinsicality to be reductively analyzable in terms of local intrinsicality.[18] However, there is no *logical* contradiction in taking some primitive notions to correspond to global intrinsicality, while others correspond to local intrinsicality. For instance, even if the primitivist believes that for a property to be globally intrinsic is for it to necessarily be locally intrinsic when exemplified, she may still deny that facts about global intrinsicality are grounded, if at all, in facts about local intrinsicality (thus violating the grounding constraint from section 1.1). Likewise, one could still maintain that some truths about the essence of primitive notions of local intrinsicality include at least some notions of global intrinsicality (thus violating the essence constraint).

Which grammatical categories express the relevant notions?

Suppose that there is some primitive notion of local intrinsicality. Even so, there might still be a number of ways to express the grammatical structure of sentences expressing this notion, and thus many possible primitive notions of local intrinsicality to choose from. For instance, one may take it to be expressed with a relational predicate ("…is intrinsic to…"). Or one may take it to be expressed with a sentential operator that takes a sequence of things and a formula and yields a closed sentence ("it is intrinsic to…that…"). Or one may take it to be expressed with an adverbial modifier that combines with one predicate to yield another ("…intrinsically"). Or one may take it to be expressed with a monadic predicate of facts ("…is an intrinsic fact"). Sorting out which one or more of these to opt for is an important theoretical task for the primitivist for at least two reasons. First, some of these primitive notions seem to bring ontological commitments along with them that one might want to reject (e.g., to properties or to facts). Second, it is not at all obvious whether every statement about local intrinsicality phrased in terms of one of these notions can be expressed with a statement phrased in

---

[18] For instance, see Witmer *et al.* (2005) and Bader (2013).

terms of any other, and thus whether some of these notions have more or less expressive power relative to the others.[19]

Are the notions comparative or non-comparative?

Yet another decision point for the primitivist is whether to take the primitive notions of intrinsicality to be *non-comparative*—stating that F is intrinsic, or that F is intrinsic to x, full stop—or *comparative*. Although comparative notions of intrinsicality are underexplored, they seem coherent, and there is no obvious reason why the primitivist could not build her account of intrinsicality around them.[20] For instance, one might take as primitive the notion that x is F intrinsically to a certain *degree*. Or one might take as primitive the notion that x is F intrinsically *more*, or *less*, or *as much as*, a given y is G intrinsically (where x might be identical to y, or F might be identical to G).

The primitivist thus has considerable theoretical work to do. (I have not even considered related questions about whether any notions of *extrinsicality* are to be taken as primitive, and which to take as primitive if so.)

One final question to consider is whether the primitivist should be a monist or a pluralist. The monist might complain that the pluralist's stock of primitive notions includes far too many, but it is not as clear as it might initially seem that the pluralist is at an inherent disadvantage to monism for this reason. First, and most obviously, it is not clear whether the various notions of intrinsicality are reductively analyzable in terms of just one. And second, it is also not clear whether a theory with less primitive notions of the same kind is *ceteris paribus* preferable to a theory with more. For instance, Sam Cowling (forthcoming) has argued that just as ontological parsimony is often taken to be judged *qualitatively* (i.e., in terms of how many kinds of entities a theory postulates) rather than *quantitatively* (i.e., in terms of how many instances of a particular kind of

---

[19] Just as it is natural to distinguish global intrinsicality from local intrinsicality, it is also natural to distinguish a property's being locally essential (i.e., an essential property of some entity) from its being globally essential (i.e., its necessarily being an essential property of all entities that have it). Fortunately, there has been some study of the logical relationships between different notions of local essentiality that may be transposed into a yet-to-be-pursued study of the logical relationships between different notions of local intrinsicality, but doing so must be left for elsewhere. See Fine (1995) and Correia (2006) for the logic of notions of essentiality.
[20] Figdor (2008, p. 699) briefly notes that her reductive analysis and others that have been recently proposed allow for local intrinsicality to be had in degrees, but does not explore the possibility further.

entity a theory postulates), ideological parsimony ought to be judged qualitatively rather than quantitatively. Suppose it can be shown that the pluralist's multiple notions of intrinsicality are all of the same kind in the sense relevant for judging ideological parsimony. (Cowling claims that a sufficient condition for belonging to the same kind is the *interanalyzability* of these notions, but perhaps there are others.) Then if Cowling is correct, no additional theoretical cost is incurred by the primitivist by opting for a larger stock of primitive notions of intrinsicality. Hence whether there is a deep dispute at all between the monist and the pluralist may not be such a deep dispute after all.

Thus completes my discussion of general questions about how to understand primitivism. The remainder of this chapter considers what reasons might be brought to bear for or against it.

2 Arguments for primitivism about intrinsicality

What kinds of support could be mustered in favor of the thesis that some notion of intrinsicality is *not* reductively analyzable? In the following section, I discuss two families of arguments (although without foreclosing the possibility that other arguments might be devised).

2.1 Arguments that appeal to past track records of failure

It is completely uncontroversial to observe that despite repeated attempts, no attempt at reductively analyzing intrinsicality garners even majority support among the practitioners, and only slightly more contentious to claim that every extant attempt faces what seem (at least *prima facie*) to be decisive counterexamples, among various other obstacles. Rather than rehash the many articles chronicling these obstacles, let us just suppose they stand and see what follows.[21]

The fact that these obstacles *do* stand is of course consistent with the existence of a hitherto unknown reductive analysis of intrinsicality. To construct a genuine *argument* for primitivism on the basis of this fact, the primitivist must

---

[21] Weatherson and Marshall (2012), Marshall (2012), and Marshall (forthcoming-a) are particularly thorough surveys of problems with the various attempts. Until recently, my own view was that intrinsicality could be reductively analyzed in terms of notions of grounding and mereology, roughly along the lines of the proposals found in Rosen (2010) and Bader (2013). However, recent criticism of such accounts due to Marshall (forthcoming-b) now give me pause.

either reason *inductively* from it (by arguing that there is a large and representative enough of a sample of repeated failures to suggest that every future attempt would result in failure too), or reason *abductively* from it (by arguing that the non-existence of a reductive analysis is the best explanation for why we have yet to discover one). And even then such reasoning may come in two broad varieties: the appeal can be either *restricted*, by focusing on the past track record of failure to reductively analyze intrinsicality in particular, or *unrestricted*, by focusing on the past track record of failure to reductively analyze *any* notion of philosophical interest. So, for instance, a restricted inductive track record argument for primitivism incorporates as a premise the claim that the sample of past attempts is both large enough (since there have been many such attempts) and representative enough (since reductive analysis has been pursued under a diverse array of approaches and has employed a diverse array of notions). In contrast, Timothy Williamson offers an unrestricted abductive track record argument when he claims that "[t]he pursuit of analyses is a degenerating research programme" that had its origins "in great philosophical visions" such as Russell's logical atomism and the principle of acquaintance, but "the philosophical visions that gave it a point are no longer serious options" that can sustain it (2000, pp. 31–32).

How should the reductivist respond, to start with, to restricted arguments for primitivism (assuming, again, that the reductivist grants that no successful account has been developed)? There are a number of strategies, each of which can be construed either as a reason to doubt that the past track record of failures is large and representative enough of a sample to support a strong inductive generalization, or as an alternative explanation to the primitivist's non-existence hypothesis.

First, the reductivist might point out that although notions of intrinsicality have been employed in philosophical conversations for centuries, the academic industry devoted to reductively analyzing intrinsicality is comparatively new, beginning in earnest only during the 1980s. Perhaps that industry has only scratched the surface of the number and variety of possibilities with some viability.

A second kind of response is this. There is no agreement about what a reductive analysis of intrinsicality should look like. However, there *is* a growing (although not unanimous) consensus that one must inevitably go beyond the "quasi" or "broadly logical" notions of logic, modality, mereology, set theory, and property exemplification in order to state one that has hope for success (given no special assumptions about the nature or ontology of properties).[22]

---

[22] Talk of "quasi" or "broadly logical" notions in this context, and argument that any such

The predominant diagnosis is that one must also appeal to notions that *hyperintensionally* distinguish intrinsic properties from those they may be necessarily co-exemplified with. The disagreement comes from whether the needed vocabulary must express notions of naturalness (Lewis 1983b; Langton and Lewis 1998), grounding and fundamentality (Witmer *et al.* 2005; Trogdon 2009; Rosen 2010; Bader 2013), an event or state of affairs "consisting in" another (Francescotti 1999), or perhaps some other exotic resources. In addition to noting how new the industry of reductively analyzing intrinsicality is, the reductionist may further note that the project of polishing the resources needed is comparatively new as well, and argue that for all the primitivist has shown, further polishing might be all that is needed for success.

A third kind of response goes as follows. As I said in section 1.2, there is also a growing consensus that there are a variety of slightly divergent notions of intrinsicality, and slightly divergent conceptions of what intrinsicality amounts to, that philosophers have targeted for reductive analysis. The reductivist may grasp hold of this observation, and argue that the presence of a past track record of failure may have more to do with mismatch between the reductive analysis offered on one hand and the conception or notion targeted, or more to do with the assumption that there is a single notion of intrinsicality that all other notions of intrinsicality are reductively analyzable in terms of. The reductionist might reasonably complain that it is too early to tell whether reductively analyzing different notions of intrinsicality independently might meet with more success.

Although they are not decisive obstacles to restricted track record arguments for primitivism, they are serious, and the primitivist who wishes to advance such arguments must grapple with them. In contrast, I will have less to say about unrestricted arguments for primitivism, since the literature dealing with these arguments is far more extensive than can be surveyed here.[23] But two notes of caution for the would-be proponent. First, those who wish to motivate primitivism, at least in part, by appealing to its reductive power (cf. section 2.2) are undermined as much by unrestricted track record arguments as the reductionist. Second, those who have advanced unrestricted track record arguments often argue on the basis of *cognitive* constraints on reductive analysis: Williamson, for instance, appeals to failures of "concept identity" between the analyzing notions and the notions to be analyzed (2000, p. 30), for instance, while many others have argued

---

account must fail, comes from Sider (1996) and Marshall (2009), respectively. For dissent, see Vallentyne (1997), Yablo (1999), Denby (2006), and Hoffmann (2010a); for discussion of whether the accounts contained in these works are both broadly logical and successful, see the discussion and references in Weatherson and Marshall (2012) and Marshall (forthcoming-a).

23 For a small sample, see many of the essays in DePaul and Ramsey (1998).

that the past track record of reductive failure is best explained by unreliability of a priori intuition as a source of evidence. But the reductionist need not require such cognitive constraints be satisfied for reductive analysis (given the conception of reductive analysis I have sketched in Section 1.1, at least).

2.2 The necessary ingredients for an analysis of intrinsicality are inapt for it to constitute a *reductive* analysis of intrinsicality

Reductionists have employed a large collection of exotic notions in attempts to reductively analyze intrinsicality, notions that have themselves been taken as primitive (see section 1.2 for a short, slightly less than comprehensive list). This observation suggests another way to support primitivism. One could argue that if intrinsicality were reductively analyzable, it would have to be done so at least partly in terms of one or more specific notions, and then argue that these notions are *inapt* to play the required reductive role.

Recalling the discussion from section 1.1, the primitivist could show that a given notion is inapt in at least one of two ways. First, the primitivist could show that one of these notions is better reductively analyzed in terms of intrinsicality rather than *vice versa*. Given the grounding constraint, it would follow that the relevant notion of intrinsicality is not reductively analyzable in terms of this inapt notion. Second, the primitivist could show that the notion is inapt by showing the relevant notion of intrinsicality is a constituent of the inapt notion's essential nature. Neither of these kinds of arguments would demonstrate that one could not illuminate what intrinsicality is in terms of these inapt notions, or even that one could not provide informative necessary and sufficient conditions of the former in terms of the latter. But either argument would demonstrate that such an account falls short of reductive analysis. Given the supposition that any viable successor account must employ these inapt notions, primitivism about intrinsicality follows.

Are there any such notions that could suit the primitivist's purposes? The most obvious candidate is *parthood*, or one or more related notions from mereology. Nearly every major purported reductive analysis of intrinsicality appeals to mereological notions, including those that appeal to the technical notions of loneliness and independence of accompaniment (e.g., Langton and Lewis 1998, Witmer *et al.* 2005, Trogdon 2009), and the notion of an isomorphism that preserves the perfectly natural properties and relations among a thing's parts (e.g., Lewis 1986). Similarly when one looks at the details of those accounts that set mereological restrictions on the ways of modally recombining properties and property instantiations, which are then taken to generate the set of intrinsic properties (Weatherson 2001 and Denby 2006). Or set mereological restrictions on the kinds of objects that cannot be "removed" from or "ignored" in a thing's environment without varying its intrinsic properties (e. g., Vallentyne 1997, Yablo 1999, and Figdor 2008). Or set mereological restrictions on the kinds of facts that can serve as the reduction or grounding base for facts about a thing's intrinsic properties (e.g., Francescotti 1999, Skow 2007, Rosen 2010, and Bader 2013). I have no argument that one *cannot* reductively analyze intrinsicality without some mereological notion, but it is difficult (at best) to see how a viable reductive analysis would go.

So, could the primitivist convincingly argue that for any notion of mereology, the collection of truths that characterize its essence must express some notion of intrinsicality? Perhaps surprisingly, indications that the correct answer is *yes* are intuitively strong. It is routine for philosophers to make appeal to truths about intrinsicality when attempting to convey truths about the essential nature of central mereological notions such as that of parthood. For instance, Fine observes when introducing "the intuitive notion of part" that "[w]hen one object is a part of another, there is a sense in which it is *in* the other—not in the sense of being *enclosed by* the other, as when a marble is in an urn, but more in the sense of being *integral to* the other" (2010, p. 560, his emphasis). Although Fine does not further characterize what "integrality" consists in, it is tempting to take it as expressing a notion of intrinsicality. Similarly, Theodore Sider observes that parthood seems constrained by a principle that he dubs "the inheritances of intrinsicality": if property *F* is intrinsic, then the property *having a part that has F* is also intrinsic. In this sense at least, part of what it is to be a part is for its intrinsic nature to be "reflected in the whole" (2007, p. 70).[24] For a third example, one that returns us to the intrinsicality literature, Stephen Yablo notes three connections between parthood and intrinsicality, and claims them to be "nonaccidental" and "as de jure as anything":

- If x is part of y, then x cannot change intrinsically without y changing intrinsically as well.
- If x is part of y, then x and y have a region of intrinsic match.
- If x is properly part of y, then x and y have intrinsic differences. (1999, p. 482)

---

24 Similarly, Fine claims that "[i]n the case of the 'intrinsic' character of a thing—such as its mass and its color—the character of the whole will be some sort of function of the character of the parts" that varies from case to case, and then adds that "I am inclined to regard these various principles as definitive of the form of composition in question. It will lie in the nature of any form of composition to conform to various principles of this sort" (2010, p. 571).

(One might add to Yablo's list. For example, it seems "nonaccidental" and "as de jure as anything" as well that if x is a part of y, then this is an intrinsic relationship between x and y—one needn't look "beyond the borders" of x and y taken together to see that one is a part of the other. But let us settle for Yablo's list for now.) By "nonaccidental", Yablo is explicit that he does not mean *contingent*. Contrasting what he takes to be "de facto" connections between intrinsicality and the Lewisian notion of naturalness, Yablo claims that there is "nothing in the nature of intrinsicness" that prevents this connection from coming apart (1999, p. 481), and adds that this would strike us as so even if the connection happens to hold with necessity (fn. 4).

Although there seems to be a strong intuitive case for the claim that notions of mereology violate the essence constraint with respect to intrinsicality, the reductionist may resist in a number of ways. First, the reductionist may simply reject the essence constraint, although doing so would require explaining away the *prima facie* support for it, and (ideally) motivating an alternative account of reductive analysis that is unfettered by it. Second, the reductionist might claim that although the connections state *necessary* truths about the relevant notions of mereology, they do not state *essential* truths about them. Third, the reductionist might claim that although these connections *do* state essential truths, they state essential truths about intrinsicality rather than about notions of mereology—presumably, truths that can be derived from a reductive analysis of the former in terms of the latter.

Could the primitivist instead argue that the notions of mereology relevant for reductively analyzing are inapt because they are reductively analyzable in terms of notions of intrinsicality rather than *vice versa*? Here again, the primitivist seems to be able to make a surprisingly strong case. I will briefly consider five accounts—although I cannot explore all the issues they raise here, or whether any variation of one of these accounts is successful, they are worth the primitivist's effort to explore in more detail (although ultimately the last pair of accounts at least initially seem more worth effort than the first three).

First, recall Fine's observation that a part of a thing is in some sense "in" or "integral" to the thing it is a part of. Normally when one speaks of a thing, x, being *intrinsic to* another thing, y, one takes "x" to range only over properties (as, for example, (CKL) does from section 1.1). But one could remove this restriction, and take "x" to range not only over properties, but rather over objects of *any* arbitrary ontological category. One might then claim that x is a proper part of y iff: x is intrinsic to y, and x is not a property. Although straightforward, this account has at least one major disadvantage that a thing cannot possibly have any properties as parts. Some might see this as an attractive result, taking only spatially locatable material objects to enter into mereological relations. Those who instead wish to evade this apparent problem could remove the qualification that *x* not be a property, but then the difficulty is to distinguish cases in which a thing has a property intrinsically from cases in which a thing has a property as a part. For the two cases can come apart: even if the two-membered set {Socrates, *being a philosopher*} has the property of *being a philosopher* intrinsic to it in the mereological sense, the set clearly does not itself have this property (let alone have this property intrinsically). Cashing out this distinction without mereological notions will be challenging.

One might instead look to the de jure connections that Yablo lists for further insight into how to reductively analyze parthood in terms of intrinsicality. For instance, a second and third kind of attempt start with Yablo's claim that if *x* is part of *y*, then *x* cannot change intrinsically without *y* changing intrinsically as well. There are at least two ways to read Yablo's claim. One reads it as the claim that intrinsic changes to *x necessitate* intrinsic changes to *y*, while the other instead reads it as the weaker counterfactual claim that intrinsic changes to *x would* lead to intrinsic changes to *y*. In a similar fashion, one may attempt to reductively analyze parthood in terms of intrinsicality as follows:

(YP-1) *x* is part of *y* iff: □(*x* undergoes intrinsic change → *y* undergoes intrinsic change)

(YP-2) *x* is part of *y* iff: (*x* undergoes intrinsic change □→ *y* undergoes intrinsic change)

Although perhaps an account in the vicinity of (YP-1) and (YP-2) could be made to function properly, at minimum it must avoid at least the following problems (and perhaps others: e.g., the implication that things which could *not* undergo intrinsic change trivially count as part of every other object). First, (YP-1) does not specify a *necessary* condition for parthood, and is thus too strong. Suppose that *x* is a piece of iron that is actually part of the Eiffel Tower. Clearly, it is possible for *x* to undergo intrinsic change without the Eiffel Tower undergoing intrinsic change: suppose *x* were part of the Hancock Tower instead. Second, (YP-2) does not specify a *sufficient* condition for parthood, and is thus too weak. Presumably, the closest counterfactual circumstances in which the Eiffel Tower undergoes intrinsic change are circumstances in which at least one of the pieces of iron that compose it undergoes intrinsic change (say, some slight increase in temperature). Let *x* be such a part. Then since *x* would undergo intrinsic change if the Eiffel Tower undergoes intrinsic change, (YP-2) entails that the Eiffel Tower is part of *x*.

The final two accounts I will consider take the more promising route of starting with Yablo's claim that if *x* is part of *y*, then *x* and *y* have a region of intrinsic match. Although Yablo does not further gloss what he means by "having a region of intrinsic match", one might try to flesh it at least in one of the following two ways. The first way brings in Sider's observation that a thing somehow "inherits" the intrinsic properties of its parts. Although Sider's inheritance principle employs the notion of parthood, a nearby principle does not. Again, let x be a piece of iron that is part of the Eiffel Tower. If *being a piece of iron* is intrinsic to x, it seems not only to be the case that *having a piece of iron as a part* is intrinsic to the Eiffel Tower. It also seems to be the case that *being such that a piece of iron exists* is intrinsic to the Eiffel Tower. One does not need to "look beyond the boundaries" of the Eiffel Tower, or inspect anything other than how the Eiffel Tower is "in and of itself", to determine that a piece of iron exists. One might attempt to reductively analyze parthood in terms of intrinsicality by claiming that it is necessary and sufficient if this holds for *every* property intrinsic to x, as follows:

(YP-3) x is part of y iff: for every property F, if F is intrinsic to x, then the property *being such that an F exists* is intrinsic to y.[25]

To devise an account of *proper* parthood, one may either add the condition that x and y are distinct, or (to evoke Yablo's third de jure connection, that a thing and its proper parts must have "intrinsic differences") add the condition that there is some property, G, that is intrinsic to x even though the property *being such that a G exists* is not intrinsic to y.

Another way to make sense of the phrase "having a region of intrinsic match" that might be useful in this context reads the phrase much more literally. It is intuitive to think that things can exemplify properties not *simpliciter*, but rather only *relative to a particular region of space:* after all, a checkerboard does not exemplify blackness and whiteness, but rather blackness *here* and whiteness *there*. A tempting thought is that for a thing, x, to have a property F in a spatial region r is just for x to have a proper part, y, that is F and exactly occupies r. However, a number of philosophers have independently argued that having a part in a spatial region does not imply, and therefore does not reduce to, having a proper part that exactly occupies that region, by arguing that applying the distinction yields a number of philosophical benefits.[26] The thought

---

[25] Variations on (YP-3): those who take there to be things that do not exist might instead state the account in terms of the property *being such that there is an F*, while those who take there to be merely possible things might instead state the account in terms of the property *being such that an F actually exists*. Thanks to Dan Marshall for discussion here.

[26] For instance, Parsons (2000; 2004), Sider (2001), and McDaniel (2004) all suggest that the distinction can help explain how extended objects that are either temporally or spatially simple

seems directly applicable to reductively analyzing parthood, for if a black piece of the checkerboard is black, square-shaped, felt-covered, and so forth in a square-shaped region, then presumably the checkerboard *also* has all those properties in that region as well. Generalizing this thought to all the *intrinsic* properties of a part in a region, one might attempt to reductively analyze parthood as follows:

> (YP-4) x is part of y iff: for every property F and every spatial region r, if x has F in r intrinsically, then y has F in r intrinsically.

The main challenge for a proponent of (YP-4) will be to motivate the claim that it is possible for an occupant of a region to have properties in that region *intrinsically*. However, there is an extensive literature defending the claim that a thing can have properties relative to a particular *time* or *possible world* intrinsically, and there seems no immediately obvious reason why a proponent of (YP-4) could not co-opt some of these familiar maneuvers.[27]

So far I have only considered whether the primitivist could reasonably *attempt* to reductively analyze parthood in terms of intrinsicality. But to argue against reductionism, the primitivist must show further that one *should* reductively analyze parthood in terms of intrinsicality, which would require asking whether one should take parthood to be reductively analyzable at all, and comparing how primitivist-friendly accounts stack up against reductionist-friendly accounts if so. Rather than pursue this question further, I will spend the remainder of the chapter considering some arguments against primitivism that the reductionist may try to mount.

3 Arguments against primitivism about intrinsicality

The best way to argue that a notion is not reductively unanalyzable is (naturally enough) to propose a reductive analysis and argue that it is successful. But reductionists might wish to rationally reject primitivism even if they are either ag-

---

can be also qualitatively heterogeneous, either in or across possible circumstances of various kinds. Hudson (2001) uses the distinction to propose a novel solution to the infamous "problem of the many".

27 See Eddon (2010) for a recent survey and discussion of the maneuvers available in the case of time-relative property exemplification.

nostic about or do not believe that any extant account is successful. In this section, I consider two such families of arguments.

3.1 Primitivism is uninformative

Perhaps the most common argument against primitivism about *any* phenomenon of philosophical interest is that it fails to do what any viable account is supposed to do: namely, provide at least some understanding of the phenomenon.[28] The argument against primitivism about intrinsicality in particular is that by refusing to specify what intrinsicality is in other terms, the primitivist either renders the phenomenon of intrinsicality epistemically opaque, or inaccessible altogether.

But what is it, exactly, about intrinsicality that primitivism does not inform us about? I do not see how the reductionist can respond that will not equally undermine accounts of intrinsicality that are reductive. The reductionist may claim that a primitivist account does not tell us much about which properties are intrinsic, or about which properties are had intrinsically on which occasions. Or the reductionist may claim that primitivism either fails to provide, or altogether precludes, any firm understanding of the essential nature of intrinsicality. But as I have emphasized before (cf. section 2.1), the vast majority of viable reductionist accounts on offer employ a variety of primitive notions (like naturalness, grounding, the "consists in" relation, and so forth) that would seem to generate the same skeptical worries. If there are epistemic obstacles to understanding intrinsicality *as* a primitive notion, understanding intrinsicality *in terms of* other primitive notions would not seem to constitute much of an advance.

Regardless, it seems clear that one can be in a position to know interesting facts about the essential nature and distribution of intrinsicality without antecedently drawing out these facts from a reductive analysis, and even if primitivism were true. First, the truth of primitivism would itself be a highly interesting truth about the essence of intrinsicality. Second, as we saw before in sections 2 and 3 (and will be re-emphasized in section 3.2), there are a considerable amount of questions about the essence of intrinsicality left open by the primitivist—about how many primitive notions of intrinsicality there are, which these are, and how they figure into interesting analyses of each other, or interesting analyses of other notions—that seem in principle resolvable (or at least, no less resolvable

---

[28] Carroll (2009) considers, and ultimately rejects, a similar argument against those who reject that causal notions are reductively analyzable; the following discussion is inspired (but diverges in some respects) from his.

than similar questions for the reductionist's primitives). Third, discussions in both philosophy and science about whether this or that notion is intrinsic typically appeal only to certain *diagnostics* about whether a notion is intrinsic (such as whether it would either apply or fail to apply to "carbon copies" of it, or whether it in some intuitive sense is "independent of what is going on around it") rather than full-blown reductive accounts.[29] There is no obvious reason why one could not be in a position to know that such diagnostics hold, even if one takes them to hold of a primitive notion. Fourth and finally, there are a number of prominent examples of informative, explicitly primitivist theories of philosophically interesting notions, along with a growing consensus that they are not immediately objectionable for that reason.[30]

3.2 Primitivism violates plausible constraints on fundamentality

A more promising tact available to the reductivist is to instead argue that there are one or more antecedently motivated necessary conditions on what is fundamental—necessary conditions either on which notions are *primitive* notions, or on which facts are *brute* (i.e., ungrounded) facts—that a reductively unanalyzable notion of intrinsicality would fail to satisfy.

It is hard to pinpoint why so many in the literature on intrinsicality have taken primitivism to be a non-starter. But I can hazard a guess that it is rooted in the thought that if some notion of intrinsicality were primitive, then (to put it roughly at first) the fundamental level of reality would somehow fail to be *minimally complete*. The idea that the fundamental is constrained by minimal completeness crops up frequently in the burgeoning literature on the metaphysics of fundamentality, and is cashed out in numerous ways. For instance, Sider observes that "[i]t is natural to assume that the fundamental must be "complete", that the fundamental must in some sense be responsible for everything", and adds that

---

[29] Parsons (2001, pp. 28–29), for instance, argues that taking facts about intrinsicality as unanalyzable would not have precluded our coming to know that facts about *weight* are non-intrinsic.
[30] See e.g. Sider (2011) on fundamentality, Williamson (2000) on knowledge, and Woodward (2003) on causation.

> Completeness seems definitive of fundamentality. It would be a nonstarter to say that the fundamental consists solely of one electron: thus conceived the fundamental could not account for the vast complexity of the world we experience. (Sider 2012, p. 105)

To claim in addition that the fundamental must be *minimally* complete is (again roughly) to claim that the fundamental must account for the vast complexity of the world we experience economically, and thus without postulating more notions or facts as fundamental than are necessary to account for it. Or as Schaffer puts it, "[t]he primary is (as it were) all God would need to create" in order to "generate an abundant superstructure of posterior entities" (2009a, p. 351). With this constraint on fundamentality in tow, the reductionist might argue that it would be incredible that in addition to specifying which particles exemplify which microphysical properties and relations, and decreeing which microphysical laws govern them, God would *also* be required to specify which microphysical properties and property exemplifications are intrinsic, and (even worse) then be required to do the same for every other subject matter to which the primitive notions of intrinsicality apply. But if facts about intrinsicality are not required to be at the fundamental level, then including them would violate the constraint that the fundamental be minimally complete. So, primitivism is false.

Thus stated, this thought is more an imprecise way of eliciting an intuition rather than a convincing argument. How might such an argument proceed? Several options present themselves. I will consider two, and argue that neither is as convincing as the initial intuition may have appeared to be.

But first, some terminology is required to distinguish between two kinds of collections about which one could ask whether it is "minimally complete" in the relevant sense. Say that a collection of facts, Γ, is a *complete grounding base* just in case (*i*) every fact in Γ is brute and (*ii*) if some fact is derivative, then it is ultimately grounded in a subcollection of facts in Γ. Say that Γ is a *minimally complete grounding base* just in case both (*i*) Γ is a complete grounding base and also (*ii*) no proper subcollection of facts in Γ is a complete grounding base.[31] Next, say that a collection of notions, Π, is a *complete structural base* just in case (*i*) every notion in Π is primitive and (*ii*) if some notion is non-primitive, then every fact in which it appears is ultimately grounded in some collection of facts in which only notions in Π appear. And finally, say that Π is a *minimally complete structural base* just in case (*i*) Π is a complete structural base and (*ii*) no proper subcollec-

---

[31] It is plausible to think that whether a fact is brute, and thus constitutes a (minimally) complete grounding base, may differ from time to time and world to world; however, for sake of readability, I will continue to suppress temporal and modal qualifications.

tion of Π is a complete structural base. Notice that the existence of a minimally complete grounding base does not logically entail the existence of a complete structural base, let alone a minimal one. (Consider a world in which there are some brute facts involving non-primitive notions.) Notice also that the existence of a minimally complete structural base does not logically entail the existence of a complete grounding base, let alone a minimal one. (Consider a world in which every fact that contains only primitive notions is grounded in further facts that involve only primitive notions.) Since the two notions of minimal completeness are logically non-equivalent, an argument that employs talk of minimal completeness must specify which notion is at issue.

Terminology in tow, I can now state and evaluate two anti-primitivist arguments. The first begins with the claim that *primitive* facts (i.e., facts about some primitive notion) are *brute* facts, and then reasons to the conclusion that since there are no brute facts about intrinsicality in a minimally complete grounding base, it follows that no notion of intrinsicality is primitive. More precisely:

Argument from constraints on a minimally complete grounding base

(1)   If some notion of intrinsicality is primitive, then at least some fact about intrinsicality is brute.

(2a) If a fact is brute, then it is included in a minimally complete grounding base.

(3a) A minimally complete grounding base includes no facts about intrinsicality.

(C)   No notion of intrinsicality is primitive.

The thought is this. Suppose that local intrinsicality is primitive. Then (1) states that there is some brute fact about local intrinsicality. Suppose it is the fact that the Eiffel Tower is intrinsically made of iron. So this fact is included in a minimally complete grounding base, as (2a) states. Let Γ be this collection of facts. But this (says the reductivist) seems absurd. Whatever facts are grounded in the fact that the Eiffel Tower is made of iron are presumably grounded in whatever collection of facts in Γ ground that the Eiffel Tower is made of iron. This fact about intrinsicality does no interesting grounding work that facts *not* about intrinsicality could carry out themselves. Generalizing, (3a) seems true as well. Thus the anti-primitivist conclusion follows.

The second argument, like the first, begins with (1), the claim that primitive facts are brute facts; however, it then reasons to the conclusion that since at least some brute facts about intrinsicality would also concern *non-primitive* notions, primitivism entails that notions beyond what would be included in a minimally complete structural base must be added. More precisely:

Argument from constraints on a minimally complete structural base

(1) If some notion of intrinsicality is primitive, then at least some fact about intrinsicality is brute.

(2b) If some fact about intrinsicality is brute, then some brute fact is about non-primitive notions.

(3b) If there is some brute fact about a notion, then that notion is included in a minimally complete structural base.

(4) No non-primitive notion is included in any minimally complete structural base.

(C) No notion of intrinsicality is primitive.

The thought is this. Suppose again that local intrinsicality is primitive, and in line with (1), suppose that the fact that the Eiffel Tower is intrinsically made of iron is a brute fact. Then in line with (2b), there is some brute fact about non-primitive notions (e.g., the property *being made of iron*). The motivation behind (3b) is the thought that one should posit a brute fact about a notion only if it is what Sider calls "pure" of non-primitive notions (2010, p. 106), and that is included in a minimally complete structural base. But as (4) states, it follows by definition that no non-primitive notion is included in a minimally complete structural base. Thus the anti-primitivist conclusion follows.

A full evaluation of these two arguments would take us deep into the burgeoning literature investigating the metaphysics of fundamentality. That said, it is worth noting that an Achilles' heel to both arguments is (1), the claim that the primitiveness of a notion entails that there be at least some brute facts about it. There are at least three observations the primitivist might make. First, the primitivist may note that there is no immediate logical or conceptual incoherence to maintaining that there are no brute facts about a primitive notion. It is widely recognized that a fact's being grounded does not entail that any notions occurring within it are reductively analyzable.[32] But if grounding of a fact

---

[32] For instance, Louis deRosset observes that "the layered structure given by grounding explanations, unlike the layered structure given by reductions, is consistent with the phenomenon known as *multiple realizability*. A fact P can be explained by a fact Q, even if it is possible that something other than Q explain P, and Q not obtain at all" (2013, p. 5). Indeed, a fact's being grounded at one time and world seems compatible with it obtaining at another time and world

does not entail there be a reductive analysis of the notions that fact is about, it is unclear at best why it should follow that *lack* of a reductive analysis of the notions involved in some fact entails that this fact *lacks* a ground.

Second, arguably there are counterexamples to the truth of (1) that concern notions other than notions of intrinsicality. Indeed, several philosophers have argued that the notion of grounding that appears in many recent attempts at reductive analysis is precisely such a case.[33]

Third and finally, nothing appears to prevent the primitivist from supplying a general account of how facts about primitive notions of intrinsicality are systematically grounded in facts that involve no notions of intrinsicality at all. One might, for instance, take the fact that a thing, x, has a property F to be grounded in facts about the *essential nature* of F, or the essential nature of the fact that x is F. Or the primitivist may simply co-opt the collections of facts that attempted reductive analyses have offered as sufficient conditions for intrinsicality, and claim that although these accounts collectively state *sufficient grounds* for x to be F intrinsically, depending on the kind of thing or property at issue, nonetheless they individually fall short of providing *necessary conditions* for a thing to have properties across all possible circumstances.

Arguments that appeal to constraints on fundamentality appear to be the most promising for supporting reductionism. However, much more needs to be said in their defense.

4 Conclusion

This chapter is intended to be exploratory rather than definitive; limited rather than exhaustive. I have not attempted to develop a complete and detailed primitivist theory; rather I have sketched some options that confront the primitivist, and presented some open questions that must be settled in order to determine whether the view is correct. Nor do I claim to have surveyed all the arguments either for or against primitivism about intrinsicality, nor have I determined which if any of those that I have are sound. Nonetheless, although my aims have been modest, I hope to have shown at least the following. There is a rich terrain of primitivist theories to map out, and the issues that they border on are among the deepest and most important in contemporary metaphysics.

---

at which it is not grounded at all. There is no obvious incoherence in taking facts about conscious phenomena to be grounded in physical properties in the actual world yet brute in other, "more distant" counterfactual possibilities.

33 Bennett (2011) and deRosset (2013).

Those attracted to primitivism have quite a bit of territory to explore. And those who still hold hope in reductive approaches to intrinsicality have much more to say about why we should continue to stick to the faith.[34]

References

Bader, Ralf (2013). "Towards a Hyperintensional Theory of Intrinsicality". *The Journal of Philosophy* 110: pp. 525–563.
Bennett, Karen (2011). "By Our Bootstraps". *Philosophical Perspectives* 25: pp. 27–41.
Carroll, John (2009). "Anti-Reductionism". In H. Beebee, C. Hitchcock, P. Menzies (eds.), *The Oxford Handbook of Causation* (pp. 279–298). Oxford: Oxford University Press.
Chisholm, Roderick. (1976). *Person and Object*. LaSalle, IL: Open Court Press.
Correia, Fabrice (2006). "Generic Essence, Objectual Essence, and Modality". *Noûs* 40: pp. 753–767.
Cowling, Sam (forthcoming). "Ideological Parsimony". *Synthese*.
Daly, Chris (2012). "Scepticism about Grounding". In F. Correia and B. Schnieder (eds.), *Metaphysical Grounding: Understanding the Structure of Reality* (pp. 81–100). Cambridge: Cambridge University Press.
Denby, David A. (2006). "The Distinction between Intrinsic and Extrinsic Properties". *Mind* 115: pp. 1–17.
Denby, David A. (2010). "Intrinsic and Extrinsic Properties: A reply to Hoffmann-Kolss". *Mind*, 119: pp. 773–782.
Dennett, D. (1988). "Quining Qualia". In A. J. Marcel and E. Bisiach (eds.), *Consciousness in Contemporary Science* (pp. 42–77). New York: Oxford University Press.
DePaul, Michael and William Ramsey (eds.) (1998). *Rethinking Intuition: The Psychology of Intuition and Its Role in Philosophical Inquiry*. Lanham, Maryland: Rowman & Littlefield.
deRosset, Louis (2013). "Grounding Explanations". *Philosophers' Imprint* 13: pp. 1–26.
Dorr, Cian (2004). "Non-Symmetric Relations". In D. Zimmerman (ed.), *Oxford Studies in Metaphysics*, volume 1 (pp. 155–192). Oxford: Clarendon Press.
Dorr, Cian (2005). "What We Disagree About When We Disagree About Ontology". In M. E. Kalderon (ed.), *Fictionalism in Metaphysics* (pp. 234–286). Oxford: Oxford University Press.
Dorr, Cian (2008). "There Are No Abstract Objects". In T. Sider, J. Hawthorne and D. Zimmerman (eds.), *Contemporary Debates in Metaphysics* (pp. 32–64). Malden, MA: Blackwell.
Dorr, Cian (manuscript). "To Be an F is To Be a G".

---

[34] Many thanks to Mark Barber, Philipp Blum (née Keller), Paolo Bonardi, Pablo Carnino, Natalja Deng, Maya Eddon, Robert Francescotti, Akiko Frischhut, Ghislain Guigon, Dan Marshall, Michaela McSweeney, Josh Parsons, Graham Peebles, Aaron Segal, Theodore Sider, Jennifer Wang, and Tobias Wilsch for helpful conversations about the topics of this paper. This article was written while funded by the Swiss National Science Foundation as a member of the *sinergia* project "Intentionality as the Mark of the Mental" (project #: CRSI11–127488), and I am grateful for its generous support.

Eddon, Maya (2010). "Three Arguments from Temporary Intrinsics". *Philosophy and Phenomenological Research* 81: pp. 605–619.

Eddon, Maya (2011). "Intrinsicality and Hyperintensionality". *Philosophy and Phenomenological Research* 82: pp. 314–336.

Ellis, Brian (1991). "Scientific Essentialism". Paper presented to the 1991 conference of the Australasian Association for the History and Philosophy of Science.

Figdor, Carrie (2008). "Intrinsically/Extrinsically". *The Journal of Philosophy* 105: pp. 691–718.

Fine, Kit (1994). "Essence and Modality". *Philosophical Perspectives* 8: pp. 1–16.

Fine, Kit (1995). "The Logic of Essence". *Journal of Philosophical Logic* 24: pp. 241–273.

Fine, Kit (2010). "Towards a Theory of Part". *The Journal of Philosophy* 107: pp. 559–589.

Francescotti, Robert (1999). "How to Define Intrinsic Properties". *Noûs* 33: pp. 590–609.

Hawthorne, John (2009). "Superficialism in Ontology". In D. Chalmers, D. Manley, and R. Wasserman (eds.), *Metametaphysics: New Essays on the Foundations of Ontology* (pp. 213–230). Oxford: Oxford University Press.

Hofweber, Thomas (2009). "Ambitious, Yet Modest, Metaphysics". In D. Chalmers, D. Manley, and R. Wasserman (eds.), *Metametaphysics: New Essays on the Foundations of Ontology* (pp. 260–289). Oxford: Oxford University Press.

Hoffmann-Kolss, Vera (2010a). *The Metaphysics of Extrinsic Properties*. Frankfurt: Ontos-Verlag.

Hoffmann-Kolss, Vera (2010b). "Denby on the Distinction between Intrinsic and Extrinsic Properties". *Mind* 119: pp. 763–772.

Hudson, Hud (2001). *A Materialist Metaphysics of the Human Person*. Ithaca: Cornell University Press.

Humberstone, I. L. (1996). "Intrinsic/Extrinsic". *Synthese* 108: pp. 205–267.

Jacobs, Jonathan D. (2010). "A Powers Theory of Modality—or, How I Learned to Stop Worrying and Reject Possible Worlds". *Philosophical Studies* 151: pp. 227–248.

Kim, Jaegwon. (1982). "Psychophysical Supervenience". *Philosophical Studies* 41: pp. 51–70.

King, Jeffrey (1998). "What is a Philosophical Analysis?". *Philosophical Studies* 90: pp. 155–179.

King, Jeffrey (2007). *The Nature and Structure of Content*. Oxford: Oxford University Press.

Ladyman, James and Don Ross (2007). "Ontic Structural Realism and the Philosophy of Physics". In J. Ladyman and D. Ross (eds.), *Every Thing Must Go: Metaphysics Naturalized* (pp. 130–189). Oxford: Oxford University Press.

Langton, Rae and David Lewis (1998). "Defining 'Intrinsic'". *Philosophy and Phenomenological Research* 58: pp. 333–345.

Lewis, David (1983a). "Extrinsic Properties". *Philosophical Studies* 44: pp. 197–200.

Lewis, David (1983b). "New Work for a Theory of Universals". *Australasian Journal of Philosophy* 61: pp. 343–377.

Lewis, David (1986a). *On the Plurality of Worlds*. Oxford: Blackwell.

Lowe, E. J. (1998). *The Possibility of Metaphysics: Substance, Identity and Time*. Oxford: Oxford University Press.

Lowe, E. J. (2012). "Asymmetrical Dependence in Individuation". In F. Correia and B. Schnieder (eds.), *Metaphysical Grounding: Understanding the Structure of Reality* (pp. 214–233). Cambridge: Cambridge University Press.

Marshall, Dan (2009). "Can 'Intrinsic' Be Defined Using Only Broadly Logical Notions?". *Philosophy and Phenomenological Research* 78: pp. 646–672.

Marshall, Dan (2012). "Analyses of Intrinsicality in Terms of Naturalness". *Philosophy Compass* 7: pp. 531–542.
Marshall, Dan (forthcoming-a). "Analyses of Intrinsicality without Naturalness". *Philosophy Compass*.
Marshall, Dan (forthcoming-b). "Intrinsicality and Grounding". *Philosophy and Phenomenological Research*.
Melia, Joseph (2005). "Truthmaking without Truthmakers". In H. Beebee and J. Dodd (eds.), *Truthmakers: The Contemporary Debate* (pp. 67–84). Oxford: Oxford University Press.
McDaniel, Kris (2004). "Modal Realism with Overlap". *Australasian Journal of Philosophy* 82: pp. 137–152.
Merricks, Trenton (1998). "Against the Doctrine of Microphysical Supervenience". *Mind* 107: pp. 59–71.
Ney, Alyssa (2010). "Are There Fundamental Intrinsic Properties?". In A. Hazlett (ed.), *New Waves in Metaphysics* (pp. 219–239). London: Palgrave McMillan.
Parsons, Josh (2000). "Must a Four-Dimensionalist Believe in Temporal Parts?". *The Monist* 83: pp. 399–418.
Parsons, Josh (2001). *Theories of Persistence*. Ph. D. thesis, Canberra: Australian National University.
Parsons, Josh (2004). "Distributional Properties". In F. Jackson and G. Priest (eds.), *Lewisian Themes: The Philosophy of David K. Lewis* (pp. 173–180). Oxford: Oxford University Press.
Rayo, Agustín (2013). *The Construction of Logical Space*. Oxford: Oxford University Press.
Rosen, Gideon (2010). "Metaphysical Dependence: Grounding and Reduction". In B. Hale and A. Hoffmann (eds.), *Modality: Metaphysics, Logic, and Epistemology* (pp. 109–136). Oxford: Oxford University Press.
Schaffer, Jonathan (2009a). "On What Grounds What". In D. Chalmers, D. Manley, and R. Wasserman (eds.), *Metametaphysics: New Essays on the Foundations of Ontology* (pp. 347–383). Oxford: Oxford University Press.
Schaffer, Jonathan (2009b). "Spacetime the One Substance". *Philosophical Studies* 145: pp. 131–148.
Schroeder, Mark (2005). "Realism and Reduction: The Quest for Robustnes". *Philosophers' Imprint* 5: pp. 1–18.
Sider, Theodore (1993). *Naturalness, Intrinsicality, and Duplication*. Ph.D Thesis, Amherst: the University of Massachussetts at Amherst.
Sider, Theodore (1996). "Intrinsic Properties". *Philosophical Studies* 83: pp.1–27.
Sider, Theodore (2001). *Four-Dimensionalism: An Ontology of Persistence and Time*. Oxford: Oxford University Press.
Sider, Theodore (2007). "Parthood". *Philosophical Review* 116: pp. 51–91.
Sider, Theodore (2011). *Writing the Book of the World*. Oxford University Press.
Skow, Bradford (2007). "Are Shapes Intrinsic?". *Philosophical Studies* 133: pp. 111–130.
Taylor, Barry (1993). "On Natural Properties in Metaphysics". *Mind* 102, pp. 81–100.
Trogdon, Kelly (2009). "Monism and Intrinsicality". *Australian Journal of Philosophy* 87: pp. 127–148.
Vallentyne, Peter (1997). "Intrinsic Properties Defined". *Philosophical Studies* 88: pp. 209–219.
Wasserman, Ryan (2005). "Humean Supervenience and Personal Identity". *Philosophical Quarterly* 55: pp. 582–593.

Weatherson, Brian (2001). "Intrinsic Properties and Combinatorial Principles". *Philosophy and Phenomenological Research* 63: pp. 365–380.

Weatherson, Brian and Dan Marshall (2012). "Intrinsic vs. Extrinsic Properties". In E. Zalta (ed.), *The Stanford Encyclopedia of Philosophy* (Spring 2013 Edition), available online at <http://plato.stanford.edu/archives/spr2013/entries/intrinsic-extrinsic/>

Wedgwood, Ralph (2007). *The Nature of Normativity.* Oxford: Oxford University Press.

Williams, J. R. G. (2013). "Part-Intrinsicality". *Noûs* 47: pp. 413–452.

Williamson, Timothy (2000). *Knowledge and its Limits.* Oxford: Oxford University Press.

Witmer, Gene, William Butchard and Kelly Trogdon (2005). "Intrinsicality without Naturalness". *Philosophy and Phenomenological Research* 70: pp. 326–350.

Woodward, James (2003). *Making Things Happen: A Theory of Causal Explanation.* Oxford: Oxford University Press.

Yablo, Stephen (1999). "Intrinsicness". *Philosophical Topics* 26: pp. 479–505.

Michael Esfeld
Physics and Intrinsic Properties

Abstract: The paper sketches out an ontology of physics in terms of matter being primitive stuff distributed in space and all the properties physics is committed to being dispositions that fix the temporal development of the distribution of matter in space. Whereas such properties can be conceived as intrinsic properties of particles in classical mechanics, in quantum physics, there is a holistic property or structure that relates all matter and that fixes its temporal development.

1 Classical Physics and Intrinsic Properties

At the end of *Opticks* (1704), Newton writes:

> ... it seems probable to me, that God in the Beginning form'd Matter in solid, massy, hard, impenetrable, moveable Particles ...; no ordinary Power being able to divide what God himself made one in the first Creation. ... the Changes of corporeal Things are to be placed only in the various Separations and new Associations and Motions of these permanent Particles. (Question 31, p. 400 in Cohen's 1952 edition)

According to Newton, matter consists in particles that are distributed in a background space, a particle being a material object that is so small that it is localized at a point in space, thus being indivisible. Hence, some points of space are occupied—a particle is localized at them—whereas other points are empty. The distribution of matter in a background space develops in a background time. That is to say, as time passes, there is a change in which points of space are occupied and which are empty. That change is furthermore such that each particle moves on a continuous trajectory. Consequently, each particle has an identity in time by which it distinguishes itself from all the other particles.

If one adopts a sparse view of physical properties, there is no reason to make use of the notion of properties as far as this basic characterization of matter is concerned—the primitive ontology of Newtonian mechanics, to take up an expression introduced by Dürr, Goldstein and Zanghi (2013, ch. 2, end of section 2.2, originally published 1992). Matter is primitive stuff, and it is a primitive matter of fact that some points of space are occupied whereas others are not. There is a good reason for conceiving matter in terms of particles, that is, in terms of points of space being occupied or empty. If one considered matter to be a continuous stuff distributed all over space (that is, gunk), then one would have to maintain that there is more stuff at some *points* of space and less stuff at others in order to be able to accommodate variation. But it could not be a primitive matter of fact that there is more stuff at some points of space and less at others; a property of the stuff would be needed to account for that difference. However, as I shall argue shortly, all the properties that classical mechanics attributes to matter concern its temporal development, not simply the fact that there is matter. The view of matter consisting in particles can easily pay heed to the fact that there is more matter in some *regions* of space than in others: in some regions of space, more points are occupied than in others.

Newton's theory seeks to account for the temporal development of the distribution of matter in space. It does so by starting from a certain stipulation: Newton assumes that a certain form of motion of the particles does not call for an explanation, namely inertial motion, that is, constant motion on a straight line (Newton's first law). Only change in the state of motion, that is, the acceleration of the particles (change in their velocity) has to be accounted for. Newton's theory does so by introducing forces (Newton's second law).[1] It hence is a second order theory, being concerned with the temporal development of the velocity of the particles, by contrast to a first order theory that would be concerned with the temporal development of the position of the particles (velocity being the first temporal derivative of position, acceleration being the second temporal derivative). The forces, in turn, are traced back to properties of the particles. Thus, in virtue of possessing a mass, the particles exert a force upon each other, namely a force of attraction, that is, gravitation. Mass manifests itself in the mutual attraction of the particles (gravitational mass) as well as in their resistance to acceleration (inertial mass).

In brief, a property is attributed to the particles in the form of mass to account for change in their state of motion. Here I gloss over the question of whether or not forces should be admitted as properties in addition to properties of the particles such as their mass.[2] If one seeks for a parsimonious ontology, there is no reason to recognize forces over and above properties of the particles such as their mass, since given the distribution of mass in space at a time, a certain change of the state of motion of the particles—their acceleration as described by the law of gravitation—ensues.

Is mass an intrinsic property of the particles? A world in which only one point of space is occupied at any time—that is, a world with only one particle—is a possible world of Newtonian mechanics, given that Newton admits a back-

---

[1] See Maudlin (2012, chs.1–2) for an excellent recent examination.
[2] See notably Bigelow, Ellis and Pargetter (1988), Wilson (2007) and Massin (2009) on the ontology of Newtonian forces.

ground space and a background time. That one particle would forever continue to be in inertial motion (or to be at rest). Consider the widespread view according to which an intrinsic property is a property that an object possesses independently of being alone in a world or being accompanied by other objects.[3] On this view, mass counts as an intrinsic property.

However, a world in which there is only one particle with mass would be indiscernible from a world in which there is only one massless particle. In other words, taking the particle to be equipped with the property of mass over and above the fact of a point of space being occupied makes no difference as long as one limits oneself to considering possible worlds in which only one point of space is occupied at a time. But the lack of a difference in the case of a one particle world does not decide against mass being an intrinsic property of the particles.

On the way in which I've introduced the ontology of Newtonian mechanics above, the theory starts with the distribution of matter in a background space, that distribution consisting in the fact that some points of space are occupied by primitive stuff, whereas others are not. Properties then are called for only to account for the form of the temporal development of the distribution of the primitive stuff in space, more precisely, to account for changes in the state of motion of the particles. Properties that are needed in order to do that job are dispositions in the sense of properties for which it is essential to play a certain role as described by a law. Hence, the answer to the question of whether mass is an intrinsic property in Newtonian mechanics depends on whether or not dispositions are intrinsic properties.

One can with good reason take dispositions to be intrinsic properties. The fact that it is essential for them to perform a certain role as described by a law—make matter accelerate in a certain manner in the case of mass—does not turn them into relations. Any theory of dispositions has to acknowledge the possibility of situations (possible worlds) in which the disposition in question exists, but is not manifest. That is to say, any theory of dispositions has to allow for situations (possible worlds) in which the disposition in question exists, but which are indiscernible from a situation (possible world) in which the disposition in question does not exist—as in the case of a Newtonian world with one particle that has mass and a Newtonian world with one particle that does not have mass. To put it differently, if one could make a case for the following conclusion, that would constitute a sufficient reason not to take mass to be

---

[3] See Langton and Lewis (1998 and 2001), as well as Hoffmann-Kolss (2010, first part) for a detailed discussion.

an intrinsic property in Newtonian mechanics: consider a situation—or a sequence of possible worlds—that starts from there being several particles, but which is such that the number of particles is subsequently reduced to only one; one would have to argue for the conclusion that the one particle that is left has lost its mass as a consequence of the annihilation of the other particles that accompany it. However, I don't know an argument that could establish that conclusion.

Instead of regarding mass as a disposition, one may maintain that it is an intrinsic property, but that it exercises the role of changing the state of motion of the particles as described by the law of gravitation only contingently. That is to say, in other possible worlds, mass plays another role. More precisely, considering two different properties (say, mass and charge), it is possible that they swap their roles: in a world w_2, mass plays the role that charge plays in the actual world w_1, and charge plays in w_2 the role that mass exercises in the actual world w_1. This view implies that the essence of a property—what the property is—is separated from the role that it exercises in a world as described by a law. But what then is the essence of a property? The answer to this question that is dominant in the literature holds that it is a pure quality, known as quiddity (Lewis 2009); but one may also suggest that properties have a primitive numerical identity (Locke 2012).

However, neither of these answers seems convincing: one may contemplate admitting a primitive numerical identity when it comes to primitive stuff filling space, for that stuff is nothing else but what occupies space, as are Newtonian particles as sketched out above. But if one attributes properties to that stuff, it seems odd to admit a primitive numerical identity for these properties as well, for there would then be no reason to take the primitive stuff that occupies space to be equipped with properties at all; one has a reason to recognize properties of the stuff if and only if one wants something that performs a certain job for the temporal development of the stuff. As far as the view of properties being pure qualities is concerned, the problem is that it is not intelligible what could constitute a purely qualitative difference between two properties (say, mass and charge), given that all the accessible difference that justifies recognizing two different properties consists in a difference in the function that these properties exercise for the temporal development of the distribution of matter in space as expressed by a law.

The same objection applies to the mixed view of properties of Martin (1997) and Heil (2003, ch. 11 and 2012, ch. 4) according to which properties are both qualitative and dispositional in one. Again, the question is what could constitute a difference in the qualitative aspect of properties such as mass or charge, or what could constitute a reason for admitting a qualitative difference that accompanies the difference in the role that properties such as mass and charge exercise. Again, one needs properties in one's ontology of the natural world only if one wants something that performs a certain function for the behaviour (that is, the temporal development) of the objects that have the properties in question. But then it is sufficient to admit properties that are dispositions, that is, properties whose essence it is to exercise a certain role as described by a law (see notably Bird 2007).

The view of properties being pure qualities is usually put forward in the context of Humeanism, in order to avoid recognizing objective modality. If one considers properties as dispositions, by contrast, one is committed to admitting objective modality, since a disposition plays the same role in any possible world in which it is instantiated—although it is questionable whether this objective modality amounts to metaphysical necessity or whether there is a genuine dispositional modality that is weaker than metaphysical necessity.[4] However, if one wants to eschew objective modality, one can do so in a much simpler way than by subscribing to a rather baroque metaphysics of pure qualities, namely by recognizing no physical properties at all: the Humean mosaic is the distribution of primitive stuff—such as particles occupying points of space—throughout the whole of space and time. Laws are the axioms of the description of the distribution of that stuff in space and time that achieves the best balance between simplicity and empirical content.[5] No properties are needed over and above primitive stuff occupying points of space as truth-makers for laws of nature on this view of laws. In any case, the *whole* distribution of stuff in space-time has to be accepted as primitive on this view of laws, there being nothing that, given an initial distribution of matter in space, determines the temporal development of that distribution.

Let us turn back to the issue of whether properties such as mass in Newtonian mechanics are intrinsic or relations. One can indeed try to make a case for them being relations along the following line: mass is a property of the particles that manifests itself in the form of mutual attraction among the particles. The strength of the force of gravitational attraction between two objects in space depends on their distance (the force diminishes with the square of the distance), but the force is supposed to be transmitted instantaneously through empty space without a medium. That is why Newton's theory is taken to be committed to action at a distance: the presence of a mass in space at a given time t changes the state of motion of all the objects elsewhere in space at that very t.

---

4 See Mumford and Anjum (2011, ch. 8).
5 Cf. the view of laws of Lewis (1973, sec. 3.3, pp. 72–75).

However, one may question whether the notion of an *instantaneous* action at a distance makes sense: when there is an object with a certain mass somewhere in space at a given time t, the manifestation of its mass is present strictly speaking in all the other objects in the universe *at that very instant t*. Consequently, there is no room for an interaction in the sense of the transmission of something. Instead, the correct analysis is to say that the property of mass, including its manifestation, simply is present in all the objects of the universe at any given time t. Consider what van Fraassen points out in another context (the context is the discussion of non-local quantum correlations to which I will turn in the next section):

> To speak of instantaneous travel from X to Y is a mixed or incoherent metaphor, for the entity in question is implied to be simultaneously at X and at Y—in which case there is no need for travel, for it is at its destination already. ... one should say instead that the entity has two (or more) coexisting parts, that it is spatially extended. (van Fraassen 1991, p. 351)

These considerations suggest taking mass to be a relation among the objects in space rather than an intrinsic property of each object. That is to say, there is one instantiation of a holistic property of mass distribution at any t that relates all the objects in the universe and that fixes how each of them changes its state of motion at t. This relational view of mass can admit a possible world with only one particle as a limiting case: there is exactly one instantiation of mass distribution at any t also in that universe, but since there is only one particle that instantiates the mass distribution, there is no change in its state of motion.

However that may be, in any case, Newton's view of particle interaction at a distance was considered to be an anomaly and was replaced by the view of local action among particles transmitted through fields in the 19th and early 20th century. Thus, according to Maxwell's field theory of electromagnetism, in virtue of instantiating the property of charge, each particle builds up a field, the field propagates with a finite velocity (the velocity of light in vacuum is the upper limit), and it is through the field that the charge of a given particle manifests itself in the change of the state of motion of other particles. As regards mass, Einstein achieves a local field theory of gravitation with the theory of general relativity, by identifying the field through which gravitation propagates with the metric field of space-time. In local field theories, the argument rehearsed above for considering the properties attributed to the particles in order to explain the temporal development of their state of motion—such as mass and charge—as intrinsic properties holds firm. In other words, these theories abandon the Newtonian anomaly of instantaneous action at a distance not in favour of developing the idea of one holistic property being instantiated by all the particles in the universe at any time that determines the temporal development of the state of motion of each particle, but in favour of the idea that each particle instantiates an intrinsic property that manifests itself in the change of the state of motion of other particles through the local propagation of a field.

2 Quantum Physics and Intrinsic Properties

Let us now turn to quantum mechanics. Any discussion of the issue of what quantum mechanics tells us about the world faces the problem that on the one hand we have a precise formalism for the calculation of probabilities for measurement outcomes at our disposal, but that on the other hand this formalism does not wear an ontology on its sleeves—it is not possible to read any ontological consequences directly off of the formalism. The following, easily accessible thought experiment suggested by Einstein at the Solvay conference in Brussels in 1927 illustrates this situation (the following presentation is based on the reconstruction of de Broglie's version of Einstein's argument in Norsen 2005). Consider a box prepared in Brussels with exactly one particle inside the box. The box is split in two halves in Brussels, one half is sent to New York, the other half is sent to Tokyo. Suppose that Alice in New York opens the box she receives and finds it to be empty. It then is a fact that there is a particle in the box that Bob receives in Tokyo.

The quantum formalism represents the particle in the box by means of a wave-function. When the box is split and the two halves are sent to New York and to Tokyo, the wave-function represents the particle in terms of a superposition of its being in the box that travels to New York and its being in the box that travels to Tokyo. The operational meaning of this representation is that there is a 50% chance of finding the particle in the box that travels to New York and a 50% chance of finding the particle in the box that travels to Tokyo. When Alice in New York opens the box she receives and finds it to be empty, the representation by means of the wave-function changes such that the wave-function represents the particle to be in the box that travels to Tokyo. That sudden change is known as collapse of the wave-function.

One may try an ontological reading of the wave-function in the sense that it provides a literal and thus complete representation of what happens with the particle in this situation. But one then faces the consequence that the collapse of the wave-function means that Alice's action of opening the box she receives in New York instantaneously brings it about that the particle is localized in the box in Tokyo. That is what Einstein considered to be spooky action at a distance. One may therefore turn to an epistemological reading of the wave-function in the sense that it provides all the information about the temporal development of the particle that we can obtain, without being able to represent the actual trajectory that the particle takes. On this reading, the collapse of the wave-function upon Alice's opening of the box she receives in New York simply represents a change in the state of knowledge of the observer—once one box has been opened, we know where the particle is, whereas before opening the box, we were ignorant of where it is. This reading implies that the particle always travels on a classical trajectory, being in one box and not being influenced by whatever operation is performed on the other box. This is Einstein's reading of this thought experiment—according to him the only reading that avoids having to acknowledge spooky action at a distance.

However, that reading has been refuted by Bell's theorem in 1964 (reprinted in Bell 2004, ch. 2). In order to understand that refutation, it is not sufficient to consider Einstein's thought experiment of one particle in a box, but one has to turn to the thought experiment that Einstein published together with Podolsky and Rosen in 1935: that thought experiment is about a situation in which two particles are prepared at a source and sent in opposite directions, with the possibility of measuring at least two different parameters on each particle; these parameters are fixed only shortly before the measurement, that is, when the particles are already separated by a distance in space that can be arbitrarily big. Bell's theorem establishes that it is not possible to account for these correlations on the basis of the particles travelling on classical trajectories so that the preparation of the particle pair at the source of the experiment would constitute the cause of the correlations, that is, a cause in the common past of the two measurement events that accounts for the measured correlations. On the contrary, Bell's theorem proves that the fixing of the parameter and the measurement outcome in one wing of the experiment influences the probabilities for the measurement outcome in the other wing of the experiment, even if the events of fixing the parameter and obtaining a measurement outcome between these two wings are separated by a spacelike interval; thus, no signal travelling at most with the speed of light can connect them.[6]

There is no space in this paper to discuss the different proposals for an ontology of quantum mechanics, and there is no need to do so. For the purpose of this paper, it is sufficient to consider the minimal change to the ontology of classical mechanics that is necessary in order to accommodate the quantum mechanical algorithm for the calculation of probabilities for measurement out-

---

[6] See Bell's papers in Bell (2004, especially ch. 24), Goldstein et al. (2011) for an easily accessible presentation of Bell's theorem and Maudlin (2011) for a detailed examination.

comes. We can do so on the basis of Bell's own way out of the mentioned dilemma into which an epistemological as well as an ontological reading of the wavefunction in the quantum mechanical formalism run—that is, a way that pays on the one hand heed to the fact that classical particle trajectories cannot yield the quantum probabilities and that on the other hand avoids the commitment to spooky action at a distance.

One can reconstruct Bell's reasoning in the form of the following four steps:

(1) Any measurement outcome consists in the fact of something having a precise localization in physical space, such as, for instance, a pointer pointing upwards instead of downwards (see e. g. Bell 2004, p. 166). In other words, any measurement outcome consists in a certain distribution of matter in space.
(2) Macroscopic objects—such as the devices that are used as measurement apparatuses—can be localized in physical space if and only if the microscopic objects that compose them are also localized.
(3) If one adopts common sense realism as well as experimental realism, macroscopic objects are localized even if no one observers them. Hence (from (2)), the microscopic objects that compose macroscopic objects are localized independently of whether or not anyone makes a measurement.
(4) Microscopic objects can be localized when they build up macroscopic objects if and only if they are *always* localized. Otherwise, one would be committed to spooky action at a distance—a measurement operation at a certain location could then have the effect that a microscopic object instantaneously adopts a precise localization arbitrarily far apart in space.

This reasoning shows that there is no need to abandon the basic or primitive ontology of classical mechanics when passing from classical to quantum mechanics. The basic ontology consists in matter distributed in a background space, more precisely in particles existing at points in space. The particles are primitive stuff: that a particle exists at a point in space simply means that a point is occupied. Consequently, the distribution of matter in space is nothing more than the fact that some points of space are occupied, whereas others are empty.

What has to be changed when passing from classical to quantum mechanics is the law for the temporal development of the distribution of matter in space, since classical trajectories of particles cannot yield the quantum mechanical probabilities for measurement outcomes. It is possible to add simply a specific quantum force to the classical forces in order to obtain particle trajectories that yield the quantum mechanical probabilities for measurement outcomes. This is done in that version of the quantum theory that goes back to Bohm (1952) in which a specific quantum force is admitted, known as quantum potential or pilot wave.[7] However, one can with good reason object that simply adding a quantum force when passing from classical to quantum mechanics is an *ad hoc* move: that force acts in a non-local manner, thus amounting to action at a distance, without a treatment being possible that matches the manner in which Einstein turned gravitation into a local interaction in the general theory of relativity. Furthermore, that force violates in any case Newton's third law: it acts on the particles without a reaction from the particles on it.

Let us therefore go one step back and recall the motivation for taking the primitive stuff in space to be endowed with properties at all. We need the commitment to properties if we want something that determines the temporal development of the distribution of the primitive stuff in space. But it is a particular choice made by Newton and further pursued throughout classical physics to take the properties that do so to be such that they give rise to forces—such as mass giving rise to the force of gravitation, or charge giving rise to the force of electricity and magnetism. In other words, it is a particular choice made by Newton and further pursued throughout classical physics to go for a law of motion that is second order, that is, being about acceleration, namely the temporal development of the velocity of the particles. A much simpler choice would be to examine simply the temporal development of the position of the particles, that is, to put forward a law of motion that is first order, being concerned with what determines the velocity of the particles, given their position. In other words, properties in this case are needed as that which fixes the velocity of the particles given their position.

There indeed is a quantum theory available that implements this choice, namely the dominant contemporary version of the theory going back to Bohm (1952), known as Bohmian mechanics.[8] In the Bohmian law for the temporal development of the distribution of matter in space, the quantum mechanical wave-function Ψ has the job to determine the velocity of the particles at a time t, given their position at t. If it has to be acknowledged that we are ignorant of the exact initial particle configuration and if one makes a mathematically precise typicality assumption about that initial particle configuration, one can derive the quantum mechanical algorithm for calculating probabilities for measurement outcomes in Bohmian mechanics.[9] Consequently, Bohmian mechanics grounds textbook quantum mechanics in the sense that it provides an ontology of the distribution of matter in space and a law for the temporal development of that dis-

---

[7] See notably Holland (1993) for a detailed account and Belousek (2003) for a defence.
[8] See Goldstein (2006) for a brief presentation and the papers in Dürr, Goldstein and Zanghì (2013) for a detailed exposition.
[9] See Dürr, Goldstein and Zanghì (2013, ch. 2).

tribution from which the textbook formalism of quantum mechanics can be deduced.

It is possible to regard the quantum mechanical wave-function as referring to a property, namely a dispositional property of the particles that determines their temporal development by fixing their velocity.[10] However, the wave-function that figures in the Bohmian law is the universal wave-function; consequently, it applies to the configuration of *all* the particles in the universe. That is to say, the property that fixes the velocity of any particle at a time t given its position at t is not an intrinsic property of that particle, but there is only one instantiation of a holistic property of all the particles at t, represented by the universal wave-function at t, that determines the velocity of each particle at t, given the position of all the particles at t. That is how Bohmian mechanics accounts for the non-local correlations brought out by the Einstein-Podolsky-Rosen thought experiment and Bell's theorem. In other words, the trajectory of the particles is not fixed by forces acting locally on the particles, but by a holistic property of all the particles taken together.

Nonetheless, Bohmian mechanics allows for the introduction of what is known as effective wave-functions, that is, wave-functions that apply to particular local configurations of particles while abstracting from the rest of the universe. Bohmian mechanics thereby is in the position to account for both the non-local correlations as brought out by Bell's theorem and for the classical, local character of the environment with which we are familiar.[11] However, when it comes to ontology by contrast to adopting an attitude that is sufficient for all practical purposes when dealing with the environment with which we are familiar, the availability of effective wave-functions does of course not mean that the temporal development of the particles is determined by intrinsic or local properties instead of one holistic property that takes all the particles in the universe as its relata. Hence, as far as what is specific to quantum mechanics is concerned, there is no room for intrinsic properties instantiated by the objects in space; instead, there is only one holistic property of all these objects taken together that determines their temporal development.

Coming back to the anomaly of instantaneous action at a distance in Newtonian mechanics, whereas classical field theory overcomes this anomaly by conceiving local action induced by intrinsic properties of the particles building up fields that propagate with a finite velocity, quantum theory can be taken to overcome that anomaly by radicalizing the holism that is already available for New-

---

[10] See Belot (2012, pp. 77–80) for a sketch and Esfeld et al. (2013) for a detailed argumentation.
[11] See Dürr, Goldstein and Zanghì (2013, ch. 5).

tonian mechanics: as mentioned at the end of the previous section, one can conceive an ontology of Newtonian mechanics in terms of one instantiation of a holistic property of mass distribution at any time t that relates all the objects in the universe and that fixes how each of them changes its state of motion at t. By the same token, one can take the universal wave-function in quantum mechanics to refer to one instantiation of a holistic property that relates all the objects in the universe and that fixes the velocity of each of them, given the position of all the particles.

This holism is more radical than the one that one can contemplate with respect to Newtonian mechanics, since the universal wave-function in quantum mechanics does not represent the distribution of a property of objects (as there is in any case a mass distribution in Newtonian mechanics such that each object has mass), but exactly one instantiation of a holistic property of all the particles taken together. That property determines the velocity of each particle, but it is not a property possessed by each particle—due to the non-separability of the wave-function, there is only one wave-function for the whole particle configuration. Nonetheless, quantum mechanics, like Newtonian mechanics, admits a possible world with only one particle as the limiting case: that particle has a wave-function, and that wave-function represents the property of that particle which fixes its temporal development. To put it differently, for any possible world, there is exactly one universal wave-function representing the property that fixes the temporal development of the objects in that world, whatever their number may be.

This holism holds whatever view one adopts with respect to the distribution of matter in space in quantum mechanics. One does not have to take that distribution to consist in particles in the sense of primitive stuff occupying points of space; other proposals notably include a continuous distribution of stuff [12] and sparsely distributed discrete point events, known as flashes, making up no continuous trajectories or worldlines.[13] In any case, whatever the distribution of matter in space may be, its temporal development is fixed by a holistic and dispositional property instantiated by the matter distribution as a whole and represented by the universal wave-function. That is why quantum physics lends support to the view known as ontic structural realism: that holistic property is a structure, because it relates everything that makes up the distribution of matter in space. However, of course, that property or structure is instantiated by something, namely the distribution of matter in space, in whatever entities that

---

12 See Ghirardi et al. (1995) and Monton (2004).
13 See Bell (2004, ch. 22) and Tumulka (2006).

distribution may consist. The only reason for admitting that property or structure is that it does the job of determining the temporal development of the distribution of matter in space and thereby also is able to account for measurement outcomes.[14]

Elaborating on the mentioned holism in terms of ontic structural realism can help to bring out the contrast with action at a distance. Bell's theorem rules out Einstein's epistemological view of the quantum mechanical wave-function, but we are thereby not committed to falling back to what Einstein considers as spooky action at a distance. Bohmian mechanics, conceived as a first order theory without a specific quantum force as sketched out above, can illustrate this issue: there is no question of a direct interaction among the particles in Bohmian mechanics—such an interaction would indeed be action at a distance. Instead of interacting directly with each other, the particles are related through the holistic property or structure that determines the velocity of each of them at a time t given the position of all of them at t. There is of course indirect interaction among the particles in that a local change in the arrangement of particles (e.g. fixing a parameter in a Bell-type experiment, opening or closing one slit in a double slit experiment, etc.) can influence the velocity of strictly speaking all the other particles, whatever their distance in space is—but it does so through the mentioned structure or holistic property instantiated by all the particles, by contrast to direct interaction among the particles. Operationally speaking, there is no difference between a second order theory that adds a specific, non-local quantum force to the classical forces and a first order theory that takes the temporal development of the distribution of matter in space (such as the velocity of particles) to be determined by a structure or holistic property instantiated by the matter distribution as a whole; both theories agree in their predictions of measurement outcomes. But operational agreement can go with a profound difference in the ontology of these theories.

In any case, the quantum mechanical wave-function cannot be conceived as representing a field in physical space that mediates the interaction among the particles. The quantum mechanical wave-function is defined on configuration space—a high dimensional mathematical space (if there are N particles, the dimension of configuration space is $3N$)—without it being possible to take that wave-function to assign field values to points in physical space (three-dimensional space, or four-dimensional space-time). Nonetheless, an analogy with classical fields is possible, if one adopts the attitude of regarding the formalism

---

[14] See Esfeld and Lam (2011) as well as Esfeld (2013) for setting out ontic structural realism in that sense and references to the discussion about ontic structural realism in general.

of classical field theory as expressing how the dispositional properties of the particles such as their charge and mass perform the function of fixing the temporal development of the velocity of the particles, without subscribing to the ontological commitment of fields existing as concrete objects in physical space over and above the particles.[15] In that case, the field value assigned to a given space-time point does not represent a physical property existing at that point, but expresses only the information about what would happen to the motion of a particle if a particle were present at that point. The truth-maker for these counterfactual propositions are the dispositional properties of the particles such as their charge and mass. If one takes fields to be nothing more than the mathematical representation of such dispositional properties of the particles, the fact that the quantum mechanical wave-function can only be conceived as a field on configuration space poses no problem.

When one passes from quantum mechanics to quantum field theory and quantum gravity, the mentioned holism is not only confirmed, but moreover strengthened. In what is known as relativistic quantum field theory, despite its being relativistic, Bell's theorem applies: there are correlations between space-like separated events which cannot be accounted for in terms of local common causes (see Bell 2004, ch. 24). The main change with respect to quantum mechanics is the following one: whereas the quantum mechanical algorithm for calculating probabilities for measurement outcomes can be derived from an ontology that is committed to a fixed number of particles whose trajectories are determined by a holistic property instantiated by the configuration of all the particles, it seems that one has to make room for events of particle creation and annihilation in quantum field theory. Nonetheless, whatever one takes the distribution of matter in space to be, that distribution instantiates as a whole a structure or holistic property that fixes its temporal development and that is represented by the universal wave-function. In other words, there is in any case a good reason in quantum field theory to endorse the commitment to a holistic property of the distribution of matter in space that fixes its temporal development, even if that property no longer provides for an intertemporal identity of particles (as it does in Bohmian mechanics).[16]

In quantum gravity, there no longer is a background space and a background time in which matter is inserted, but space and time are themselves quantum ob-

---

[15] See Lange (2002) for a good introduction to the discussion about whether or not one should subscribe to an ontological commitment to classical fields.
[16] For attempts to formulate a Bohmian quantum field theory, see Bell (2004, ch. 19) and Dürr, Goldstein and Zanghì (2013, ch. 10) as well as Struyve (2011) for an overview of the state of the art.

jects. Accordingly, there no longer is a universal wave-function that develops itself in a background time, but the universal wave-function is stationary, the Schrödinger equation being replaced with the Wheeler-deWitt equation. Nonetheless, the universal wave-function can still be regarded as referring to a configuration of elementary objects, such as a configuration of elementary parts of space (or a configuration of elementary parts of space-cum-matter), and representing a holistic property of such a configuration that fixes the transition from one such configuration to the next one such that something approximating the classical space-time of general relativity theory is built up. In such a scenario, the holism that is characteristic of quantum physics is strengthened, since whatever relationship holds between the subsequent configurations of elementary objects is given entirely by the mentioned holistic property that is instantiated by any such configuration and that is represented by the universal, stationary wave-function.[17]

In sum, the crucial difference between classical and quantum mechanics is this one: in classical mechanics, there are dispositional properties of the particles that fix their temporal development in the sense of fixing the temporal development of their velocity (acceleration), and these properties can be conceived as intrinsic properties of each particle. As far as what is specific for quantum physics is concerned, there are no intrinsic properties of particles, but only one structure or holistic property that determines the temporal development of the distribution of matter in space (determining in the case of particles the temporal development of their position by fixing the velocity of each particle). Since Bell's theorem can with reason be conceived as putting a constraint on any future physical theory, there seems to be no prospect of going back to intrinsic properties in the ontology of physics.

References

Bell, John S. (2004). *Speakable and Unspeakable in Quantum Mechanics* (second edition). Cambridge: Cambridge University Press.
Belot, Gordon (2012). "Quantum States for Primitive Ontologists: A Case Study". *European Journal for Philosophy of Science* 2: pp. 67–83.
Belousek, Darrin W. (2003). "Formalism, Ontology and Methodology in Bohmian Mechanics". *Foundations of Science* 8: pp. 109–172.
Bigelow, John, Ellis, Brian and Pargetter, Robert (1988). "Forces". *Philosophy of Science* 55: pp. 614–630.

---

[17] See Dürr, Goldstein and Zanghì (2013, ch. 11) and Vassallo (2014) for a sketch of a Bohmian ontology of quantum gravity.

Bird, Alexander (2007). *Nature's Metaphysics. Laws and Properties.* Oxford: Oxford University Press.

Bohm, David (1952). "A Suggested Interpretation of the Quantum Theory in Terms of 'Hidden' Variables". *Physical Review* 85: pp. 166–193.

Dürr, Detlef, Goldstein, Sheldon and Zanghì, Nino (2013). *Quantum Physics without Quantum Philosophy.* Berlin: Springer.

Einstein, Albert, Podolsky, Boris and Rosen, Nathan (1935). "Can Quantum-Mechanical Description of Physical Reality be Considered Complete?". *Physical Review* 47: pp. 777–780.

Esfeld, Michael (2013). "Ontic Structural Realism and the Interpretation of Quantum Mechanics". *European Journal for Philosophy of Science* 3: pp. 19–32.

Esfeld, Michael and Lam, Vincent (2011). "Ontic Structural Realism as a Metaphysics of Objects". In: A. Bokulich and P. Bokulich (eds.), *Scientific Structuralism* (pp. 143–159). Dordrecht: Springer.

Esfeld, Michael, Lazarovici, Dustin, Hubert, Mario and Dürr, Detlef (forthcoming). "The Ontology of Bohmian Mechanics". *British Journal for the Philosophy of Science* 64. Paper available at http://philsci-archive.pitt.edu/9381/

Ghirardi, Gian Carlo, Grassi, Renata and Benatti, Fabio (1995). "Describing the Macroscopic World: Closing the Circle within the Dynamical Reduction Program". *Foundations of Physics* 25: pp. 5–38.

Goldstein, Sheldon (2006). "Bohmian Mechanics". In: E. N. Zalta (ed.), *Stanford Encyclopedia of Philosophy.* http://plato.stanford.edu/entries/qm-bohm

Goldstein, Sheldon, Norsen, Travis, Tausk, Daniel Victor and Zanghì, Nino (2011). "Bell's Theorem". http://www.scholarpedia.org/article/Bell's_theorem

Heil, John (2003). *From an Ontological Point of View.* Oxford: Oxford University Press.

Heil, John (2012). *The Universe as We Find It.* Oxford: Oxford University Press.

Hoffmann-Kolss, Vera (2010). *The Metaphysics of Extrinsic Properties.* Frankfurt: Ontos-Verlag.

Holland, Peter R. (1993). *The Quantum Theory of Motion. An Account of the de Broglie—Bohm Causal Interpretation of Quantum Mechanics.* Cambridge: Cambridge University Press.

Lange, Marc (2002). *An Introduction to the Philosophy of Physics.* Oxford: Blackwell.

Langton, Rae and Lewis, David (1998). "Defining 'Intrinsic'". *Philosophy and Phenomenological Research* 58: pp. 333–345.

Langton, Rae and Lewis, David (2001). "Marshall and Parsons on Intrinsic". *Philosophy and Phenomenological Research* 63: pp. 353–355.

Lewis, David (1973). *Counterfactuals.* Oxford: Blackwell.

Lewis, David (2009). "Ramseyan Humility". In: D. Braddon-Mitchell and R. Nola (eds.), *Conceptual Analysis and Philosophical Naturalism* (pp. 203–222). Cambridge, Massachusetts: MIT Press.

Locke, Dustin (2012). "Quidditism without Quiddities". *Philosophical Studies* 160: pp. 345–363.

Martin, C. B. (1997). "On the Need for Properties: The Road to Pythagoreanism and Back". *Synthese* 112: pp. 193–231.

Massin, Olivier (2009). "The Metaphysics of Forces". *Dialectica* 63: pp. 555–589.

Maudlin, Tim (2011). *Quantum Non-Locality and Relativity.* Third edition. Chichester: Wiley-Blackwell.

Maudlin, Tim (2012). *Philosophy of Physics. Volume 1. The Arena: Space and Time.* Princeton: Princeton University Press.

Monton, Bradley (2004). "The Problem of Ontology for Spontaneous Collapse Theories". *Studies in History and Philosophy of Modern Physics* 35: pp. 407–421.

Mumford, Stephen and Anjum, Rani Lill (2011). *Getting Causes from Powers*. Oxford: Oxford University Press.

Newton, Isaac (1952). *Opticks or a Treatise of the Reflections, Refractions, Inflections and Colours of Light*. Edited by I. B. Cohen. New York: Dover.

Norsen, Travis (2005). "Einstein's Boxes". *American Journal of Physics* 73: pp. 164–176.

Struyve, Ward (2011). "Pilot-Wave Approaches to Quantum Field Theory". *Journal of Physics: Conference Series* 306, p. 012047.

Tumulka, Roderich (2006). "A Relativistic Version of the Ghirardi-Rimini-Weber Model". *Journal of Statistical Physics* 125: pp. 825–844.

van Fraassen, Bas C. (1991). *Quantum Mechanics: An Empiricist View*. Oxford: Oxford University Press.

Vassallo, Antonio and Esfeld, Michael (2014). "A Proposal for a Bohmian Ontology of Quantum Gravity". *Foundations of Physics* 44: pp. 1–18.

Wilson, Jessica (2007). "Newtonian Forces". *British Journal for the Philosophy of Science* 58: pp. 173–205.

M. Eddon
Intrinsic Explanations and Numerical Representations

1 Introduction

In his (1980), Hartry Field argues that good explanations of physical phenomena are "intrinsic explanations." Roughly, an *intrinsic explanation* of some phenomenon is one that invokes objects that are causally relevant to the phenomenon to be explained. For instance, an explanation of the structure of spacetime that appeals to spacetime points and the relations they stand in is an intrinsic explanation, while one that appeals to causally irrelevant entities like numbers is an extrinsic explanation. More carefully, let us say that a predicate F is an *intrinsic predicate iff* whether $F(x_1, ..., x_n)$ obtains does not depend on anything other than $x_1, ..., x_n$, and the relations among them. Let us say that a fact is an *intrinsic fact iff* the predicates it involves are intrinsic predicates. Finally, let us say that an explanation is an *intrinsic explanation iff* it only involves intrinsic facts and intrinsic predicates.[1]

Field argues that his treatment of quantity is able to provide intrinsic explanations of the structure of space, spacetime, and other quantitative properties, as well as intrinsic explanations of why certain numerical representations of quantities (distances, lengths, mass, temperature, etc.) are appropriate or acceptable while others are not.

In contrast, Brian Ellis (1960) and (1966) argues that certain quantitative predicates are not intrinsic,[2] and that numerical representations of quantitative features are largely a matter of convention. In a similar vein, Peter Milne (1986) uses arguments like Ellis's to argue that both of Field's claims are false—that

---

[1] These notions of "intrinsic" are those employed by Field and Milne. They are not particularly explicit about what they mean by these terms, but the characterizations given above are suggested by the passages in Field (1980, pp. 27–8 and pp. 41–6) and Milne (1986, pp. 344, 346). (Of course, to make these characterizations completely precise, one needs to spell out the relevant notions of "involves" and "depends.")

[2] Ellis does not put it in quite this way. Rather, he suggests that "grounds of convenience" (1966, p. 82) and "the roles of the various quantities in physical theory" (p. 86) are "the only kind [s] of justification that can be given" (p. 83) for the choice of fundamental scale and fundamental measuring procedure. This entails that certain length relations are, on his view, not intrinsic.

Field's account cannot provide intrinsic explanations of either our numerical representations of quantity or the structure of quantity.

In this paper, I show where the arguments put forth by Ellis and Milne go wrong, and where they go right. Their arguments that one cannot provide an account of quantity in "purely intrinsic" terms fail for the same reason: they take the conventionality of numerical representations of quantitative features to reveal conventionality of the features themselves. Both Ellis and Milne infer from the fact that choice of measurement scale is a matter of convention that the underlying quantitative features the scale represents must also be a matter of convention.

On the other hand, Ellis's claim that the numerical representations of quantitative features that we employ are merely conventional, and Milne's claim that Field's framework does not provide an intrinsic explanation of our use of certain numerical representations over others, are both right. I will show that Field is mistaken to claim this as a virtue of his framework. That said, I will tentatively suggest a way to modify Field's framework so that it can provide such intrinsic explanations.

In sections (2) and (3), I present two questions Ellis raises about measurement, concerning the structure of quantity and the numerical representation of quantity. In section (4), I show how, contrary to what Ellis claims, these questions are orthogonal to one another, and I show how this undercuts Ellis's argument that one cannot provide an account of quantity in "purely intrinsic" terms. In section (5), I describe Field's framework. In sections (6) and (7), I present and assess Milne's objections to it. Finally, in section (8), I suggest one way to modify Field's framework so that it can provide an intrinsic explanation for why some numerical representations are better than others.

2 Two Fundamental Measuring Procedures

Consider three rods—a, b, and c. Suppose that a and b are the same length. When placed end to end, the distance from the leftmost tip of a to the rightmost tip of b is the same as the length of c:

This procedure for measuring the lengths of rods is what Brian Ellis calls a "measuring procedure."[3] Roughly, a measuring procedure is a physical procedure for adding objects together, with respect to some magnitude.[4] Let us call the particular measuring procedure used above the "standard measuring procedure." When a is added to, or concatenated with, b using the standard measuring procedure, the result is c. And it seems plainly clear that when two rods of equal length are added together, the resulting rod is twice as long as each of the individual rods. So, it seems plainly clear that we can deduce from this procedure that c is twice as long as a and b.

But is that so? Consider a different measuring procedure. Begin again with rods a and b, and now add another rod, d. Suppose that instead of placing a and b end-to-end, we place them perpendicular to one another. When perpendicular to one another, the distance from the leftmost tip of a to the topmost tip of b is the length of d:

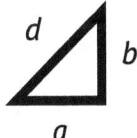

Call this way of "adding" or "concatenating" objects the "right-angle measuring procedure." When a is added to, or concatenated with, b using the right-angle measuring procedure, the result is d. And if we assume, as we did above, that concatenating two objects of equal length yields an object that is twice as long, then it seems we are committed to saying that d—not c—is twice as long as a and b.[5]

---

3 See Ellis (1960) and (1966, pp. 74–89).
4 Ellis writes: "All fundamental measurement depends upon the existence of a procedure for producing equality in respect of the fundamentally measureable quantity. In the fundamental measurement of length, the object to be measured is equaled in length by a line produced by a series of repeated procedures with a standard or set of standard objects (i.e. measuring rods)" (Ellis 1960, p. 42).
5 Suppose one claims that only c is twice as long as a and b, and this is why that standard measuring procedure is the correct one to use. But whether c really is twice the length of a and b, irrespective of some choice of measuring procedure, is precisely the question at issue. As Ellis notes, to maintain that "the notion of 'twice as long as' has a significance which is independent of measuring operations" (Ellis 1966, p. 83) is simply to say that there *is* an objectively correct measuring procedure. If the standard measuring procedure is the fundamental one, then c is twice as long as a and b; while if the right-angle measuring procedure is the fundamental one,

So is the length of *a* and *b* added together the same as the length of *c*, or is it the same as the length of *d*? Is there some reason to think that the standard measuring procedure, and not the right-angle measuring procedure, is the "correct" measuring procedure? This is one of two questions Ellis poses in his (1960) and (1966, pp. 74–86):

> Question 1: What is the fundamental measuring procedure? Is there some reason to think that the fundamental measuring procedure is the standard one as opposed to the right-angle one?

What does Ellis mean by a "fundamental measuring procedure"? A measuring procedure is a physical procedure for adding together the lengths of objects. Of course, there are many different procedures one may carry out to measure length. What makes a particular measuring procedure *fundamental* is that it tracks the *fundamental* facts about length. In other words, the fundamental measuring procedure is interesting because its method of "adding" rods lines up with the fundamental concatenation relation.[6] So, Ellis's question about which fundamental measuring procedure is the correct one to use is, at bottom, a question about the fundamental concatenation relation. Here is Ellis's first question, reformulated:

> Question 1, reformulated: What is the fundamental concatenation relation? Is there some reason to think that it is the one that lines up with the standard measuring procedure, where rods are placed end-to-end, as opposed to the one that lines up with the right-angle measuring procedure, where rods are placed perpendicular to one another?

In what follows, I use "measuring procedure" and "concatenation relation" (or "concatenation predicate") interchangeably.

3 Scales of Measurement

How might one argue that the standard concatenation relation (or, in Ellis's terms, the "standard measuring procedure") is the one linked to the objective notion of length, while the right-angle concatenation relation (or, in Ellis's terms, the "right-angle measuring procedure") is not? One thought is to appeal to our

---

then *d* is twice as long as *a* and *b*. And if there is no fact of the matter about which of these is fundamental, then there is no fact of the matter as to which rod is twice as long as *a* and *b*.
6 In this context, I use "fundamental" to mean something akin to Lewis's "perfectly natural." See Lewis (1983).

use of certain scales of measurement. Consider, for instance, the inches scale. Suppose that a and b are both one inch long, and c is two inches long. So a and b are assigned the number 1 on the inches scale, and c is assigned the number 2. Now, one might say, the inches scale accords with the standard concatenation relation in an important way. The concatenation of a and b, each one inch long, yields an object that is two inches long. More generally, the inches scale is *additive* over the standard concatenation relation: when the lengths of rods are measured in inches, the number assigned to the concatenation of x and y is the sum of the numbers assigned to x and y individually.

In contrast, the inches scale is not additive over the right-angle concatenation relation. The right-angle concatenation of a and b is d, which is $\sqrt{2}$ inches long. So the number assigned to d is not the sum of the numbers assigned to a and b (1+1≠$\sqrt{2}$). Therefore, one might claim, since we want our scale to be additive over the fundamental concatenation relation, the right-angle concatenation relation is to be rejected.[7]

As Ellis points out, however, this attempt to justify the standard concatenation relation is unsuccessful. There are two reasons. First, although it is true that the inches scale is not additive over the right-angle concatenation relation, one can construct scales that *are* additive. Ellis offers one candidate: the so-called *dinches* (or "diagonal inches") scale. The dinches scale is related to the inches scale in the following way:

1 inch = 1 dinch
2 inches = 4 dinches
3 inches = 9 dinches

and more generally:

n inches = n^2 dinches

Since a and b are both one inch long, they are also both one dinch long, and so are assigned the number 1 on the dinches scale. And d—the hypotenuse of the right triangle formed by concatenating a and b using the right-angle measuring procedure—is two dinches long, and so is assigned the number 2 on the dinches scale. The number assigned to d is the sum of the numbers assigned to a and b (1 +1=2), and so we see that the dinches scale is additive over the right-angle concatenation relation.

So, even if we grant the assumption that a satisfactory measurement scale must be additive over the fundamental concatenation relation, this does not

---

7 This appears to be the move suggested by Fox (2007).

give us a reason to reject the right-angle concatenation relation. For we can construct a scale—the dinches scale—that is additive over the right-angle concatenation relation. Regardless of which concatenation relation is the fundamental one, we can construct a scale that is additive over that relation.

The second reason this attempt to defend the standard concatenation relation falters is that the assumption that an adequate measurement scale be additive over the fundamental concatenation relation is unjustified. Why must our scale be additive in this way? There are plenty of satisfactory scales that seem to fail to satisfy this criterion: decibels (of sound), Richter magnitudes (for earthquakes). As Ellis (1960, p. 47) points out, the requirement that certain measurement scales be additive seems to be a matter of convention more than anything else.[8]

That said, the dinches scale surely seems odd, and it would be interesting if there were some independent justification for rejecting it. This leads to the second question Ellis poses:

> Question 2: What is the correct measurement scale to use when measuring lengths? Is there some reason to think that scales like the inches scale are the correct ones to use as opposed to scales like the dinches scale?

4 Two Paths to a Dinches Scale

Ellis takes these two questions—the question of the correct fundamental measuring procedure, and the question of the correct measurement scale—to be related to one another, such that an answer to one of these questions entails an answer to the other.[9] In particular, Ellis says that the intrinsic facts about lengths do not give us any reason to use one measurement scale over another, and therefore that the intrinsic facts about lengths do not give us any reason to use one concatenation relation over another. But in fact these two questions are orthogonal to one another. In this section, I show how one can construct both inches and dinches scales from the standard concatenation relation, and also how one can construct both inches and dinches scales from a non-standard concatena-

---

[8] See also Krantz *et al.* (1971, p. 100).
[9] Ellis: "The two problems of choice involved in fundamental measurement are, of course, very closely linked together. For to choose a fundamental scale for the measurement of any quantity, both of these choices have to be made. Consequently, they are both parts of the more general problem of choosing a scale, and the same considerations are likely to be relevant to both choices" (Ellis 1966, p. 81). See also remarks in Ellis (1960, pp. 46–7) and (1966, pp. 82–6).

tion relation. In sections (6) and (7), this result is used to evaluate Milne's objections to Field.

Let us begin with the canonical treatment of measurement. Following Krantz et al. (1971), there are two primitive predicates: *greater than or equal to* ($\geq$) and *concatenation* ($\circ$). To say that $x \geq y$ means, intuitively, that the length of x is greater than or equal to the length of y. And to say that $\circ(x, y, z)$ means, intuitively, that the length of z is the length of x concatenated with the length of y. The concatenation predicate, $\circ$, corresponds to what Ellis calls the standard fundamental measuring procedure.

Consider a set of rods, A, over which the length relations $\geq$ and $\circ$ are defined. In order to represent the objects in A using numbers, we want a function that maps the relational structure $\langle A, \geq, \circ \rangle$ to some numerical structure. A natural way to do this is to carry the objects in A to the positive real numbers, carry $\geq$ to $\geq$, and carry $\circ$ to $+$. One can then prove representation and uniqueness theorems—theorems specifying the constraints on numerical representations of the objects and relations of A. In this case, the representation theorem states that $\langle A, \geq, \circ \rangle$ is a model of the axioms of extensive measurement *iff* there is a function ϕ_1 from $\langle A, \geq, \circ \rangle$ into $\langle Re^+, \geq, + \rangle$ such that:

(a_1) $x \geq y$ iff $\phi_1(x) \geq \phi_1(y)$

(b_1) $\circ(x, y, z)$ iff $\phi_1(x) + \phi_1(y) = \phi_1(z)$

The corresponding uniqueness theorem states that for any two functions ϕ_1 and ϕ_1' defined over A, ϕ_1 and ϕ_1' satisfy these constraints *iff* they differ only by a positive multiplicative constant (i.e., $\phi_1 = n\phi_1'$ where $n > 0$). This uniqueness theorem captures the fact that if the inches scale, say, is an acceptable measurement scale for lengths, then so is the centimeters scale, the yards scale, the miles scale, and so on. (Of course, some of these scales may be more convenient in some circumstances. If you ask someone how far away the moon is from the earth, you might be irritated if she gives you the answer in millimeters.)

While this may be the most obvious way to numerically represent the objects in A, it is not the only one. We could, for instance, choose to map $\langle A, \geq, \circ \rangle$ onto $\langle Re^+, \geq, \# \rangle$, where $\#$ is defined as follows:

$n \# o$ $= p$ iff $(\sqrt{n} + \sqrt{o})^2 = p$ (where n, o, and p are variables ranging over numbers)

In this case, one can prove a representation theorem that states that $\langle A, \geq, \circ \rangle$ is a model of the axioms *iff* there is a function ϕ_2 from $\langle A, \geq, \circ \rangle$ into $\langle Re^+, \geq, \# \rangle$ that satisfies the following analogues of (a_1) and (b_1) above:

(a_2) $x \geq y$ iff $\phi_2(x) \geq \phi_2(y)$

(b_2) $\circ(x, y, z)$ iff $\phi_2(x) \# \phi_2(y) = \phi_2(z)$

The corresponding uniqueness theorem is the same as the one above: for any two functions ϕ_2 and ϕ_2' defined over A, ϕ_2 and ϕ_2' satisfy these constraints *iff* they differ only by a positive multiplicative constant (i.e., $\phi_2 = n\phi_2'$ where $n > 0$).

ϕ_1 and ϕ_2 are functions that map the same relational structure, $\langle A, \geq, \circ \rangle$, onto different numerical structures. And they are related in the following way: $\phi_1 = \phi_2^2$. If ϕ_1 is the inches scale, then ϕ_2 is the dinches scale. So we see that the relational structure in which the standard concatenation predicate figures permits the construction of both inches and dinches scales.

Now let's see how one can construct both inches and dinches scales from a non-standard concatenation relation. Suppose that instead of $\circ$, we introduce a different sort of concatenation predicate, $*$. Intuitively, $*$ corresponds to Ellis's right-angle measuring procedure. Consider again our set of rods, A, but rather than define $\geq$ and $\circ$ over A, we define $\geq$ and $*$ over A. As before, in order to represent the objects in A using numbers, we want a function that maps the relational structure $\langle A, \geq, * \rangle$ to some numerical structure. One way to do this is to carry the objects in A to the positive real numbers, carry $\geq$ to $\geq$, and carry $*$ to $+$. The representation theorem in this case states that $\langle A, \geq, * \rangle$ is a model of the axioms *iff* there is a function φ_1 from $\langle A, \geq, * \rangle$ into $\langle Re^+, \geq, + \rangle$ such that:

(a_1) $x \geq y$ iff $\varphi_1(x) \geq \varphi_1(y)$

(b_1) $*(x, y, z)$ iff $\varphi_1(x) + \varphi_1(y) = \varphi_1(z)$

The corresponding uniqueness theorem states that, for any two functions φ_1 and φ_1' defined over A, φ_1 and φ_1' satisfy these constraints *iff* they differ only by a positive multiplicative constant (i.e., $\varphi_1 = n\varphi_1'$ where $n > 0$).

Just as $\langle A, \geq, \circ \rangle$ could be mapped to various numerical structures, so can $\langle A, \geq, * \rangle$. Suppose that instead of carrying $*$ to $+$, we carry $*$ to a different mathematical procedure, $\$$, where $\$$ is defined as follows:

$n \$ o = p$ iff $\sqrt{(n^2+o^2)} = p$ (where n, o, and p are variables ranging over numbers)

Now one can prove that $\langle A, \geq, * \rangle$ is a model of the axioms *iff* there is a function φ_2 such that:

(a_2) $x \geq y$ iff $\varphi_2(x) \geq \varphi_2(y)$

(b_2) $*(x, y, z)$ iff $\varphi_2(x) \$ \varphi_2(y) = \varphi_2(z)$

φ_1 and φ_2 are functions that map the same relational structure, $\langle A, \succeq, *\rangle$, onto different numerical structures. And they are related in the following way: $\varphi_2 = \varphi_1^2$. If φ_2 is the inches scale, then φ_1 is the dinches scale. So we see that a structure using the right-angle concatenation predicate, *, permits the construction of both inches and dinches scales.

Ellis takes the existence of the dinches scale to demonstrate that distances among lengths is not an intrinsic matter—it is not settled by the objects and the length relations that hold among them. If it is settled at all, he believes, it can only be due to considerations of simplicity of mathematical formulations of the laws of nature.[10] But we see now that this doesn't follow. The fact that we can construct non-standard measurement scales like the dinches scale implies nothing about the underlying length relations, since both dinches and inches scales can be constructed from structures with the standard concatenation predicate as well as structures with the right-angle concatenation predicate. True, the inches scale is more convenient and familiar than the dinches scale. But both are just numerical representations—and there are no metaphysical insights to be gleaned from the obvious fact that some numerical representations are more convenient and familiar than others.

5 Hartry Field and Intrinsic Explanations

Like Ellis, Milne takes the existence of the dinches scale to show that certain facts about lengths are not "intrinsic facts," or "facts about the world which are statable independently of ... the use of particular mathematical representations" (Milne 1986, p. 341). Milne's criticisms are directed at Field's claim that his framework provides "intrinsic explanations"—explanations that appeal only to "intrinsic facts"—of relevant phenomena.

Field takes his framework to provide intrinsic explanations of two sorts of things: first, an intrinsic explanation of our standard numerical representations of lengths, mass, temperature, and so on;[11] second, an intrinsic explanation of the structure of space, spacetime, and various scalar magnitudes.[12]

---

10 See Ellis (1966, pp. 82–3).
11 "[O]ne of the things that gives plausibility to the idea that extrinsic explanations are unsatisfactory if taken as *ultimate* explanation is that the functions invoked in many extrinsic explanations are so arbitrary. For example, in the case of geometry, the choice of one distance function over any other one which differs from it by positive multiplicative constant is completely arbitrary; it reflects in effect an arbitrary choice of units for distance" (Field 1980, p. 45). Concerning his treatment of Euclidean geometry, Field writes that the associated uniqueness

Milne argues that Field's framework fails on both counts. In broad outline, Milne's argument goes as follows: first he argues that Field's framework fails to provide intrinsic explanations of our standard numerical representations of various quantities. Then he infers that some of the predicates invoked by Field are not intrinsic, and thus any explanations involving them are not intrinsic explanations.

In the following sections, I show that while it's true that Field's framework does not provide an intrinsic explanation of our use of certain numerical representations, this does not entail that it fails to provide intrinsic explanations of the structure of space, spacetime, and various scalar magnitudes. I begin with a rough sketch of Field's framework, and then show where Milne's criticisms of Field go awry.

5.1 Field's Framework

Field's treatment of space, spacetime, and other quantitative properties is modeled on Hilbert's axiomatization of Euclidean geometry. Let's here consider Field's treatment of Euclidean geometry (in section (7) we see how this account is modified to apply to other quantitative properties). Field takes the basic predicates to be the 3-place predicate *betweenness* (Bet) and the 4-place predicate *congruence* (Cong). To say that y Bet xz means, intuitively, that the spatial location of y is between that of x and z. And to say that xy Cong zw means, intuitively, that the spatial distance between x and y is the same as that between z and w.[13]

---

theorem "gives an *explanation* of the fact that the laws of Euclidean geometry, when stated in terms of coordinates, are invariant under shift of origin, reflection, rotation, and multiplication of all distances by a constant factor" (Field 1980, p. 50).

12 Concerning his treatment of Newtonian space-time, Field writes: "The position that we arrive at, then, is that the only spatio-temporal relations needed to describe Newtonian space-time are the three invoked in this axiom system... [T]he coordinate system and the distance function can be viewed as merely devices for deriving conclusions about spatio-temporal betweenness, simultaneity, and spatial congruence, conclusions which could be derived without ever bringing in numbers at all" (Field 1980, p. 53). Concerning temperature, Field says that the relevant question is, "what must the intrinsic facts about temperature differences between physical objects be if it is appropriate to think of temperature as being represented by real numbers?" (1980, p. 58). And after providing his account of these intrinsic facts, he writes: "We have specified the continuity of temperature with respect to space-time in a completely intrinsic way, a way that never mentions spatio-temporal coordinates or temperature scales. In my view this fully intrinsic character of the method makes it very attractive even independently of nominalistic scruples" (Field 1980, p. 63).

13 Field (1980, pp. 25–6)

One can provide representation and uniqueness theorems for Field's account of Euclidean geometry. Roughly, the representation theorem says that, given a domain of points A over which betweenness and congruence are defined, there is a function d that maps pairs of points onto numbers such that:

(a) for any points x, y, z, and w, xy Cong zw iff $d(x, y) = d(z, w)$

(b) for any points x, y, and z, y Bet xz iff $d(x, y) + d(y, z) = d(x, z)$

The corresponding uniqueness theorem for betweenness and congruence says that, given a model of the axiom system and any two functions d and d' defined over A, if d satisfies (a) and (b), then d' satisfies (a) and (b) iff d and d' differ by a positive multiplicative constant.

Field takes these representation and uniqueness theorems to have philosophical significance. The representation theorem, he says, "shows that statements that talk about space alone, without reference to numbers, are equivalent to certain 'abstract counterparts' which do talk about numbers." (Field 1980, p. 27) So, if we think of d as a distance function (as intuitively it is), then we see that all the geometrical laws stated in terms of numbers can be restated in terms of betweenness and congruence. The uniqueness theorem guarantees that the inches scale satisfies (a) and (b) *iff* the centimeters scale does as well, since they differ by only a multiplicative constant. Field takes this to show that, given his treatment of geometry, "the fact that geometric laws, when formulated in terms of distance, are invariant under multiplication of all distances by a positive constant, but are not invariant under any other transformation of scale, receives a satisfying *explanation*: it is explained by the *intrinsic facts* about physical space, i.e. by the facts about physical space which are laid down without reference to numbers in Hilbert's axioms" (Field 1980, p. 27).[14]

So, given Field's account, we can prove that there is a range of numerical representations that satisfy certain constraints. This, says Field, shows that we are *justified* in using the numerical representations that we do. In other words, he claims that his account provides an intrinsic explanation for why certain numerical representations of distance, length, etc., are permissible while others are not.

---

[14] Elsewhere Field writes that the uniqueness theorem "explain[s], in terms of intrinsic facts about space which are statable without such arbitrary choices, why the choice of functions to be invoked in the extrinsic theory will be arbitrary to precisely the extent that it is" (1986, pp. 45–6).

6 Milne's First Objection: Differential Congruence

In section (4), we saw that different kinds of numerical representations of length can be constructed independently of the underlying length relations. So we already have reason to be skeptical of Field's claim that the length facts themselves explain why we use one representation rather than another. And indeed, Milne challenges Field's claim, showing that one can numerically represent betweenness and congruence using either an inches or a dinches scale.

We've seen that the standard representation theorem associated with betweenness and congruence maps pairs of points onto numbers in the ways constrained by (a) and (b) above. But this is only one of many ways we can numerically represent betweenness and congruence. Milne offers an alternative, which replaces (b) above with (b'):

(b')   for any points x, y, and z, y Bet xz iff $\sqrt{d(x, y)} + \sqrt{d(y, z)} = \sqrt{d(x, z)}$

Note that if we replace (b) with (b'), we've effectively constructed a dinches scale (where the length in dinches is the distance between pairs of points). Consider any function d that satisfies (a) and (b); then a function d' satisfies (a) and (b') iff $d(x, y) = d'(x, y)^2$. If d is the inches scale, then d' is the dinches scale.

Nothing about the axioms governing betweenness and congruence rules out (b') as opposed to (b). As Milne says, neither (b) nor (b') "represent an intrinsic constraint on distance functions, *i.e.* an intrinsic feature of length measurement" (Milne 1986, p. 343). And so we reach the same moral as in section (4): the fundamental distance relations (whether Bet and Cong, or $\geq$ and ∘) can be mapped onto many different numerical structures. The relations themselves do not place constraints on the numbers we may use to represent them. So the pattern of betweenness and congruence relations simply cannot explain why we use certain numerical representations rather than others. Field's claims to the contrary are mistaken.

While this is all correct, Milne goes on to draw a much more radical conclusion: Field's framework fails to provide an intrinsic explanation of the structure of space. In particular, Milne says, the fact that there are multiple ways of numerically representing the pattern of betweenness and congruence relations entails that the obtaining of some of these relations is a matter of convention. As a result, certain facts about geometry are not "intrinsic facts," and explanations that invoke these facts are not intrinsic explanations.

To illustrate this, Milne introduces the relation of *differential congruence*. To say that pairs of points xy and $x'y'$ are differentially congruent to zw and $z'w'$ means, intuitively, that "the difference between the distance from x to y and the distance from x' to y' is congruent to the difference between the distance from z to w and the distance from z' to w'" (Milne 1986, p. 343). Milne then claims that the dinches scale does not preserve the differential congruence relation:

> If one obtains in inches the difference in length between, say, two rigid rods by measuring their lengths then subtracting the smaller from the greater and finds it congruent to the difference between another pair usually the result disagrees with that obtained when the lengths are measured in dinches... *Differential congruence is not independent of the measuring procedure by which it is ascertained*... What is of the utmost importance here is that differential congruence is not fixed by the intrinsic facts, the facts about betweenness and congruence. (1986, pp. 343–4)

But Milne's conclusion at the end of the paragraph is not warranted. To see this, note that differential congruence may be defined in terms of congruence:

> points xy and $x'y'$ are *differentially congruent* to points zw and $z'w'$ iff for some points u and v, $x'u$ Cong xy, $z'v$ Cong zw, and uy' Cong vw'

Given this, facts about differential congruence *must* be fixed by the facts about congruence.

It is easier to see exactly where Milne's argument goes awry if we use the notion of concatenation, which is interdefinable with differential congruence:[15]

> points xy and $x'y'$ are *differentially congruent* to points zw and $z'w'$ iff for any objects l_1, l_2, l_3, l_4, whose endpoints are xy, $x'y'$, zw, $z'w'$, respectively, and for some object o, $\circ(o, l_1, l_2)$ and $\circ(o, l_3, l_4)$

Now consider the following four rods:

---

15 This interdefinability claim works only if we make some ontological assumptions. For instance, we must assume that every object has endpoints, and that for every pair of points (x, y), there is an object that has x and y as endpoints (this object might be the fusion of points between x and y). Since these ontological issues are irrelevant to the issues I'm concerned with, I put these complications aside.

Suppose that *e* is one inch long (one dinch long), *f* is two inches long (four dinches long), *g* is four inches long (sixteen dinches long), and *h* is five inches long (25 dinches long). The difference in the lengths of *e* and *f* is one inch, and the difference in the lengths of *g* and *h* is one inch. Since one inch = one dinch, the difference in the lengths of *e* and *f* is one dinch long, and likewise for the difference in the lengths of *g* and *h*.

Milne writes that "condition (b) corresponds to the *convention* that differences in length are treated as distances themselves and their congruence ascertained directly, *e.g.*, one can place rods side by side and measure the overlap of the longer over the shorter. Such a procedure fails for dinches: the directly measured difference in lengths between two rods (in dinches) is not equal to the absolute difference in length of the two rods (again measured in dinches)" (Milne 1986, p. 343). The "directly measured difference" in lengths between rods *x* and *y* is, intuitively, the length value one would obtain by lining up the rods and using a ruler, say, to measure the length of the part of the longer rod that does not overlap the shorter one. In contrast, the "absolute difference" in length between rods *x* and *y* is the length value one would obtain by calculating $|d(x) - d(y)|$, where *d* is a distance function from rods to numbers.

If *d* maps rods onto the dinches scale, the "absolute difference" in length between rods *e* and *f* is $|4 - 1| = 3$, and the "absolute difference" in length between rods *g* and *h* is $|25 - 16| = 9$. In each case, the "absolute difference" in length between the rods differs from the "directly measured difference" in length between the rods, which in both cases is 1 dinch. If, on the other hand, *d* maps rods onto the inches scale, the "absolute difference" in length between rods *e* and *f* is $|2 - 1| = 1$, and the "absolute difference" in length between rods *g* and *h* is $|5 - 4| = 1$, both of which equal the "directly measured difference" in length, which is also 1 inch. So, whether the "directly measured difference" value is the same as the "absolute difference" value depends on the scale we use to numerically represent the lengths of these objects.

Milne takes this to show that differential congruence is somehow conventional. But it shows no such thing. The fact that the number assigned to the "directly measured difference" and the number assigned to the "absolute difference" varies with choice of measurement scale does not show that the underlying length facts vary with choice of measurement scale as well.

So what *does* this show? It shows that the "absolute difference" in length yields the same value as the "directly measured difference" in length only when the measurement scale *d* is additive. To see this, let's go through two examples. Consider the inches scale, d_{in}. The "directly measured difference" in inches between l_1 and l_2 is the value the inches scale assigns to *x* ($d_{in}(x)$). The "absolute difference" in inches between l_1 and l_2 is the value we get when we subtract the value the inches scale assigns to l_1 from the value it assigns to l_2 ($d_{in}(l_2) - d_{in}(l_1)$). As we've seen, the inches scale d_{in} is additive over the concatenation relation: $\circ(x, l_1, l_2)$ iff $d_{in}(x) + d_{in}(l_1) = d_{in}(l_2)$. It follows from this that $d_{in}(x) = d_{in}(l_2) - d_{in}(l_1)$, and thus that the "directly measured difference" in inches ($d_{in}(x)$) will always equal the "absolute difference" in inches ($d_{in}(l_2) - d_{in}(l_1)$).

Now consider the dinches scale, d_{din}. The "directly measured difference" in dinches between l_1 and l_2 is the value the dinches scale assigns to x ($d_{din}(x)$). The "absolute difference" in dinches between l_1 and l_2 is the value we get when we subtract the value the dinches scale assigns to l_1 from the value it assigns to l_2 ($d_{din}(l_2) - d_{din}(l_1)$). As we saw in section (4), the dinches scale is not additive over the concatenation relation. Instead, the dinches scale is such that $\circ(x, l_1, l_2)$ iff $(\sqrt{d_{din}(x)} + \sqrt{d_{din}(l_1)})^2 = d_{din}(l_2)$. It is obvious that, in general, $d_{din}(l_2) - d_{din}(l_1)$ does *not* equal $d_{din}(x)$. The fact that the dinches scale is not additive over the concatenation relation entails that the "directly measured difference" in dinches will not generally equal the "absolute difference" in dinches.

So Milne is correct to say that the "absolute difference" in dinches does not equal the "directly measured difference" in dinches. But all this means is that the dinches scale is not additive over the standard concatenation relation. And, as we have seen, the fact that one can construct a scale of measurement that is not additive over the relevant concatenation relation does not entail anything at all about the fundamental length predicates; and in particular, it does not entail that the "differential congruence is not fixed by the intrinsic facts, the facts about betweenness and congruence." Differential congruence *is* fixed by the intrinsic facts. What is not fixed by the intrinsic facts is the numerical structure we use to represent those facts. So far, we've seen no reason to think that Field's framework does not provide an intrinsic explanation of the structure of Euclidean geometry.

7 Milne's Second Objection: Congruence

Field extends Hilbert's strategy for axiomatizing Euclidean geometry to scalar magnitudes like mass, temperature, and so on. For scalar magnitudes, the basic idea is to introduce different families of *betweenness* and *congruence* predicates: intuitively, *mass-betweenness* and *mass-congruence* predicates hold among objects with mass, *temp-betweenness* and *temp-congruence* predicates hold among objects with temperature, etc.[16]

---

16 Note that for quantitative features that require an ordering – such as length, mass, tem-

The axiom system for these scalar notions of betweenness and congruence that Field adopts is in essence the axiom system for an "absolute difference structure" described by Krantz et al. (1970, pp. 171–3). (See also Field 1980, p. 58 and pp. 119–120.)[17] And the representation theorem for scalar betweenness and congruence is slightly different from the one used in Euclidean geometry, as it assigns numerical values to individual objects rather than pairs of points:

<A, Bet, Cong> is a model of the axioms *iff* there is a function f from A into the real numbers, such that:

(a) for any x, y, z, and w, xy Cong zw iff $|f(x)-f(y)| = |f(z)-f(w)|$

(b) for any x, y, and z, y Bet xz iff $f(x) \leq f(y) \leq f(z)$ or $f(z) \leq f(y) \leq f(x)$

The corresponding uniqueness theorem for scalar betweenness and congruence says that, given a model of the axiom system and any two functions f and f' defined over A, if f satisfies (a) and (b), then f' satisfies (a) and (b) iff f' is a linear transformation of f.[18]

Milne's second objection to Field targets the scalar congruence predicate. He argues that whether xy Cong zw obtains depends on the scale of measurement we use; and since choice of measurement scale is a matter of convention, then so is the obtaining of the congruence predicate. Therefore, any fact involving congruence is not "an intrinsic fact," and thus congruence is "not intrinsic" (Milne 1986, p. 344).[19, 20]

(It is interesting to note that while Milne challenges the intrinsicality of congruence, he does not doubt the intrinsicality of betweenness.[21] It is unclear why

---

perature, etc. – the predicate *less than or equal to* (Less) is used in place of *betweenness* as a primitive notion. (*Betweenness* can then be defined: y Bet xz iff x Less y Less z or z Less y Less x.) For ease of exposition, I follow Milne and ignore this complication.

17 Krantz et al. employ one primitive: $\geq$. To say that $xy \geq zw$ means, intuitively, that the distance between x and y is greater than or equal to the distance between z and w. As Field notes, the system Krantz et al. describe can be modified so as to employ Field's primitives instead. One way to do that is to define Bet and Cong in terms of $\geq$: xy Cong zw iff $xy \geq zw$ and $zw \geq xy$; x Bet yz iff $yz \geq xy$, xz.

18 φ is a linear transformation of ϕ *iff* $\varphi = a\phi + b$, where a and b are real numbers (and $b \neq 0$).

19 Recall that, for Milne, xy Cong zw is intrinsic *iff* xy Cong zw obtains in virtue of the objects and the relations that hold among them, and nothing else.

20 This line of thought is similar to Ellis's, who likewise appeared to believe that if choice of measurement scale is a matter of convention, then so is the fundamental measuring procedure.

21 "It is abundantly clear from Field's discussion that he regards ϕ-betweenness and ϕ-congruence as relations whose obtaining is an intrinsic fact. About ϕ-betweenness there is no ground for complaint. ϕ-congruence is quite another matter" (Milne 1986, p. 344).

congruence is a target of suspicion while betweenness is not. If the fact that there are multiple different relations among numbers that can be used to represent facts about congruence shows that these facts about congruence are not intrinsic, as Milne believes, then the same can be said for betweenness.[22])

Milne's argument goes as follows. One can measure the same scalar using different measurement scales, where these measurement scales are not linear transformations of one another. Such scales differ not only on the values they assign to the same interval, but on whether congruent intervals are assigned the same value. One example Milne offers is the Dalton temperature scale, which is "logarithmically related to the absolute scale." Suppose that a, b, c, and d are objects with temperature, and suppose that ab Temp-Cong cd. The absolute scale assigns the same number to ab and cd, while the Dalton scale does not. From this fact, Milne draws the following conclusion: "The moral is that [scalar]-congruence is not independent of the manner in which it is ascertained. And so, it seems, it is not the case that [scalar]-congruence is intrinsic" (Milne 1986, p. 345).

But this argument is not valid. The fact that intervals assigned the same value on the absolute scale are assigned different values on the Dalton scale does not entail anything about the intrinsicality of congruence. All it shows is that a relational structure <A, Temp-Bet, Temp-Cong> can be mapped to many different numerical structures. Some will represent congruent intervals with the same number, others will not. Some are more familiar and convenient in some contexts, while others are more familiar and convenient in other contexts. But the fact that the choice of numerical structure is a matter of convention does not entail that the obtaining of the underlying temperature relations is not intrinsic.[23]

In sum, Milne is correct in pointing out that the choice of numerical structure is not fixed by the pattern of betweenness and congruence relations, and thus that the pattern of betweenness and congruence relations cannot provide an intrinsic explanation of our standard numerical representations of length, mass, temperature, and so on. But this does not show that the underlying betweenness and congruence relations are in any way extrinsic, conventional, or non-objective. Any argument for this conclusion—that the underlying betweenness and congruence relations fail to provide intrinsic explanations for the struc-

---

[22] A similar point applies to Ellis: Ellis doubts the objectivity of concatenation, but not of ordering ($\geq$). But again, if the fact that there are multiple different relations among numbers that can be used to represent facts about concatenation shows that these facts about concatenation are not objective, as Ellis believes, then the same can be said for ordering.
[23] See also Krantz et al. (1971, p. 152).

ture of space and the structure of scalar magnitudes—that relies on premises concerning our representation of this structure is invalid.

8 A Suggestion

There seems to be a kind of tension prompting much of the preceding discussion of measurement scales. On the one hand, certain kinds of measurement scales seem, at least at first, to do a worse job of representing reality than others. For instance, the dinches scale seems, intuitively, to represent the underlying length relations in a particularly opaque way, while the inches scale does so in a particularly transparent way. Similarly, the Dalton temperature scale, while surely useful in many contexts, nonetheless does not seem to represent the underlying temperature relations as perspicuously as the absolute temperature scale (there is a reason only one of these scales is called the "absolute" scale).

On the other hand, there does not seem to be any way to justify the intuition that some scales fail to represent the world in as transparent a manner as other scales. The underlying relations of distance, length, mass, temperature, and so on, can be represented by many different numerical structures. Consider the axiomatization of extensive measurement, from Krantz et al., that employs the basic predicates $\succeq$ and $\circ$. Why should $\succeq$ be carried to the numerical relation $\geq$, and why should $\circ$ be carried to the numerical relation $+$? Or consider the congruence and betweenness predicates of Field's framework. Why should Temp-Cong, say, be carried to the numerical relation given by (a), and why should Temp-Bet be carried to the numerical relation given by (b)?

If there were some way to justify the intuition that some scales do a better job at representing reality than others, then we would have grounds for rejecting odd or unnatural scales like the dinches scale. Even better would be some way to vindicate Field's claim that the underlying relations themselves provide an *intrinsic explanation* that justifies the use of some scales over others.

Let me here suggest a route that one might take. The standard representation theorem for extensive measurement carries $\succeq$ to $\geq$, and $\circ$ to $+$. One way to argue that this representation is *better* than others is to claim that $\succeq$ stands in a privileged relationship with $\geq$, and $\circ$ stands in a privileged relationship with $+$. But what is this privileged relationship?

One could claim that this relationship is *sui generis*, but that would not be particularly explanatory. A more interesting option is to claim that this relationship is identity: $\succeq$ is identical to $\geq$, and $\circ$ is identical to $+$. In other words, the *greater than or equal to* and *addition* relations that numbers stand in simply are the *greater than or equal to* and *concatenation* relations invoked in extensive measurement. Similarly, one might say, the *betweenness* and *congruence* relations among numbers (which we rather clumsily analyze in terms of ≤, subtraction, and absolute value) simply are the *betweenness* and *congruence* relations invoked in Field's framework. If that is so, then it seems we *do* have an intrinsic explanation for why we use some scales rather than others: the perspicuous scales are the ones where the numbers representing the scalar magnitudes stand in the *very same* relations as the scalar magnitudes themselves.

This suggestion, however, requires some revision of Field's framework. Field's primary aim is to provide a nominalistic treatment of spacetime and of quantity—an account of these that does not quantify over properties or relations. In order to accommodate various families of quantities, Field introduces a different betweenness and congruence predicate for each family: Mass-Bet is distinct from Temp-Bet, Mass-Cong is distinct from Temp-Cong, and so forth. But if there are multiple distinct betweenness and congruence predicates, then we cannot implement the suggested strategy. Given Field's framework, Mass-Bet and Temp-Bet are not identical. But, by transitivity of identity, if Mass-Bet is identical to the betweenness relation among numbers, and Temp-Bet is identical to the betweenness relation among numbers, then Mass-Bet must be identical to Temp-Bet.

So in order to implement this strategy, we must accommodate the fact that there are various families of quantities, without having different betweenness and congruence predicates for each family of quantities. To do this, we introduce determinate properties for every family: *one gram mass*, *two grams mass*, etc., *one degree Fahrenheit*, *two degrees Fahrenheit*, etc., and so on. These properties stand in second-order betweenness and congruence relations: *two grams mass* is between *one gram mass* and *three grams mass*, and so a perspicuous mass scale is one where the number used to represent *two grams mass* is between the numbers used to represent *one gram mass* and *three grams mass*.[24] Likewise for temperature, charge, length, and all other scalar magnitudes. On this proposal, then, we do not have to introduce different betweenness and congruence relations for each family of quantities. Since there is only one betweenness relation, and only one congruence relation, we can identify these relations with the corresponding relations that hold among numbers.

---

[24] Mundy (1987) offers an account of quantity that posits first-order determinate properties that stand in second-order relations. Rather than use second-order betweenness and congruence relations, he uses second-order less than or equal to and concatenation relations, modeling his account on Krantz *et al.*'s treatment of extensive measurement.

If we adopt this proposal, we must quantify over first-order properties, and so we must give up on Field's nominalism. Whether one is amenable to this move depends on one's other metaphysical commitments. I've argued elsewhere that there are independent reasons to be a realist about determinate quantitative properties, and to take the relations that these properties stand in as part of the fundamental structure of the world.[25] To the extent to which one feels that scales like the dinches scale do not latch onto reality in quite the right way, whereas scales like the inches scale do, one might take this to be yet another reason to reject the nominalist position.[26]

References

Eddon, M. (2013). "Fundamental Properties of Fundamental Properties." In K. Bennett and D. Zimmerman (eds.), *Oxford Studies in Metaphysics*, Volume 8 (pp. 78–104). Oxford: Oxford University Press.

Ellis, Brian (1960). "Some Fundamental Problems of Direct Measurement." *Australasian Journal of Philosophy* 38: pp. 37–47.

Ellis, Brian (1966). *Basic Concepts of Measurement*. Cambridge University Press.

Field, Hartry (1980). *Science Without Numbers*. Princeton University Press.

Fox, John (2007). "Why We Shouldn't Give Ellis a Dinch." *Analysis* 67: pp. 301–303.

Krantz, D., Luce, R. D., Suppes, P, and Tversky, A. (1971). *Foundations of Measurement: Volume I*. NY: Academic Press.

Lewis, David (1983). "New Work for a Theory of Universals." *Australasian Journal of Philosophy* 61: pp. 343–377.

Milne, Peter (1986). "Hartry Field on Measurement and Intrinsic Explanation." *British Journal for the Philosophy of Science* 37: pp. 340–346.

Mundy, Brent (1987). "The Metaphysics of Quantity." *Philosophical Studies* 51: pp. 29–54.

---

25 Eddon (2013).
26 Many thanks to Chris Meacham and Katia Vavova for comments and discussion.

Contributors

The new essays in this collection are from:
David Denby (Tufts University)
Maya Eddon (University of Massachusetts at Amherst)
Michael Esfeld (Université de Lausanne)
Carrie Figdor (University of Iowa)
Robert Francescotti (San Diego State University)
Vera Hoffmann-Kolss (Universität zu Köln)
Dan Marshall (University of Hong Kong)
Alexander Skiles (Université de Neuchâtel)
D. Gene Witmer (University of Florida)

The previously published classics reprinted here are by Rae Langton & David Lews, Peter Vallentyne, Stephen Yablo, and Brian Weatherson

Rae Langton's and **David Lewis**' "Defining 'Intrinsic'" was published in *Philosophy and Phenomenological Research* 58: 333–345 (1998), and is reprinted here with permission of Rae Langton and Stephanie Lewis, and Wiley & Sons, Inc.

Peter Vallentyne's "Intrinsic Properties Defined" appeared in *Philosophical Studies* 88: 209–219 (1997). Reprinted with permission of Peter Vallentyne and Springer.

Stephen Yablo's "Intrinsicness" is from *Philosophical Topics* 26: 479–505 (1999). Reprinted with permission of Stephen Yablo and Edward Minar (editor of *Philosophical Topics*).

Brian Weatherson's "Intrinsic Properties and Combinatorial Principles" appeared in *Philosophy and Phenomenological Research* 63: 365–380 (2001). Reprinted with permission of Brian Weatherson and Wiley & Sons.

Name Index

Aristotle 87, 88
Anjum, Rani Lill 257, 269
Armstrong, David 25, 26, 29, 77, 85

Bader, Ralf 179, 197, 223, 228, 232, 234, 236, 238, 249
Barcelo Aspeitia, Axel Arturo 139, 154
Bell, John S. 260, 261, 263, 264, 265–267
Belot, Gordon 263, 267
Belousek, Darrin 262, 267
Benatti, Fabio 268
Bennett, Karen 248, 249
Bohm, David 261, 262, 268
Bigelow, John 47, 254, 267
Bird, Alexander 257, 268
Bradley, Ben 149, 154
Braun, David 38
Bricker, Phillip 101, 109, 199, 206, 219
Butchard, William 5, 9, 16, 93, 109, 138, 143, 155, 161, 173, 181, 183, 185, 187, 198, 220, 252

Cameron, Ross 90, 109
Carroll, John 243, 249
Casullo, Albert 36
Chisholm, Roderick 3, 31, 225, 249
Contessa, Gabriele 109
Copi, Irving 106, 109
Correia, Fabrice 91, 92, 109, 111, 138, 179, 197, 219, 229, 233, 249
Cowling, Sam 233, 234, 249

Daly, Chris 223, 249
Dancy, Jonathan 151, 154
Danto, Arthur 153, 154
Della Rocca, Michael 91, 92, 109
Denby, David 8, 9, 14, 15, 91–93, 101, 104, 109, 154, 161, 173, 236, 238, 249, 250
Dennett, Daniel 13, 15, 92, 109, 223, 249
DePaul, Michael 236, 249
deRosset, Louis 247–249
Dorr, Cian 226, 228, 249
Dorsey, Dale 148, 154

Dunn, J. Michael 2, 7, 10, 15, 19, 33, 91, 109, 113, 138, 158, 173, 178, 197, 199, 219
Dürr, Detlef 253, 262, 263, 266–268

Ellis, Brian 139, 154, 231, 250, 254, 267, 271–279, 286, 287, 290
Esfeld, Michael 13–15, 263, 265, 268, 269
Eddon, Maya 11, 12, 14, 15, 144, 154, 158, 162–165, 167, 170, 171, 173, 177, 178, 179, 194, 197, 199, 219, 222, 223, 242, 250, 290
Edelberg, Walter 36, 40
Eistein, Albert 258–260, 262, 263, 265, 268, 269

Fara, Michael 215, 219
Feldman, Fred 149, 154
Field, Hartry 14, 271, 272, 277, 279–282, 285, 286, 288, 289, 290
Figdor, Carrie 10, 11, 14, 15, 139, 140, 147, 154, 158, 173, 178, 179, 184, 197, 231, 233, 238, 250
Fine, Kit 9, 15, 52, 53, 58, 87, 88, 90, 92, 94, 95, 97, 108, 109, 226, 229, 233, 238, 239, 250
Fletcher, Guy 148, 154
Forbes, Graham 50, 67, 214, 215, 219
Fox, John 275, 290
Francescotti, Robert 15, 91, 93, 109, 113, 127, 138, 140, 143, 153, 154, 161, 165, 169, 170, 173, 175, 190, 197, 222, 223, 231, 236, 238, 250
Frankena, William 150, 154

Ghirardi, Gian Carlo 264, 268, 269
Goldstein, Sheldon 253, 260, 262, 263, 266–268
Gorman, Michael 90–92, 106, 109
Grassi, Renata 268

Hawthorne, John 136, 138, 145, 147, 154, 223, 250
Harris, Roger 176, 177, 191, 192, 197

Hazen, Allen   22, 215, 219
Heil, John   256, 268
Hilbert, David   280, 281, 285
Hoffmann-Kolss, Vera   12, 14, 15, 139, 154, 170, 173, 176, 179, 182, 190, 197, 249, 250, 255, 268
Hofweber, Thomas   223, 250
Holland, Peter   262, 268
Hubert, Mario   268
Hudson, Hud   242, 250
Humberstone, Lloyd I.   10, 15, 17, 19, 24, 51–53, 154, 158, 173, 178, 183, 197, 199, 219, 221, 225, 250

Jacobs, Jonathan   230, 250
Jenson, Karsten Klint   154
Johnson, Michael   208

Kagan, Shelly   148, 149, 154
Khamara, E. J.   19, 183, 197
Kim, Jaegwon   3, 15, 17, 18, 24, 26, 29–32, 41, 42, 117, 138, 142, 146, 149, 154, 197, 225, 250
King, Jeffrey   226, 227, 250
Korsgaard, Christine   148, 149, 153, 154
Krantz, David   276, 277, 286–290

Ladyman, James   221, 250
Lam, Vincent   265, 268
Lange, Marc   266, 268
Langton, Rae   4, 14, 15, 17, 19, 33, 41–43, 51, 63, 69–75, 77, 78, 80, 81, 83–85, 117, 138, 145, 154, 155, 157, 164, 170, 173, 176, 181, 194, 195, 197, 236, 237, 250, 255, 268
Lazarovici, Dustin   268
Lewis, David   3–5, 15, 17, 18, 20, 25, 26, 28, 29, 31–33, 41–43, 45–48, 50, 51, 60, 62–64, 66, 69–75, 77, 78, 80, 81, 83–85, 90, 91, 95, 98, 99, 109, 113, 117, 138, 140, 144–146, 154, 155, 157, 161, 162, 164, 166, 170, 171, 173, 175, 176, 181, 194, 195, 197, 199, 200, 202–211, 214, 219–223, 225, 231, 236, 237, 239, 250, 251, 255–257, 268, 274, 290
Lippert-Rasmussen, Kasper   151, 154
Locke, Dustin   256, 268

Lowe, E. J.   229, 230, 250
Luce, R. Duncan   290

Marshall, Dan   7, 12, 14, 15, 16, 69, 72, 75, 76, 78, 85, 92, 109, 113, 114, 117, 119, 127, 128, 129, 133, 137, 138, 140, 141, 145, 155, 160, 171, 173, 175, 184–186, 188, 189, 194–198, 200, 201, 211, 220, 221, 231, 234, 236, 241, 250–252, 268
Massin, Olivier   254, 268
Martin, C. B.   256, 268
Maudlin, Tim   254, 260, 268
Melia, Joseph   226, 251
McDaniel, Kris   241, 251
McGowan, Mary Kate   20
Menzel, Christopher   216, 220
Merricks, Trenton   221, 251
Milne, Peter   271, 272, 277, 279, 280, 282–287, 290
Molnar, George   60
Monton, Bradley   264, 269
Moore, G. E.   2, 3, 15, 148–151, 153–155, 195, 197
Mumford, Stephen   257, 269
Mundy, Brent   289, 290

Newton, Issac   253, 254–258, 262–264, 269, 280
Ney, Alyssa   221, 251
Norsen, Travis   259, 268, 269

Pargetter, Robert   254, 267
Peacocke, Christopher   214, 215, 220
Podolsky, Boris   260, 263, 268
Parson, Josh   7, 12, 15, 69, 72, 75, 76, 78, 85, 145, 155, 196, 197, 222, 241, 244, 251, 268

Quine, W. V. O.   90, 109

Rabinowicz, Wlodek   155
Ramsey, William   236, 249
Rayo, Agustin   226, 228, 251
Robinson, Denis   22
Rønnow-Rasmussen, Toni   155

Rosen, Gideon 22, 111, 112, 137, 138, 180–182, 184–186, 196, 197, 202, 220, 228, 234, 236, 238, 251
Rosen, Nathan 260, 263, 268
Ross, Don 221, 250

Salmon, Nathan 65
Schaffer, Jonathan 180, 197, 221, 245, 251
Schnieder, Benjamin 111, 138
Schrödinger, Erwin 267
Schroeder, Mark 226, 251
Shoemaker, Sydney 21, 41, 60
Sider, Theodore 5, 7, 15, 33, 37, 38, 69, 73, 75, 76, 85, 135, 138, 145, 155, 176, 194, 195, 197, 199, 206, 211, 220, 221, 222, 236, 238, 241, 244, 245, 247, 251
Skow, Bradford 161, 173, 199, 220, 221, 238, 251
Skiles, Alex 13, 14, 187, 197
Struyve, Ward 266, 269
Suppes, Patrick 290
Swoyer, Chris 21

Tausk, Daniel Victor 268
Taylor, Barry 20, 70, 85, 224, 251
Thomson, Judith 52, 56, 58
Trogdon, Kelly 5, 9, 16, 93, 109, 127, 138, 143, 155, 161, 173, 181, 182, 185–187, 197, 198, 220, 236, 237, 251, 252
Tumulka, Roderich 264, 269
Tversky, Amos 290

Vallentyne, Peter 5, 6, 7, 14, 15, 20, 25, 30, 36, 41, 59, 112, 138, 141, 145, 155, 160, 161, 170, 173, 176, 177, 194, 198, 200, 220, 236, 238, 251
van Fraassen, Bas 258, 269
Vassallo, Antonio 267, 269

Wasserman, Ryan 221, 251
Weatherson, Brian 7, 8, 14, 15, 16, 113, 117, 119, 122, 127, 133, 138, 140, 142, 145, 155, 171, 173, 175, 188, 189, 194, 196, 198, 201, 220, 221, 231, 234, 236, 238, 252
Wedgwood, Ralph 226, 252
Williams, J. R. G. 221, 251
Williamson, Timothy 215, 219, 235, 236, 244, 252
Wilson, Jessica 112, 138, 254, 269
Witmer, D. Gene 5, 9, 10, 14, 16, 93, 109, 111, 127, 130, 138, 143, 155, 161, 173, 179, 181, 182, 185, 187, 195, 196, 198, 201, 220, 228, 232, 236, 237, 252
Woodward, James 244, 252

Yablo, Stephen 5, 6, 7, 12, 13, 14, 16, 69, 71, 72, 78, 80, 83–85, 113, 115, 138, 140, 155, 161, 173, 195, 198, 199–204, 206–214, 217–220, 236, 238–241, 252

Zalta, Edward 88, 91, 92, 109
Zanghi, Nino 253, 262, 263, 266–268
Zimmerman, Michael 155

www.ingramcontent.com/pod-product-compliance
Lightning Source LLC
Chambersburg PA
CBHW050854160426
43194CB00011B/2152